West of Camelot

The Historical Paintings of Kenneth Riley

by Susan Hallsten McGarry

Foreword by James K. Ballinger

Published by

Eiteljorg Museum of American Indian and Western Art
Indianapolis, Indiana

Settlers West Galleries
Tucson, Arizona

Published on the occasion of the exhibition "West of Camelot: The Historical Paintings of Kenneth Riley" at the Eiteljorg Museum of American Indian and Western Art, July 18-September 12, 1993.

Published by the Eiteljorg Museum of American Indian and Western Art, Indianapolis, Indiana, in conjunction with Settlers West Galleries, Tucson, Arizona.

Printed in Singapore.

ISBN: 0–9635642–1–8

Library of Congress Catalogue Card Number: 92–063281

Frontispiece: 1. *Portrait of Kenneth Riley,* 1992, by Harley Brown, pastel, 16 x 12.
Dedication: 2. *Peruvian Mother,* 1986, oil, 6 x 7.

Note on illustrations: All dimensions are stated in inches, height preceding width. Reproductions are referenced by plate number throughout the text.

First Edition

"Historical painting is the noblest and most comprehensive branch of art, as it embraces man, the head of the visible creation. The historical painter, therefore, must study man, from the anatomy of his figure, to the most rapid and slightest gesture expressive of feeling, or the display of deep and subtle passions. He must have technical skill, a practised eye and hand, and must understand so to group his skillfully executed parts as to produce a beautiful whole. And all this is insufficient without a poetic spirit, which can form a striking conception of historical events, or create imaginary scenes of beauty." —Anna Douglas Ludlow, *A General View of the Fine Arts* (New York: G. P. Putnam, 1851).

Kenneth Riley

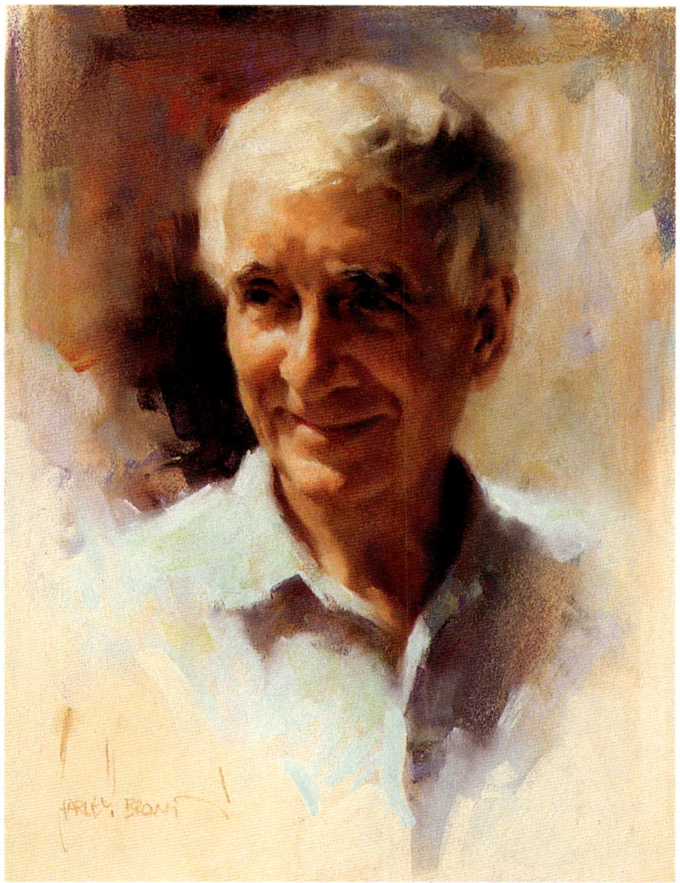

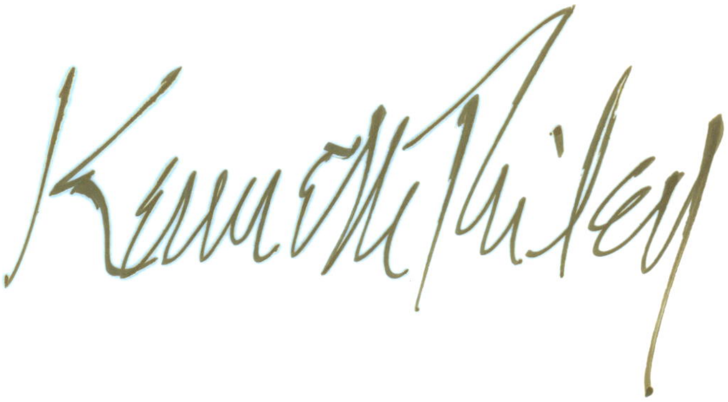

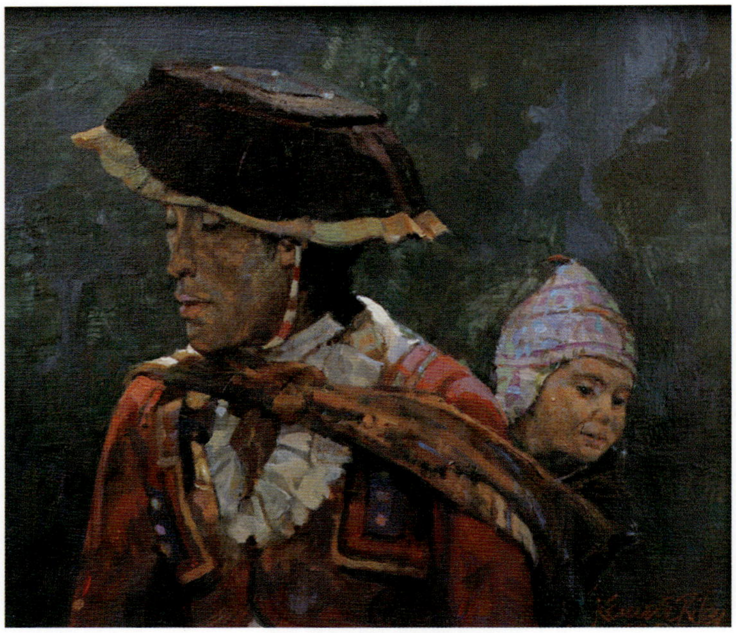

To MarCyne
who has made life itself
a work of art.

TABLE OF CONTENTS

Introduction by Michael Duty 2

Foreword by James K. Ballinger 6

Preface by Susan Hallsten McGarry 14

The Life and Art of Kenneth Riley
by Susan Hallsten McGarry 18

- Growing Up in the Midwest 24
- Searching for a Method in Kansas City 38
- Learning to Paint in New York 48
- Life and Death in the Pacific 56
- A Professional Life in Illustration 62
- Resurrection in Tombstone 92
- Yin and Yang 114
- History Painting as Storytelling, Allegory and Poetry 118

Communicating the Idea by Kenneth Riley 156

Appendix

- Chronology 195
- Selected Bibliography 200
- Prints and Posters 204

Alphabetical Index of Illustrations 206

Acknowledgments 212

INTRODUCTION

MICHAEL DUTY
EXECUTIVE DIRECTOR, EITELJORG MUSEUM

A few years ago while visiting the annual exhibition of the National Academy of Western Art in Oklahoma City, I was repeatedly drawn to a particular painting. In an exhibition of outstanding examples of contemporary western American art, this painting, for me, was the most compelling. It was titled ***Ancestors [95],*** and it seemed to me that the artist had imbued the painting with such profound content that I felt a certain reverence in its presence, almost as if I was witnessing an actual event. Since then I have attended a number of Western art exhibitions and visited countless galleries, but that painting still holds as much power for me today as it did the first time I saw it. The artist who created it is Kenneth Riley. During the ensuing years, I have sought out Ken's work, and on each occasion I have found it to be every bit as compelling as my first encounter with his art.

As this book affirms, Ken has created a remarkable body of work over the course of his career and continues to work at the same high level today. He has been recognized by his peers, by collectors who actively seek his work and by museum directors and curators who acquire his paintings for their institutions. His skill as both painter and historian are much evident in this book. What is also evident through the story of Ken's life and career is the quality of the man himself: his dedication to his art, his devotion to his wife, MarCyne, and his sensitivity to the world around him.

Looking at paintings reproduced in this book offers the reader a remarkable opportunity to visit the historic West, to gain insight into Native American culture, and to simply appreciate the skill of a consummate artist. The American West and its native cultures have always been rich fields for artistic expression and interpretation. In recent years, art that reflects the West—its heritage, traditions and people—has gained wide recognition for its quality. What Western art collectors and historians have known for some time—that art of the American West deserves the same critical attention as any other form of American art—is now being perceived by a widening circle of critics, curators, historians and the public at large. As more and more people become aware of the excellent work being done by contemporary interpreters of the American West, the esteem for Ken's paintings can only grow.

3. Detail of *Camelot [4].*

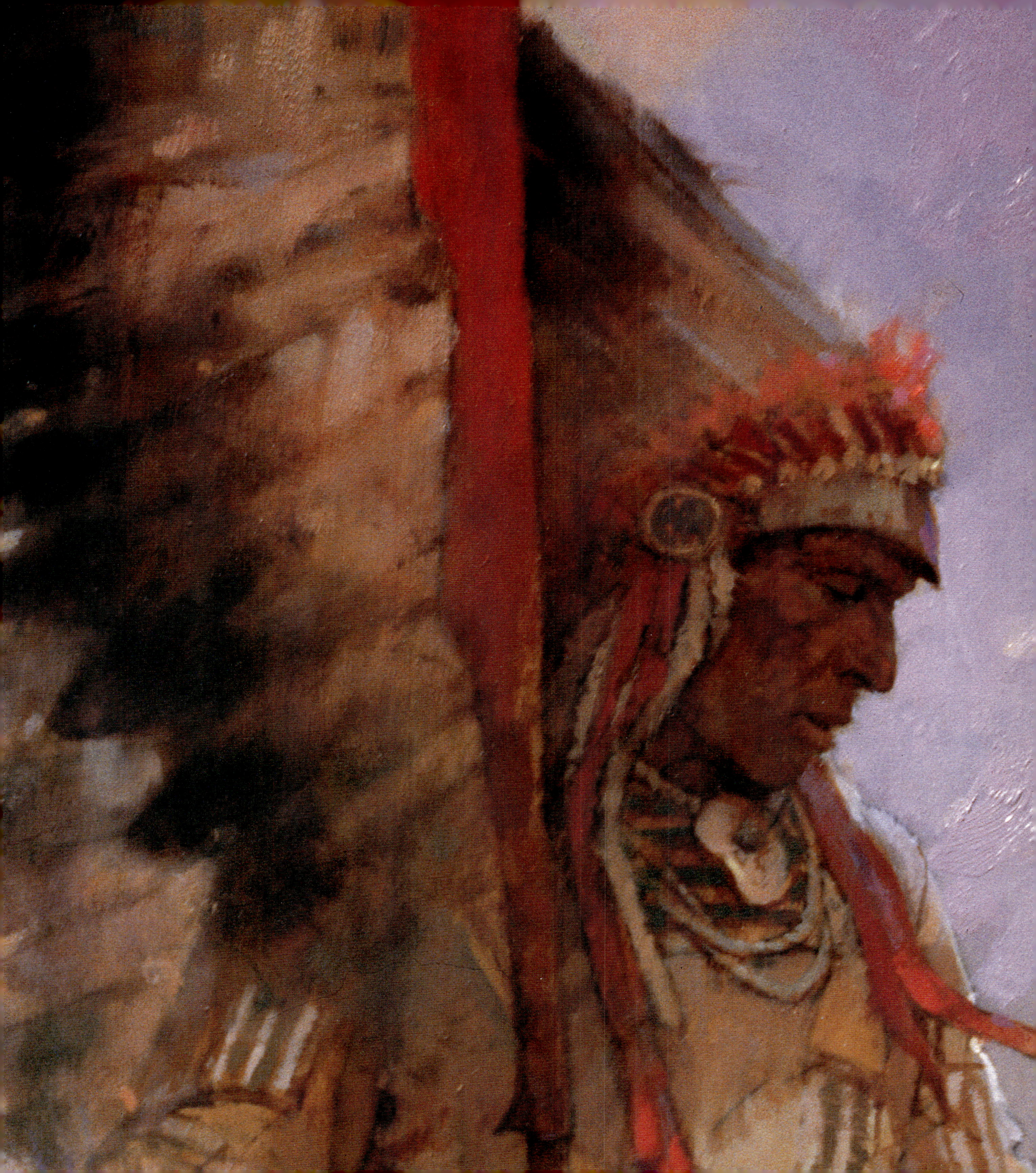

4. *Camelot*

1987

oil, 38 x 40

On a trip to Morocco, MarCyne and I attended the re-creation of a competition honoring the king. Tents flying tribal banners were filled with exotic weavings and adornments, providing a magnificent setting for Berber horsemen who fired antique muskets and rode with the pomp and ceremony of the ages. The pageantry of the Berbers has a parallel among the Plains Indians, who likewise decorated themselves and their mounts in celebration of a successful war party or in preparation for a parade on horseback at the midsummer Sun Dance. Beadwork glinting in the sun, ermine fringes and scalp locks flying in the wind, along with painted shields, beaded bow cases and feathered warbonnets and lances must have presented a formidable spectacle of not only power and status, but color and texture.

We at the Eiteljorg Museum of American Indian and Western Art are proud to be part of this deserved recognition of a great artist. Many of the paintings in this book were part of a major exhibition of Ken's work at the museum in the summer of 1993. The exhibition was organized to coincide with the bestowal of the museum's highest honor, the Eiteljorg Award for Excellence, which is given every two years to a living artist whose entire career is worthy of the highest praise. There is no more deserving artist than Ken Riley, and we are pleased to be able to share his work with the public and the readers of this book.

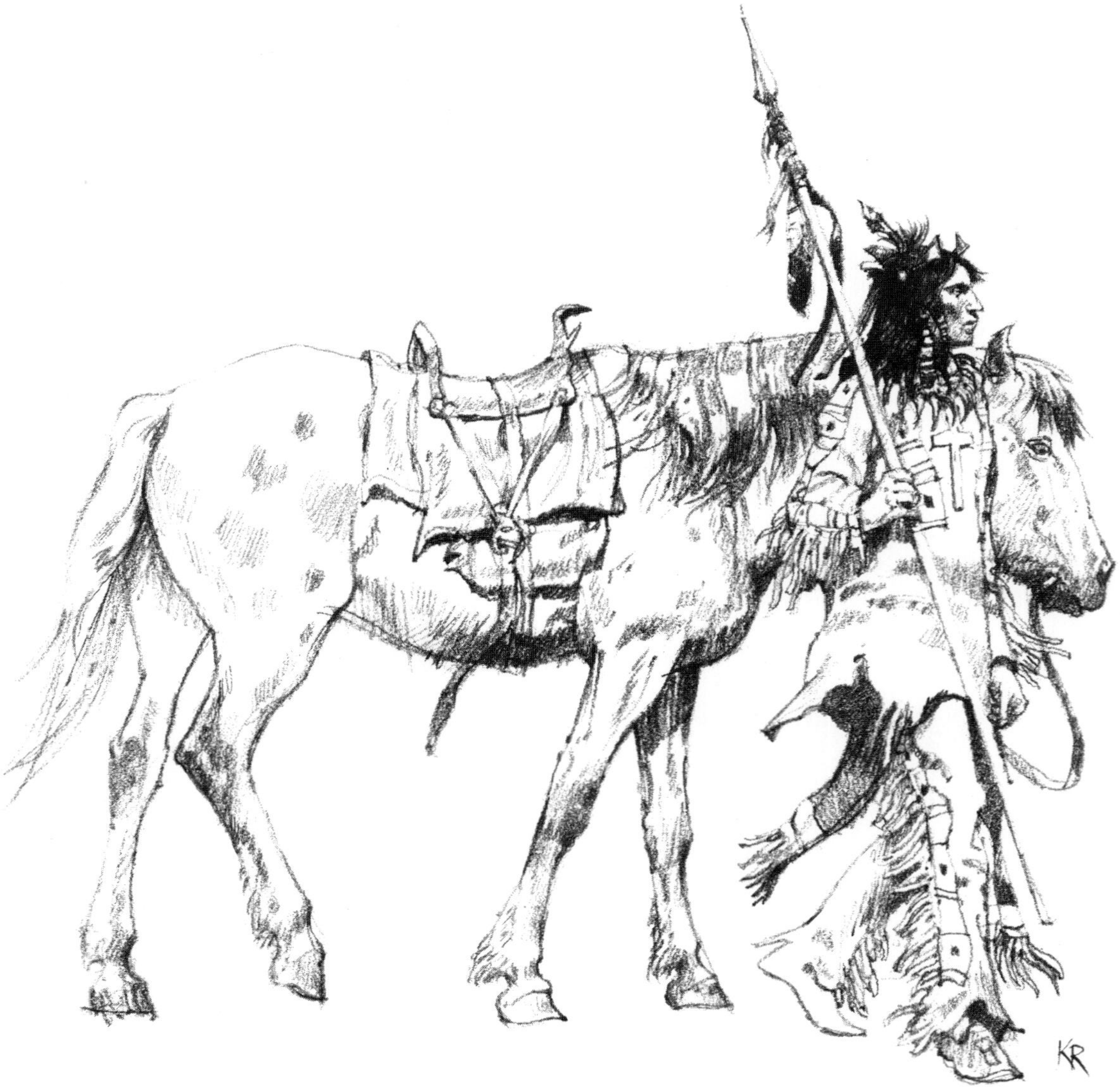

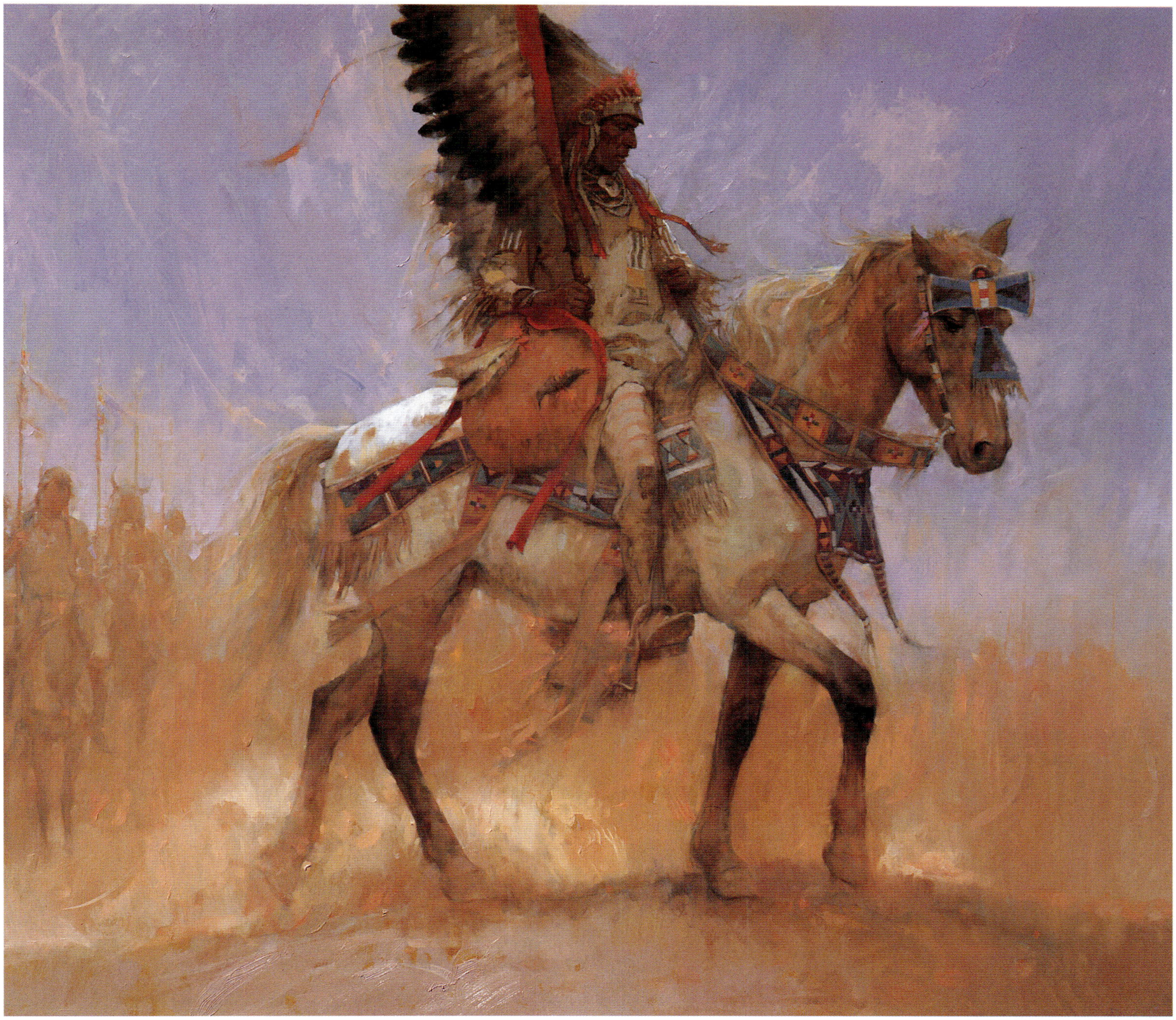

FOREWORD

JAMES K. BALLINGER
DIRECTOR, PHOENIX ART MUSEUM

During the past decade, Ken Riley has become one of America's greatest painters of the American West and its history. His career as the ultimate professional can be traced almost step-by-step since his student days. Thus, it has been a delight to know this sensitive painter, as well as to watch his rise to success.

When Ken Riley exhibited his tremendous painting ***Bodmer Paints the Piegan Chief [6]*** in the 1986 Cowboy Artists of America exhibition at the Phoenix Art Museum, it was quickly acquired for the museum's permanent collection. An examination of the reasons for selecting this work serves as a case study for understanding the importance of Ken Riley among his peers. Museum acquisition of works by living artists is quite often a waiting game. The curator of the institution with the assistance of various committees knows the artists desired for the collection, as well as the level of quality that deserves inclusion. Riley had been exhibiting at the museum for five years, and each year his body of work improved significantly. This was noted by the museum —and by his colleagues—based on a special award from the membership of the Cowboy Artists of America for the overall quality of his submissions to the annual exhibition. Thus, when the right painting came along, it was purchased, and we still consider this painting to be Riley's finest.

Bodmer Paints the Piegan Chief depicts a young Swiss artist named Karl Bodmer at work making a watercolor portrait of Piegan Chief Mehkskéhme-Sukáhs ("Iron Shirt"). The actual event took place on August 11, 1833, at Fort McKenzie, an outpost located near the Great Falls of the Missouri River in what is today Montana. Bodmer felt this dignified chief to be the most distinguished of the Piegans, and Riley has re-created the scene constructing the composition around his own interpretation of the Bodmer watercolor, which is today in the collection of the Joslyn Art Museum, Omaha, Nebraska. Because a museum most often tries to amass a collection that documents the history of a culture, a style or a type of object, a picture such as ***Bodmer Paints the Piegan Chief*** is highly desirable. It ties together the development

5. Detail of *Bodmer Paints the Piegan Chief [6]*.

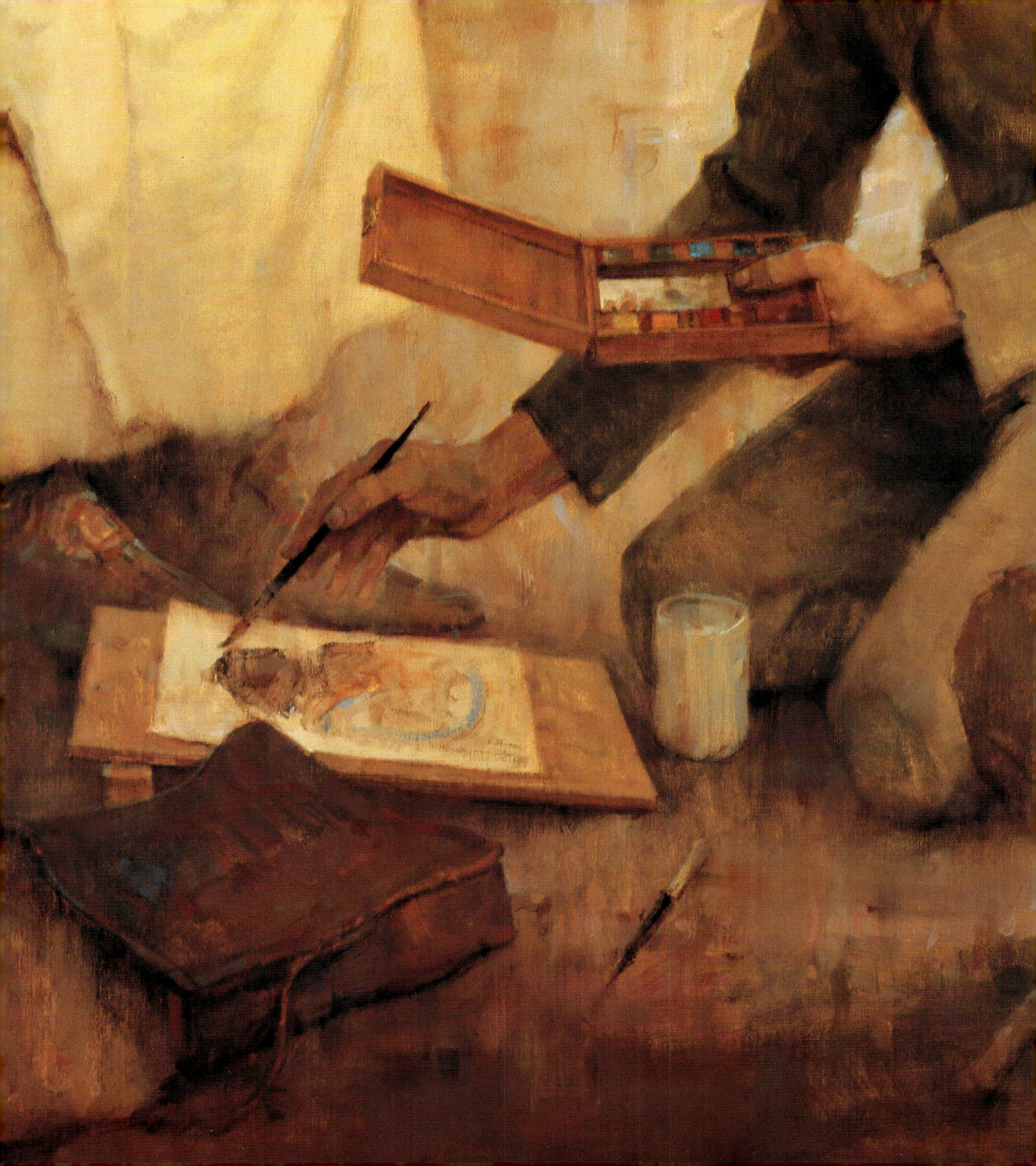

of, in this case, the history of Western American art from its very earliest days of explorer artists, to the most current artists, who reflect upon earlier events to create a narrative. Riley often refers to the original journals of Western American adventurers, artists and residents of the past century so that his narratives spring from actual events. He adds the detail based on research. But, he also brings to the work a special sense of universality which enables the story to remain poignant a century and a half later. And here, even an allegory is created. Riley uses an earlier artist, Bodmer, allegorically in order to put himself even closer to the place and time he has chosen for his painting. This insight and interpretation sets Ken Riley apart from his contemporaries.

Riley has always sought to place himself side-by-side with his subjects by understanding history and utilizing primary sources. The Phoenix Art Museum picture demonstrates this characteristic quite well. Among the first painters to venture into the arid West were George Catlin and Karl Bodmer. Catlin moved into the upper Midwest by steamer around 1830, while Bodmer chose a more common approach. He was the "staff artist" of the Prince Maximilian du Wied expedition of 1832–33—which covered much of the same area as had Catlin—and was charged with providing illustrations for the Prince's proposed volume on the natural history of the region. Thus Bodmer was called upon to visually document flora, fauna and the Native American population. These explorer artists became the first "Western" artists.

As expansion of American society forced Native Americans off of their homelands, more artists came into the area, eventually settling there. Missouri painter George Caleb Bingham was probably the greatest resident artist of the West during the middle years of the nineteenth century. Finally, as the initial conquest of the West came to a close toward the end of the century and great wealth was realized from cattle, mining and tourism, a more nostalgic look at life in the region was adopted by artists. Frederic Remington, Charles M. Russell and others carefully combined firsthand experiences on the Great Plains and in the Southwest with subtle, personal interpretations of a life they saw as passing. The power of these works captivated American audiences for several generations, until very recently when the face of the West began to be redrawn, especially by historians.

Ken Riley's art can perhaps be viewed as providing an end point of this narrative. His earliest work was that of an illustrator following his training at

6. *Bodmer Paints the Piegan Chief*
1986
oil, 48 x 40
Phoenix Art Museum, Arizona

On August 11, 1833, in a room at Fort McKenzie, Swiss painter Karl Bodmer set about painting the portrait of Mehkskéhme-Sukáhs ("Iron Shirt"), a principal chief of the Piegan Blackfeet. With great affection for the record that Bodmer left us of those early times, I did this painting of him at work on the portrait. Despite the tough conditions under which he worked, I would have liked to have been in Bodmer's shoes!

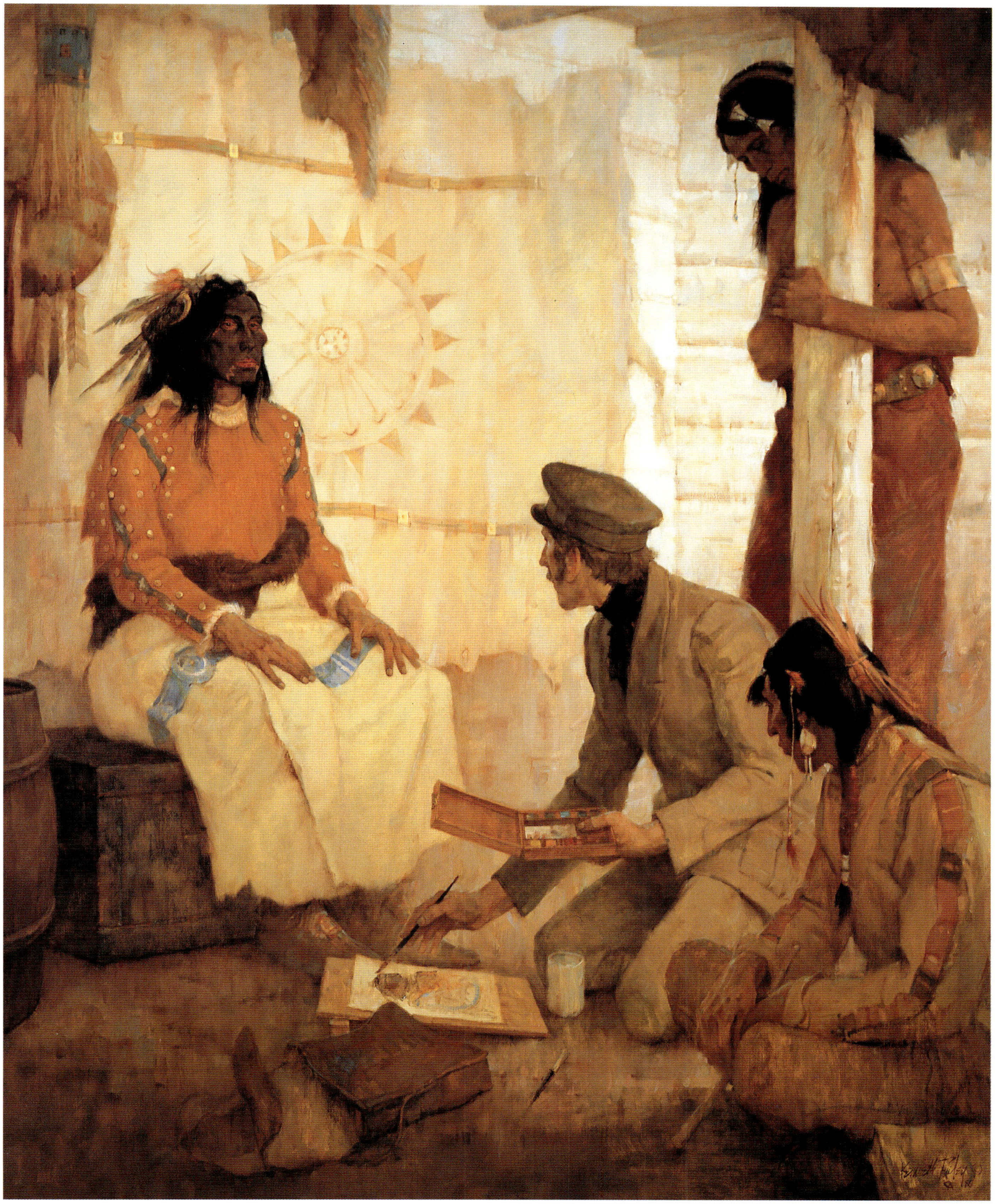

7. *Evening Calm*

1983

acrylic, 16 x 36

Seated around the campfire, a banjo player provides the evening's entertainment along with a friendly jug. Though this is a night scene, I tried to keep it from getting too dark. The spirit of this work is perhaps reminiscent of George Caleb Bingham whose paintings I first encountered while studying at the Kansas City Art Institute. Scenes of men reveling on the river were Bingham's stock-in-trade.

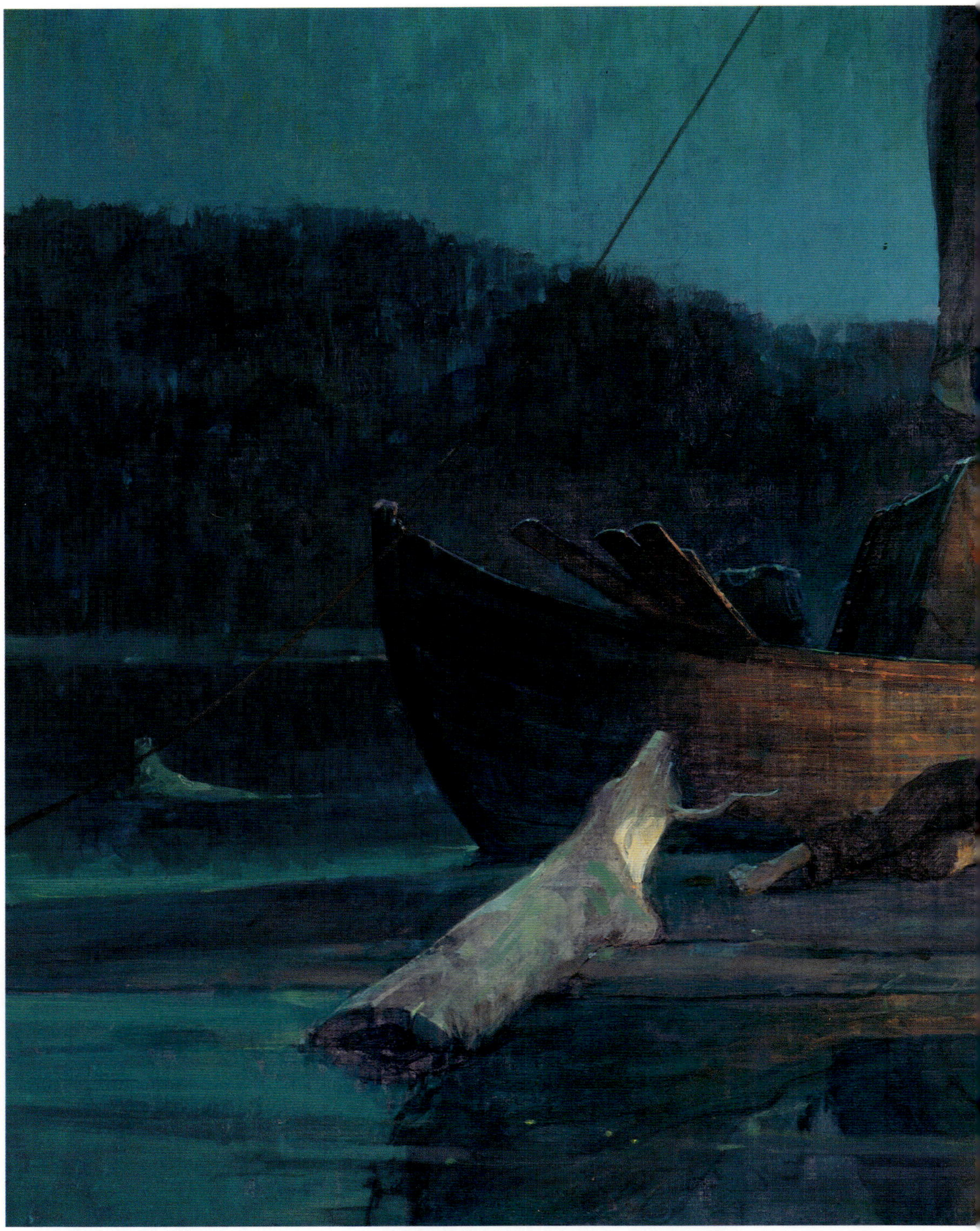

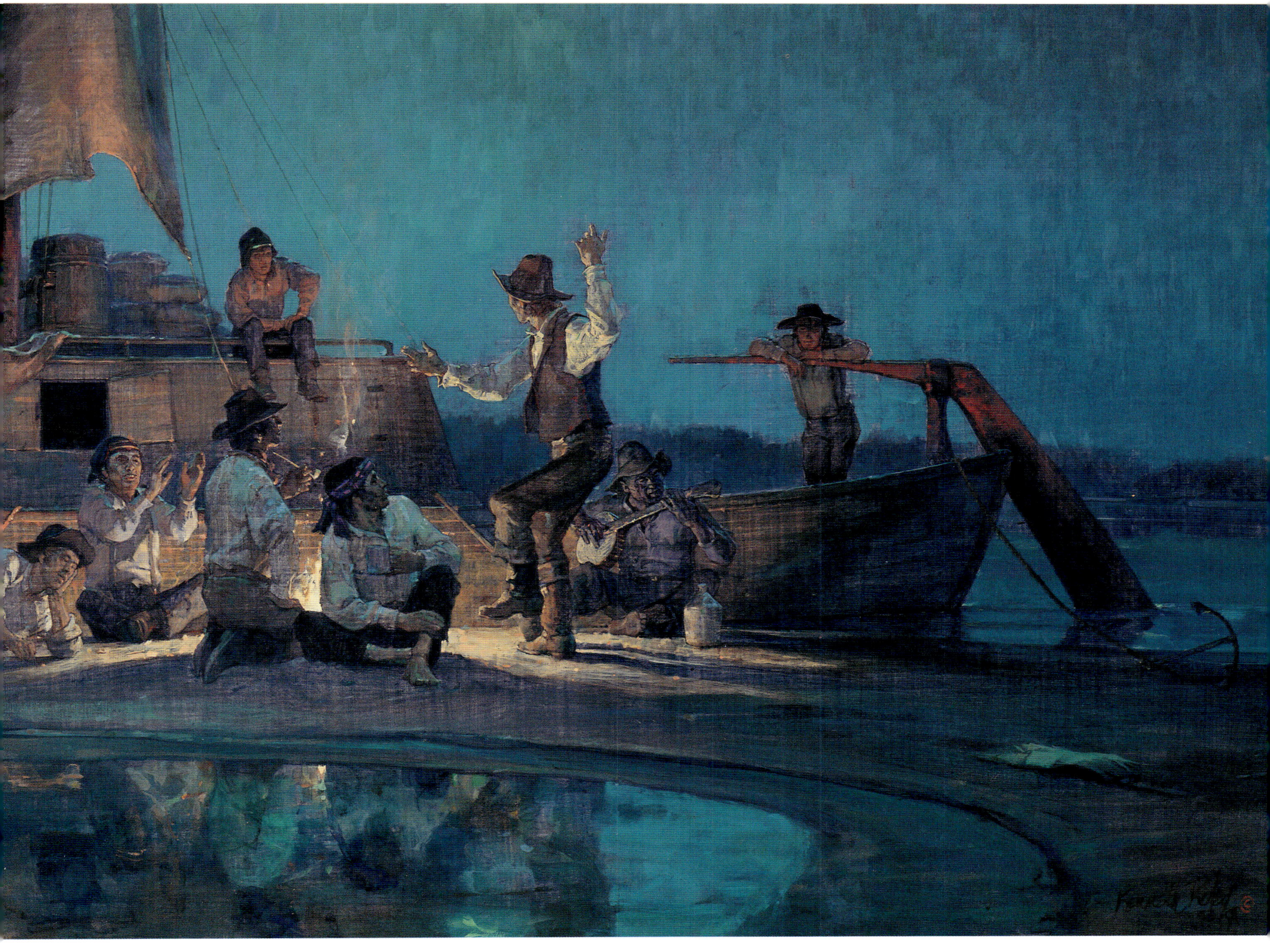

the Kansas City Art Institute under the tutelage of Thomas Hart Benton. This association is important. Benton's overt rejection of modernism during the 1930s in favor of the development of a regionalist style celebrating the agricultural life of the Midwest was a crucial dividing point in American art history. Riley, as did other students, learned from Benton the importance of being able to draw in a classical manner, to compose figures to create a narrative and to create a rhythm of line and color in his work. Riley then chose not to participate in the avant-garde but to become an illustrator. He made his decision at a time when this commercial outlet for an artist was still attainable. Interestingly, Jackson Pollock, the innovator of Abstract Expressionism, America's most radical break in the art world, also studied with Benton during these years. A close examination of Pollock's work also demonstrates the importance of the rhythmic use of color and line.

Illustration quite often provides a dead end for the truly creative artist. Spending time, as did Riley, providing visual equivalents of a creative writer's image can thwart the visual artist's own imagination. Faced with this predicament, Riley turned to the American West as a subject. By relying on firsthand descriptions of the region, he was freed from others' work to create his own images and interpretations based on a region in which he was comfortable. Over the years, two eras of nineteenth-century American history have especially intrigued Riley: the Plains Indians' activities and the decades of the Apache Wars in the southwestern states.

As Riley's subject interests shifted, so did his lifestyle. He moved from the East to Arizona, where he lives today. His career literally exploded with this geographical change and the freedom it provided. By placing himself literally in the middle of his artistic inquiry, his style matured. His narrative works have often gone against the traditions of Western American art, which for so many years have focused on the action and "wild west" aspects of the region. Rather, Riley has chosen to capture scenes of quiet, reflective moments in an attempt to show the humanity of Native Americans and Anglos on the frontier, two groups who were often combatants. Coming to understand Riley's work is actually an act of knowing the painter, who is a quiet, articulate and introspective artist. His careful research and his attempt to capture individual lives based on personal journals and letters create the one-on-one connection he also strives for with his audience. And, no one does it better.

8. *Four Lances*
1988
oil, 48 x 42

A few years ago I attended a Hopi kiva ceremony. It was a dark night and the drumming and chanting hypnotically united the crowd. The movement of the dancers that night inspired this work. The warm and cool reds pulsate around this Mandan warrior who seeks the spiritual realm by dancing between lances indicating the four cardinal points.

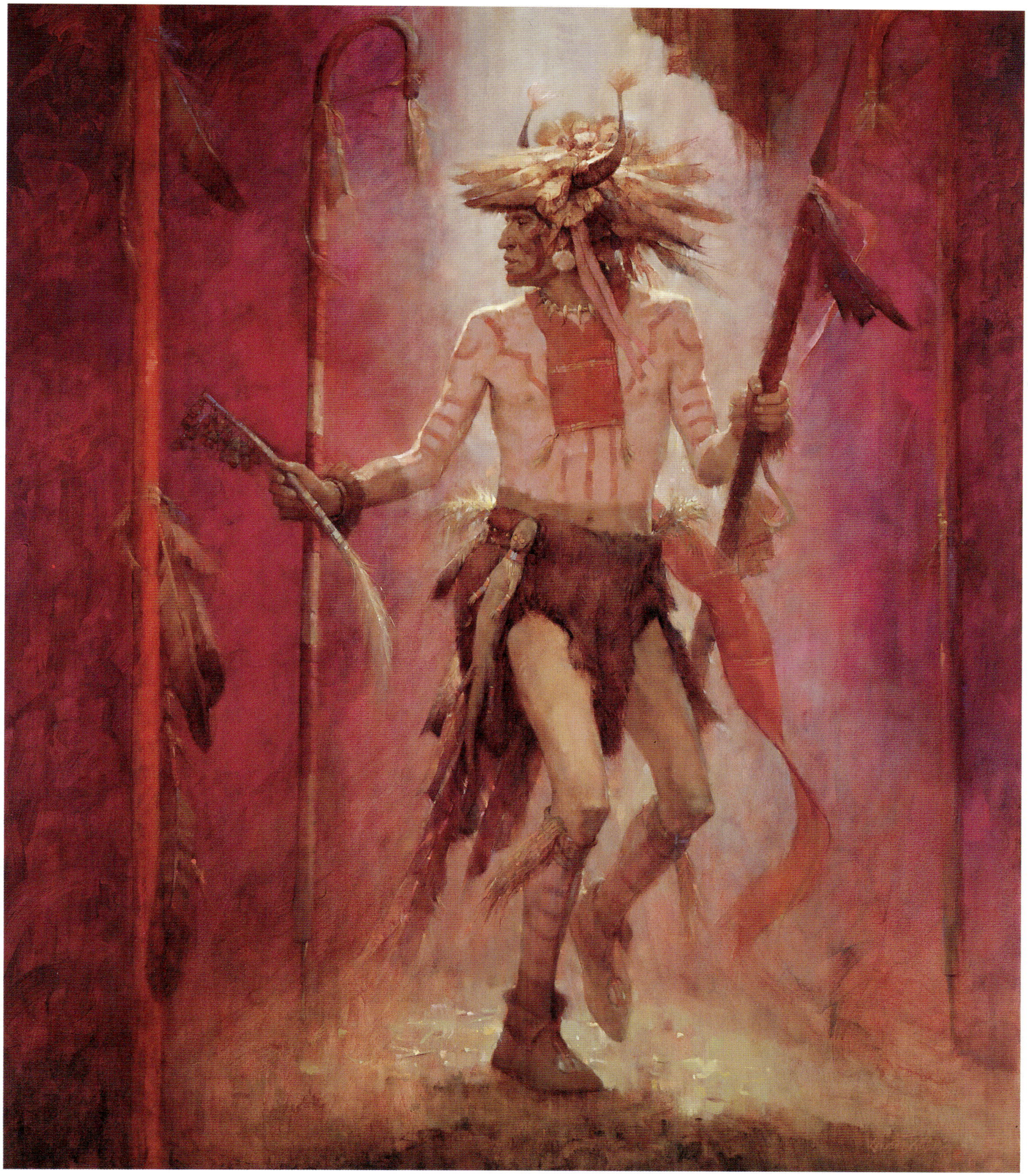

PREFACE

SUSAN HALLSTEN McGARRY

Enjoy this master storyteller by design
SH McGarry

More than ever before, western American art is receiving the critical attention it merits. A growing list of museum exhibitions, in particular, have focused on living and deceased artists who depict the American frontier experience. The benchmark in this regard was the 1991 exhibition and catalog *The West As America*, organized by the National Museum of American Art. Focusing on the nineteenth century, catalog essayists offered novel, sometimes outrageous but always provocative reinterpretations of frontier imagery. Scenes formerly believed to be innocent and idyllic were described instead as replete with latent and blatant symbols of religious and sexual supremacy, wanton despoliation of the landscape, decimation of the Native American and more.

Such revisionist thinking adds tremendously to our enjoyment of art. By forcing a new perspective, we question the baggage of stereotypes we bring to a subject. This fuels not only expanded interpretation of the past but of today's material, as well. No longer can we simply accept a superficial two-dimensional reading of western American subjects. Rather it is imperative to explore the three-dimensional depth, searching not only for the artist's point of view, but our personal response to what appears to be going on in an artwork. I use the word "appears" because anyone involved in the creative process admits that while some aspects of selectivity and presentation are predictable and understandable, others remain a mystery. Art is, therefore, both discovered revelation during its making and a revelation of additional discoveries once it is viewed by others.

Discovery was at the heart of the collaboration between Ken Riley and myself in compiling this book. Hours of taped dialogue between us was unrehearsed and spontaneous. His candor in responding to my assumptions and interpretations was cordial and unlimited. Only on occasion did he chide, "Just remember, you said that, not me."

The downside to working with a living artist, particularly one as private as Riley, is the reluctance to pry. This would have been especially problematic to the writer whose agenda included imposing some religious significance on the oft-used cross shapes in Riley's paintings. Or finding some lingering

9. Detail of *The Legend of Manabozho [11]*.

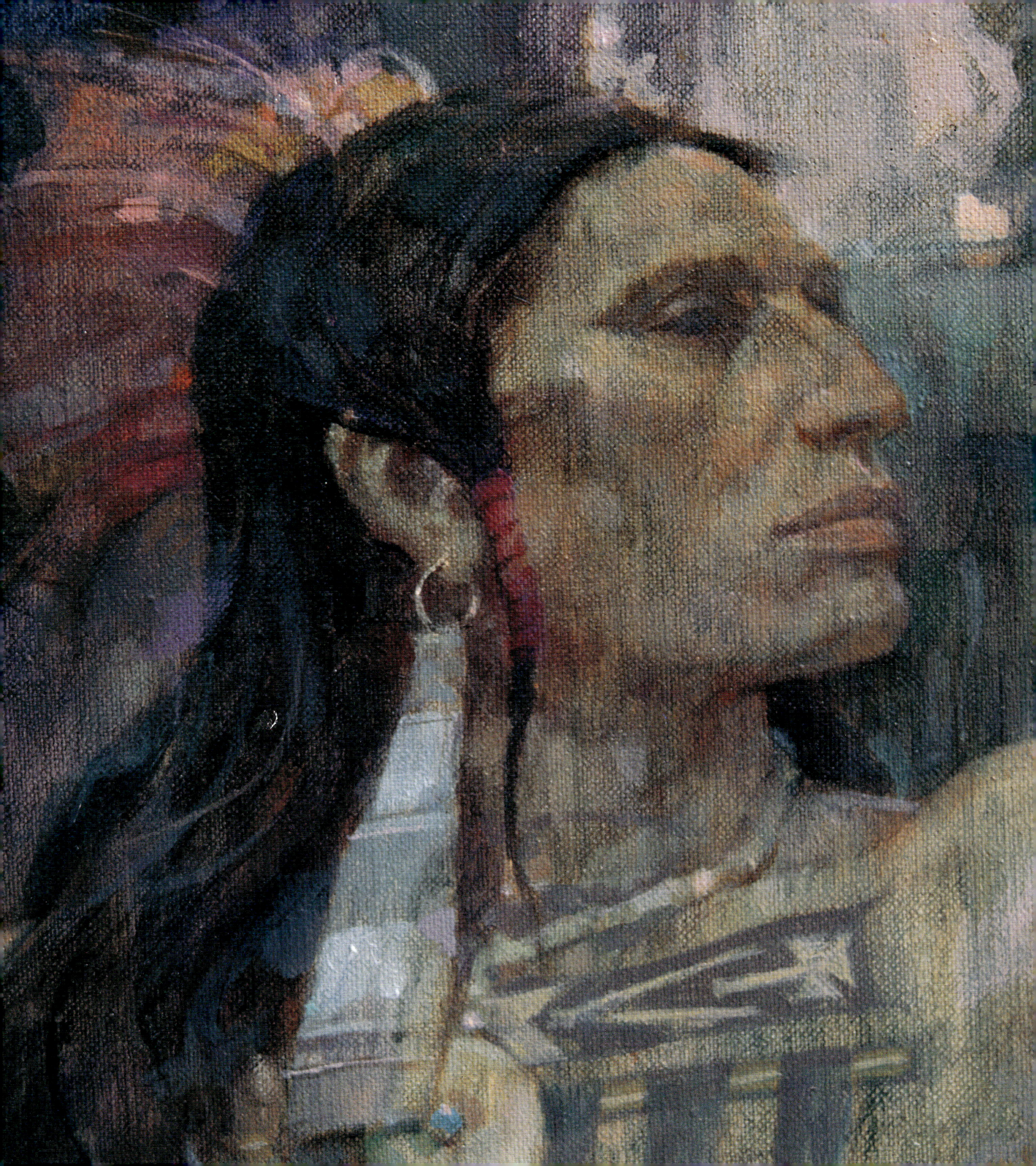

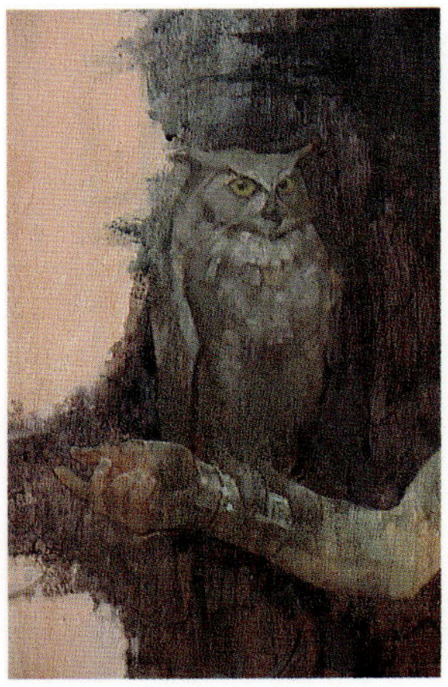

10. Detail of *The Legend of Manabozho [11].*

11. *The Legend of Manabozho*

1992

oil, 46 x 42

Although I was familiar with the *Song of Hiawatha*, I had no idea that Longfellow's poem was based upon the Woodland legend of Manabozho. Originally recorded and published by Henry R. Schoolcraft, the legend of Manabozho tells of a mercurial warrior who communicated with animals and changed his form at will. When I was commissioned to paint the legend, I decided to focus on the three guises of Manabozho—shaman, warrior and old woman—encircled by forest creatures and an abstract suggestion of northern woods. Since the owl is regarded as a storyteller in many Indian legends, I've shown it looking out at the viewer with the wisdom of a soothsayer.

childhood trauma that causes Riley to rarely paint figures that meet you face to face. While I frequently broached such observations during our interviews, I did not feel cheated when Riley laughed and assured me he had "never thought of that." Likewise, where there was a discrepancy in corroborating dates or events, I more often than not opted for Riley's recollection.

When I spoke of my involvement in this project to other artists, they were anxious to offer opinions about what makes Riley's work so special. The adjectives "classical," "sophisticated," "gentle" and "sensitive" came up more than once, as did the notion that Riley is "not just another western artist." The foundation for such comments comes, I believe, from Riley's dedication not to the hard lines of authenticity and ethnography but to the more fluid nuance of allegory and spirituality. Unlike many of his peers who pride themselves on an historical incident well-told or an artifact well-copied, Riley uses the past as inspiration and then passes through it to personal revelation about the harmony and perfection to be found in the human condition. On the pediments of the Parthenon and on the ceilings and walls of Renaissance churches we find the classical ideal Kenneth Riley portrays in the guise of a legendary Indian shaman named Manabozho.

The story that follows introduces you to Kenneth Riley today. It is organized chronologically thereafter, beginning with his childhood. The chapter "History Painting as Storytelling, Allegory and Poetry" examines the three forces that inspire Riley to paint. "Communicating the Idea: Notes on Composition and Design" was written by Riley as a refresher course in elements of design as well as a synopsis of how he himself composes his ideas.

It has been an honor to collaborate on a project that commemorates the July-September 1993 retrospective of Riley's work at the Eiteljorg Museum of American Indian and Western Art. Through the experience I have learned much about the greatness of the human spirit and the power of artists to convey that spirit through ideas expressed in paint on canvas.

Susan Hallsten McGarry
16 August 1992

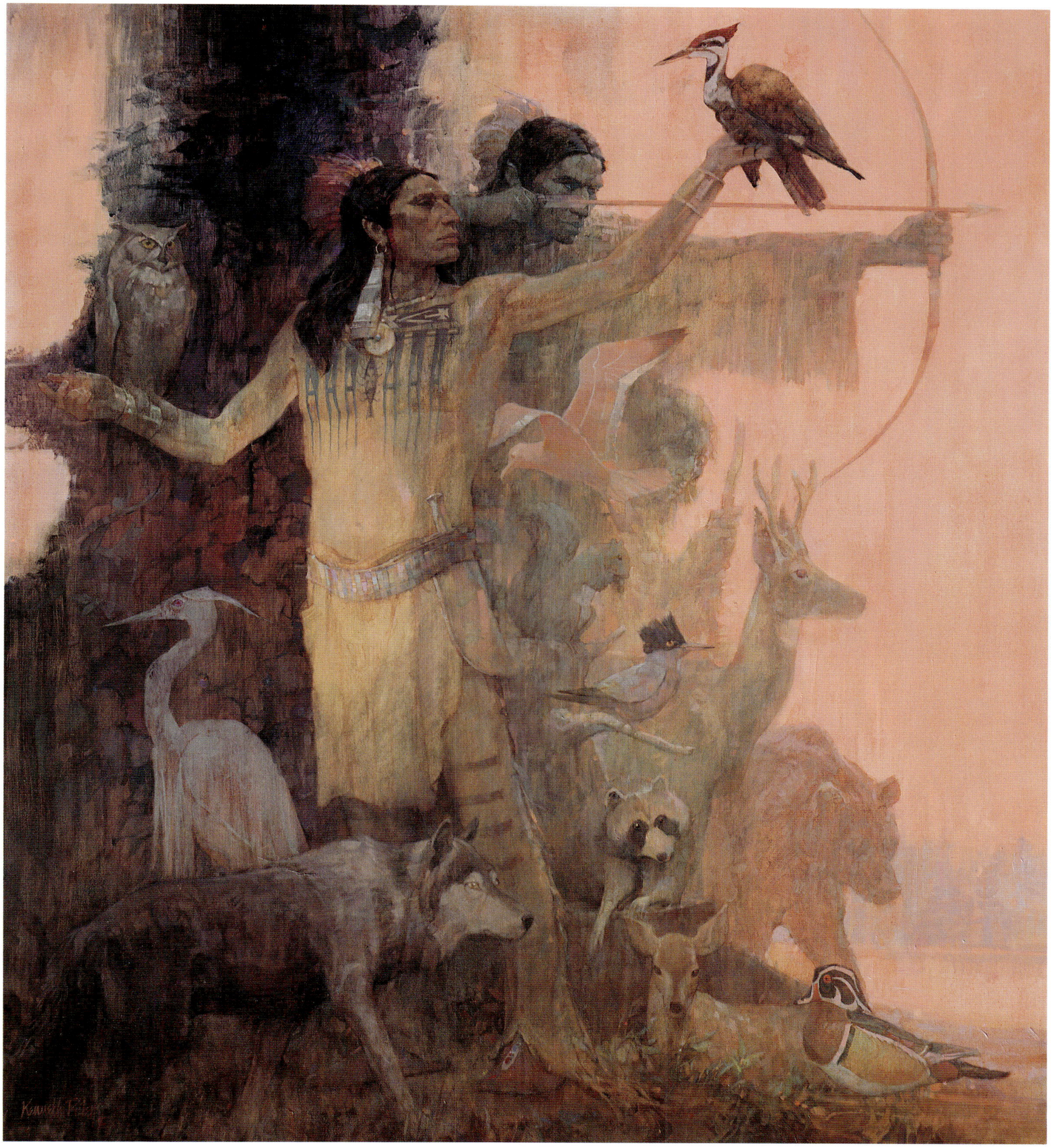

THE LIFE AND ART OF KENNETH RILEY

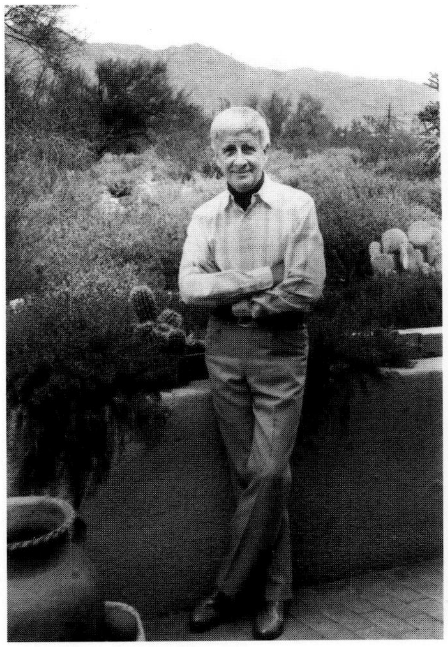

12. Kenneth Riley on his patio in Tucson with a view of the Santa Catalina Mountains, ca. 1990.

Ken and MarCyne Riley's front door opens to a prodigious corridor that stretches from the foyer to the hearth at the far end of the house. With high ceilings and softly lit by skylights, "the gallery," as the Rileys call it, gives access to the other rooms: rooms that offer a 360-degree view of the mountain ranges surrounding the Santa Cruz Valley of southern Arizona.

Situated atop a hill landscaped with gravel and sand, pale-green paloverde and rose-colored Santa Rita cacti, the Riley home was designed by Ken and MarCyne with a southwestern flair. Ceiling vigas are rough-hewn and the exterior walls surfaced in adobe-colored stucco. Hints of an international sensibility can be observed in the functional simplicity of the facade, the Art Deco-styled gate and the Oriental restraint of the pebbled garden. The aesthetic here, like the Rileys themselves, is far from formulaic.

Indeed, the cool, Spanish-tiled gallery is decorated with an eclectic array of Middle Eastern rugs and dhurries, elaborately embellished trunks, polished brass lanterns and carved wood Shivas. Their range of cultural origin bespeaks the Rileys' fascination with color, texture and design. The objects also confirm their interest in the native artisans across the world who crafted these items with skill and attention to detail.

In this large, almost reverent space in an otherwise intimately-scaled home, a tangle of green plants flourishes in the humidity created by a lap-pool. Resting on its blue-tiled ledge is a sculpture of an Indian in trance-like ritual. Nearby is a Hopi maiden whose smooth, clean lines are carved in moss-colored stone. Above it, on the wall, is a tin-covered burro that once served as the sign for MarCyne's "Silver Burro" gift shop in Tombstone.

13. Detail of *The Witches Market, Bolivia [14].*

The walls are hung with small paintings, drawings and oil sketches. Many are by friends and professional colleagues. Mixed among them are paintings by both Ken and MarCyne. Ken's on-location studies invite escape into moody rock-lined canyons, while MarCyne's richly layered mixed-media paintings bring the visitor face-to-face with the colorful Third World women who made the objects so proudly displayed here. With inherent curiosity

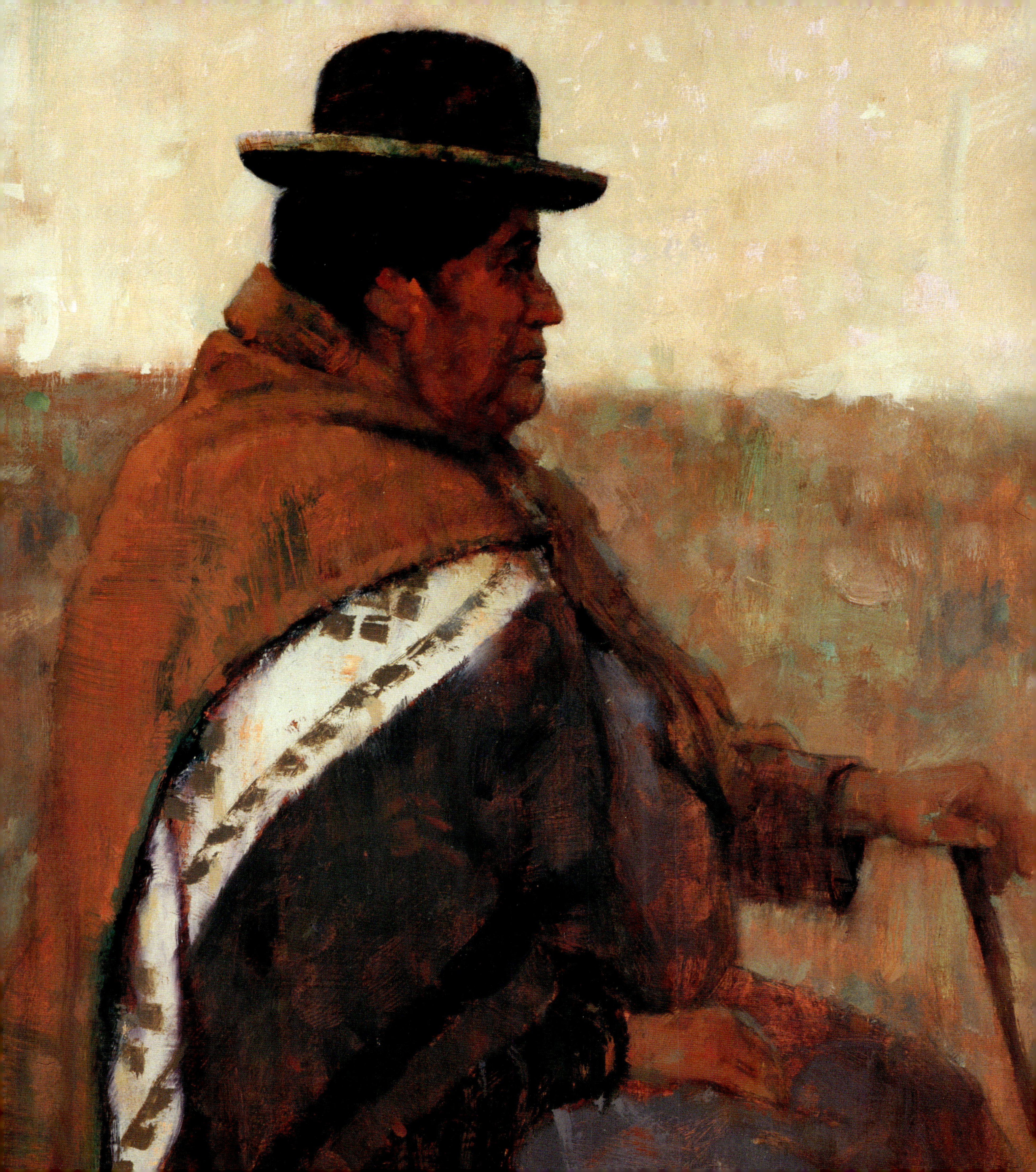

14. *The Witches Market, Bolivia*
1983
oil, 20 x 40

At twelve thousand feet above sea level, La Paz, Bolivia, is the highest national capital in the world. Ringed by snow-capped peaks that rise twenty thousand feet, the city sits in a volcanic crater. The business district and wealthy are found in the central lower elevation, while the poor live at the top. Every day people come down through a maze of narrow streets to market their services and wares. Most fascinating of all was the Witches Market where this woman was evidently a resident of considerable standing. She occupied a prominent corner from which she sold all manner of potions and cures and sat on her little platform with the regality and aplomb of a practicing physician.

about global humanity, Ken and MarCyne have explored life—near and far, familiar and foreign—and surrounded themselves with evidence of its finest moments.

Their extensive travels having taken them literally around the world, the Rileys' view of the city is likewise circumscribed only by the cycles of day and night. They observe pale late-morning sunrises above the Rincon Range and blood-red sunsets behind the Tucson Mountains. During the summer monsoon season circling clouds scud across the Santa Rita Mountains bringing the desert a goodly portion of its scant eleven inches of rainfall. And throughout the day when Ken looks up from his easel out his huge north window he watches the shifting light transform the Santa Catalina Mountains from cool, bleached white to warm, rosy beige.

Here, in the studio, Riley's experiences of some seven decades distill into paintings. To communicate these things, he speaks in a language of rhythmic line, provocative design and poetic color. "The challenge," he says, "is to become articulate in these terms and to use them as tools to sing."

As a bard savors the details of a story about a hero, arranging them to elucidate the underpinnings of a society, Riley takes the bare skeleton of history and fleshes it out with the soul of humanity. Communicating our common humanity is what Ken Riley's art is all about, and in so doing he reveals much about himself. "No artist works in a vacuum," he observes. "We are constantly responding to and stimulated by things around us. The artist must be aware of and pursue the business of knowing himself."

We all fall back on clichés and tried-and-true solutions. Therefore, it is critical to put in the energy necessary to doing your pictures not just differently but better. —KR

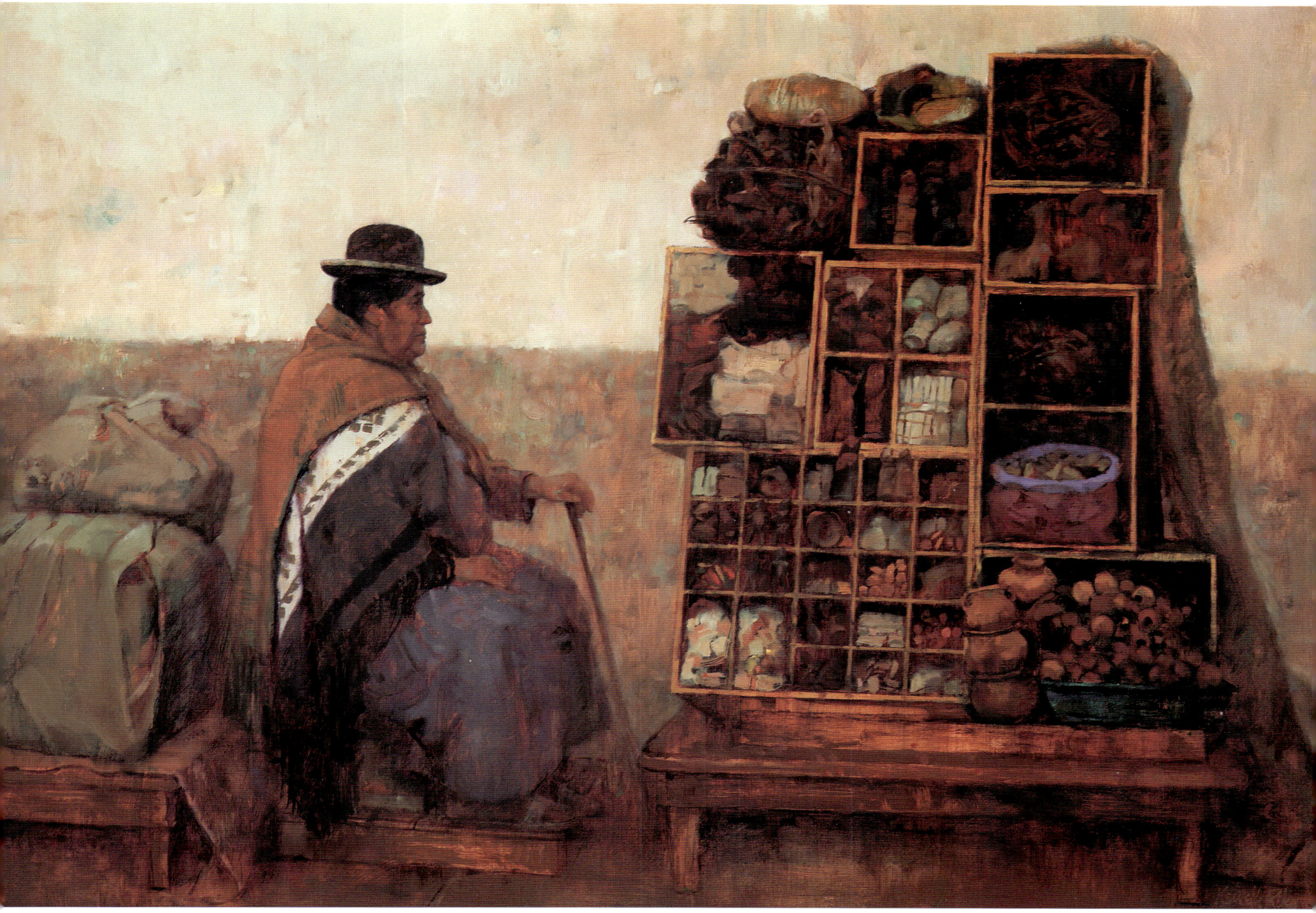

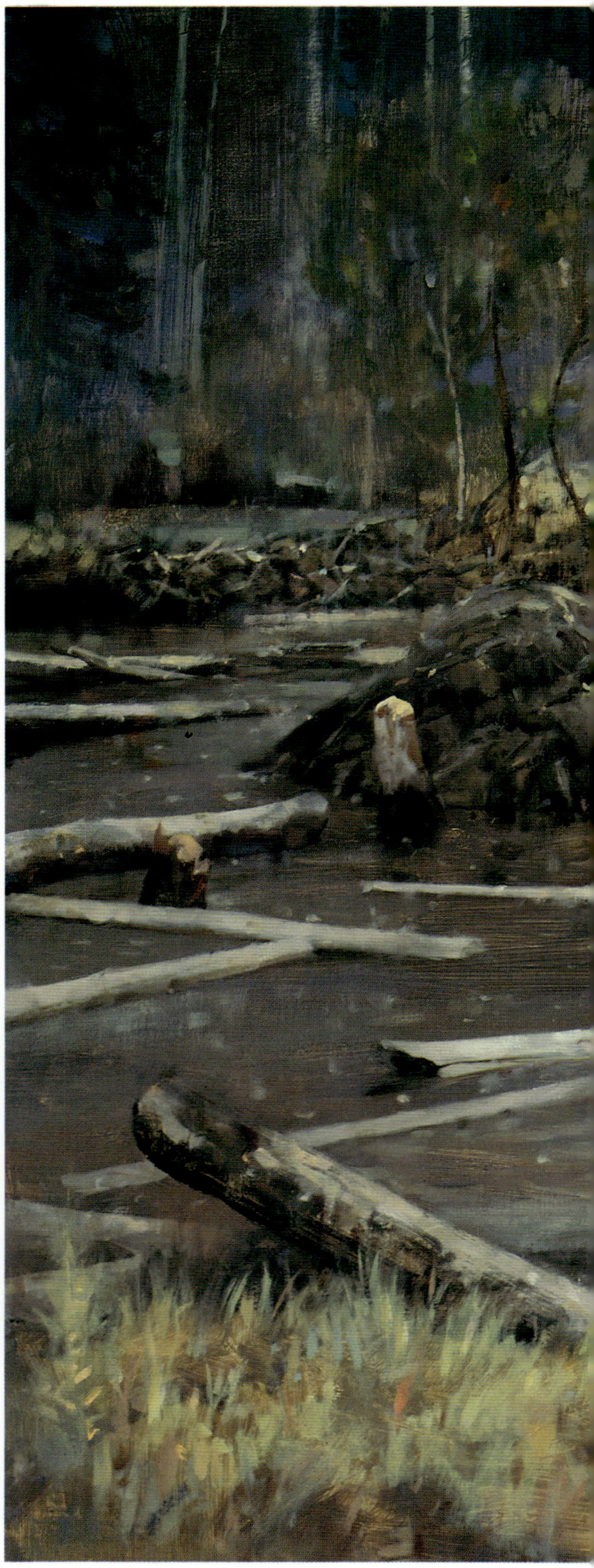

15. *Season's End*
ca. 1981
oil, 20 x 30

I had been hiking and sketching in Mancos Valley in southern Colorado when I came across this beaver pond. It was raining and the atmosphere was heavy and moody—a perfect spot to imagine trappers. Back in the studio, I arranged the logs in the foreground to create an interesting design, splashed the pond with rain drops and added trappers on horseback headed to rendezvous in a primeval wilderness.

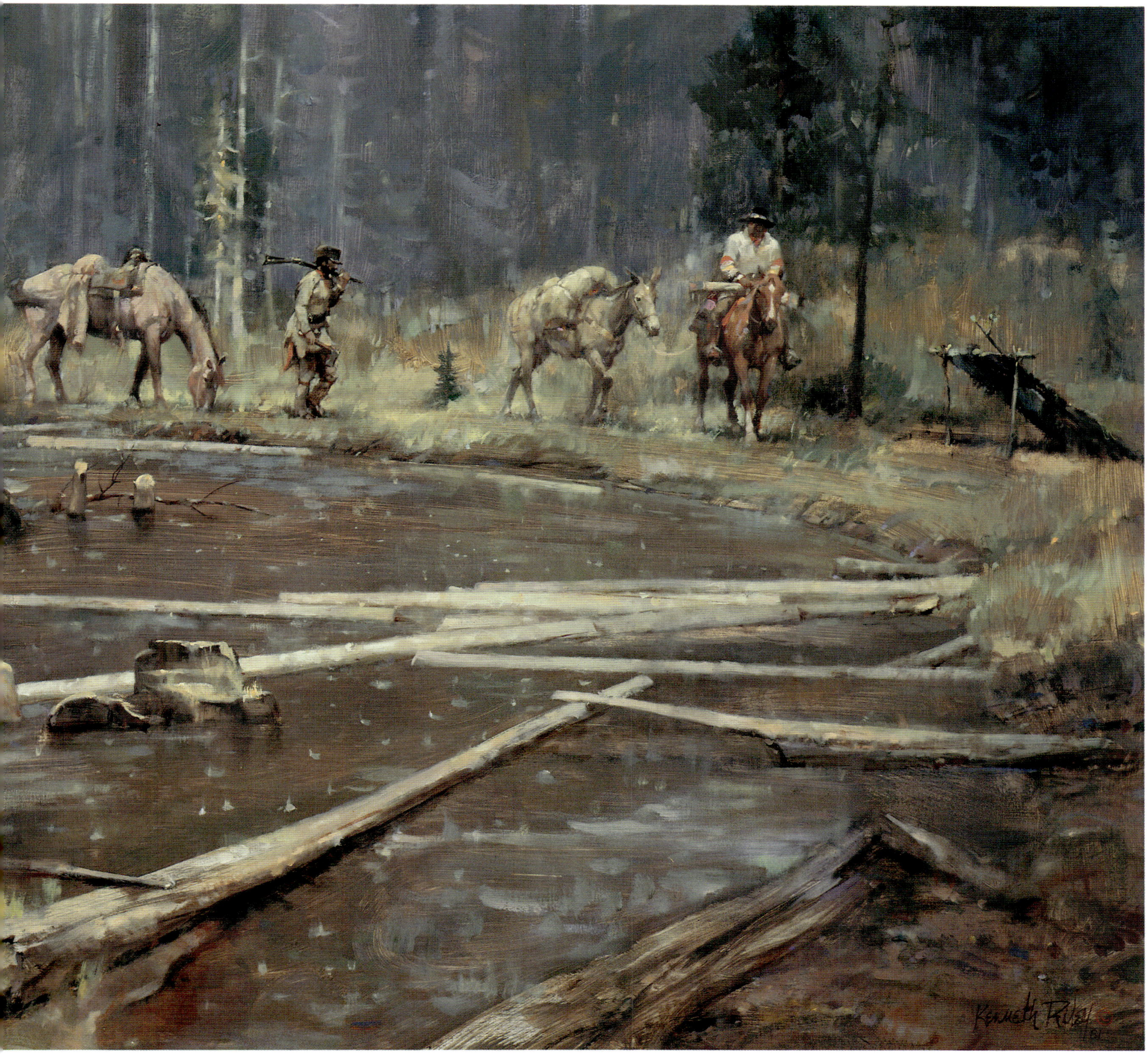

GROWING UP IN THE MIDWEST

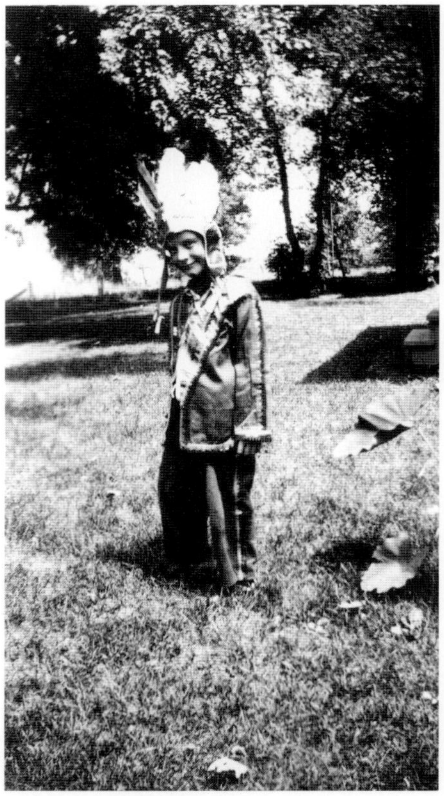

16. Five-year-old Ken Riley dressed as an Indian.

17. Detail of *Romancing the West [18].*

Fall 1924 ... Stars dissolve into a band of faint lavender expanding on the eastern horizon. Plates clatter, and the fragrance of coffee seeps through the floorboards, alerting the boy to morning. Bolting down the stairs, the five-year-old races into the warm glow of the kitchen where Grandmother Pauling peels carrots and potatoes for the noon meal while Grandfather enjoys a breakfast of home-cured bacon and eggs.

Downing a glass of cream-topped milk, Ken lets the screen door slam behind him and heads out to the yard. Pails are lined up near the cistern. While Uncle Joe irrigates the great throat of the pump, Ken reaches for the handle and begins a rhythmic swing that gets harder and harder until water gushes out the spigot. Distant voices merge with the sound of splashing until suddenly a monster lurches over the hill, its wood fires belching and steaming, its fly wheels whirring. "The threshers are here!" the boy announces ... and so begins the ritual of the harvest.

Though many decades and miles away from his maternal grandparents' farm in north-central Missouri, Ken Riley's childhood memories are permeated by a nostalgia for the "pre-television, pre-airplane era that is so foreign to contemporary society." Like a young Tom Sawyer, his years of innocence were defined by small-town life on a bend in a great river. In this nurturing rural environment, he came to appreciate the turn of the seasons and the endless cycles of withering and decay that make possible the rebirth of spring.

Descended from Irish immigrants on his father's side and Dutch farmers on his mother's, Kenneth Pauling Riley was born during the September harvest of 1919, the only child of Elwin and Marie Pauling Riley who lived in the small town of Waverly, Missouri. Located twenty miles east of historic Lexington, where Civil War cannon-balls are still embedded in the courthouse walls, Waverly was a supply station for area farmers during the 1920s. Elwin had grown up in this town where his father before him had served as a justice of the peace. Ken's memories of the area single out stories of steam-powered barges trafficking goods from St. Louis to Kansas City, and Grandfather Pauling's sleigh, which transported the family across the frozen Missouri for Christmas celebrations.

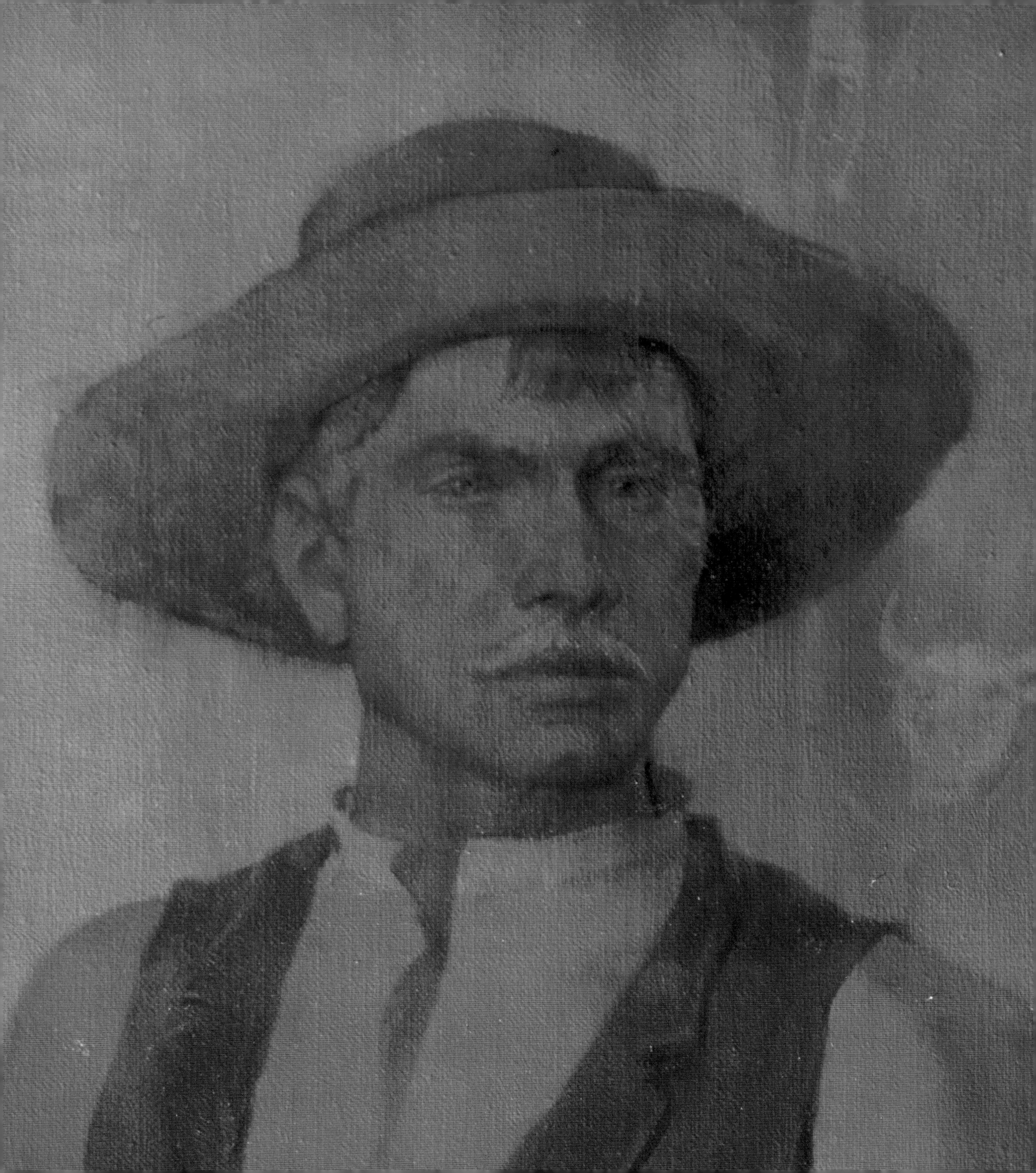

He better remembers Carrollton, where the Riley family moved when Ken was two. Ten miles north of Waverly, Carrollton was the county seat. Band concerts filled the summer nights in the town square, along with radios and mass advertising. Elwin took advantage of an emerging industry that fueled the tanks and fixed the flats of America's newly developed love-affair with the automobile. A race-car aficionado as a young man, he became an auto mechanic and then a Chevrolet car salesman, who helped keep motoring America chugging along the newly improved county roads.

"Touring," as driving was called in the 1920s, was a weekend pastime for the Rileys, as well. Piling Marie and Ken into the Chevy, Elwin regularly left the hustle of town for the solitude of the Pauling farm fifteen miles south. Passing fields planted in corn and grain, across the Missouri, into the Osage Plains, they came upon the classic red barn and clapboard farm house just north of Blackburn. There the Paulings raised everything from milk cows, hogs and chickens, to corn, wheat, fruit trees and vegetables. When Ken began visiting the farm there was no electricity, nor any indoor facilities. Within a matter of years, however, kerosene lamps gave way to fluorescent tubes, the ice-chest was replaced by a refrigerator, and the horse-drawn buckboard that Uncle Joe let Ken drive into town was exchanged for horse-power supplied by Ford.

Riley remembers a black-and-white print of Rosa Bonheur's (1822–1899) ***Horse Fair*** that hung in the Pauling dining room and the feed-store calendars nailed to the barn walls. Stronger, however, are sensory memories of "the shack" where Uncle Joe and the hired hands slept. Wall-papered in newsprint and appointed with iron beds and hay-tick mattresses, the place had a manly smell of chewing and pipe tobacco. Similarly, Riley recalls the fragrant oat bins and hayloft and the musty smelling cave where the cheese and milk were stored. "If I had to attach colors to that time," he offers in retrospect, "I'd say the warm russets and golds of wheat."

Though living in a relatively rural area, Ken could not escape knowledge of the larger world. The Missouri River had long been a busy corridor of shipping and commerce, establishing St. Louis as the "Gateway to the West." Nearby trading centers such as Independence, Kansas City and St. Joseph retained evidence of their roles as the embarkation and outfitting points of major overland routes such as the Santa Fe and Oregon Trails. Paralleling these earlier migrations westward were thousands of miles of railroad lines

18. *Romancing the West*

1992

oil, 48 x 44

My idea here was to do a triptych within one painting. The three heroes of the West—cowboy, Indian and cavalryman—are set into formal poses, each with his own saddle and color context. Hints of the action and atmosphere in which each operated are diffused by light in the background, which also unifies the whole into a single statement.

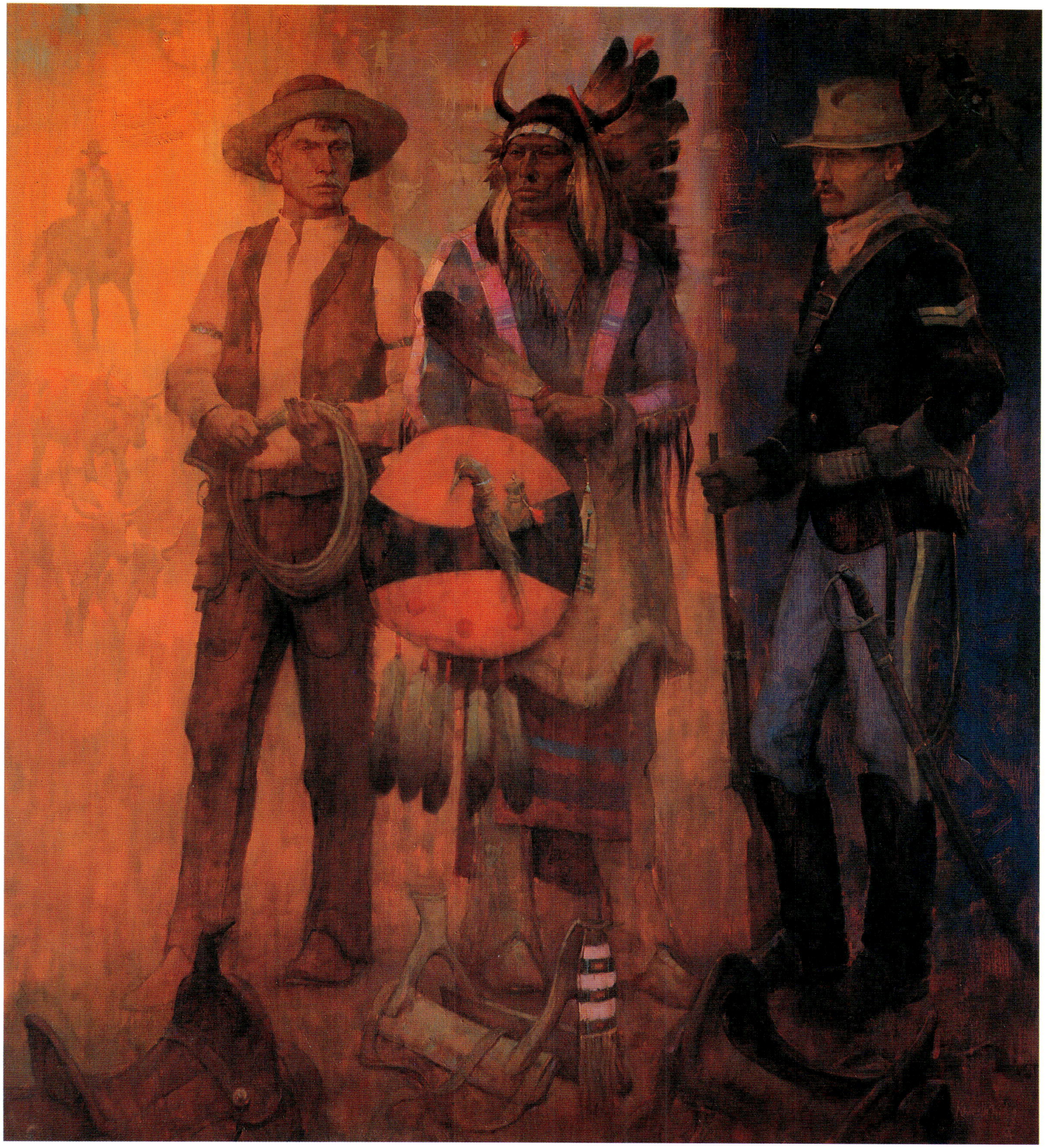

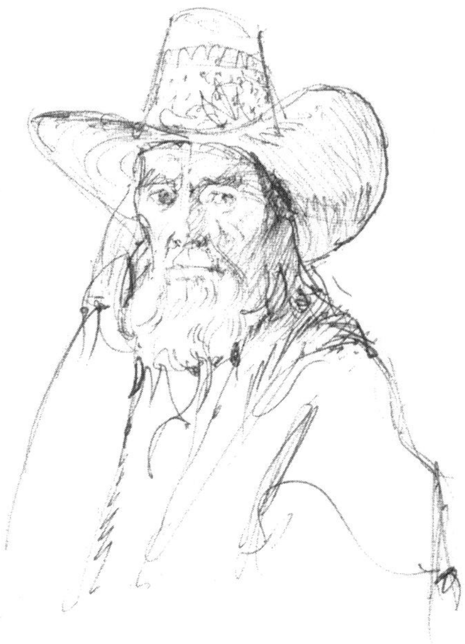

with commensurate stockyards, grain elevators and railway stations where goods made in the East were exchanged for those grown in the West.

The romance of the railroad became a fixation for adolescent Ken Riley. In 1926 Elwin took a job with the Chevrolet dealership in Parsons, Kansas. Located in the mineral-rich Cherokee plateau in the southeastern corner of the state, Parsons had been founded in 1870 by the Union Pacific Railroad as the major switching point for its southern Missouri-Kansas-Texas line between Junction City, Kansas, and Dennison, Texas. The Parsons roundhouse was one of the largest in the area, capable of servicing some fifteen engines at a time. Riley remembers their funnel-shaped smokestacks lined up for what seemed like miles and the Fred Harvey-type dining room where travelers ate their meals. In the mid-1920s, Parsons supported an all-time high population of some twenty thousand people. The billiard parlors, restaurants, hotels and shops that encircled the train depot buzzed with activity. In this new environment, Riley, a shy country boy, was about to give up his Tom Sawyer ways. He'd become, in his words, "a city kid" whose attentions turned to the science-fiction adventures of Tom Swift and the matinee idols of the western movies.

Despite the cosmopolitan nature of Parsons, the state of Kansas was closely tied to its frontier past—a colorful period with an odd assortment of heroes and villains. One legend Riley vividly recalls is that of the "Bloody Benders," namesake of the grassy hillocks just west of Parsons. Kate Bender was the owner of a road-house serving hot meals to travelers. This auburn-haired, green-eyed temptress would distract diners while son John axed them to death and stole their belongings. The burial sites, believed to be in the family orchard, gave rise to the legend of the "Bender Mounds," an eery specter that haunted the dreams of young children.

And the Benders weren't alone. They had other "Kansas cousins" in the likes of gun-toting abolitionist John Brown and hatchet-carrying prohibitionist Carrie Nation. The state's history echoed with the whine of the Winchester and the crack of the six-gun. Cowboys were known to lose their earnings and occasionally their lives when the cattle drives hit the railheads of Abilene and Dodge City. Legendary lawkeeper Bat Masterson emerged from these quintessential western towns, as did the Daltons, remembered for their 1882 holdup of two banks at once in Coffeeville, forty miles southeast of Parsons.

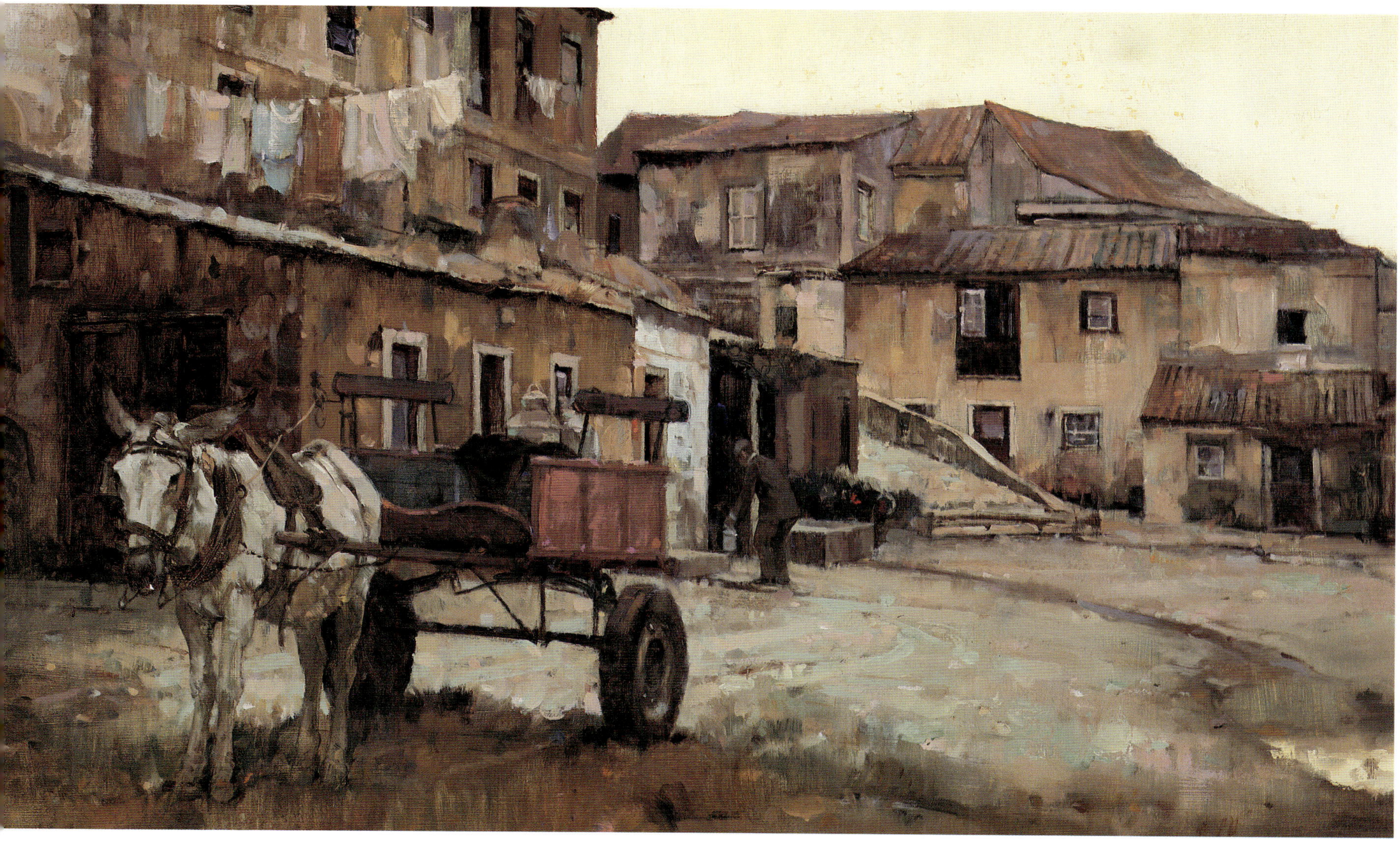

19. *Morning Delivery*

1982

oil, 12 x 20

We live in an age when cardboard cartons, neatly lined up on pristine shelves in a climatically controlled cooler, say "milk" to a couple of generations of young people. So, I admit that there was no small amount of nostalgia in hearing the rattle of milk cans in this small Portuguese village. It reminded me of my grandparents' farm where the milk cans were chilled in water troughs until the horse-drawn cooperative wagon picked them up.

Ken Riley came to know these Old West charactertypes in the western movies that played during Saturday matinees at Parsons' downtown Orpheum Theater. Melodramatic conflicts between ranchers and farmers, settlers and Indians, nature and culture, freedom and restriction, gave visual basis to his earliest history lessons. Actors would personify the triumph of good, whether in the guise of bashful Ken Maynard or daredevil stuntman Tom Mix and his horse Tony. With such heroes in mind, Ken begged his parents for a rifle. His disenchantment with its power of destruction came quickly. One day he and a friend were roaming in the woods and Riley took bead on a bird. "I guess I was feeling really macho so I shot the thing right off the line ... that cured me of hunting."

When you paint a figure or an inanimate object, you must empathize or become a part of what you paint. That is pure Howard Pyle, transferred through Harvey Dunn, and I've carried it with me all along. —KR

The Stock Market crash of 1929 and the onslaught of the Great Depression dealt a fierce blow to Parsons' economy. Railway lines were consolidated and employees laid off. Bank credit for buying cars dried up and with it went Elwin's job, forcing the family to move in with the Paulings, now living in the hamlet of Blackburn.

During these tough times, "Old Jim" became a bright spot in the ten-year-old's life. "It was quite a triumph to ride him from the farm back to town," Riley recalls of his first and only horse. Now a "kid-cowboy," Riley decided he'd get his "school marm" to swoon at his feet by galloping down the hill past her front porch. "I was just about there when the cinch gave way and I was deposited in the dirt. She came running out to help me—and my ego—dust off."

The two years in Blackburn were Riley's introduction to "Main Street Americana." At its center was Grandfather Pauling's Atwater-Kent radio and the Golden Age of radio programming. Riley recalls his extended family gathered around the radio on Sunday evenings, laughing at "Amos 'n' Andy" and later cowering in fear as doors creaked and chains rattled in "Lights Out." "The radio honed a kid's imagination," recalls Riley. The weekly serials and

20. *Spring Song*
1989
acrylic/oil, 48 x 38

Native American flute playing has become popular these days. Recordings feature haunting melodies that offer a glimmer of the old days when flute playing was a form of courtship. Many an artist has depicted this courtship ritual in the woods. Perhaps the lyrical flute is best conveyed in relationship to the hollowed out tree branch from whence it comes.

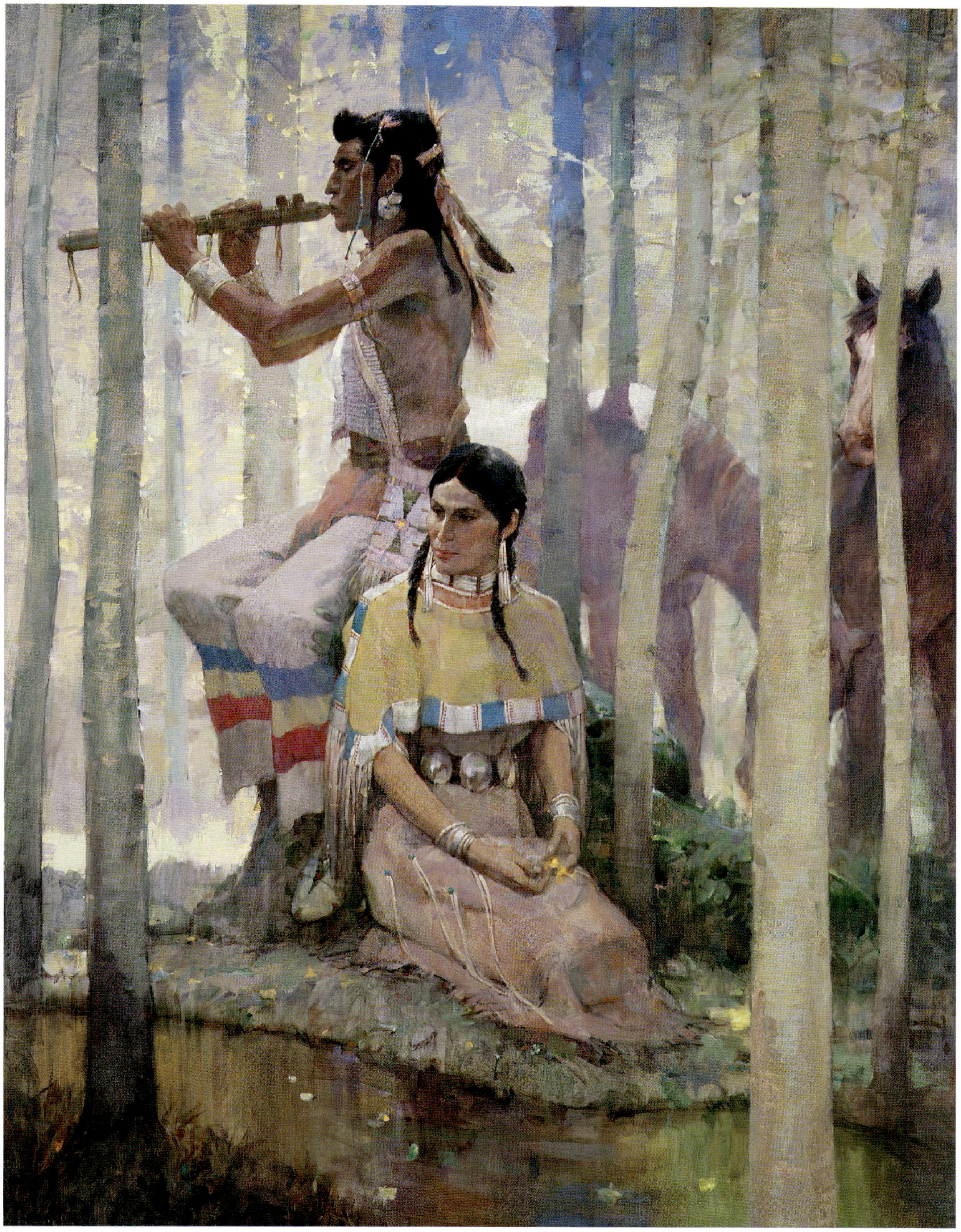

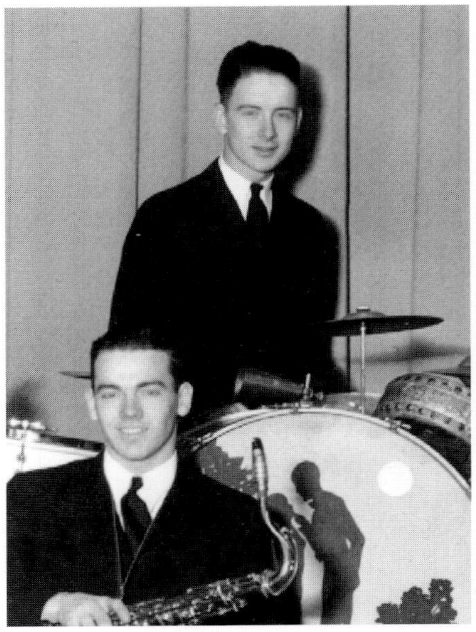

21. Kenneth Riley (in rear) with another member of Eddie Lain and His Orchestra, December 23, 1937.

dramas would exercise the imaginative visualization he'd later call upon in his career as an illustrator.

Just as significant as news and drama, however, was music. Suddenly the New York Philharmonic was available to farmer and factory worker alike. As the decade of the '20s danced into the Depression, the radio became a forum for a new sound. Jazz had been born of African-American ragtime and blues singers in Chicago and New Orleans. When Riley became aware of it, jazz had given birth to its free-wheeling daughter dubbed "swing." With its percussion counterpoints, trumpet melodies and clarinet decorations, swing crooned across the airwaves turning musicians and vocalists such as Ben Bernie and Mildred Bailey into household names. With Big Band melodies as a backdrop, Ken drew Tom Swift's space laboratories in the margins of his school books.

In 1931 the Rileys returned to Parsons, in time for the first of the Dust Bowl "black blizzards." Riley recalls going to the mailbox for his weekly edition of *The Saturday Evening Post* and finding it covered with west Kansas topsoil. He eagerly anticipated Norman Rockwell's (1894–1978) homey covers of Thanksgiving dinners and identified with John Falter's (1910–1982) recollections of Fourth of July celebrations in Nebraska. The artistry of Haddon Sundblom (1899–1976), who created the Coca-Cola Santa Claus, and the Brown and Bigelow calendars that Elwin brought home from the car dealership were Ken's introduction to art and illustration. Though he was still in junior high school, Ken apprenticed with sign-painter Ray Scroggins who encouraged him to experiment with his materials. However, there would be yet another creative outlet competing for his attention.

Riley's school buddies were members of the high-school band. They had been experimenting with the new rhythms and decided to form a dance band, and since Ken had no formal training in music they suggested he play the drums. With his practice pad set up by the Fada floor model radio topped by a revolving forest-fire lamp, Ken tapped away in silence, picking up the craft as a "matter of feel by listening to Gene Krupa and Buddy Rich." Eventually he got a set of traps decorated with a man and woman silhouetted by the light of the moon and joined in the practice sessions at trombonist Eddie Lain's house. Lain had the most "euphonious-sounding name," so the ten-member ensemble appointed him bandleader. Soon Eddie Lain and His Orchestra started playing for high school dances.

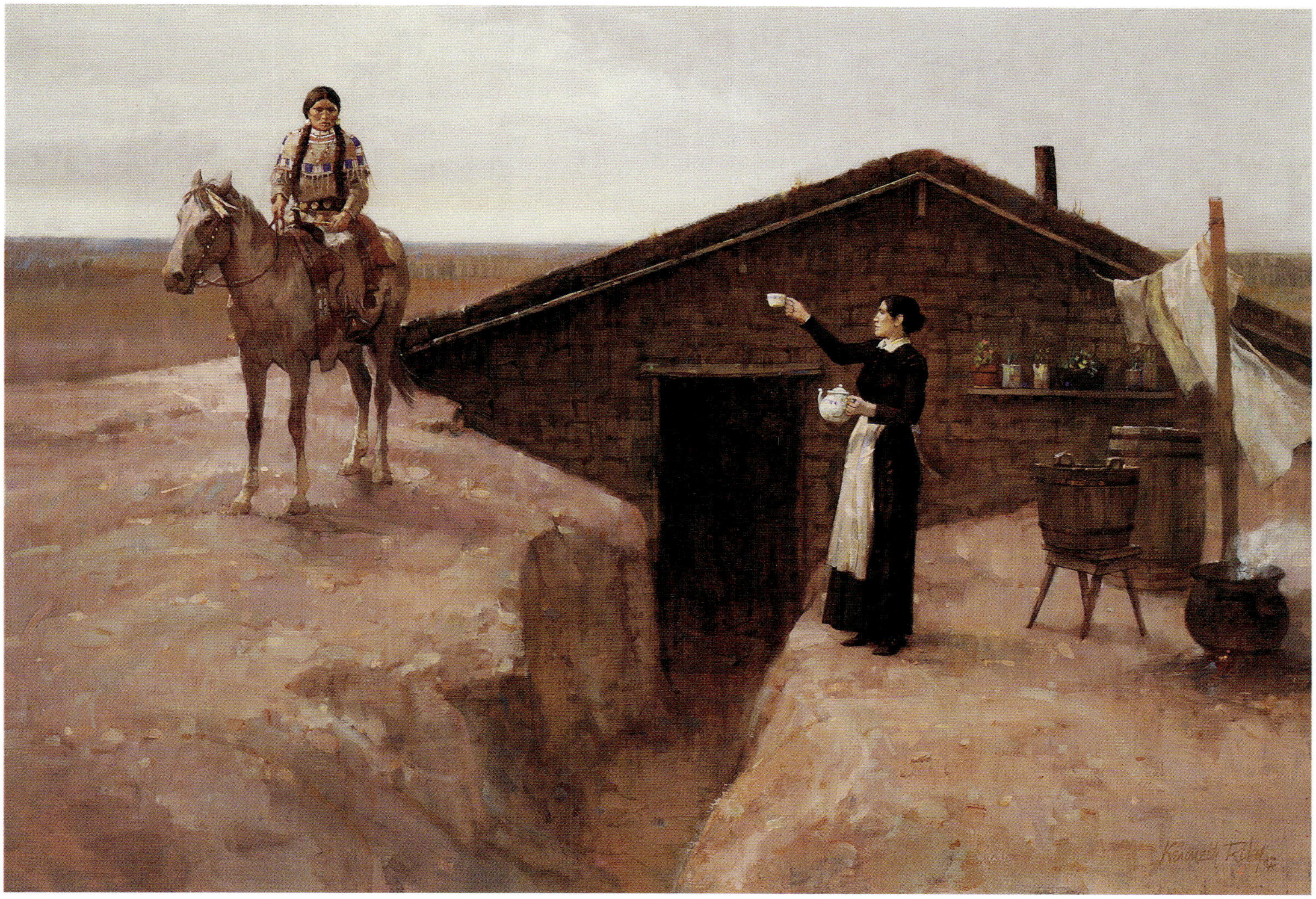

Playing drums had a profound influence on Ken Riley. In an era when music allowed the depressed to escape and the troubled to forget, Eddie Lain and His Orchestra became enormously popular. They played nearly every weekend from Ken's sophomore year in high school through his first year at the Kansas City Art Institute. Traveling in their own bus, they worked for union scale, each member receiving roughly $3 per gig, or $6 per weekend—decent spending money for a young man at the time. Wearing white coats and black bow ties, the band played at college fraternity parties, Missouri hotels and Oklahoma dance halls. As their reputation grew, a bandleader from Kansas City hired them for a week at the Lake Worth Casino between Dallas and Fort Worth. And during the summer of 1938, they played in the Ozarks resort town of Bella Vista, Arkansas—no ordinary assignment.

22. *Tea for Two*
1991
acrylic/oil, 18 x 27

The settlers who homesteaded the Plains built their dugouts into the earth. I've often thought about all the bugs and discomforts that must have visited these people who brought their tea services with them, hoping to re-create East Coast lifestyles in the West. The loneliness and feeling of infinity on the treeless plains of western Kansas were known to drive people mad.

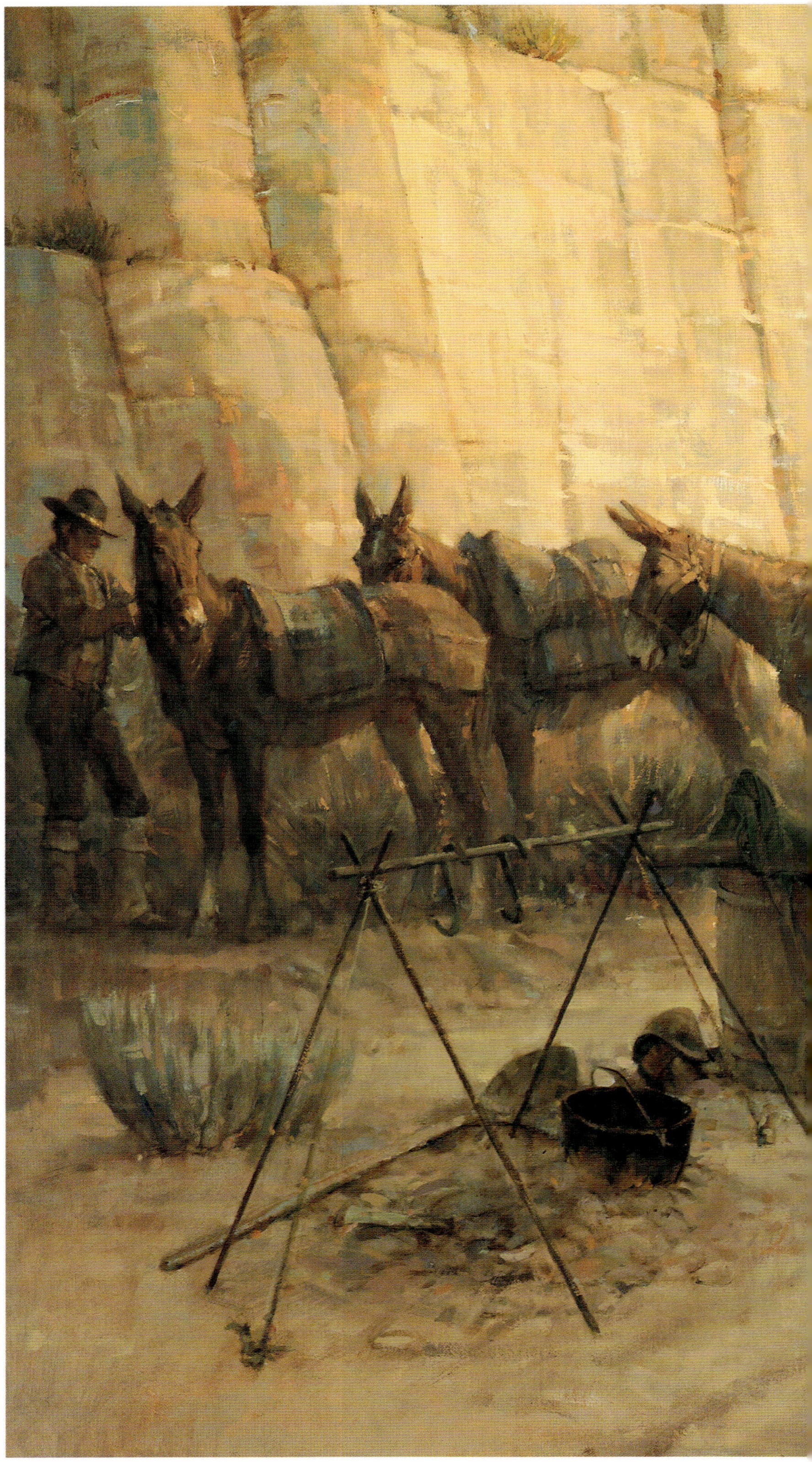

23. *Annie Laurie*

1982

oil, 26 x 46

The rhythm of life in the frontier West was set by Indian drummers. To their primal heartbeats, settlers added the twang of the fiddle and banjo, and the cavalry brought the strains of the harmonica. After the Civil War new tunes were heard around the campfires—a melding of cadence and lyric from the South and the North.

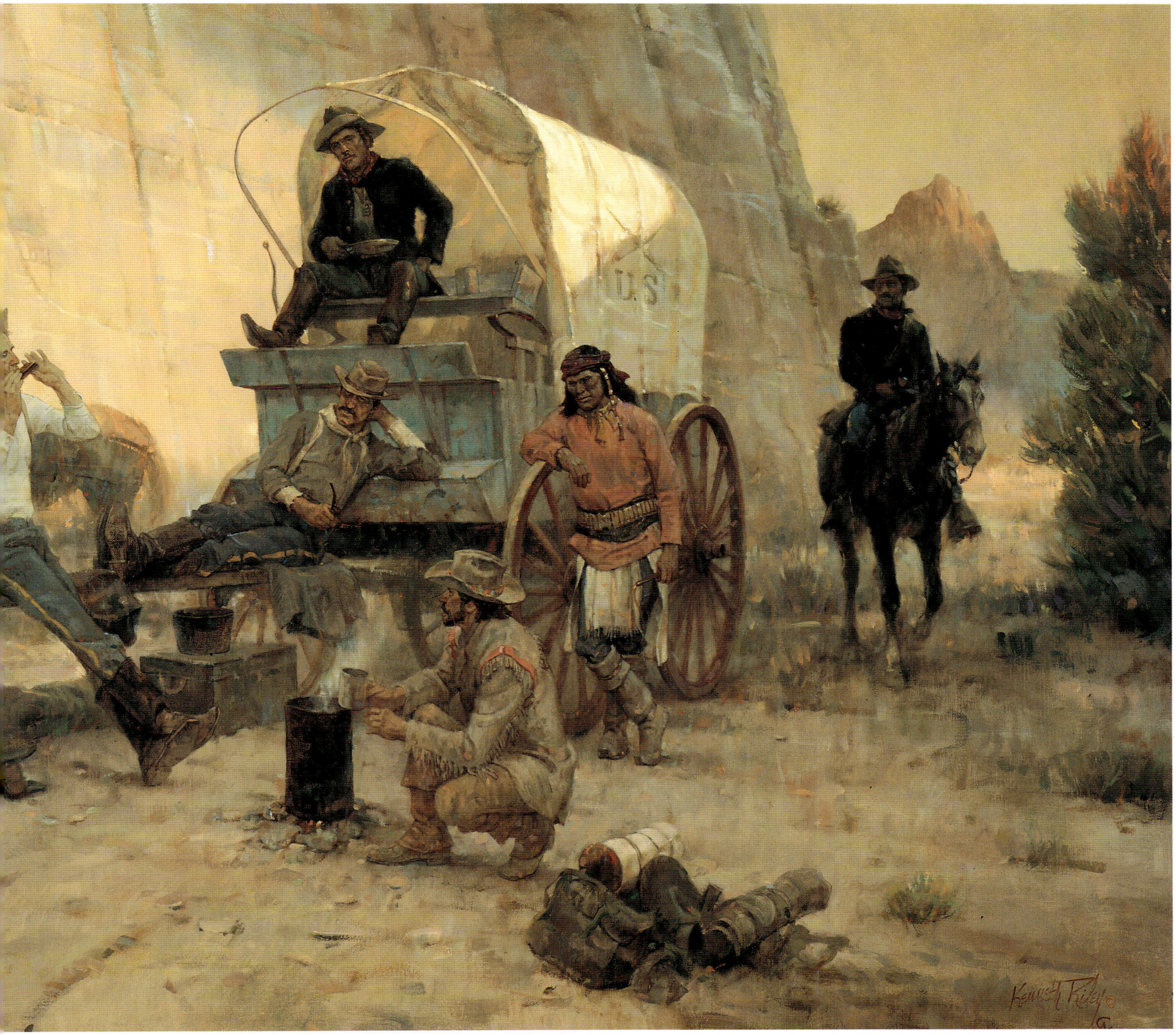
U.S

24. *Morning Call*
1985
oil, 24 x 36

With unprecedented fervor, today's scholars and journalists routinely turn heroes into anti-heroes. A case in point is the cavalryman of 1950s movie-stardom. Once wearing a white hat while riding in to save the world from the "red menace," the cavalryman has more recently been assigned a black hat for suppressing the rights of the "noble savage." Since nothing is ever purely black nor solely white, I am sure there is ample evidence to support both points of view. For me, the historic horseman offers an empathetic subject and a chance to depict the human form in action ... sans politics.

"The resort consisted of a nice hotel on a cliff, high up a hill," recalls Riley. "In the valley below was the golf course and a lake with a pavilion on it. We played week nights in the pavilion and in the hotel during lunch. On weekends, we moved into a cave in the Arkansas Hills." Dodging stalactites and stalagmites, the band hauled its equipment in about a quarter mile to a dance floor. "People came from all around to dance under the drips and listen to snares and traps that sounded like beating on soggy leather!"

By the time he was a senior, Riley was relatively well-traveled and had chalked up some memorable experiences—good and bad. Sickened by the smell of stale beer and the tragic humiliation of drug-broken musicians, he had decided against music as a career. But all that late-night drumming hadn't left much time for other pursuits. Luckily, a guardian angel by the name of Olive Rees had decided his future for him.

Rees taught arts and crafts at Parsons High School and had recognized an inherent skill for draftsmanship beneath the batiks and wall-hangings that Ken made in a tenth-grade class. She encouraged him to dabble in watercolors and recommended him to the Orpheum Theater when they needed a show-card painter. Seated behind the movie screen, in a loft with no windows, Ken copied romantic love scenes between actors such as Claudette Colbert and Clark Gable from photographic stills. Painted in dazzling colors, the pictures were placed on a tripod in front of the theater to advertise coming attractions.

Ken likewise turned a profit from his drawing by depicting bucking broncos on storefront windows advertising the Tri-State Fair held in Parsons. With a classmate who sold his services, the "ad company" prospered until the rains washed away evidence of Ken's hard work. Despite the setback, Ken began to think he might make a profession out of drawing and painting. His plans were fed by a friend named William Porter, who wrote for the pulps. Porter mapped out the route Ken would have to follow to gain the coveted title of magazine illustrator and recommended he begin his career at the Kansas City Art Institute.

Though Elwin wasn't convinced that Ken could make a living as an artist, there was ample evidence to the contrary. The Midwest had recently become the focus of American painting in the form of the Regionalists, so named in a December 1934 cover story of *Time* magazine. The populist art movement had been fostered by artists Thomas Hart Benton (1889–1975) from Missouri,

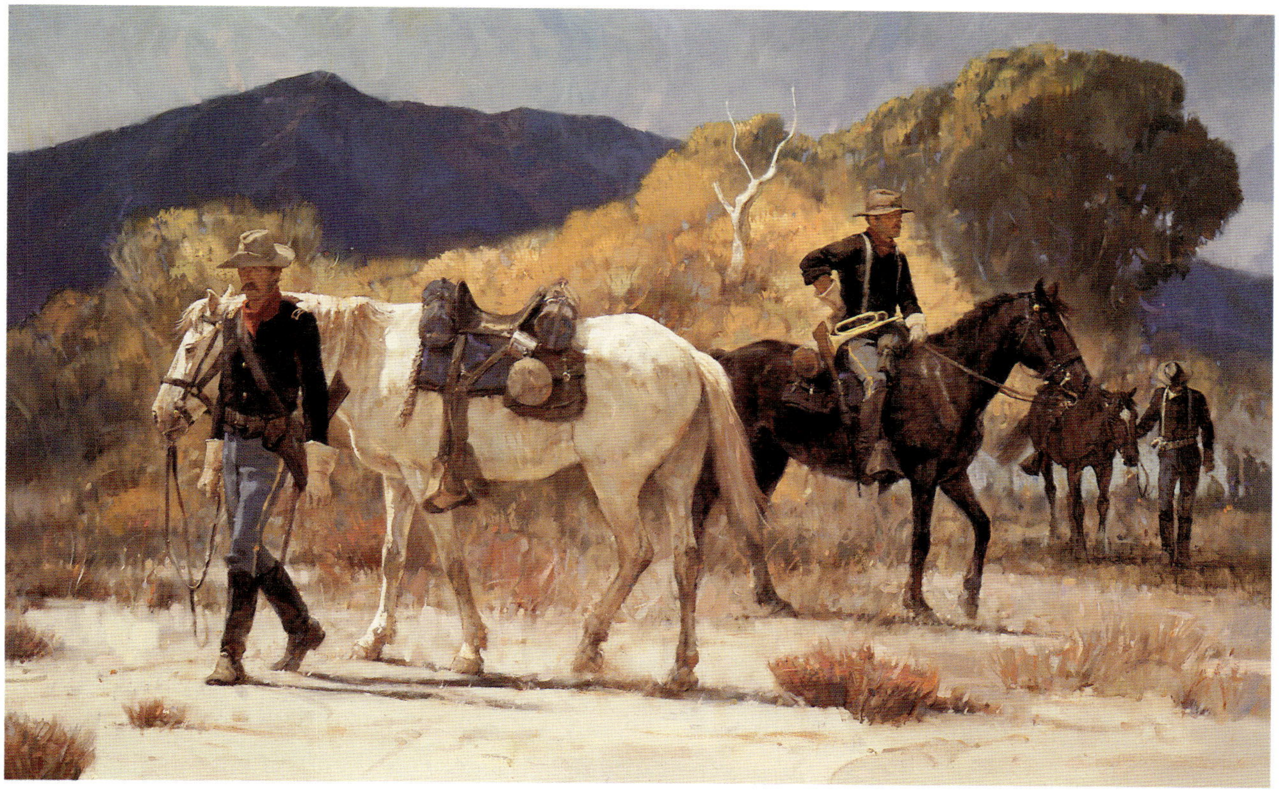

Grant Wood (1892–1942) from Iowa, and John Steuart Curry (1897–1946) from Kansas. Identified as flag-waving realists, each monumentalized the rural American scene with which he was familiar. Curry would be a featured artist in a 1936 issue of *Life* magazine, just at the time when Elwin enrolled Ken in a pre-med program at the junior college located in the same building as the high school. Olive Rees stood by waiting for the right moment. It came in the fall of 1938 when she saved enough money to pay Ken's first semester tuition to the Kansas City Art Institute. Elwin relented and Ken Riley entered a fine arts program at a school noted for the controversial hard-drinking Thomas Hart Benton and in a town resounding with the four-beat jazz of Charlie Parker and Count Basie.

SEARCHING FOR A METHOD IN KANSAS CITY

Every aspiring artist, according to Thomas Hart Benton, goes through three phases in his career. "The first is devoted to a search for method," Benton wrote in *An American in Art*. "In the second phase the method is developed and its formal and representational potentialities are explored. In the third, the developed method is applied to the expression of those human meanings that the artist's life and beliefs provide. The first two phases are primarily technical, the last largely communicative."

When Ken Riley stepped off the train into Kansas City's huge Beaux Arts-style Union Station, he was in "search of a method" for expressing himself in art. Though his knowledge of musical communication was considerable and would continue to grow in Kansas City's 12th Street jazz clubs, Riley was an acolyte when it came to picture-making. During the next three years at the Kansas City Art Institute studying with Benton and others, he would follow a yellow-brick road destined for the Wizard's knowledge of communicating through pigments on canvas.

Kansas City was a good place to embark on his odyssey. Filled with contrasts, the busy commercial center had acres of stockyards, elegant residential neighborhoods, lavish parks and a honeycomb of underground limestone caverns used as cold storage and a Duty Free Trade Zone. It was also something of a Continental replica, with miles of boulevards and parkways decorated with European statues imported by City Beautiful advocate J. C. Nichols. Country Club Plaza, the nation's first shopping mall, also developed by Nichols, added to the international feel with its Moorish-style buildings, Italian fountains and manicured gardens.

Just a few blocks from Country Club Plaza, the Institute, which had been founded in 1885, was located in a large old home on several acres of lawns dotted by vintage trees. A center of culture, the first floor of the Vanderslice mansion hosted exhibitions by KCAI teachers and regional painters and sculptors. Across the street the continental flair was emphasized in the Nelson-Atkins Museum with its collections of European and Oriental art, as

25. Detail of *Cottonwood Crossing [27]*.

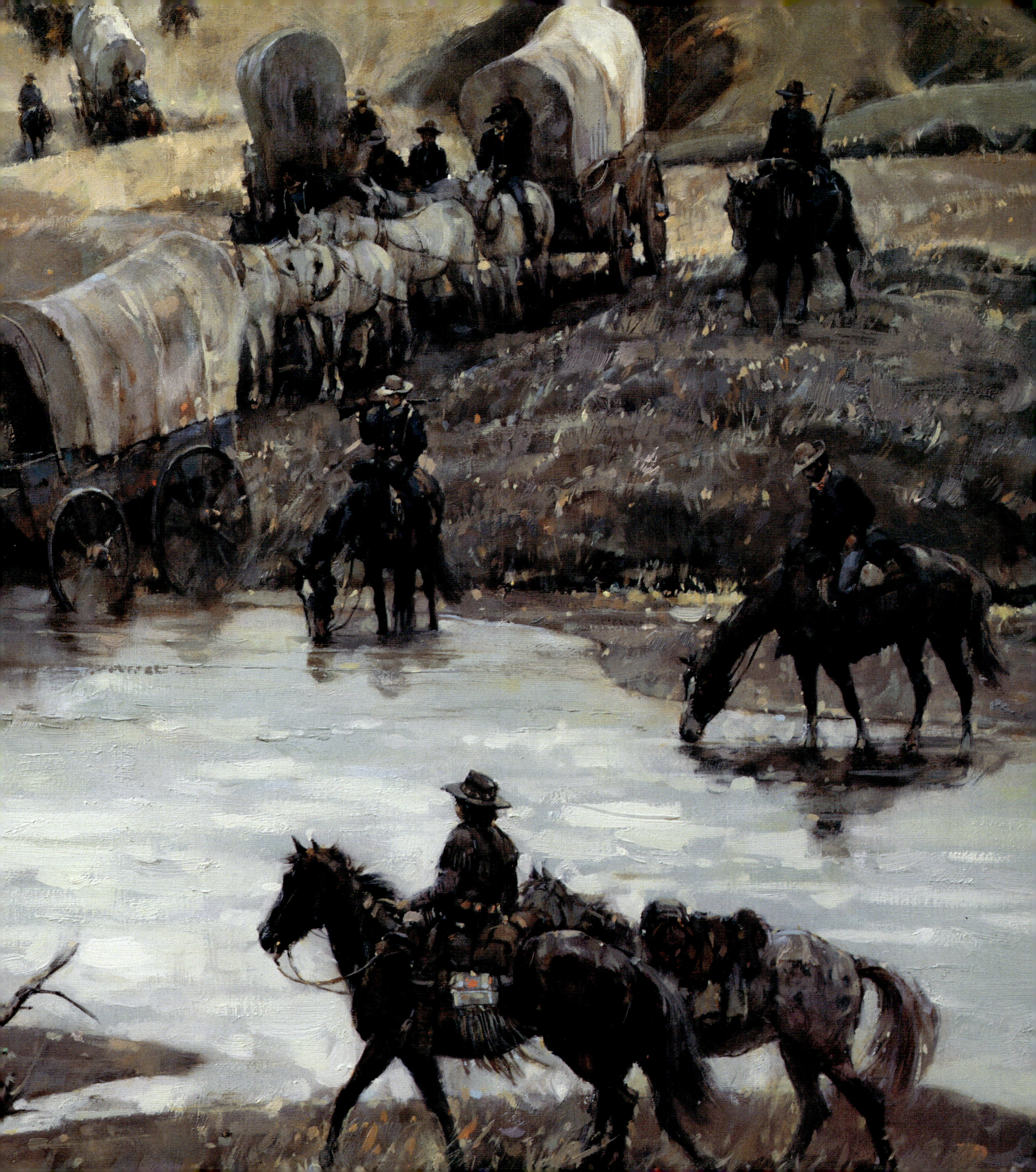

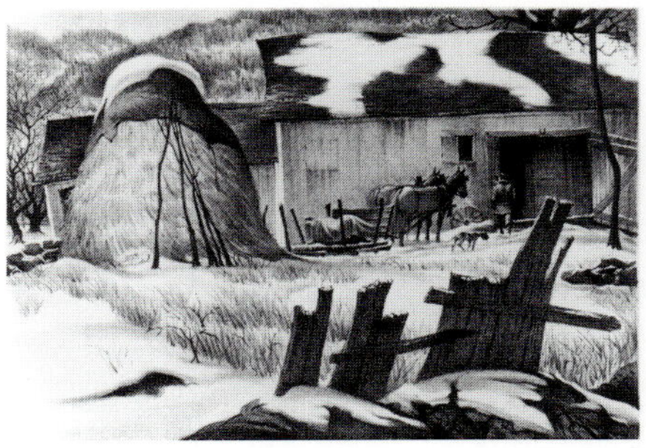

26. *Farmyard,* ca.1940, stone lithograph, 11 x 16.

well as a fine selection of works by Missouri genre painter George Caleb Bingham (1811–1879).

Riley spent considerable time in the museum, studying the refined draftsmanship of French Neo-Classicist J. A. D. Ingres (1780–1867) and compositional brilliance of French Post-Impressionist Edgar Degas (1834–1917). The human dignity found in Bingham's river-boatmen and townspeople was of special interest to Riley, who was commissioned to make a pastel copy of one of Bingham's river-barge scenes. "After so many reproductions of Norman Rockwell, it was exciting to finally see the real thing," Riley recalls. "I began to understand what quality art looked like."

Although he entered the Institute wanting to become an artist, the career path ahead of Riley branched in two directions: teaching or commercial work. Early on, he expressed a preference for commercial illustration, though at the time the school had no illustration teacher. The classes that would take him one step closer to "developing his method" included sculpture from Wallace Rosenbauer (1900—), design from Mildred Welsh Hammond (taught 1933–1939), stone lithography from John De Martelly (1903–1980), and a private class in portraiture from Austin Ketcham (1898—). His principal focus, however, was drawing. For the duration of his studies, Riley spent at least half of each day in life-drawing class. "The Institute," he says in retrospect, "was the breeding ground for my decision to focus on the human form as the subject of my art."

In the beginning an art student is fascinated by the technical aspects of development. Eventually, the technical means are used almost unconsciously to further what we say in paint. The artist is constantly drawing from a subliminal source that frees him to concentrate on expression. —KR

Thomas Hart Benton had been an instructor of drawing and painting at the Institute since 1935. When Riley arrived in September 1938, the irascible 5-foot 2-inch, 49-year-old titan had already evaded an attempt by the Institute Board to dismiss him. Recently finished with his controversial Missouri State

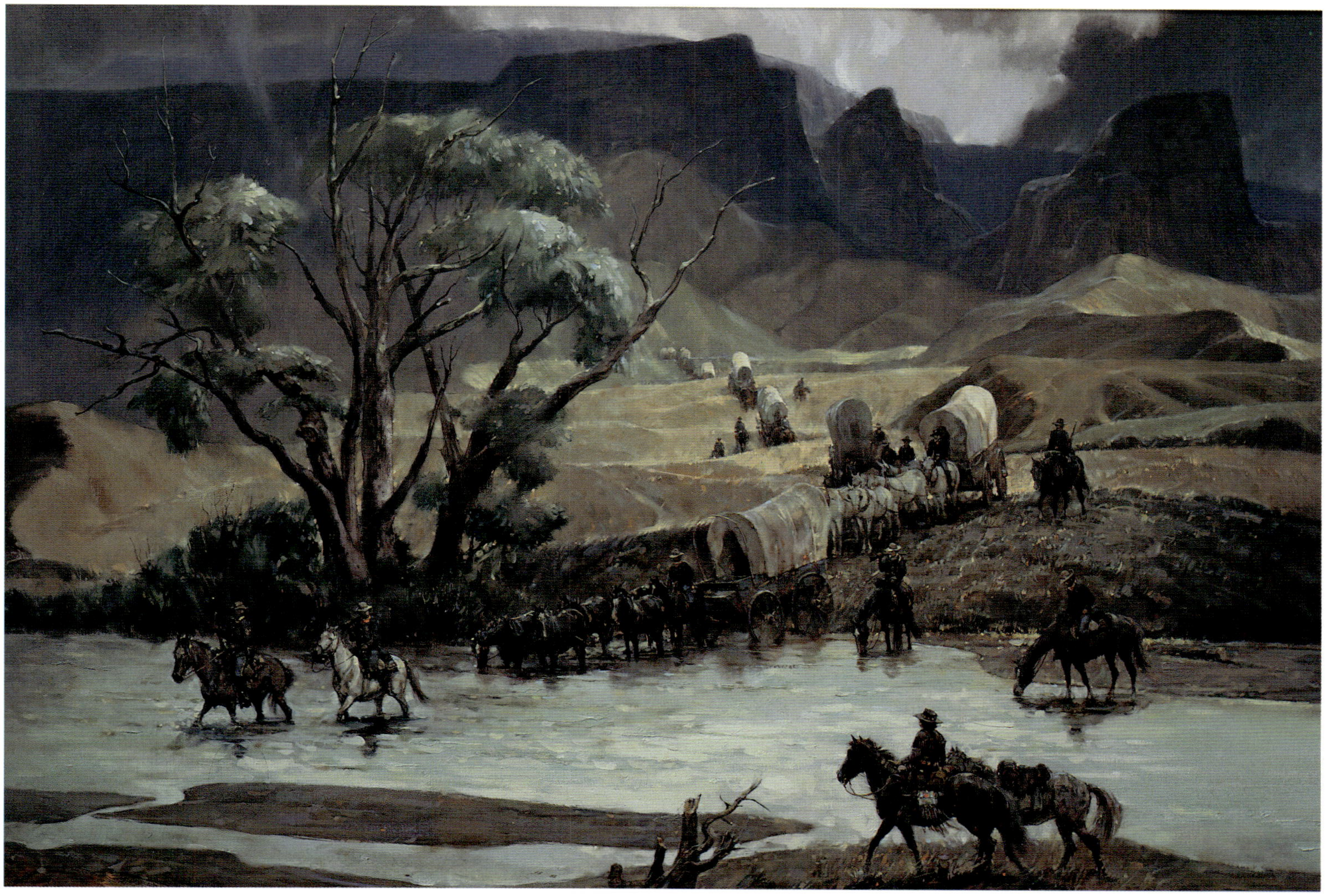

Capitol murals, in which he had used a number of his students as models, Benton was beginning work on the even more controversial 6-by-5-foot nude titled ***Persephone***. Set up with a model in the Institute's old greenhouse studio during the winter of 1939, Benton painted surrounded by students from his advanced painting class, who made smaller versions of the same subject.

"There was never any middle ground with Benton," says Riley. "You either loved him or hated him." Riley purposely avoided Benton's painting class because he didn't wish to become one of the "little Bentons" that the charismatic painter couldn't help but clone. He did, however, study drawing with Benton for an entire year. "He liked certain people who would go home with him for lunch. The rest of us were on the fringe, trying to catch little crumbs of what he was saying."

27. *Cottonwood Crossing*
ca. 1980
oil, 24 x 36

The mood in this landscape came from a camping trip MarCyne and I made into the east end of the Chiricahua Mountains, where dramatic canyons open to plains that roll into New Mexico. The high point of view and the size of the figures set a scale that aggrandizes the landscape. With so many wagons and supplies, this cavalry column is on a major expedition.

Even if they were crumbs, Benton's comments in drawing class were undoubtedly fortified with his well-entrenched theories of reconciling the abstract qualities of art with a meaningful subject. Decrying what he called "phony avant-garde bug-house" painting, Benton stressed the value of fundamental structure and overall design. Proselytizing for honest emotion and painting, he promoted what he termed "logical principles" of organization and design that had been passed down from the Renaissance.

Benton's theories were the antithesis of those making headlines in New York. Modernist painters of the 1930s looked at subject matter, and particularly the American history that Benton pursued, with scorn. "Evocative subject matter ... which suggested meanings beyond painting itself was particularly frowned upon," Benton wrote in *An American in Art*. He countered such criticism based on his studies of pre-Renaissance Italian muralists. The form utilized by Giotto (ca. 1267–1337), he declared, "resulted quite as much from the meanings that inspired him as from his technical discoveries or his observations of nature.... Giotto's religious stories had a constructive as well as a communicative place in his art. Form was, therefore, to a much greater degree than our modern artists realized, a 'function' of the subject."

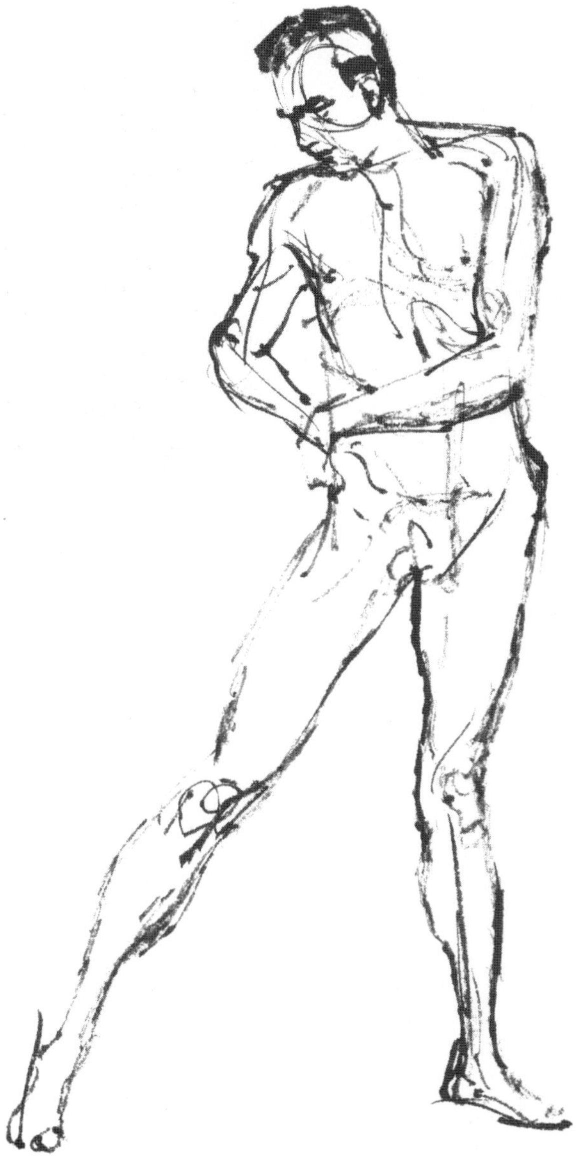

Within this theory of form, Benton also espoused an idiosyncratic design concept of dynamic sequences and interlocking/opposing lines and curves. His primary ambition, writes biographer Henry Adams, was to "orchestrate pictorial rhythms in depth." Using visual pathways created by lines and points of connection between verticals, horizontals and diagonals, Benton sought to create sequences of positive and negative shapes. The resulting movement and counter-movement conveyed depth as well as an undulating pattern across the flat plane of the two-dimensional surface.

Although Riley wasn't aware of it at the time, Benton's theories took root in the fertile ground of his "developing method." Not only does Riley concentrate heavily on interlocking shapes and rhythmic patterns in his own works (see "Communicating the Idea"), he has an equally abiding passion for Italian painters such as Cimabue (ca. 1272–1302) and Piero della Francesca (1416–1492). It was the frescoes of these religious muralists that were the focus of a pilgrimage Ken and MarCyne would make to Italy in 1959.

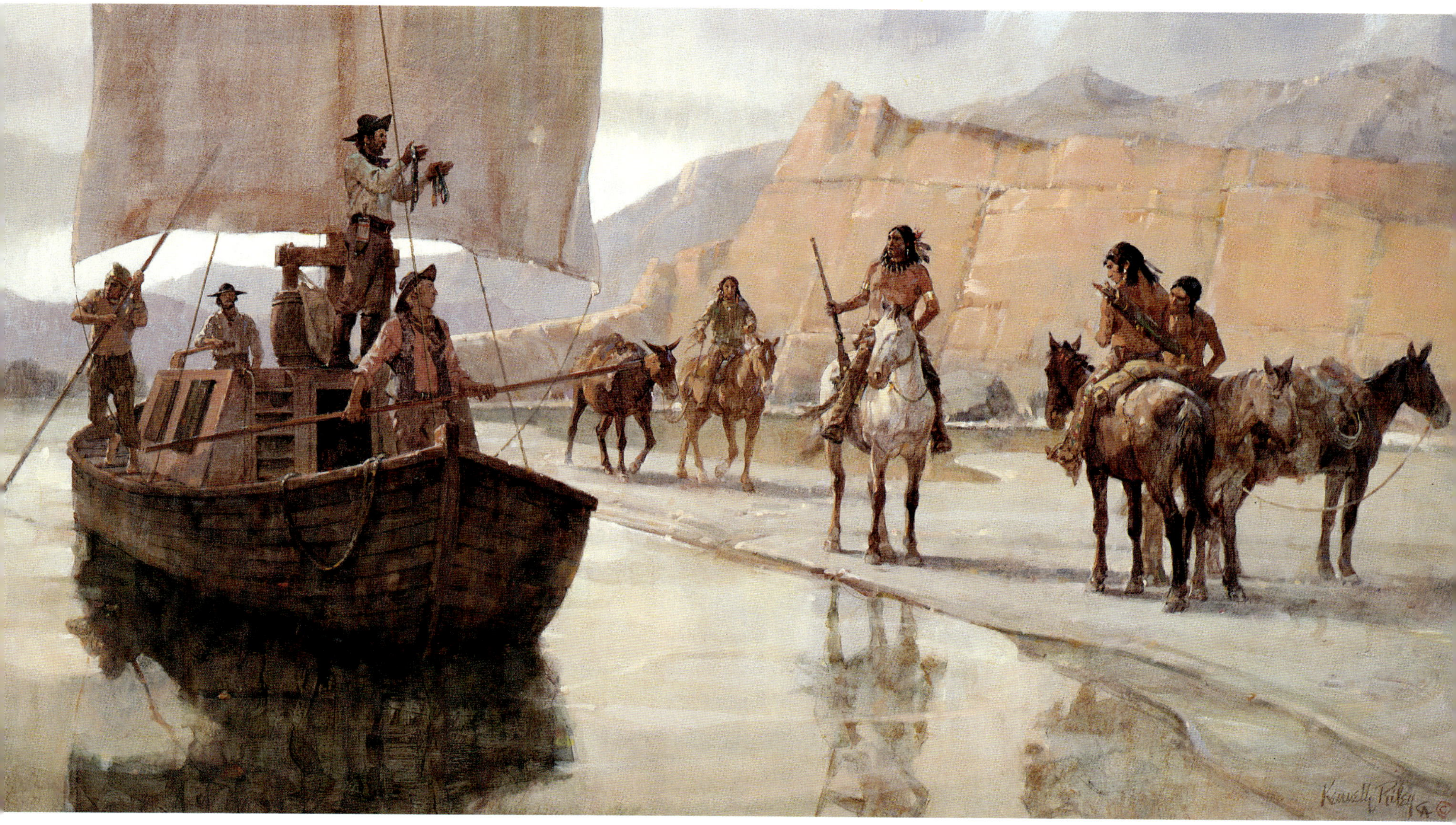

28. *Trinkets*

1988

acrylic/oil, 15 x 27

Before the Fort Peck Reservoir flooded the area, the bluffs of the Upper Missouri River were described by visitors as having the most fascinating shapes and colors known to man. Made of clay or sandstone, the bluffs and river reflected the pink sunset providing a colorful ambience for a keelboat navigated by traders. The shallow draft of the keelboat (18 to 24 inches) made it a floating phenomenon that could negotiate the sandbars and snags in the winding Missouri.

It seems to me that the term "master" is greatly overworked when applied to artists. Some are much better than others, but every really good artist that I have ever known, no matter at what stage of life, is essentially a student constantly striving for a new plateau of excellence. —KR

Twenty years before that trip to Italy, MarCyne Johnson, from Topeka, Kansas, was a first-year painting student at the Institute. "It was the custom for the guys to survey the first-year students," recalls Riley. "There was this lovely, fresh blonde lady, and I decided to try to date her." The romance developed mutually and that summer Riley opted to stay on campus rather than tour with the orchestra. On an Institute scholarship, he received a small stipend from his parents and made extra money doing odd jobs, including teaching Saturday morning art classes to high school students. He kept his costs low, living off campus with a couple of other art students, dining for a quarter per meal with MarCyne, and contributing whatever he could when the donation plate was passed following stirring gospel sing-alongs at the local churches.

President of the student council, Riley found himself in a delicate position in 1939. Benton was finally fired and Riley debated whether to join the student body which rallied to Benton's defense. With the specter of World War II looming on the horizon, Riley was likewise debating his own future. Though registered for the draft, he hoped to pursue additional studies and once again he had two options: Chicago or New York. Earlier, illustrator R. G. Harris (1911—), an alumnus of the Institute, had visited campus and met with Riley. Known for his empathetic illustrations of mothers and children, Harris had studied with Harvey Dunn (1884–1952) at the Grand Central Art School and George Bridgman (1864–1943) at the Art Students League. He recommended that Riley do the same and avoid the advertising agency atmosphere of Chicago. At Harris' recommendation, Riley applied for a scholarship at the League, and in the spring of 1941, he learned that he had been accepted.

29. *The Competition*
1990
oil, 52 x 42

Since the earliest days of my training I've focused on the human figure. Working with Benton I learned that the human body is itself a composition, comprising complementary and opposing curves and lines. This painting is a study in the wondrous shapes and angles found within the human form.

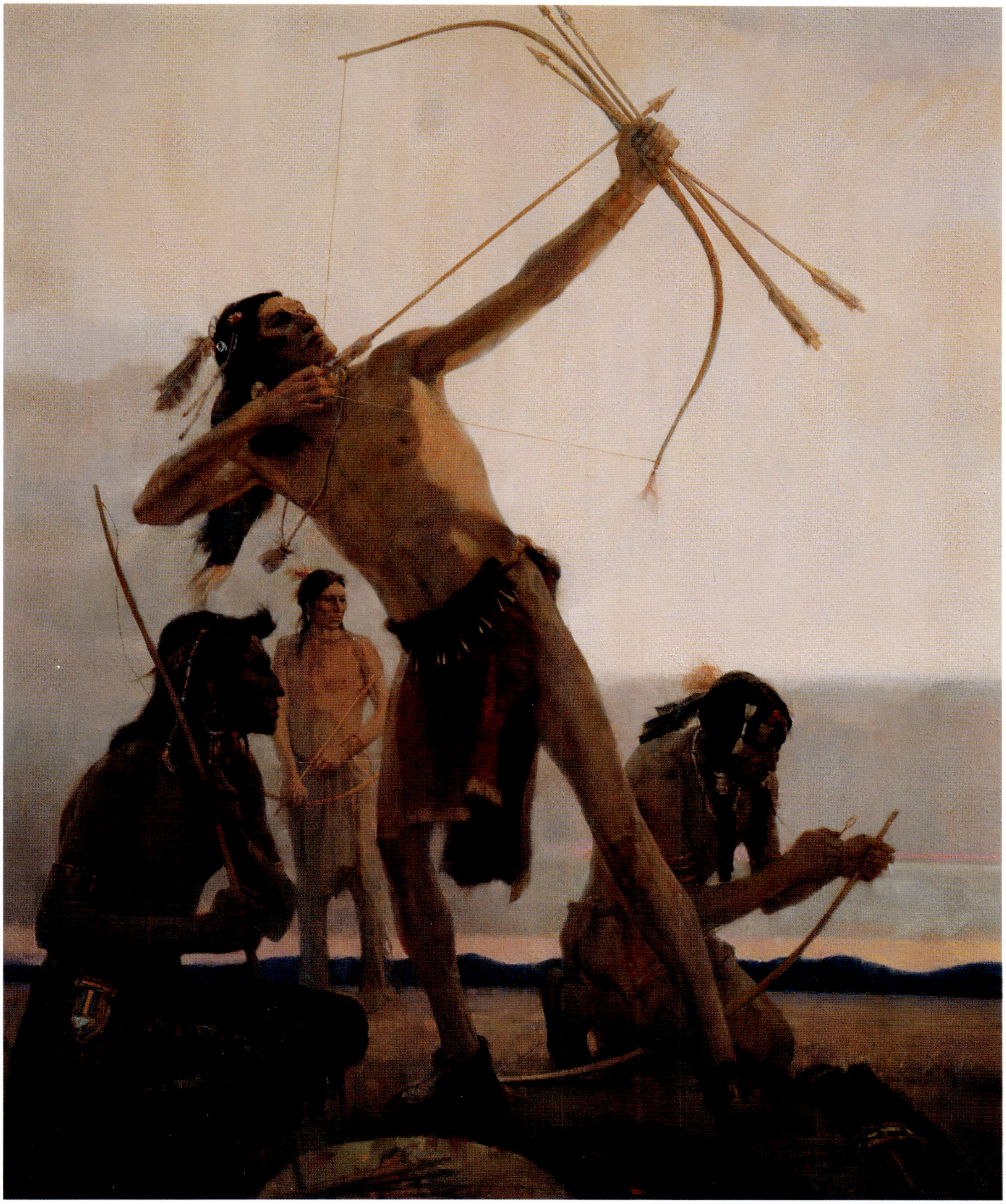

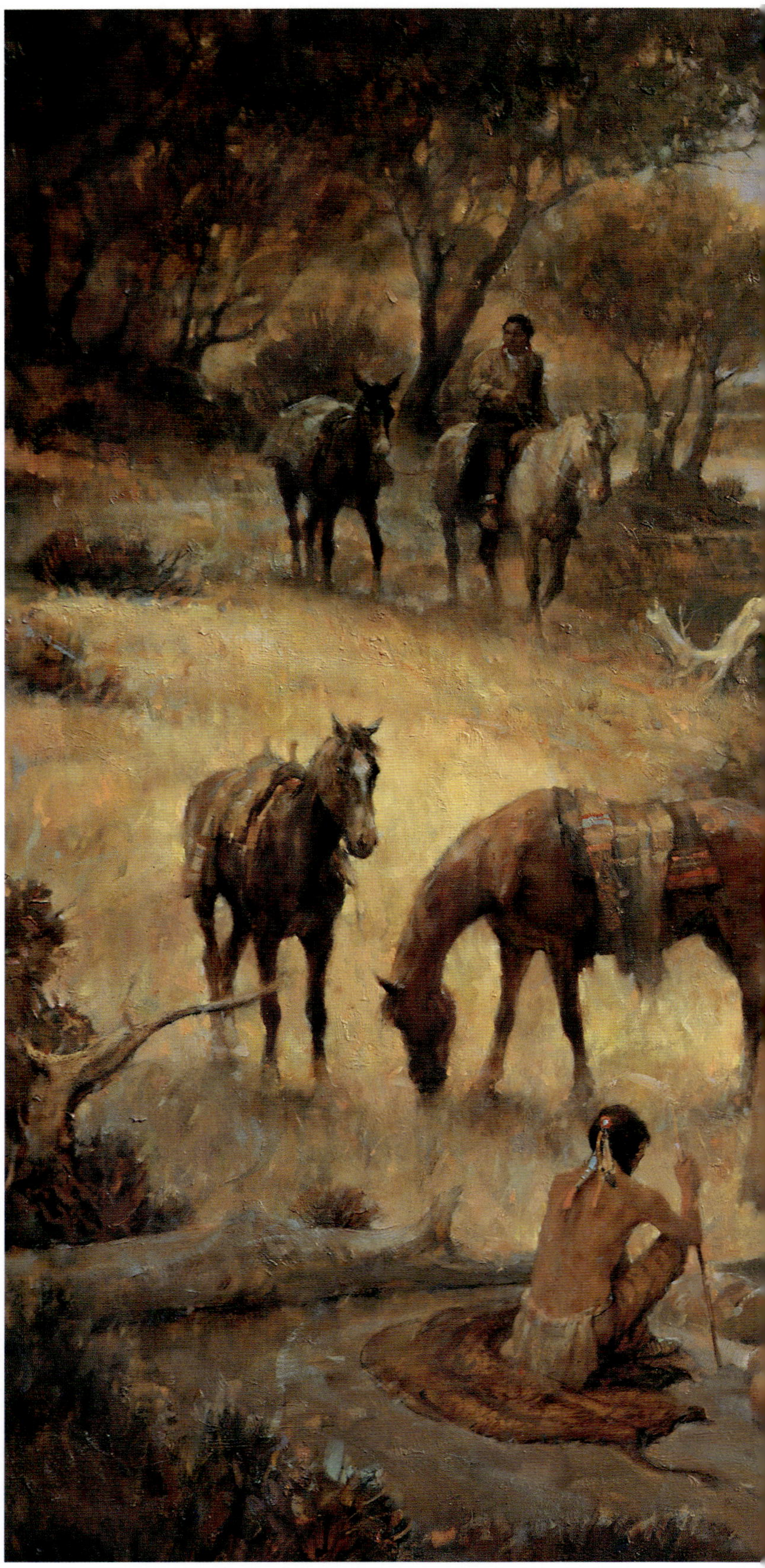

30. *Red Flannel*

1985

oil, 30 x 48

The occasion of a keelboat arriving with trade items offered me the opportunity to show an atmosphere of excitement. Traders rolled out their bundles of guns, tobacco, knives, beads and trinkets hoping to interest the Indians in trading for furs. Red flannel was a favored trade item. It gave title to the work as well as a focal point to the scene.

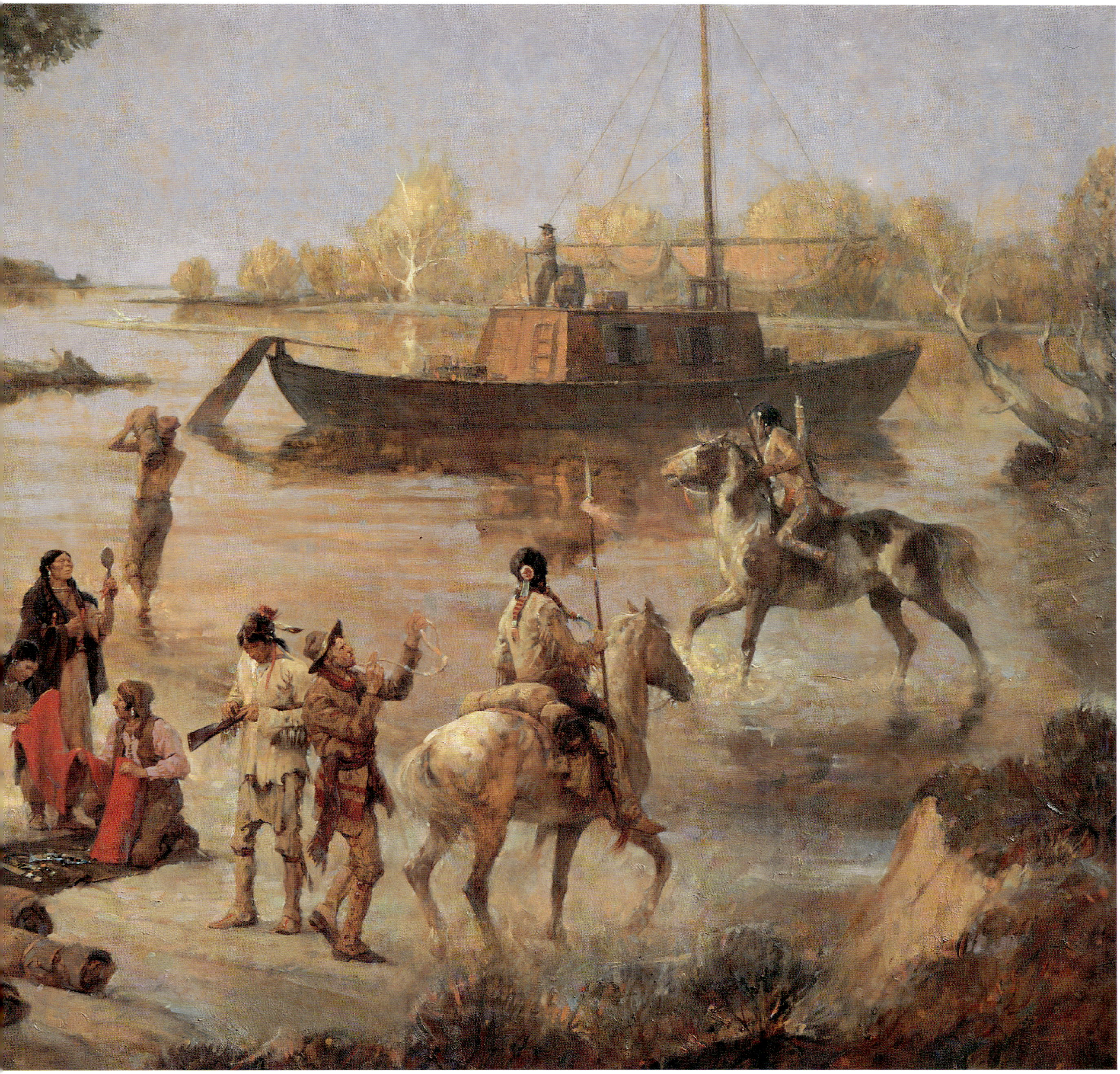

LEARNING TO PAINT IN NEW YORK

Fall 1941 ... "I'm dreaming of a White Christmas" crooned on the radio when a newscaster interrupted the record ... and the lives of Ken Riley and MarCyne Johnson. "The Japanese have bombed Pearl Harbor!" he said, his voice saddened by the news of seven battleships sunk and over 2,000 men dead. The United States was at war. Ken and MarCyne were awaiting the finalization of their marriage license. "We talked about waiting till war's end," recalls Riley. "But we decided to push forward and tough it out."

Married at the Little Church Around the Corner in New York's theater district, the couple moved out of Ken's Tin Pan Alley walk-up and settled into a small flat in Greenwich Village. MarCyne worked as a bank secretary and Ken devoted himself to learning how to paint. Enrolled in George Bridgman's anatomy class, Riley quickly decided that his drawing skills were solid enough to move into Frank Vincent DuMond's painting class instead. Also accepted into Harvey Dunn's night classes at the Grand Central Art School, Riley worked at his craft to the strains of Cole Porter's "Night and Day"—a tune that equally described the divergent approaches of these two renowned instructors.

Technique is only a means for arriving at the desired idea. —KR

DuMond (1866–1951) had been teaching at the League on 57th Street for nearly four decades when Riley signed up for a figure painting class. Paris-trained at the Académie Julian with academics Gustave Boulanger (1824–1888) and Benjamin Constant (1845–1902), DuMond was best known for meditative religious subjects, figural murals combining myth and history, and *plein air* landscapes done throughout New England. Not content with superficial appearances, DuMond stressed understanding the artistic significance of the landscape or human form and insisted that his students eliminate details. He often spoke of the figure as a unit engaged in an all-inclusive

31. Detail of *Hidden Eyes [32].*

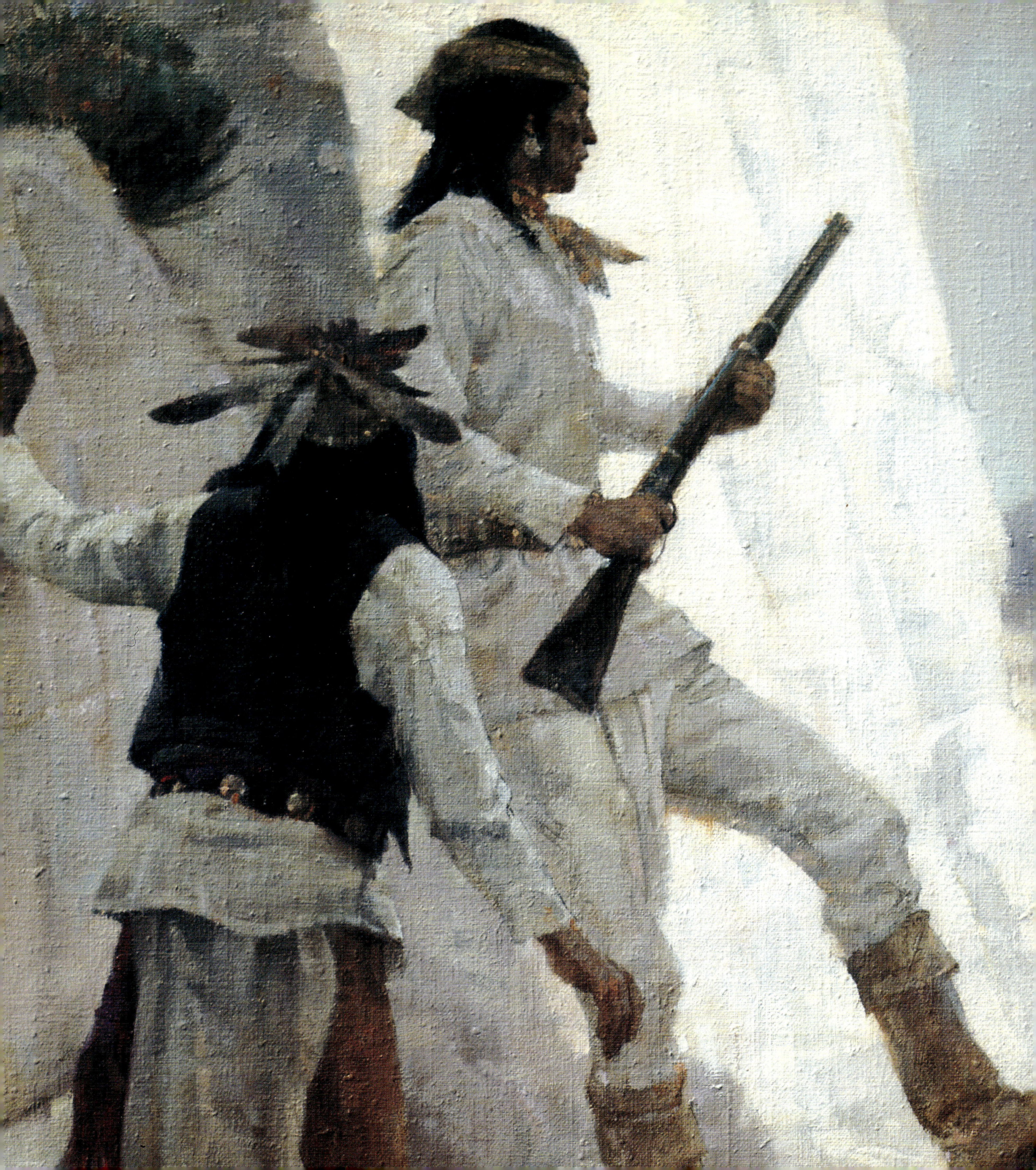

gesture which flowed from the tips of the fingers into the arms, shoulders, back of the neck and down the other arm. He also emphasized the unity of color achieved through an analytical process of "half-tone."

"The blinding light of the sun and the dark of the deepest cave are out of reach of our palette," DuMond wrote. "The only place we can directly relate to nature is through half-tone, which mysteriously weaves in and out of everything, tying it all together. When one looks backward there seems to be some sort of half-tone that covers the whole affair and makes it acceptable."

DuMond's half-tone rested at the center of a series of greys that represented five planes of light: highlight, light, half-tone, shadow and accent. "DuMond's system was very deliberate and mathematically precise," recalls Riley. "You'd have five shades of grey, from white on one end to black at the other. This was set in line with your colors—the highest keyed, like yellow, at one end, down through the ochres to the blues and purples at the deep end of the scale."

Exercises in putting this palette of values to work consisted of models set up in dramatic lighting situations. The goal, DuMond stressed, was to see the action of light as revealing form and to aim for the elusive essence. Riley recalls one modeling situation in which a black man wearing an Oriental costume was illuminated by candlelight. "The candle would be the supreme highlight of the painting with everything else receding into darkness, except that there might be sequins on the costume picking up light. The challenge was to handle the extremes of a small range in the upper scale, but a broad range in the muted low-key colors. It took real discipline."

DuMond's idol, according to Riley, was Frenchman Puvis de Chavannes (1824–1898), a follower of Ingres. Puvis, who is categorized with the Symbolist painters, was a reductivist. He arranged his nostalgic, idealized figures to create a mood of order, serenity and formal harmony characterized by decorative two-dimensionality, clear silhouettes, compressed space and subdued colors. The simplification of formal elements fundamental to Puvis' style appealed to DuMond's sense of logic. Many years later, in paintings such as ***Shadows [102]***, it would appear to have appealed to Ken Riley's logic as well.

32. *Hidden Eyes*
1985
oil, 48 x 30

Southwestern canyon country is magical! The vertical stone worlds of the Dragoon Mountains represented refuge to the Apache. Hidden among a fantasyland of ghoulish boulders colored by minerals, they could hide undetected while monitoring the movements of cavalry patrols.

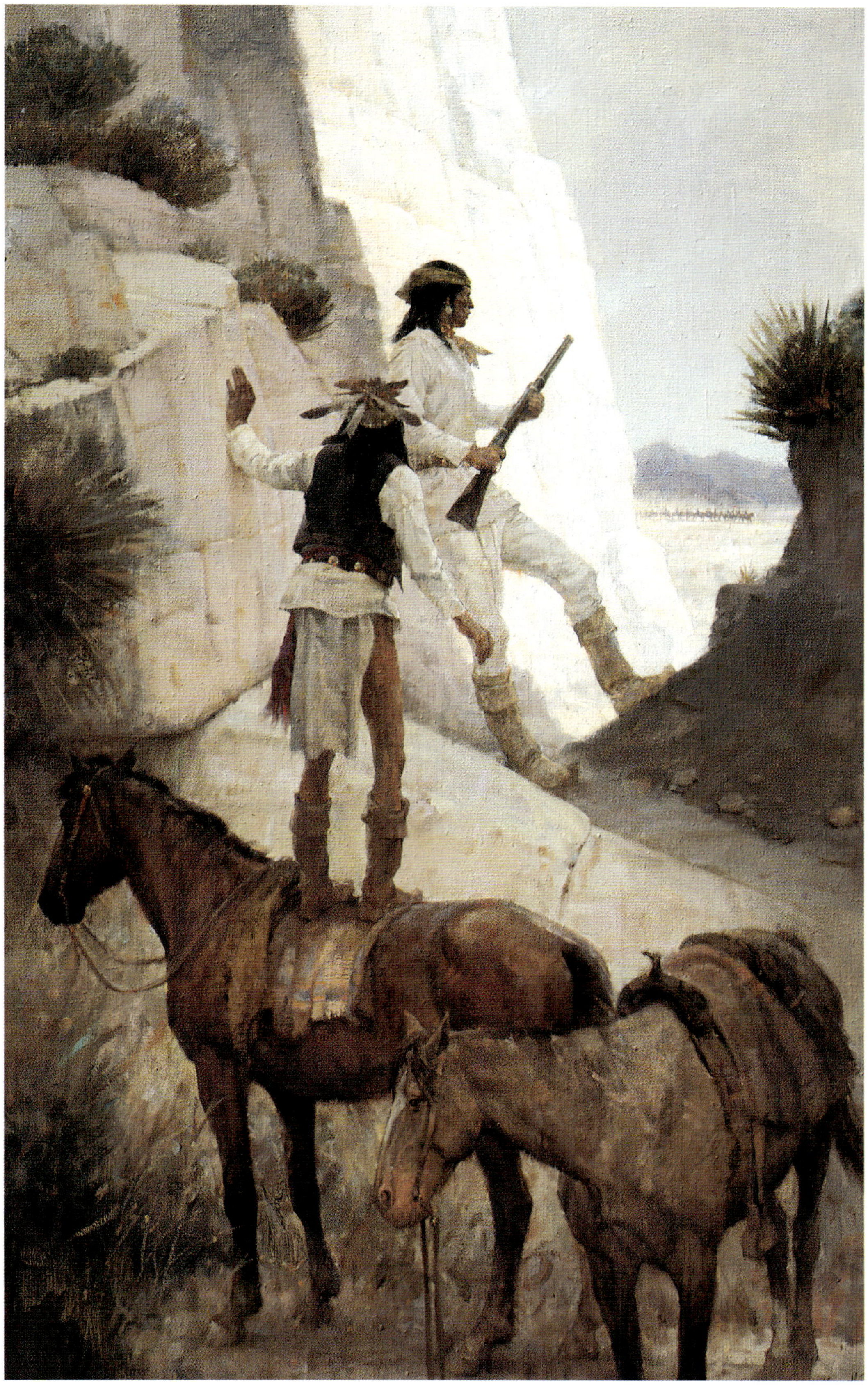

With television and photography so much a part of the visual world, our dilemma today is: How does the artist paint something so that it has its own character? How can the painter take a flat surface and make the viewer enjoy it? —KR

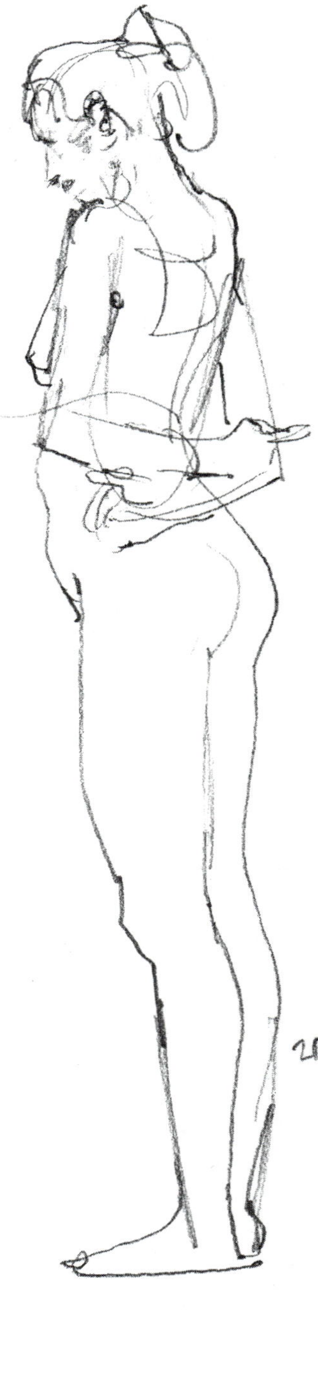

During the day, Riley watched DuMond intellectually mingle his color with delicate shades of grey. At night, he stood in awe as Harvey Dunn loaded his brush with color and attacked a painting with so much emotional abandon the easel shuddered and the students quaked. Rather than teaching his students "how" to paint, Dunn goaded them to understand "why" they paint. He was, according to biographer Robert F. Karolevitz, "a philosopher of pictures." And unlike DuMond, his approach eschewed the intellect: "When the intellect comes in, Art goes out," Dunn wrote.

A native of South Dakota, Dunn trained at the Chicago Art Institute and then at Chadds Ford with Howard Pyle (1853–1911). Illustration historian Walt Reed notes that, "Of all Pyle's students, Dunn was perhaps most deeply imbued with his philosophy, and as a teacher passed it along together with his own straightforward honesty and intolerance of pretense."

Pyle believed, much like Thomas Hart Benton, that American students should seek training and inspiration in the United States. And to convey these American subjects he insisted upon universal human themes and emotions. Pyle's theory of empathizing with both animate and inanimate objects—of "living in the picture," as he put it—greatly influenced Dunn, who likewise reminded his students that "art is a universal language because it is the expression of the feelings of man.... Fear is fear and love is love anywhere in the world."

"Mr. Dunn," as Riley still refers to him, taught these theories three nights per week, the highlight being the Friday night critique. Seated on a tall stool next to a spotlighted picture on an easel, Dunn invariably began his critique with a question: "What were you trying to say?" Then, speaking in broad terms, he urged the student to emphasize the pictorial epic or what he termed the "Idea" rather than the literary incident. The Idea supplied the form and the design of a picture, and to recognize the Idea the artist had to know himself: "If your life is full you will paint full pictures. If it is empty your pictures will be empty, too."

Noted for aphorisms, which were later compiled by a student and published in *An Evening in the Classroom* (1934), Dunn had an uncanny ability to present the opposing sides of a problem, thereby facilitating its solution. Recalls Riley, "Dunn would pace a few steps behind you and you knew he was watching what you were doing. Then he'd come over and ask where your biggest brush was. I was using my little brushes, but he took a big one and just painted all over the surface of the canvas, saying, 'Paint your broadest areas with your smallest brushes and your smallest areas with your biggest brushes.'"

33. *The Spellbinder*
1987
acrylic, 8 x 13

This is a true "vignette" or incident where the artist leaves it up to the viewer to provide his or her own story line. Is the bachelor rancher in town on Saturday to visit with local eligibles? Or is it a committee of pink people trying to enlist a blue person for civic duty? Or maybe he's being scolded for some unpardonable sin. It's up to you to decide.

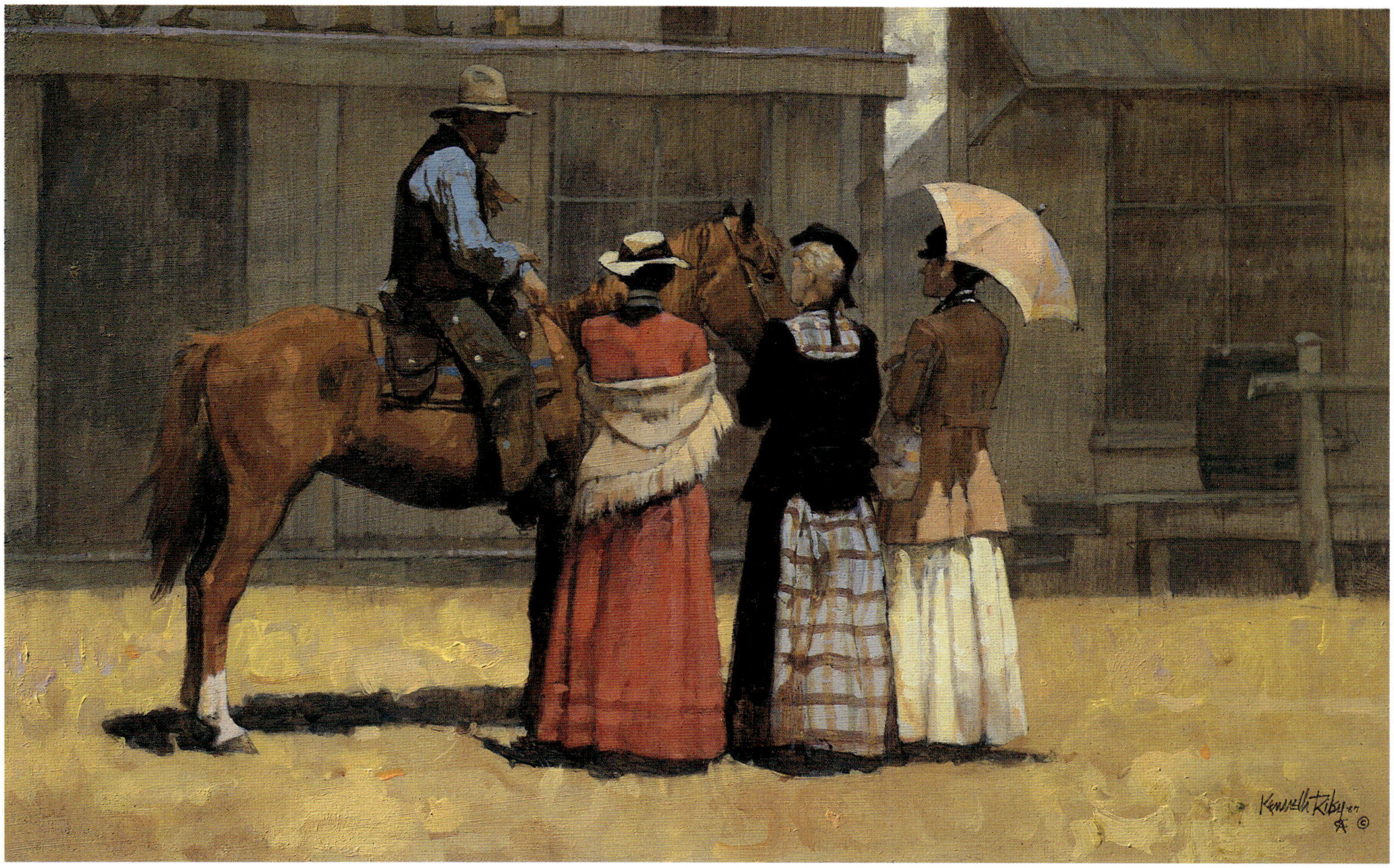

34. *The Signal*
1984
oil, 22 x 28

During the Apache campaigns, the cavalry made use of the heliograph—an apparatus that sent signals across distances by means of the sun's rays thrown from a mirror. The Apache, being an enterprising tribe, would have no doubt adapted the technique using contraband won in battle. In addition to the fun of speculating on such an event, the mirror gave me an opportunity to set up a striking high-key value in an otherwise low-key painting.

Dunn encouraged his students to stretch and not be limited by convention nor obsessed with technique. "Everything Dunn said pointed to painting from the heart, not from the head," says Riley. "Technique was irrelevant. Get it down and get it said, to hell with everything else." Technique, according to Dunn, was in service to the Idea. "Let the Idea direct your energies. Say to yourself not, 'I've an idea, what am I going to do with it?' Rather, 'Here's an idea, what is it going to do with me?'"

Other New York artists would also offer their knowledge to aspirants like Ken Riley. Leading illustrators of the day regularly lectured at the Society of Illustrators. Riley heard, among others, Robert Fawcett (1903–1967), Norman Rockwell, Al Parker (1906–1985) and Harold von Schmidt (1893–1982). Von Schmidt, who had studied with Dunn and occasionally wandered into the Friday night critiques while Riley was there, did an especially memorable lecture during which he began a painting for a serial in *The Saturday Evening Post.* "He painted for two hours and got the work halfway along," says Riley. "It was an inspiration to watch a man of his caliber give himself in that way to a student audience."

Riley's nine months in New York were dedicated to a total immersion in the various techniques needed to communicate the joys and sorrows of life. It was the sorrows of life that dominated the final session with Dunn. "Dunn's experience in World War I had been rigorous. He knew what was coming up for us kids," says Riley. "I'd never seen him quite in that mood. It was a tender parting—we all realized we might never see each other again."

Admittedly overwhelmed, Ken Riley left New York in May 1942 torn between the intellectual and emotional philosophies of DuMond and Dunn. "I couldn't have painted a picture even if I tried," he says. Providentially, at least in retrospect, Riley would put his "confusion" to work in the service of his own life story aboard a ship in the Pacific. There would be scant time to worry about technique in the tale he was about to tell.

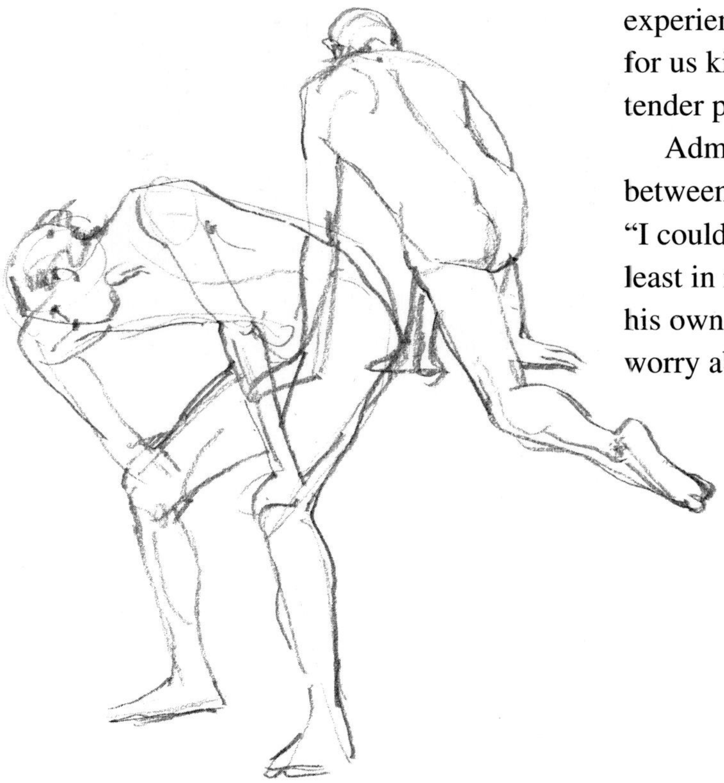

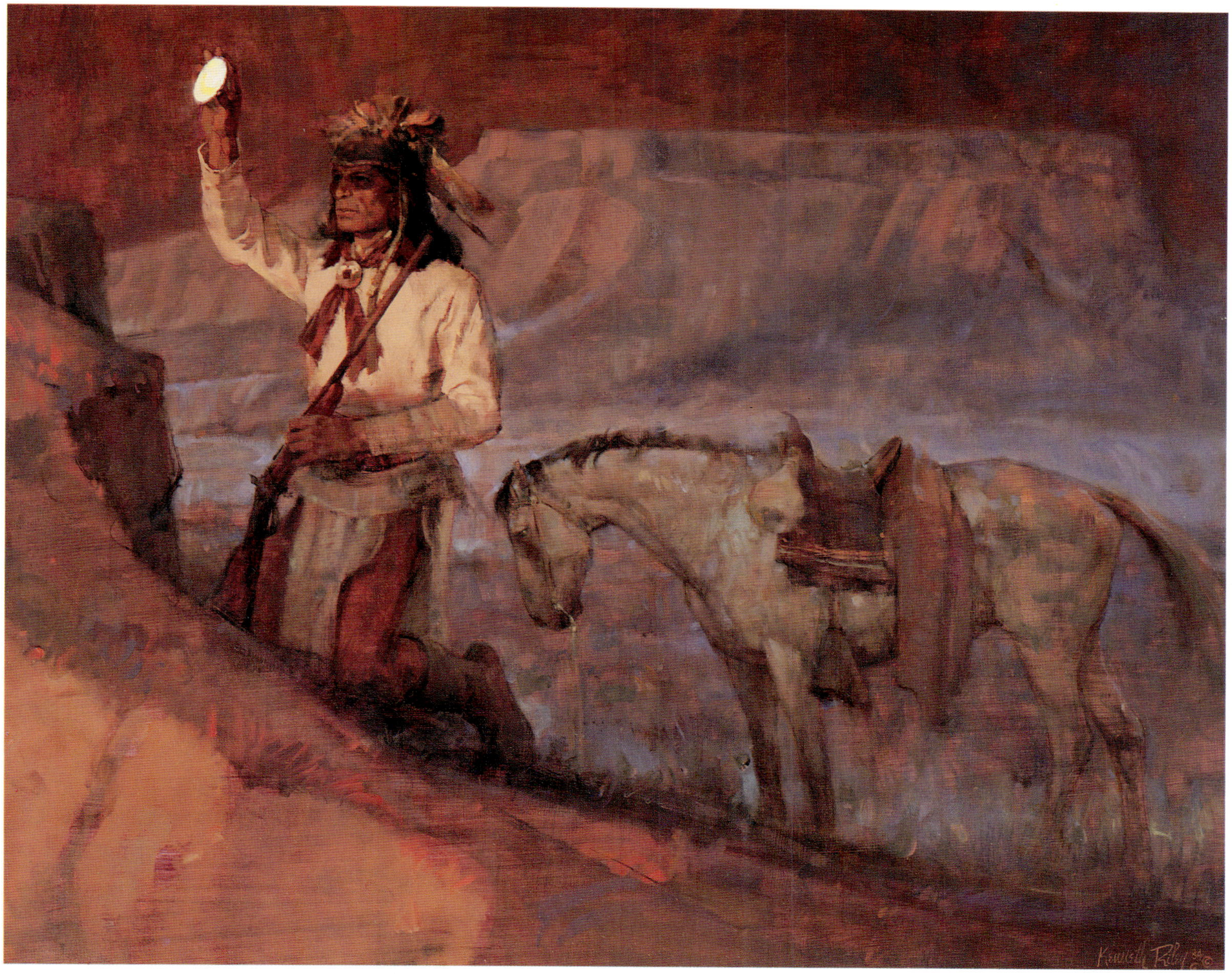

LIFE AND DEATH IN THE PACIFIC

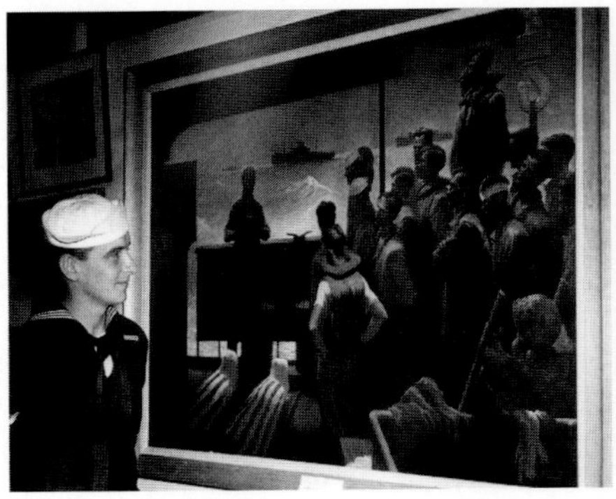

35. Kenneth Riley with his painting *For Thine Is The Kingdom,* 1944.

36. Detail of *The Catch Is Running [38].*

A headline in the *Parsons' Sun,* October 11, 1944, read, "Ken Riley Now Famed Painter." Riley had won the grand award for a painting of a burial at sea titled ***For Thine is the Kingdom [35].*** Described by the reporter as short of stature, with brown eyes, dark hair and a face "tinged by a modest, rosy blush," Specialist Second Class Riley was quoted as responding, "Gosh!" when he learned the news.

Two years earlier, when he enlisted in the Coast Guard, Riley thought of himself as neither "famed" nor necessarily a "painter." While he had visions of a career as a magazine illustrator and had even done a few action paintings for the pulps while studying in New York, he was still in search of the "representational potentialities" of his newfound method. Having chosen a "smaller branch of the service attached to the romance of the sea," Riley was paradoxically stationed in the Cascade Mountains of Washington at an outlying site called the Big Four Inn. A rambling clapboard hotel near the snowcapped Big Four Mountain, the inn served as an overflow receiving base and Riley worked in the kitchen. When he wasn't peeling potatoes or mixing powdered milk, he drew portraits, including one of the commissary officer. "He was smitten with my work and suggested that I paint something appropriate to the Coast Guard."

Riley wrote to MarCyne for canvas and paints and set up a studio in the glass-enclosed widow's walk atop the hotel roof. While snow sifted through the rafters and bears thrashed about in the garbage dump below, Riley, his hands covered with mittens and his canvas propped on chairs, embarked on a mural. In true Benton tradition, the theme was the history of the Coast Guard in the Upper Northwest. "It was fairly complicated," Riley recalls, "having to do with small boats and the Alaskan coastline."

Riley had seen neither the boats nor much of the coastline at this point. But drawing from Coast Guard literature and fortified with a healthy dose of imagination, he went at the task with gusto. A month or so later the canvas was carted through seven-foot snowdrifts to Seattle where the District Admiral pronounced the painting Riley's ticket into the public relations division.

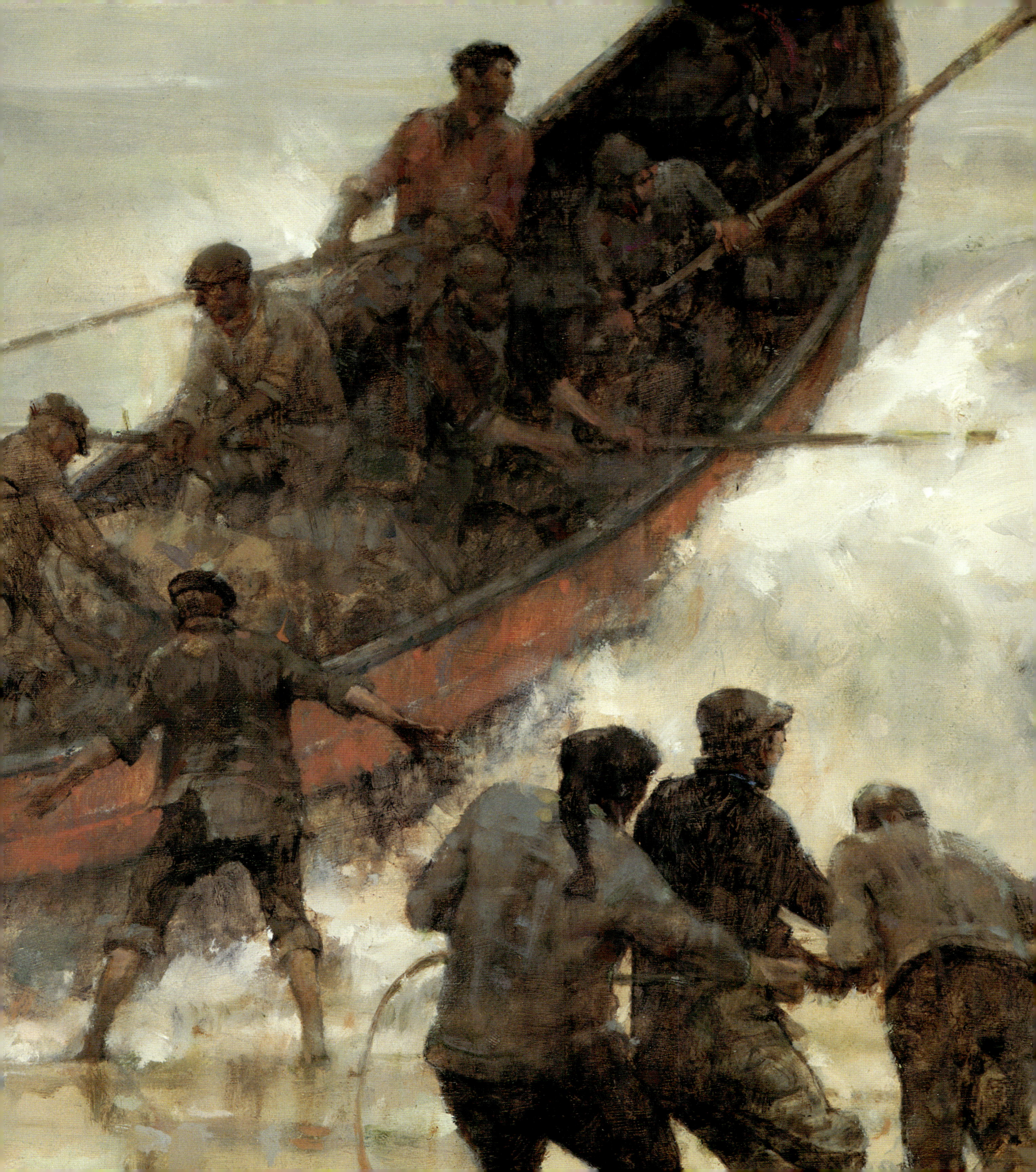

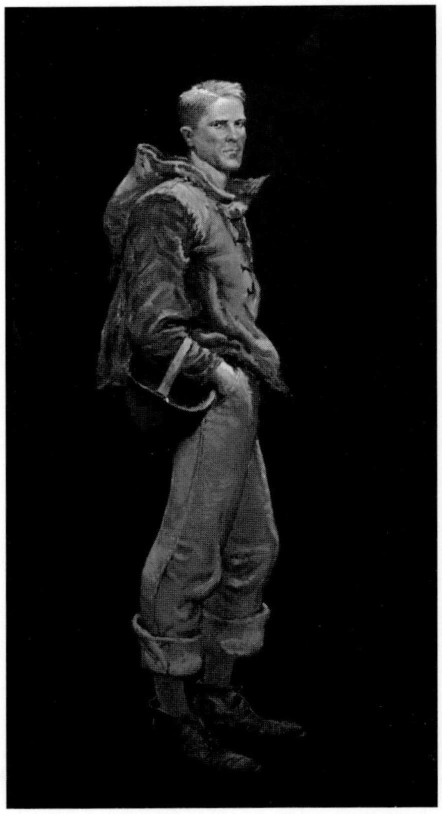

37. *Coxswain,* oil, ca. 1944.

38. *The Catch Is Running*
1985
oil, 16 x 24

Much to the delight of generations of artists, the fishermen of Nazarre, Portugal, colorfully launch their boats into the Atlantic. A brewing storm provided the inspiration for this scene. The ocean's elemental energy continues to test man's determination and brute strength.

Riley joined a seasoned crew in Seattle. "There wasn't an amateur among them," he says of the men who as civilians held jobs as editors, cartoonists and artists for major city newspapers. They took the young artist under their wing as he tackled his first illustration assignments. Riley documented military activities such as the rescue of a grounded Russian freighter, and ship-building and repair at nearby Bremerton Naval Yard. Making sketches and notes out in the field, Riley took his raw information back to the office where he composed and executed drawings in brush and ink. No longer documenting a stationary model holding a pose, he learned to respond to movement and to go for gesture and memory-jogging details. His skills quickly matured and soon his drawings were picked up by the United and Associated Presses and appeared as sepiatones in the Sunday *Seattle Times.* Expecting to remain in Seattle, Ken sent for MarCyne who had been working in a Parsons ammunition plant. She arrived a few weeks before his new orders: Riley was to ship out as a combat artist headed for the South Pacific on the Coast Guard manned invasion transport, the U.S.S. *Arthur Middleton.*

Ship life and the beach assaults that Riley would witness were a far cry from the low-pressure military duties he experienced on the mainland. The *Middleton* and its crew were themselves an adventure tale and no doubt they helped turn the Kansas landlubber into an able-bodied seaman. Introduced to boat mechanics and coxswains, Aussies and U.S. Marines, Riley turned the daily activities of survival into endless drawings done in watercolors, charcoal and pen and ink. Whether mundane or heroic—from men asleep in their bunks to those staring blankly from battlegrounds-turned-graveyards—the theme of human vulnerability dominates Riley's drawings. Against a backdrop of smoldering ships and seas pitching landing barges like bobbers in Dante's *Inferno*, Riley drew his own experiences of landing on a beach under enemy attack and the firsthand accounts told to him by Marines returning from the bloody November 1943 battle of Tarawa. "We sent out the Second Marines in barges, thinking that the battle would be over in a day," recalls Riley. "But the Japanese were dug in with coconut-log bunkers and it took two days of fighting just to get the Marines on the beaches." By the end of the third day, over two thousand casualties made Tarawa one of the most intense Pacific battles.

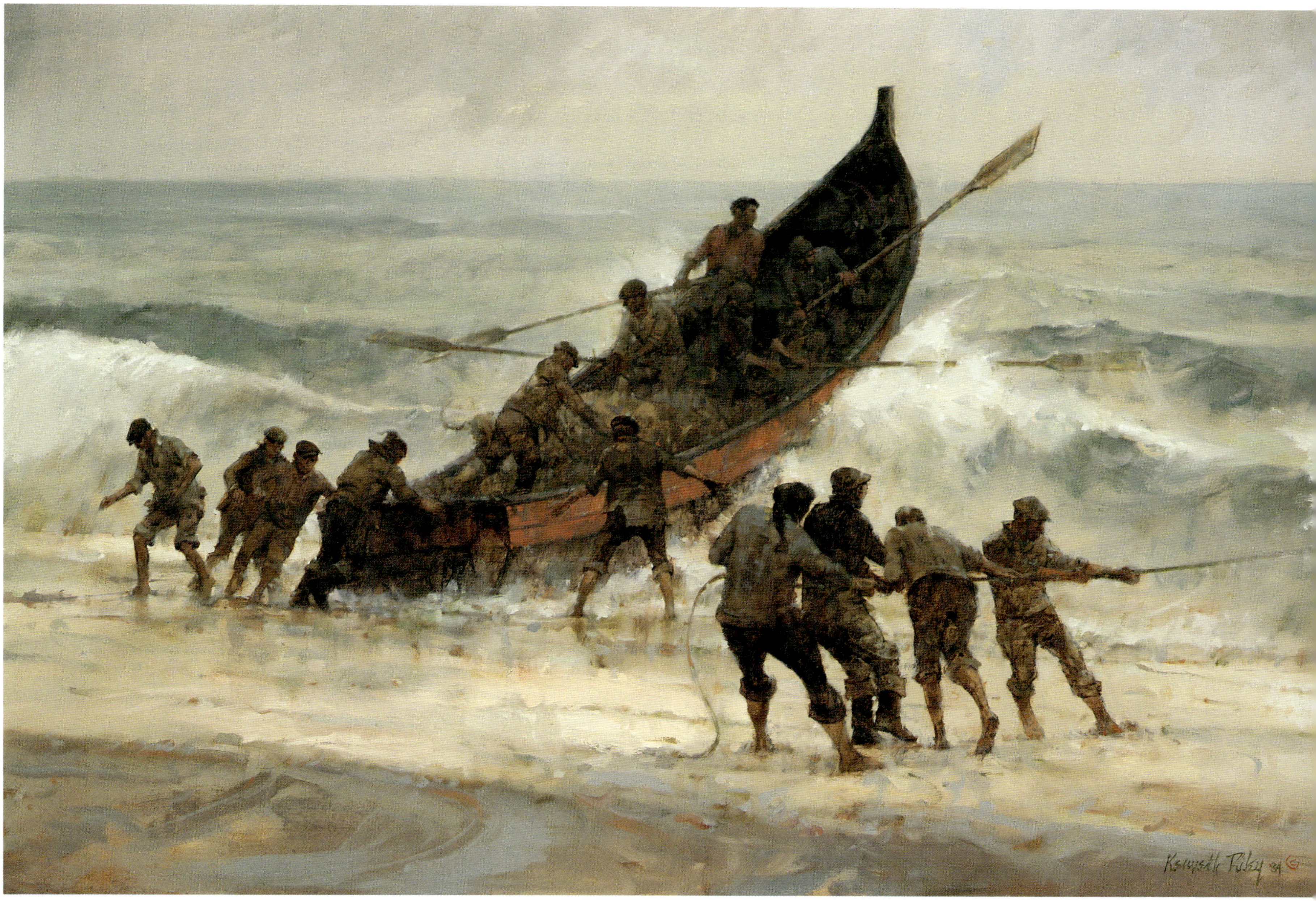
Kenneth Riley '84

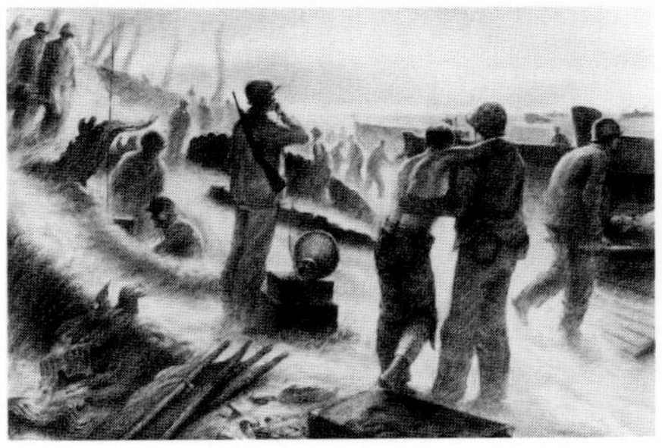

39. *Beach Scene, Engebi,* 1943.

40. *Crew Cut Aboard The U.S.S.* Middleton, ca. 1943.

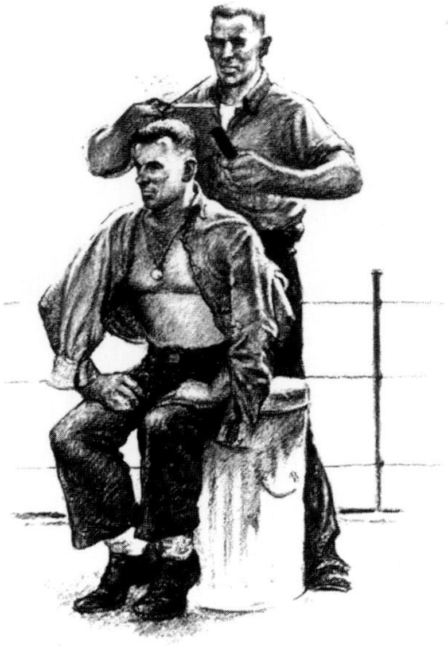

Casualties were a recurring theme in Riley's drawings: Stretcher bearers stoically carry the wounded and dying over the beaches of Eniwetok. A coxswain indicating the number of wounded holds up six fingers, as if to offer benediction over a body outstretched on the motor housing of a barge returning from the battle of Saipan. Japanese machine gunners lie where they fell in bunkers on Ebeye Island. The war drawings were Riley's first effort as an illustrator of life ... and death. Forced to summon the full gamut of emotions, he came to understand Dunn's admonition that the artist must "choose a picture and think of it from all angles, then choose the most barren, most brutal way of saying it. Say it strongly and simply with the fewest possible things necessary."

The strength and simplicity of Riley's drawings were a prelude to the more complex paintings he would undertake once the *Middleton* returned stateside and he was reassigned to Coast Guard Headquarters in Washington, D.C. With his sketches and drawings, photographs and notes, Riley spent the last several months of his duty "working out the kinks" of the formal and representational potentialities of oil painting that he had learned from Dunn and DuMond. Although he had abandoned the system of greys, Riley found that DuMond's theory helped him understand the value relationships of flame-red fires burning on a lush-green island during early morning light. Or a blazing tropical sun penetrating an awning over a helmsman on the flying bridge.

The Idea of war, as Riley came to express it, was the reality that some must die so that others might live. Thanksgiving for life became as prominent as mourning in Riley's Washington works. One of the drawings he turned into a painting was the aforementioned ***For Thine is the Kingdom [35]***. Solemn faced men, some wearing life jackets, others wrapped in bandages, listen to a chaplain who reads over two flag-draped bodies. The solid triangular shape of the living men on the right offers an organic contrast to the vacant machined shapes defined by hard edges on the left. The silhouette of the chaplain against a rolling sea is repeated in the haunting figure in the shadows who is poised to send the bodies into a watery grave. Submitted to the Seventh Annual Outdoor Art Fair sponsored by the *Times-Herald* in Washington, D.C., the piece won Best in Show out of eight-hundred entrants. As reported in the *Parsons' Sun*, the work "brought many spectators up short with a new and poignant realization of the price which some men are willing to pay for freedom and decency."

Living in a rented room off Dupont Circle, Riley was joined by MarCyne in the spring of 1945. When he wasn't engaged in assignments like designing the U.S. Coast Guard commemorative stamp, Ken and MarCyne indulged themselves in the rich atmosphere of art that was found in museums like the National Gallery, Phillips Collection and the Corcoran. Anxious to get on with his career, Riley planned to move to New York. Before his discharge, however, the road forked in yet another direction.

David Finlay, director of the National Gallery, had seen Riley's work in the 1944 exhibition "Paintings and Drawings by U.S. Coast Guard Combat Artists," at the National Gallery. In need of an artist to illustrate a book on his deceased brother-in-law, Finlay commissioned Riley to do seven drawings to accompany *The War Letters of Morton Eustis*, which was privately published in 1945. The results impressed Finlay, who offered to arrange a fellowship abroad for Riley, if he so wished to continue his education. "I was honored," recalls Riley, "but at this point I just wanted to get out of the service and into a professional life."

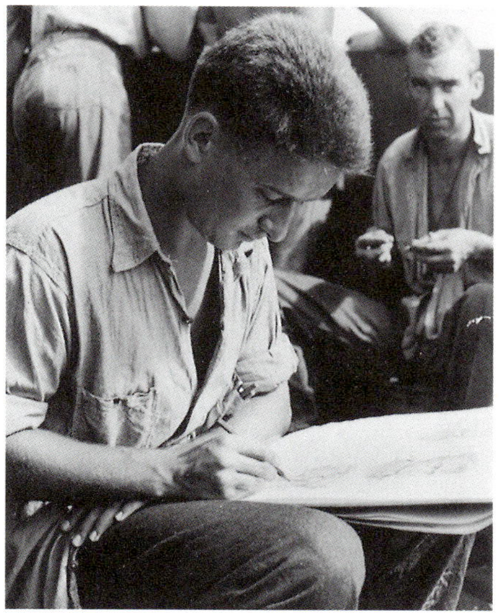

41. Kenneth Riley sketching aboard the U.S.S. *Middleton,* ca. 1943.

42. *Mess Hall on the U.S.S.* Middleton, oil, ca. 1944.

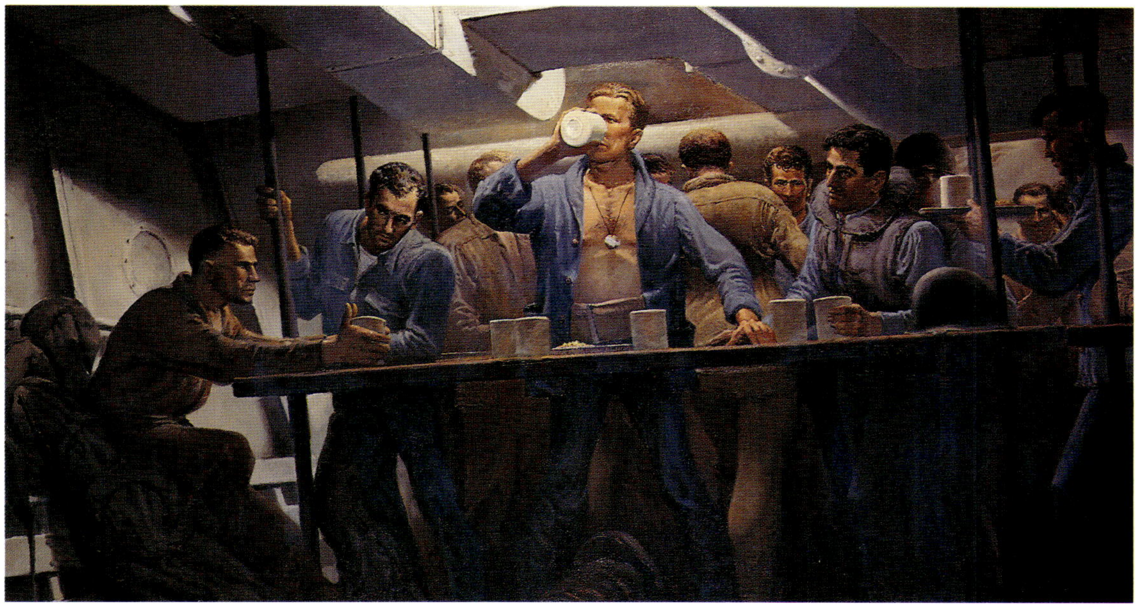

A PROFESSIONAL LIFE IN ILLUSTRATION

"I have great respect and admiration for the illustration profession and not just because I toiled in it over twenty-five years," says Ken Riley. "An illustrator is someone with the skills to render an angel dancing on the head of a pin ... and have it ready for delivery first thing on Monday morning."

Riley was twenty-seven years old when he offered his imagination and technical skills to the book and magazine editors in New York City. The post-war illustration market that he entered was, like the art world itself, evolving from the traditional, halcyon imagery of Norman Rockwell to the more modernistic, experimental approaches of Austin Briggs (1909–1973). Rejecting highly detailed images of an idealized world peopled with handsome men and gorgeous women, the avant-garde of illustration were calling attention to the creative process itself. According to Al Parker, who was among them, the innovators painted "intense, turbulent expressions that avoided photographic realism and willfully lacked polished craftsmanship, imparting an unfinished look to the finished art." Such moxie, continued Parker, "strutted amidst a pageant of plenty. Advertising budgets had skyrocketed and magazines bulged with fiction, providing work for all who painted in the style of the innovators."

To break into this fast-paced, competitive market, Riley needed a place in which to live and create a portfolio. Jack Williams, an advertising executive he had met during the war, helped by offering the young couple his rural New England guest house near Ridgefield, Connecticut. As he would for virtually the rest of his life, Riley painted at home, turning whatever available space he had into a studio. During the daylight hours he painted variations of mother-child, boy-girl, western and historical themes for his portfolio. At night and on weekends, he earned a living drawing explosive adventure comics for another military friend, publisher Joe Simon. Throughout it all, MarCyne pledged her assistance. Called upon to serve as a model and to offer critiques, she "kept all the balls in the air" so that Riley could keep his "nose to the boards."

43. Detail of *Dance Progressions [44].*

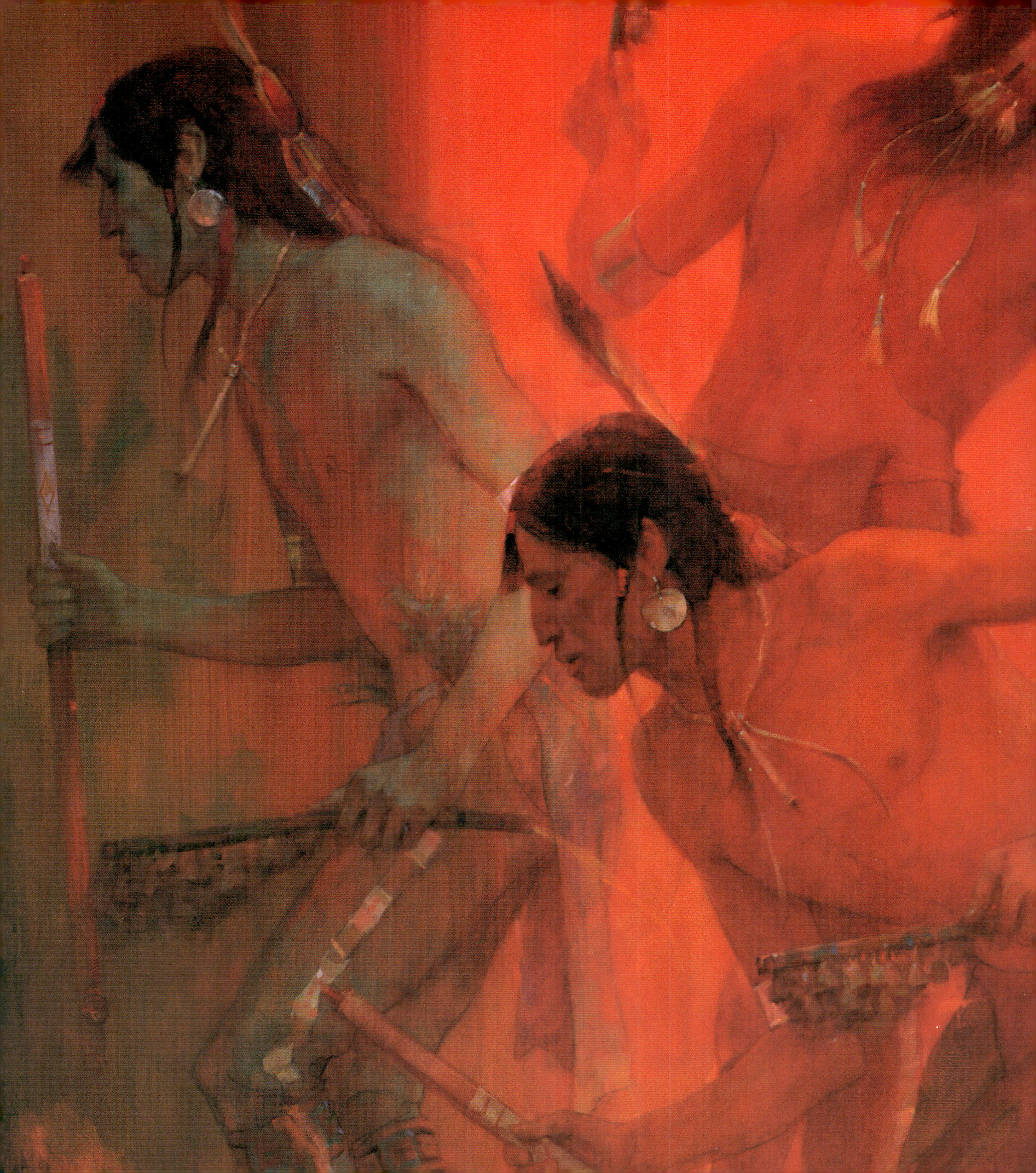

44. *Dance Progressions*

1991

oil, 50 x 42

Leanin' Tree Museum,
Boulder, Colorado

George Catlin did a wonderful job describing the powerful cadence of drum beats that stirred entire tribes into ritualistic dances. In ***Dance Progressions,*** I focused on that drum beat, speculating on the movement of a single dancer whose body traces the line of a dance in space. The agitated angles and lines formed by the dancer's limbs, rattle and pipe are intended to give this painting movement that releases into a gasp of light in the upper right.

Already in his portfolio were the war drawings and paintings which Riley thought might interest the men's magazines. And they did, securing him one of his first assignments. "It was a story about an Inuit woman for *Argosy* and I botched it so badly that they didn't accept it," says Riley. He adds that his failure turned into a success when illustrator John Clymer (1907–1990) got the story, introducing Riley to the art of a man who would later become a colleague and friend.

With his portfolio complete, Ken and MarCyne moved closer to the New York publishing houses by using their savings of $3,500 to buy a third-floor walk-up on West 75th Street. Figuring he'd start at the top, Riley gathered his samples and his courage and made an appointment with Frank Kilker, art editor of *The Saturday Evening Post*, published in Philadelphia. "I vividly recall walking down this long, tunnel-like hallway and meeting Kilker, who asked me to spread my work out on a big round table. He scrutinized it for what seemed like an eternity ... then looked up and said, 'Well, I like this. You'll be hearing from me.'" Riley didn't remember the train ride back.

Within the month, the first story came in the mail, beginning an association that continued until photography usurped the role of picture-making in the early 1960s. Looking back on those early years, Riley concedes that the art editors at the *Post* offered him a training ground in which he learned the technical craft of creating a picture that would "stop a person thumbing

45. Illustration for "Mountain Woman," *The Saturday Evening Post,* January 17, 1948.

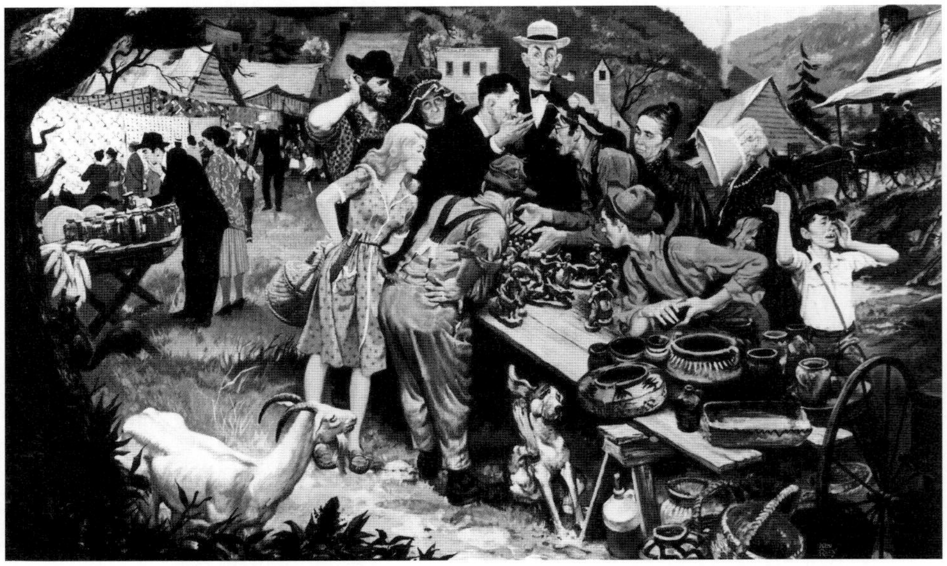

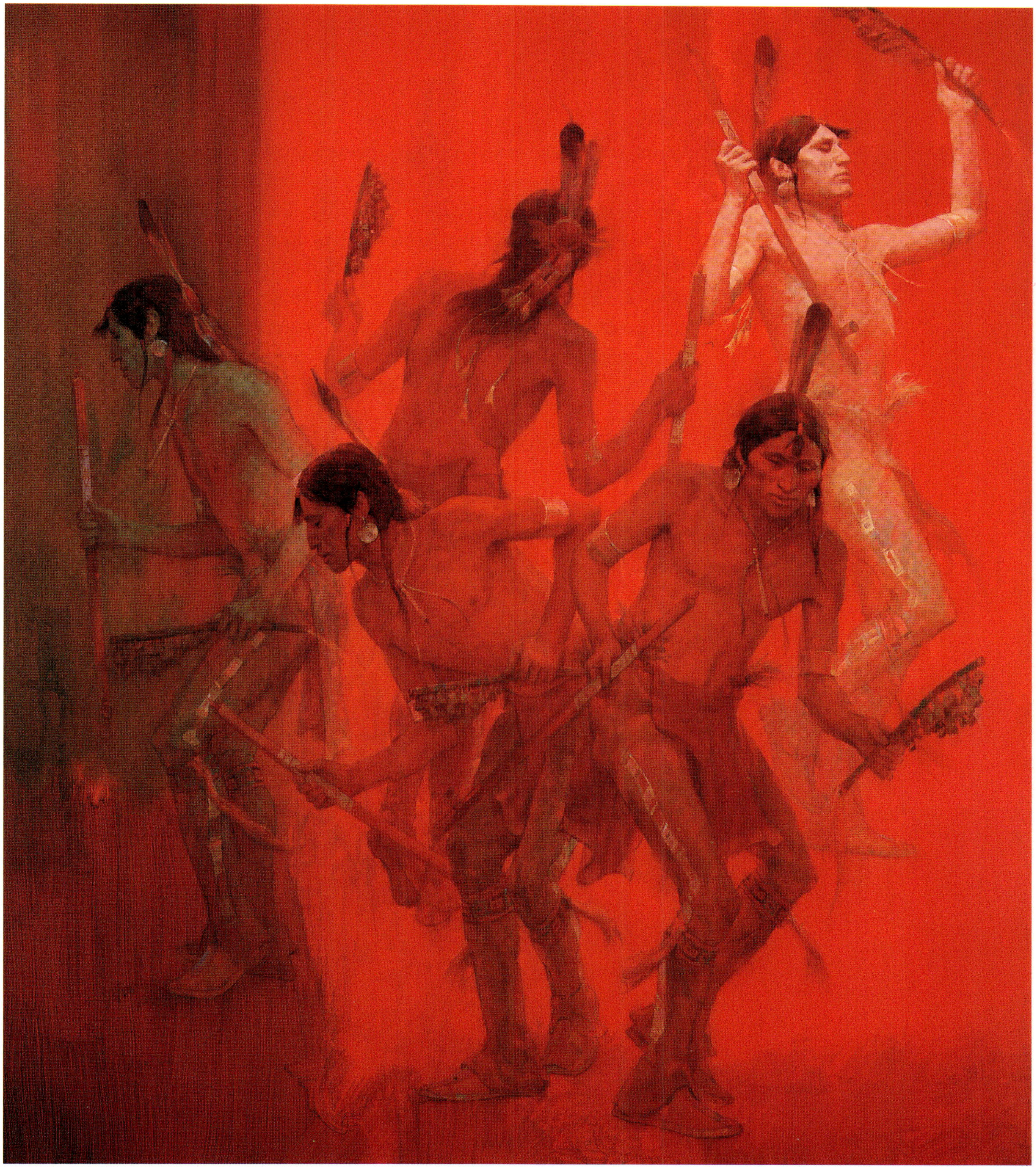

through a magazine and incite their interest to the read the story." His first assignment was for an Ozarks hillbilly story titled "Mountain Woman," printed in the January 17, 1948, issue ***[45].*** Later, the illustration was discussed by Associate Editor Ashley Halsey Jr. in the book *Illustrating for the Saturday Evening Post.* With their folksy expressions, Riley's figures hint of Norman Rockwell, who had illustrated for the *Post* since 1916. But the composition looks more Bentonesque, especially the figure groupings which form an undulating line in space, circling clockwise from the lower left and picking up speed as it pirouettes into the central focus of figures gathered around a table covered with goods.

"I was so thrilled," recalls Riley, "that I decided to leave no stone unturned. The story described handmade quilts, pottery, baskets, jars of canned fruit ... and of course I felt I had to put it all in. I ended up doing the most complicated picture I have ever done!"

A new illustration assignment appeared in the mailbox about once a month. Riley would read it through, indicating scene possibilities in the margins and preparing preliminary sketches. "The editors didn't tell you what to illustrate. It was your baby and you got to pick out your own situation," Riley says of the sketches which were sent to the editors for approval. Captions for Riley's illustrations often stressed the action about to happen, the mood of the moment or a description of the person: "The man was staggering in the middle of the road. Mike slammed on his air brakes. 'What the hell are you doing?' he shouted." Or, "Her name was Travis. Her hair was yellow and she handled a gun as though she could shoot."

46. Illustration for "Horatio Hornblower," by C. S. Forester, *The Saturday Evening Post.*

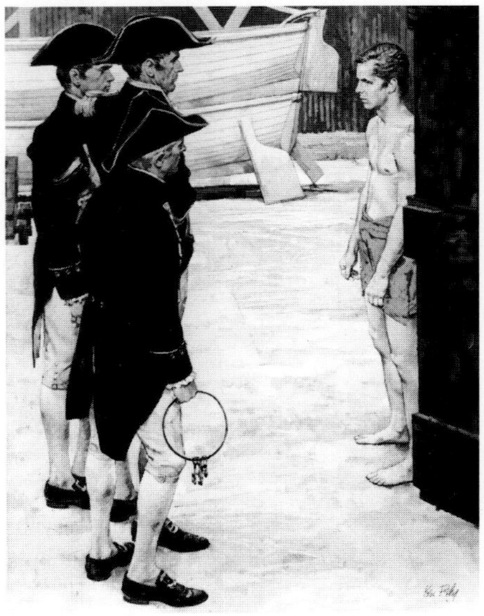

A *Post* story typically required one large illustration and occasionally a "spot" or smaller vignette, both of which were run on the opening spread. "If someone read past the first couple of paragraphs," explains Riley, "the editors felt that the art had fulfilled its purpose, since the remaining copy ran in columns in the back of the publication." For his efforts, he was paid $300 for a single page and $600 to $700 when the picture went across two pages. These larger illustrations were used on the openings of serialized stories, such as C. S. Forester's account of Horatio Hornblower, a tale of an English Naval mid-shipman who moved up the ranks to admiral ***[46].*** Harold von Schmidt had illustrated the story in the 1940s, followed by Ben Stahl (1910–1986). Riley took over the serial in the mid-1950s and did approximately ten installments.

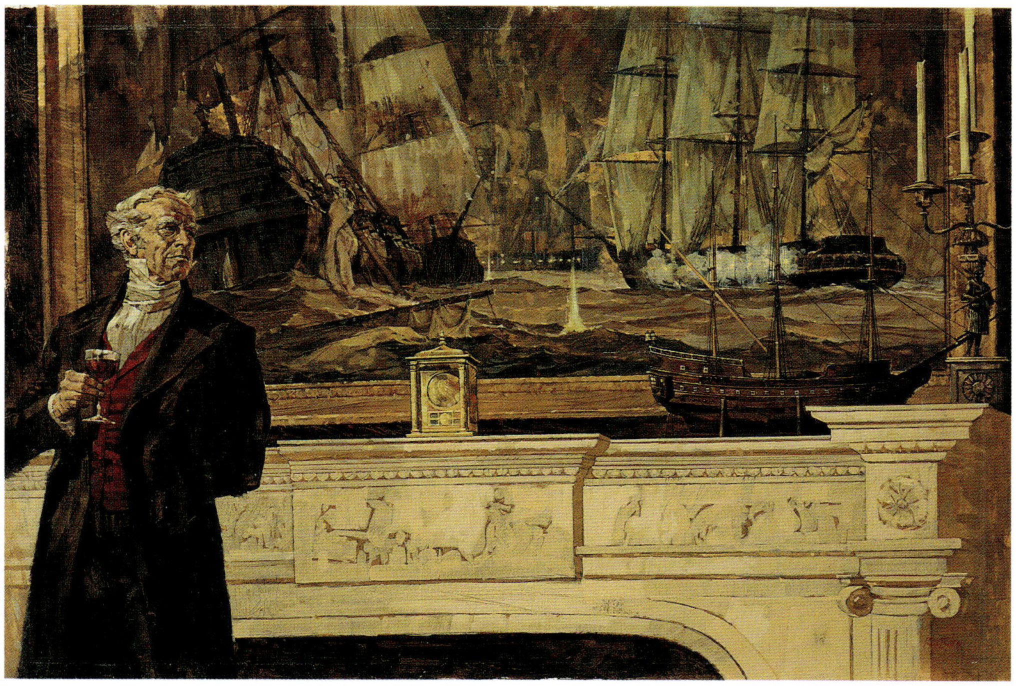

47. Illustration for a story in *The Saturday Evening Post.*

The procedure that Riley established for creating his illustrations was fairly regimented. First he selected an incident that was specific to the story, yet universal in its emotional appeal. Next he researched the time period of the story and its location, getting a feel for the landscape, costuming, architecture and accouterments. With this information he created several thumbnail sketches looking for a design whose eye-catching abstract patterns and shapes directed the readers to a focus—almost always a face—with which they could empathize.

With his concept in place, Riley painted one or more roughs measuring 6 by 8 inches that were mailed to the editors for approval. When an approved sketch was returned, models were hired and costumes rented. Riley would set up the situation and photograph the models from every angle. "I learned fairly early that it was expensive to have models sit for long periods of time and that the camera could do as good a job of recording the details," he says. "The camera was an expedient for getting the job done on time." (To this day, Riley poses and photographs models. "The artist needs to face reality or his imagination will return to boring, tried-and-true solutions," he explains. Often using MarCyne or himself as a model, Riley might throw a blanket over his shoulders and hold a garbage can lid for a shield. A Polaroid photo is enough to give him the drape of fabric or the gesture he needs.)

Using the photographs as aids in "seeing the nuances of life," Riley scaled up the drawing to around 24 by 36 inches and commenced painting. His first assignments were done in oils but he soon switched to water-based media that dried more quickly, including gouache, designers colors and casein. When acrylics first came on the market in the early 1960s, Riley tested the Liquitex version which ultimately gave him the richness and spontaneity he desired. Once finished, he either hand-carried or mailed the painting to the publishers and then lost complete track of its whereabouts.

"Back then no one wanted an illustration," Riley laughs, adding that some of his illustrations have found their way into auctions and galleries. "We painted for reproduction only, so the original didn't have any value. People threw them away or they stockpiled at the magazine and were finally given away. We were creating subject matter that was incidental—depicting nothing but a certain point in a story. The illustrations had no universal meaning whatsoever."

Artists tend to feel inferior to business people who make so many decisions. But when you stop and think about the number of decisions an artist makes in doing a painting, it is incredible. They may not be earth-shattering but they are decisions. —KR

Perhaps because the primary goal of illustration is to address specifics, Riley quickly learned that a battalion of critics was ready to puncture the egos of errant illustrators who hadn't done their homework. He laughs about it today, but when his second *Post* illustration brought a letter from an irate reader, Riley was devastated.

"I had illustrated a pioneer tale set in Oregon. The scene showed a log cabin in a clearing with the stumps of trees scattered throughout. A dentist from Oklahoma wrote that he had never seen tree stumps as I had shown them. Not a beaver, nor saw, nor ax would result in the projections I had pictured. But he concluded that it really made no difference, since the stumps were on a par with the picture ... and it stunk too! That caught my attention and from then on I was more careful."

Being more careful meant many trips to New York's central library which offered several rooms of photographs, maps and drawings categorized by

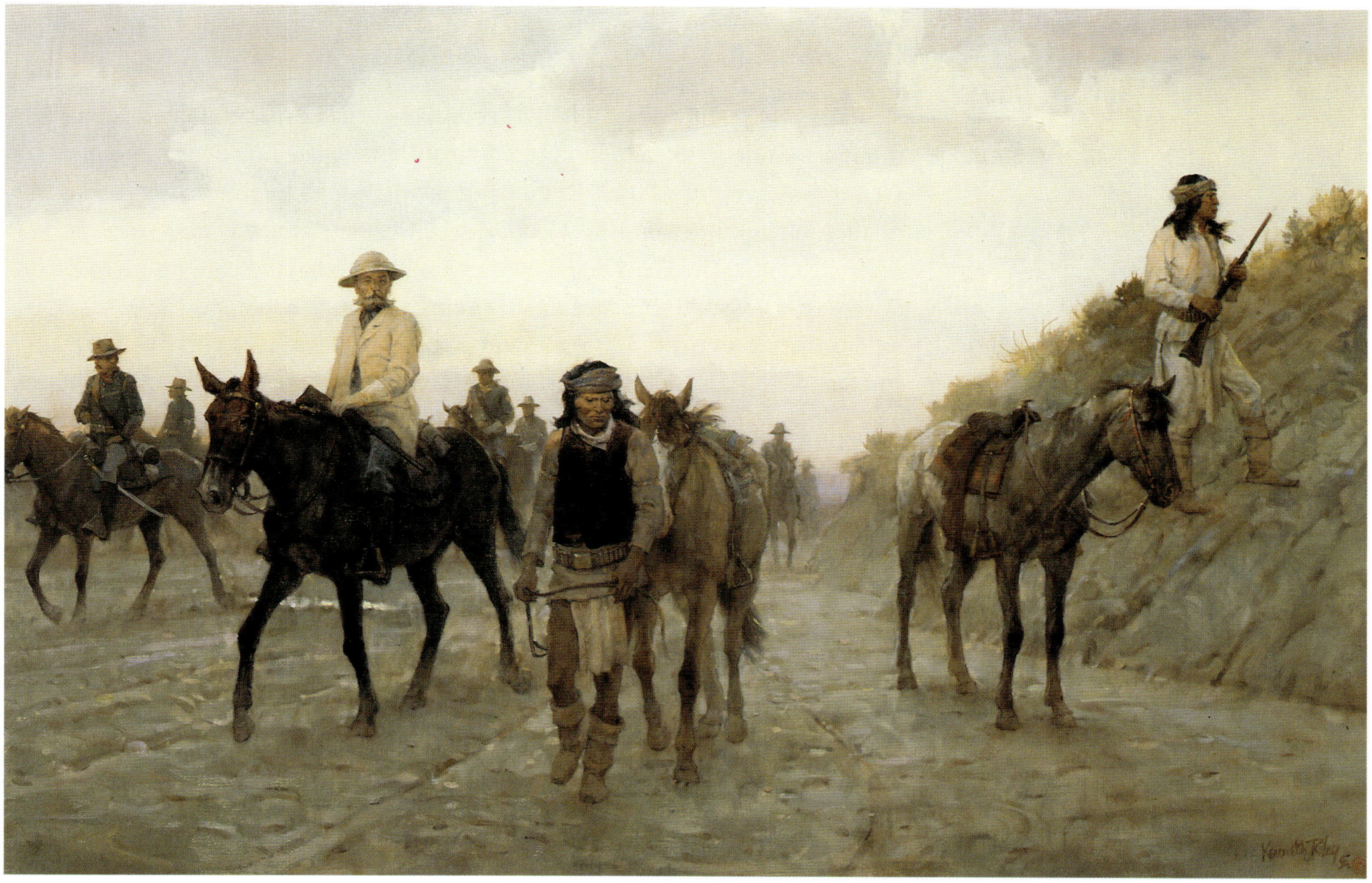

subject. “You could find just about anything you needed,” says Riley, who started building a personal library of reference books and his own “scrap file” of photos and movie stills purchased in the shops along 42nd Street near Times Square. Movie stills were excellent resources for action scenes and for charactertypes. And since period movies were costumed, Riley occasionally used a movie still as the starting point for his research. He relishes a story about illustrator Robert Fawcett who took a studio tour in Hollywood. “He was impressed with the costume and accessories department and asked the guide what resources they had for authenticating all these things. She mentioned a few, then said, ‘Of course, we look at magazine illustrations.... ’ Talk about the blind leading the blind!”

48. *General Crook*
1987
oil, 18 x 28

Much is known about General Crook through his biographer, Captain John G. Bourke, who described the commanding officer as having “muscle and sinew to the rigidity of steel and the elasticity of rubber.” Crook, who preferred to ride a mule, introduced the use of mule pack-trains for supplying the troops. His typical uniform was an army-issue, two-piece cotton-duck outfit with a helmet made of cork covered with mosquito netting.

Riley enjoyed the research involved in historical illustration and soon his diligence came to the attention of publications such as *Life* and *National Geographic.* For the latter, Riley was commissioned to do a series on English history, including a courting scene between Anne Hathaway and William Shakespeare. "The Geographic was committed to having everything as accurate as possible and, since I was doing some fairly complicated compositions, they sent my working drawings to the London Museum for approval. I had done quite a bit of research authenticating portraits, costumes, furniture and a cottage fireplace. When I got the drawing back, however, it was marked all over with little notations of things that weren't quite right ... like Anne's dress, which they said was five years too contemporary!"

A book that Riley cherishes to this day is *The Encyclopedia of Costume*. But, while it gives him information about styles, the pictures don't reveal how a costume would respond to a pose. Such was the problem when Riley was asked to illustrate a trapper in buckskins for "Violent Interlude," by Ernest

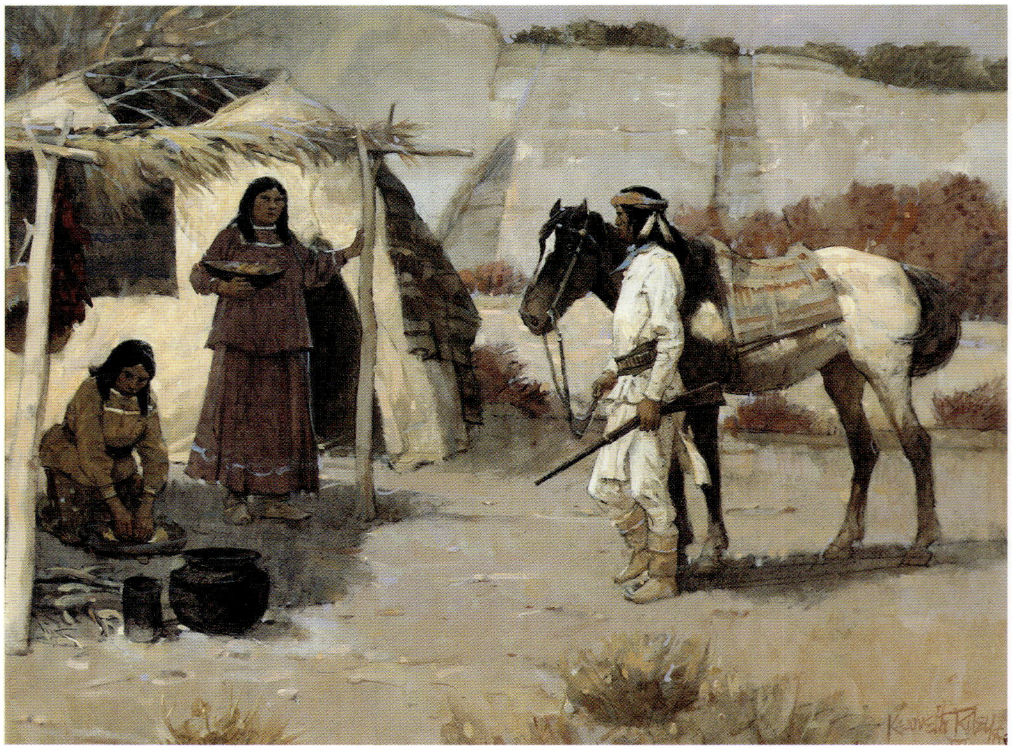

49. *Chiricahua Homestead*

ca. 1987

acrylic, 9 x 12

This work is done completely in acrylic, which for me is a drawing and design medium. Because acrylics set up so quickly, I work directly, keeping the paint moving as much as I can but recognizing that I will end up with crisper edges.

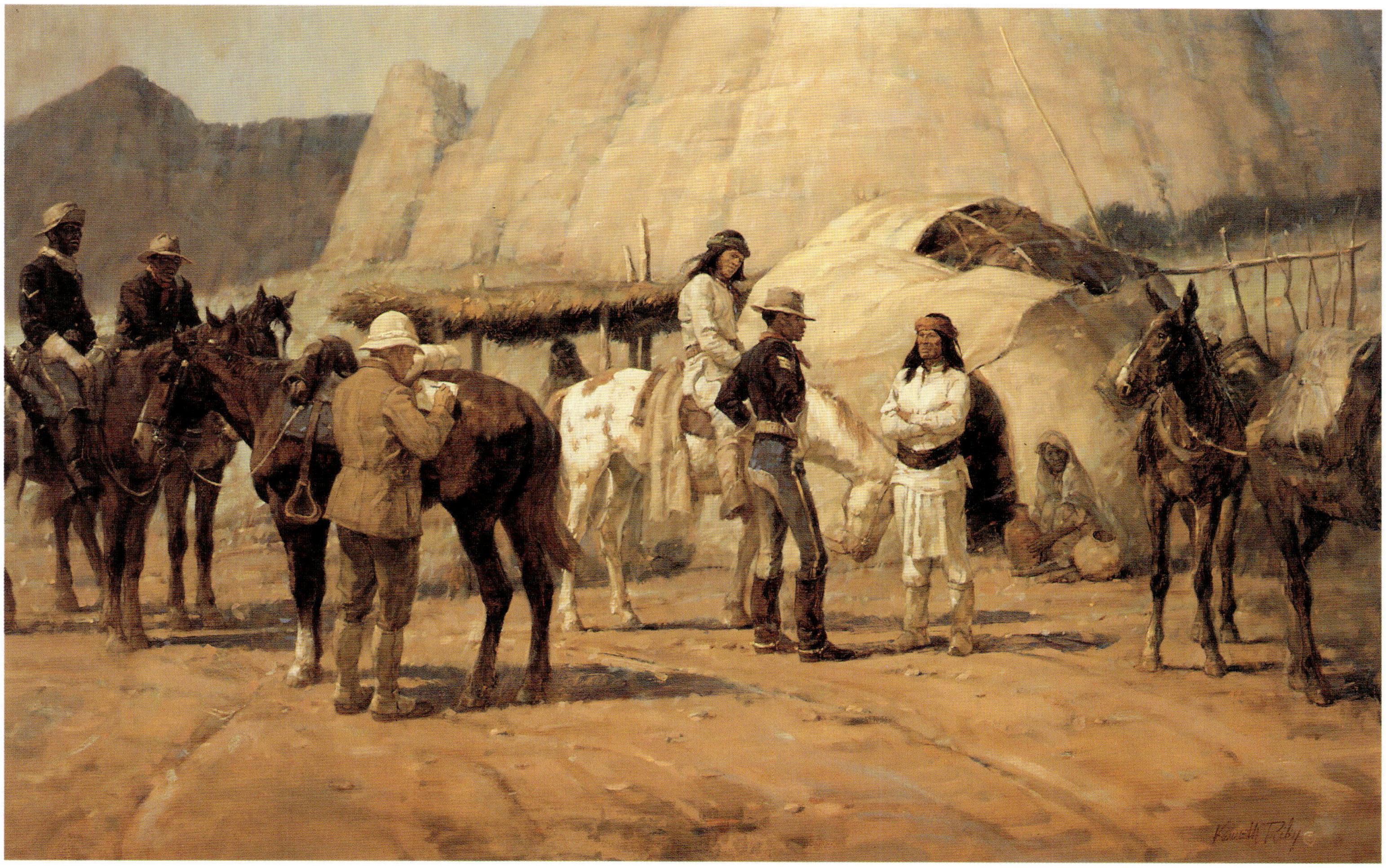

Haycox in the February 26, 1949, issue of the *Post*. Two days of searching the costume shops had uncovered only musical comedy buckskins made of suede. "Just when it seemed hopeless and I was resigned to do a Nelson Eddy trapper, I ran across some worn leather buckskins that looked like a whole tribe of Indians had war-danced on them!"

Occasionally authenticity and propriety necessitated a compromise, particularly at the *Post* whose editors were sensitive to young people among their fifteen million readers. When Riley was asked to illustrate Conrad Richter's story, "The Last Man Alive," he chose the scene when, under Indian attack, an Amish woman picks up her sleeping husband and places him in a dower chest. It happened to take place on their wedding night, and Riley asked himself what this man and woman would be wearing. Since the woman's possessions had burned in a fire, Riley "tossed her bridal nighties into the fire too" and dressed her in a petticoat. The man he put in a red nightshirt. The illustration brought letters complaining that the Amish never wear red;

50. *Frederic Remington and the Buffalo Soldiers*
1982
oil, 24 x 40

Though the name Frederic Remington is synonymous with the West, he was in fact a New Yorker who visited the area on numerous illustration assignments. Among them was an assignment from *Harper's* to accompany the Buffalo Soldiers to the San Carlos Apache reservation in the White Mountains. There, Remington endeavored to sketch the Apache undetected by hiding behind men or animals. I chose to show him not as the svelte painter he depicted in his article, but with the girth for which he came to be known.

moreover, they would sleep in their underwear or nothing at all. "In either case," wrote Ashley Halsey, "the artist stood excused."

Not everything Riley illustrated was foreign to him. His military experiences made him a logical candidate for a number of war-related illustration assignments. Among them was the 1960–64 *Life* series on Civil War battles, from which Riley's painting of the ***Surrender of Appomattox*** is in the West Point Museum. Though he had to acquaint himself with details of geography and strategy, armaments and uniforms, Riley well understood the epic of war. No doubt this contributed to his selection in 1962 for a series of prints on civilian militia in American wars. Commissioned by the Army and Air National Guard, the series comprised four works, one of which shows the Battle of Bunker Hill. Titled ***The Whites of Their Eyes***, the painting was presented to John F. Kennedy in an Oval Room ceremony in September 1962. Today it is displayed in the Kennedy Library and Museum.

"Living the part" made any illustration more vital. Riley took advantage of this fact when he started illustrating Forester's Hornblower series. In need of information about early sailing ships, Ken and MarCyne decided to sail their thirty-foot sloop, *The Whitecap*, to the Maritime Museum in Mystic, Connecticut, to study the old whalers, frigates, navigation gear and artifacts. Cruising past Coney Island, into New York harbor and then up the East River into Long Island Sound, the trip was anything but uneventful. MarCyne vividly remembers getting down on her knees and praying they'd make it on the moonless night when turbulent winds blew them adrift. Though believing himself capable of handling most any situation at sea, even Riley had some doubts that night. "When the port holes on one side are under water, you do have to worry," he says with a wry smile. The experience added tremendously to Riley's melodramatic scene of Admiral Hornblower, surrounded by flying halyards and straining crewmen, battling against a thirty-degree list to hold sight of an onrushing schooner.

By the early 1950s, Riley was working with an agent (initially Barry Stevens and later Frank Lavaty). It was a big step. The agent took a quarter of all Riley's earnings as a commission for securing additional jobs with the women's magazine and book publishers. Living in a high-rise apartment in Peter Cooper Village, on 23rd Street, Riley painted his romanticized scenes in the living room looking out to the bridges crossing the East River. On

51. *The White Pony*
1991
oil, 48 x 42

The idea for this picture was to create a white-on-white painting. The challenge was to come up with whites of such different color character and texture that each is interesting and yet all unify into a whole behind the vertical hide-and-seek trees.

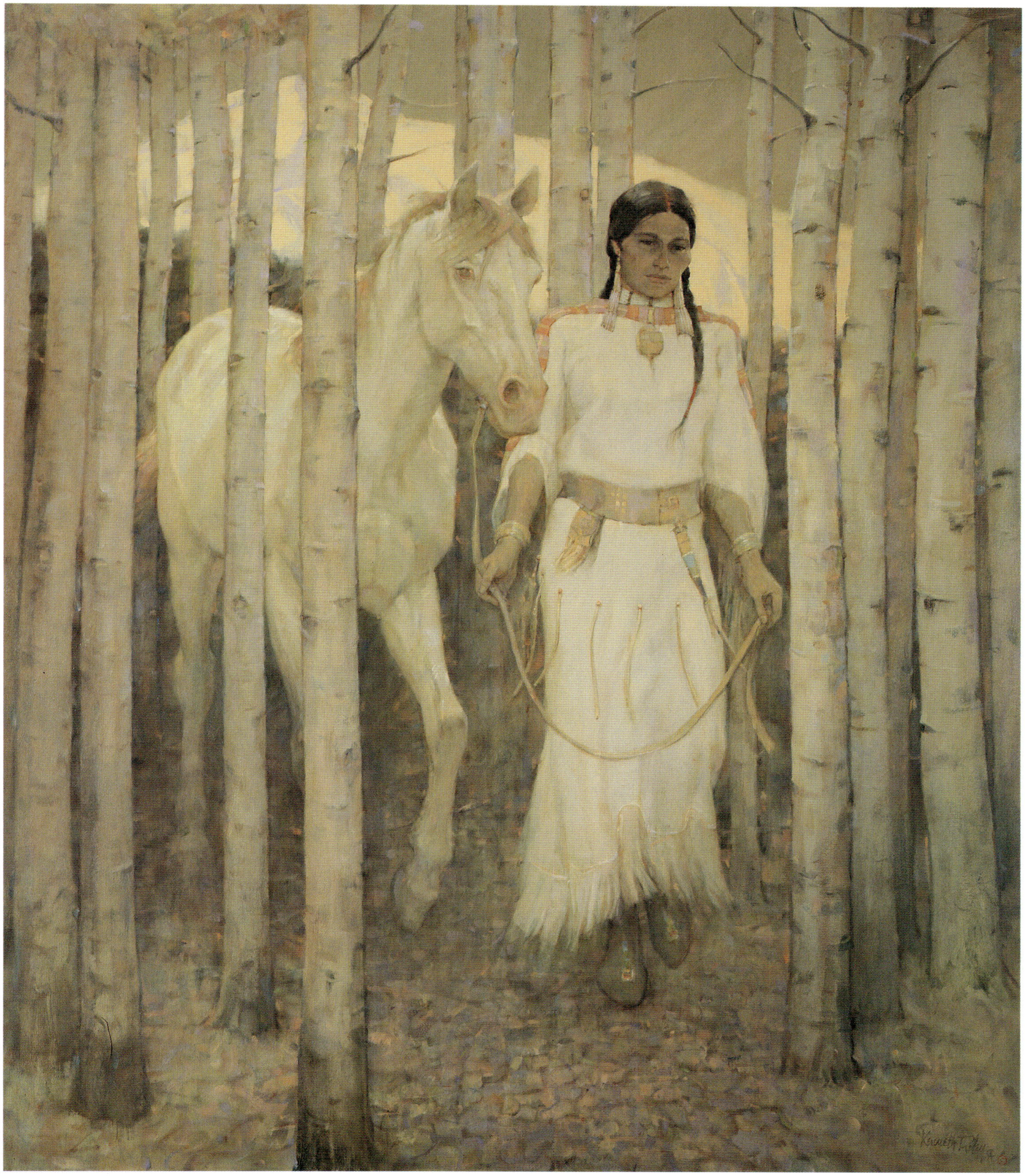

weekends, he and MarCyne escaped the flashing lights and cultural overload of the city by staying at their cottage on Lake Candlewood, near New Milford, Connecticut. In 1952 they were ready to make rural life a full-time affair. Purchasing a five-acre lot in a wooded residential area near Danbury, Connecticut, Ken and MarCyne built the home they would live in for the next eighteen years. Ken subsequently designed a studio alongside the house and dammed a small stream, creating a lake that brought them year-round entertainment. The seasons were heralded by spring ducklings, snapping turtles warming themselves in the summer sun, fall migrations of blue birds, and winter rabbits casting shadows in the steel light of a full moon.

Riley had little need to go into the city unless he was delivering a painting, but this didn't mean he was isolated from the illustrating world. Southeastern Connecticut abounded with illustrators who had likewise exited the Big Apple. Riley occasionally lunched or socialized with Tom Lovell (1909—), John Clymer, Bob Kuhn (1920—) and John Stobart (1929—). And his neighbors Cordy and Bob Lougheed (1910–1982) became very close friends and teammates when the Rileys took up indoor badminton for exercise and began competing in weekend tournaments.

It was a perfect life ... almost. By the early 1960s, Riley had become aware of a Catch 22 in his painting method that took some of the enjoyment out of illustrating: He loved color, light and subtle values ... none of which reproduced well. "After a few of my illustrations came out diluted and fuzzy I learned that a painting reproduced best with hard edges and crisp, well-defined color. I was rightly accused of putting too much into my illustrations—little accents of color, lost edges and subtleties that muddied into brown sauce when the painting was printed on the page."

52. *Baseball in Tokyo,* 1957, U.S. Air Force Art Collection, Washington, D.C.

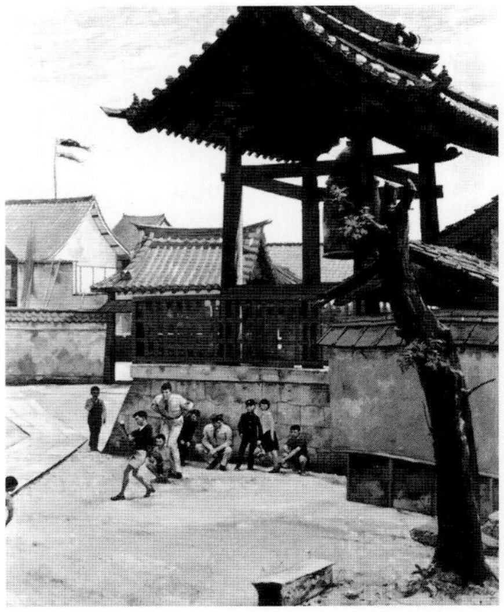

Additionally, it became clear that even when he researched a historical incident thoroughly, the "facts" were inevitably an interpretation, destined to be reinterpreted by each person who encountered them. The impossibility of identifying and then painting the "truth" resulted in some soul searching out of which Riley developed an attitude: He'd do his best to get the details correct but he would not be subservient to them. Nor would he compromise the quality of his paintings for reproduction purposes. Riley refused to give up creating what he calls "viable works of art."

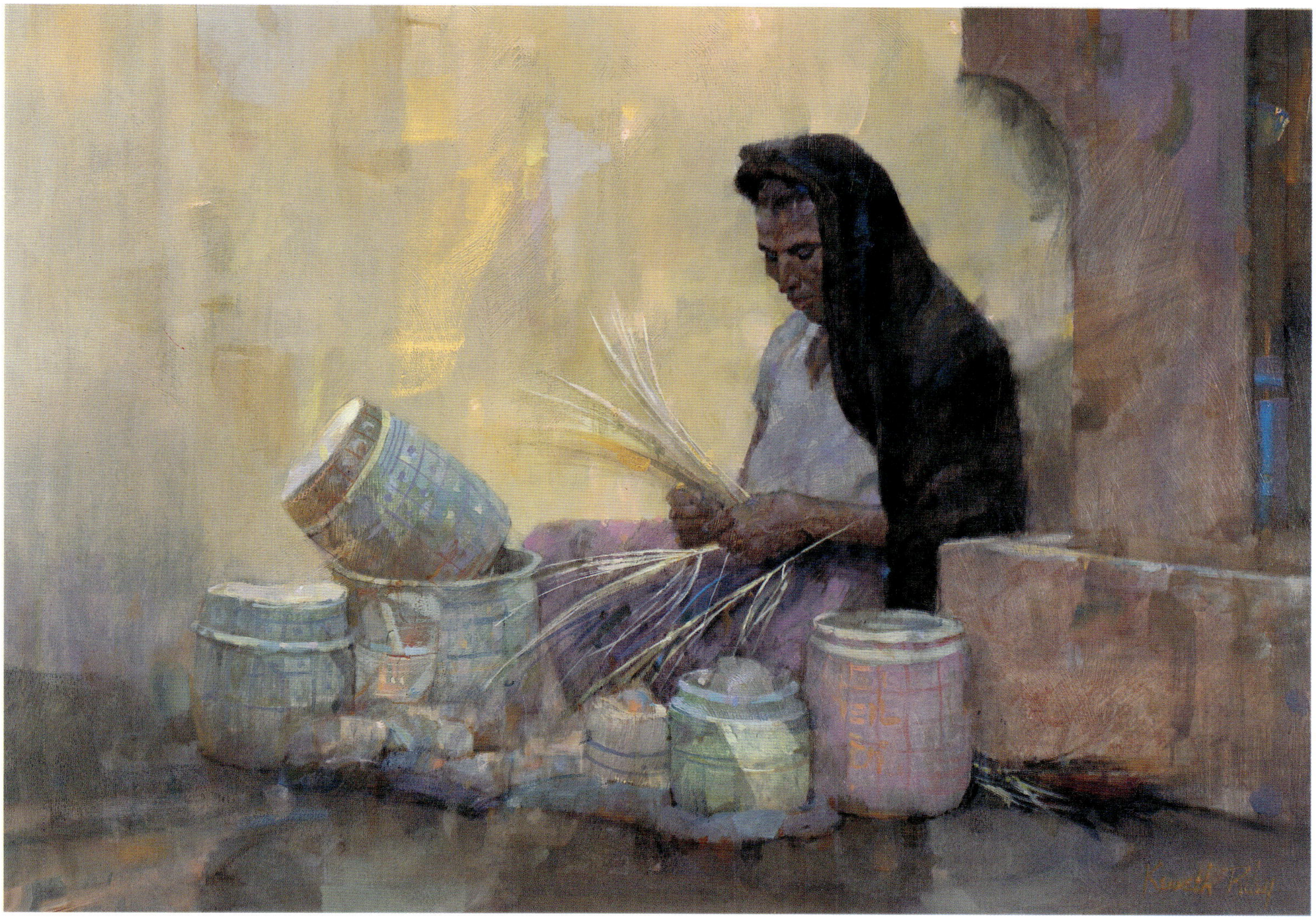

According to Walt Reed, he succeeded. Writing in *The Illustrator in America*, Reed states that Riley's works are "remarkable on many counts: strength of draftsmanship, effective composition, the color and quality of the painting and the portrayal of mood. Riley's pictures reveal that he is clearly a master of all these, particularly his use of color."

To exercise his love of painting, Riley applied to the Society of Illustrators program wherein artists were commissioned to create paintings in trade for travel opportunities. Selected on four occasions, two of which were sponsored by the United States Air Force, Riley traveled to Korea and Japan in 1956. From the trip came paintings inspired by the meeting of cultures.

53. *Basket Weaver, Mexico*
1990
acrylic, 14 x 20

This woman wove intricately colored baskets while seated on the sidewalk near our hotel. She would arrive every morning with her inventory wrapped in a blanket, slung over her shoulder. Each evening she reversed the routine, gathering up the objects and placing them in her blanket in a gesture that seemed to reflect the patience and durability of the ages.

54. *Visit of Lewis and Clark*
1983
oil, 50 x 44

When travelers came through, Indians typically dressed up, adorning themselves with their most prized garments and accouterments. Displaying their status, these Mandan warriors await a formal meeting with explorers Lewis and Clark who recorded the event in their journal of 1804. What interested me most was the large busy shape created by the three Mandan figures on the left balanced against the open space with small figures on the right.

In a painting of Japan, Riley selected a scene of servicemen teaching Japanese boys how to play baseball in a temple courtyard in Kyoto ***[Baseball in Tokyo, 52].*** Each of the carefully delineated figures responds to the umpire who is the focus of the impromptu event. Dwarfed by imposing wooden structures, curved roofs, angled sidewalks and staccato fences, the figures represent an interplay of cultures—a theme repeated in the "machined" angles and positive and negative shapes of manmade structures which contrast with the organic shape of a tree pruned back to nubs. "Kyoto being the ancient capitol retains much of the character of traditional Japan," Riley wrote of the painting. "The setting seemed to magnify the significance that we live in a shrinking world, with traditions and influences being passed back and forth."

In 1964, Riley once again traveled for the Air Force, this time to Libya. The visit to Wheelus Air Base coincided with tensions acerbated by Nasser's voice blaring out of the radios in the shops lining the narrow streets of Tripoli. The painting ***Salt Flats at Wheelus Air Base, Libya [55]*** contrasts a group of salt miners shown prominently on the left with a tiny but powerful F105 jet taking off on the right—all shimmering in the intense North African sunlight. Compared to the painting of Japan, Riley's approach had evolved. Rather than detailing individual figures engaged in an incidental moment, he selected

55. *Salt Flats at Wheelus Air Base, Libya,* 1965, U.S. Air Force Art Collection, Washington, D.C.

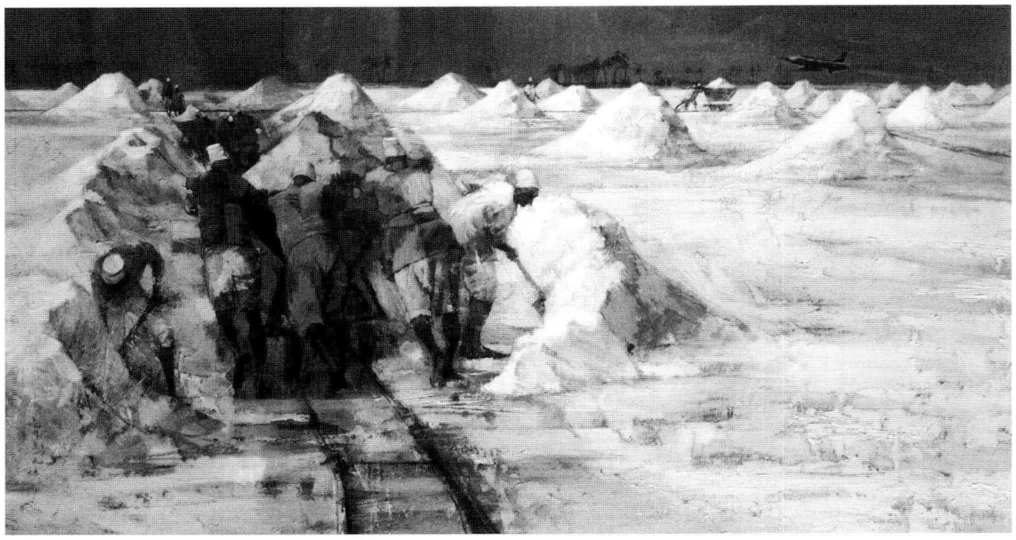

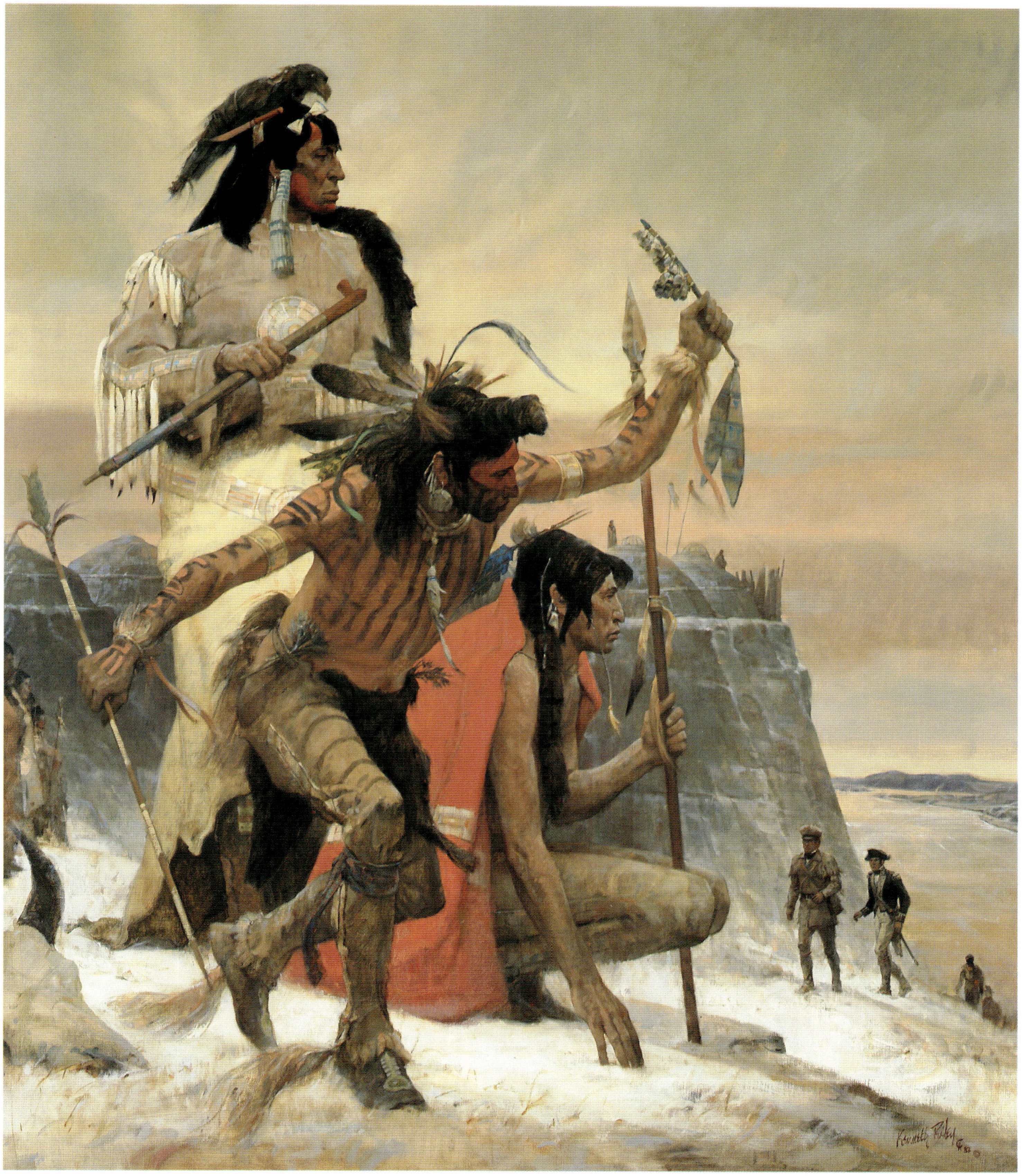

56. *Saturday in Town*
1982
oil, 18 x 24

The umbrella places this work during reservation days when a husband and wife might have traveled to the nearest trading post. The officious air of the man suggests that he finds his newly acquired trinket both a technical wonder for taking his shade with him, as well as a decoration that adds to his sense of importance. From an artist's point of view, the light passing through the umbrella made an interesting color note on the man's face.

an archetypal scene of back-breaking labor, simplified down to the shapes of clothing and head gear worn by the workers. The whole picture has a deliberate quickness of touch, especially in the gestural thick-and-thin application of paint. The power of the underlying structure is enhanced by the extremes in scale between the slow-moving curves and diagonals of workers versus the powerful speeding angle of the plane, which veers off the horizon into a narrow band of sky dotted with faint silhouettes of distant palm trees.

Essentially a white-on-white painting, Riley has introduced a tremendous amount of color in the underpainting and in touches of hot pink, rose and orange. He also tilts and flattens the ground in such a manner that it becomes a decorative backdrop. Distance is suggested through exaggerated conceptual relationships based on the relative size of objects and the forced perspective of the tracks. Rejecting mathematical and atmospheric recession, Riley's space "recedes" in three horizontal registers that move vertically up the canvas beginning with the smooth white foreground, the hilly mid-ground, and the strip of red sky in the background.

Painting a picture can be likened to playing jazz: You start with a melody and then all the instruments feed into and off one another. In a picture, you begin with an idea and all the design elements complement and respond to the idea. —KR

These three qualities: forced or exaggerated spatial relationships, arbitrary color and thin gestural layers of pigment became the hallmarks of Riley's illustrations beginning in the 1960s. There is little doubt that they were in response to the predominating art philosophy of the time: Abstract Expressionism.

Though living in the country, both Ken and MarCyne were very much aware of current art developments during the 1950s and 1960s. MarCyne had already been experimenting with abstraction in her work, and together they frequented the galleries and museum exhibitions in Manhattan where abstract art dominated the walls. "You couldn't open a newspaper or read a magazine review without getting caught up in the debate over the merits of nonobjective work," he recalls.

The mood-enhancing properties of color had already been exploited by Riley in his two-color illustrations published by the *Post*. "You used black

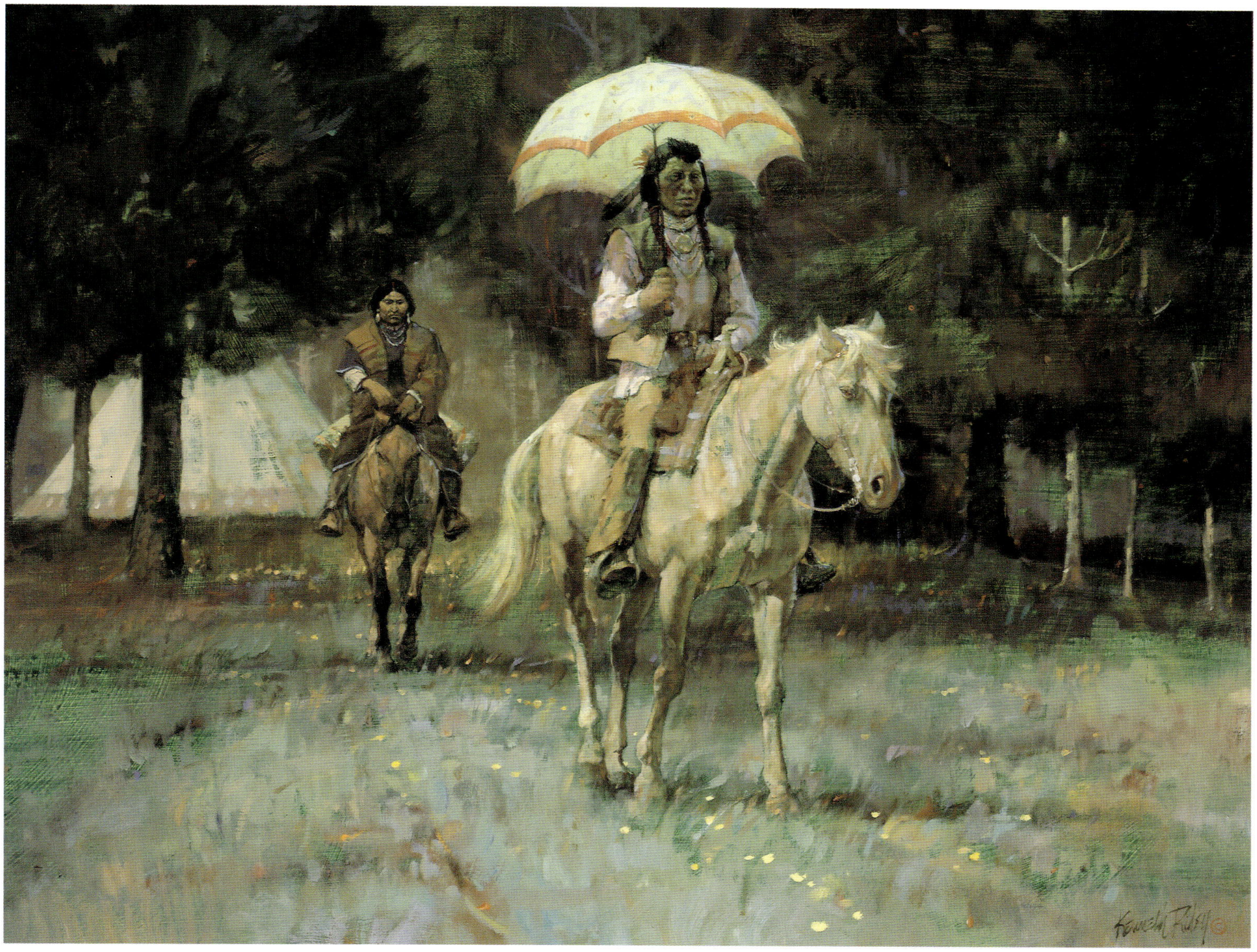

and one other color to portray the mood you were trying to get. If it was a night scene or a darker mood you would probably use blue. Happy scenes might require yellow, and red was good for dramatic situations." To better understand these and other abstract concepts, Ken and MarCyne decided to take a class in abstract art. With neighbors/illustrators Tracy Sugarman (1921—) and Arthur Shilstone the Rileys drove into New York every Friday evening to paint with Reuben Tam (1916—) at the Brooklyn Museum School.

A Japanese-American from Hawaii, Tam was a second generation Abstract Expressionist who had come back to the landscape as a subject. Addressing the geological rise and fall of land masses, light and weather, the span of the sea to the space of the sky, Tam's paintings were, according to Helen Hiller writing in *Art USA: Now,* "highly personal, emotional and lyrical.... Through provocative use of paint, line, color and shapes, he rediscovers for us the wilderness and the clearings of places we have known and forgotten. He brings us face to face with the crisis of place ... in oil paintings that are luminous, as if light and air were entrapped in the several translucent films of pigment that make up the surface of the canvas. Although the paint is not particularly thick, it gives the illusion of richness and the color is worked subtly in many variations."

For a year, Riley experimented with taking a theme and pulling it apart into its elements of mass, shape, line and color. In paintings such as ***Don Quixote [58],*** the canvas becomes an arena where realism jousts with abstraction. The tension between paint performing as "surface entertainment" and conveying the illusion of form in space creates a push-pull effect enhanced by the energetic application of bold color throughout. Mood-enhancing hues go from raw blue-black accented by fire-brand yellow on the left to the gauze-like veils of muted rose, gold and turquoise on the right. Within the boundaries of this richly tactile surface Don Quixote might be seen as a romantic symbol of the artist challenging himself to "kill off" the figural subject matter that he loves so much.

But death wouldn't come. "Painting abstractly was fun and very educational," says Riley. "It was like playing a game with shape, color and texture in the confines of a canvas. The exercise made me more conscious of not simply rendering a portrait of Aunt Mary, but of moving her around like an inanimate object and making the space around her just as interesting as the likeness."

For Riley, painting abstractly was an exercise in one artist speaking to another. He likens it to an insider sport that gets boring to the person unfamiliar with the rules. Communicating only to artists was not a fulfilling goal for Riley, even though his work has always spoken eloquently to his peers. Rather, Riley sought a broader appeal. "I couldn't give up the chance to create subject matter that communicates to a larger audience," he concludes.

His disillusionment with abstraction was put into perspective when he and MarCyne vacationed in Maine during the summer of 1962. Camera in hand, Riley wandered the shoreline looking for inspiration. He found it in tidal pools formed in granite depressions along the rocky shore ***[57].*** "They were

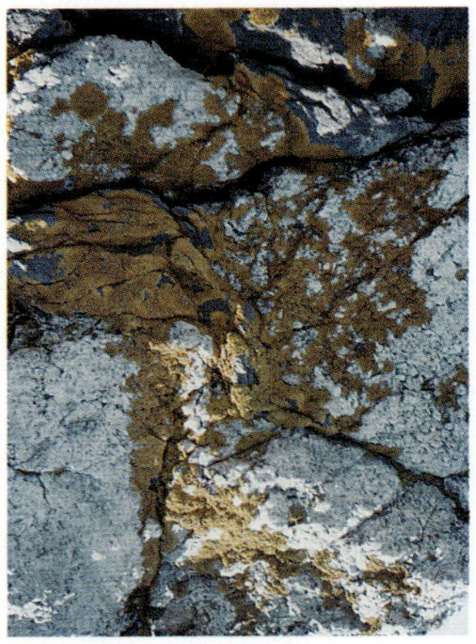

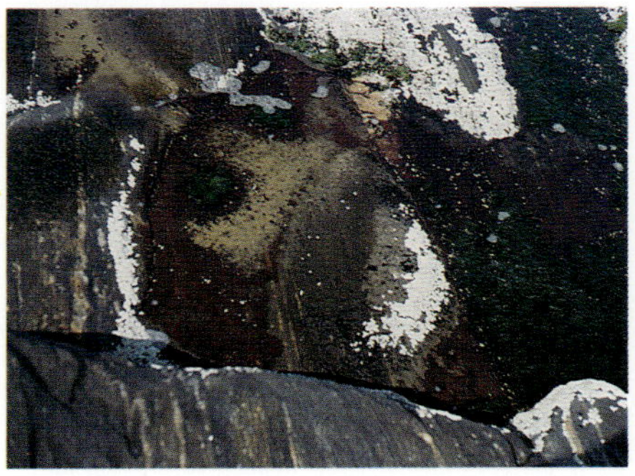

57. Tide pools on the coast of Maine.

58. *Don Quixote,* ca. 1962, acrylic, 14 x 14.

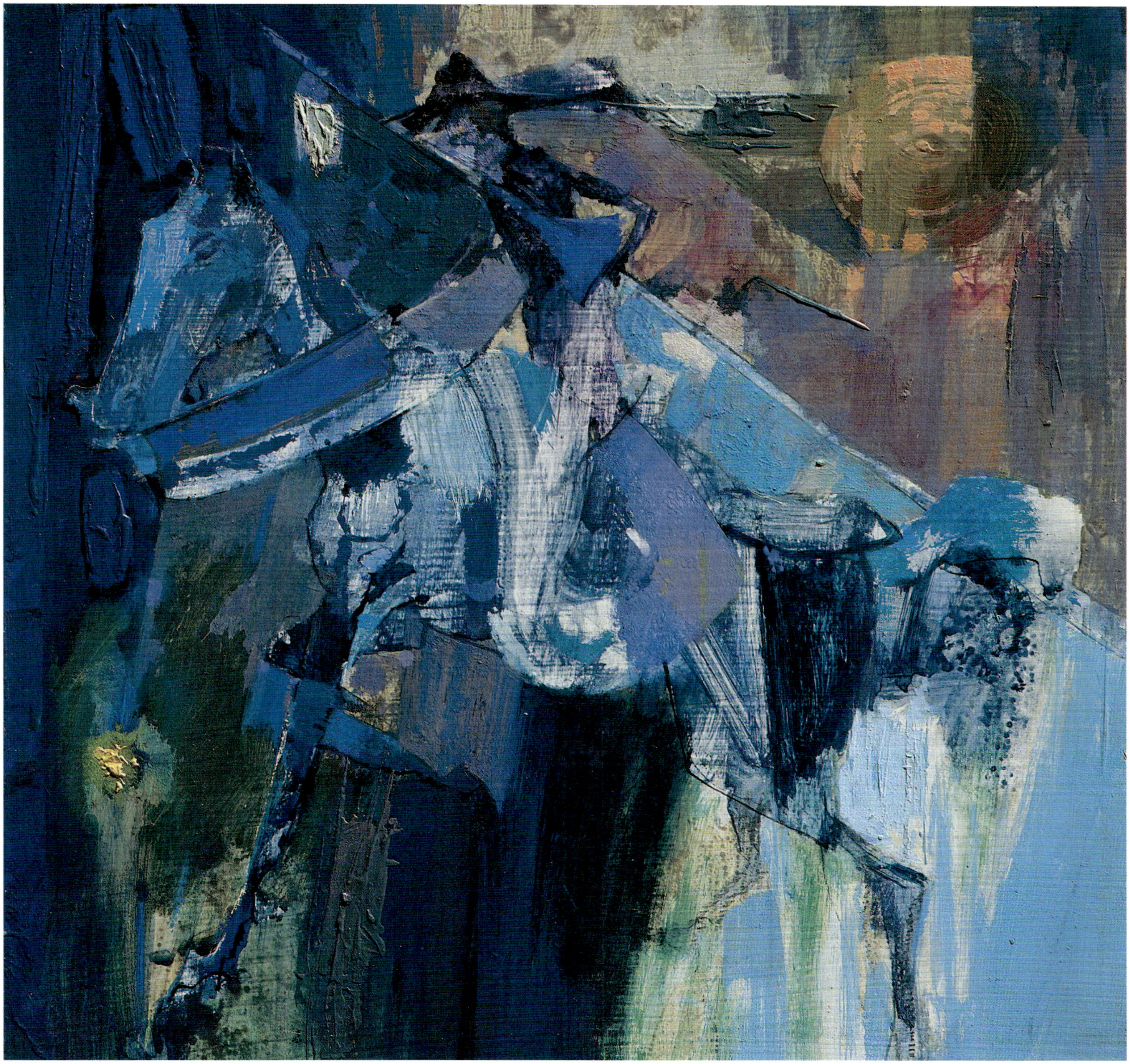

little worlds unto themselves, filled with organisms, shells, starfish, seaweed ... all manner of colorful textures mixed in with the patterns and striations in the rock itself.

"The tidal pools were the most gorgeous abstractions I had ever seen, and I thought I might use them as the gambit for a painting. When I looked at my slides, however, it was apparent that these natural abstractions could not be improved upon and that I'd be foolish to try to compete."

I take the material that comes to me, absorb it and let it come out in my own way. —KR

Whether observing tidal pools in Maine, the museums of Italy or the peasants of Portugal, travel has always played an important part in Ken and MarCyne's life together. Their first major trip came in 1959 when they spent five weeks in Italy. "It was as if we were in one big museum. I remember the thrill of seeing works by Giotto and Piero della Francesca as we traveled from Florence to Ravenna and then Venice," recalls Riley, who believes that Piero "was way ahead of his time. He didn't simply place his figures in space, he was highly conscious of what was going on around them—he designed the negative spaces to be as interesting as the figures."

In 1965, when Riley was on commission for Garrett Aircraft Company, he and MarCyne took their second overseas trip together, this time to Norway, Sweden and Denmark. Once again they absorbed the treasures of centuries tucked away behind every doorway and courtyard. Firsthand experience with history recharged Riley's batteries so, when the Society of Illustrators announced its Artists in the Parks program, he was ready to travel again. Chosen in the fall of 1966 to paint Teton and Yellowstone National Parks, Ken and MarCyne got an introduction to the American West that opened a door to the nation's past as well as a vision to the Rileys' future.

As with the Air Force program, Riley's lodging and travel expenses were covered in exchange for a painting. Hiking along the edges of Yellowstone Canyon and driving through the park to Jackson, Wyoming, where the Teton range offers its mercurial mix of ever-changing weather and overpowering views, the Rileys encountered mountains far younger than those in Europe but no less dramatic in the stories they had to tell. The following year, Riley painted ***Jackson's Big Hole [61]*** in acrylics on tissue mounted on Masonite. He signed it "Ken Riley" (the signature used on his illustrations). As with the five horsemen silhouetted as tiny celebrants amidst a band of yellow grass, Riley had felt

59. *The Algonquian Family*
1991
oil, 46 x 50

Much of my work focuses on the human tribe—a global family of peoples that divides into nationalities often distinguished by language. North American Indian tribes are likewise divided into linguistic groups. The Algonquian Family once included between forty and fifty separate languages. At the time of contact with the white man, the Plains portion of the family was identified with the tribes whose names I've included at the base of the painting. When the horse was introduced to the Algonquians, they became a nomadic hunting society. Though their lifestyle changed, they took their language with them.

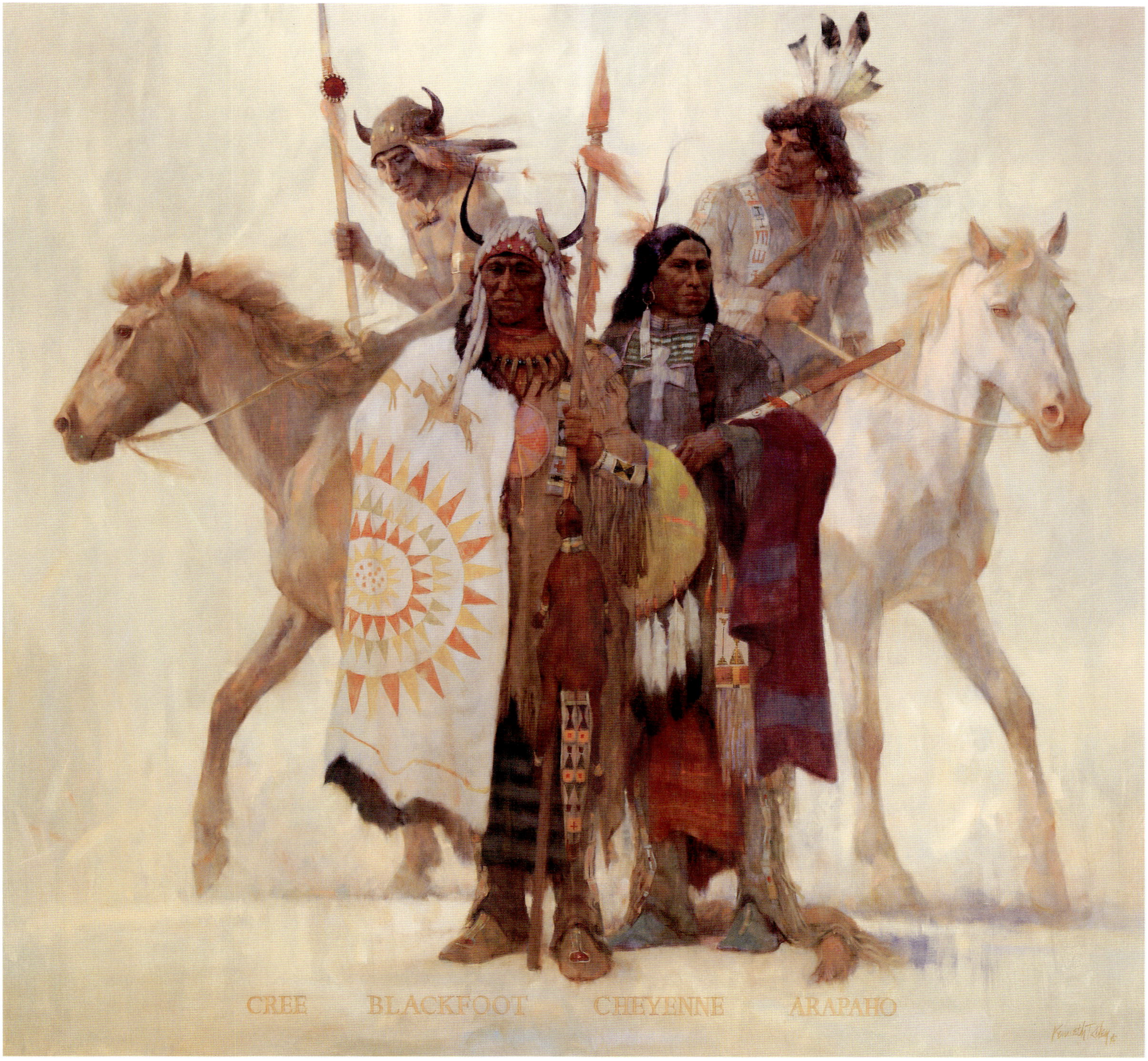
CREE
BLACKFOOT
CHEYENNE
ARAPAHO

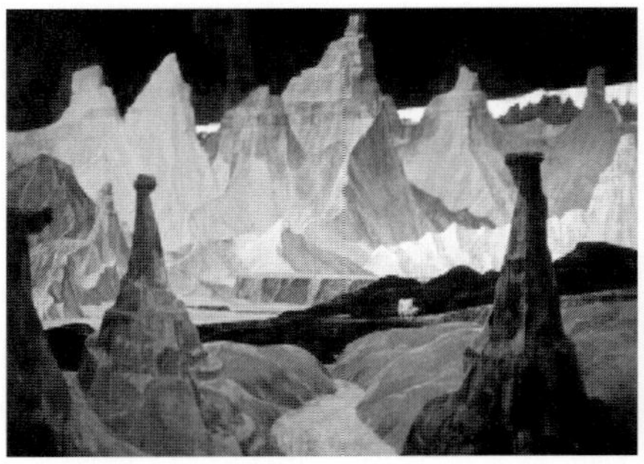

60. *Badlands National Monument,* 1968, oil, 40 x 54, U.S. Department of the Interior, National Park Service, Harper's Ferry, West Virginia.

overwhelmed by the ragged edges and hypnotic heights of these quintessential western mountains. Unlike Europe, where history was cloistered indoors with stone steps worn by centuries of traffic, the history of the American West seemed virtually untrammeled. Riley was anxious to see more and applied to the Parks Program again.

During his second trip Riley flew to Rapid City, South Dakota, and journeyed back in time to a prehistoric place called The Badlands whose story is told in pastel ribbons of sedimentation. He wasn't prepared for the grotesque pillars, chimneys and toadstool-shaped hoodoos eroded by sandpaper wind and water. Nor could he have foreseen a more graphic introduction to the meaning of it all. Hiking through a canyon, he noticed small bone fragments following along a rift created by rushing water. "The bones got larger and larger and suddenly I came upon a skull, roughly four inches in diameter, protruding out of the ground." Riley gazed at the forty-million-year-old face for some time before scrambling back to the ranger station to report his

61. *Jackson's Big Hole,* 1967, acrylic, 32 x 48, U.S. Department of the Interior, National Park Service, Harper's Ferry, West Virginia.

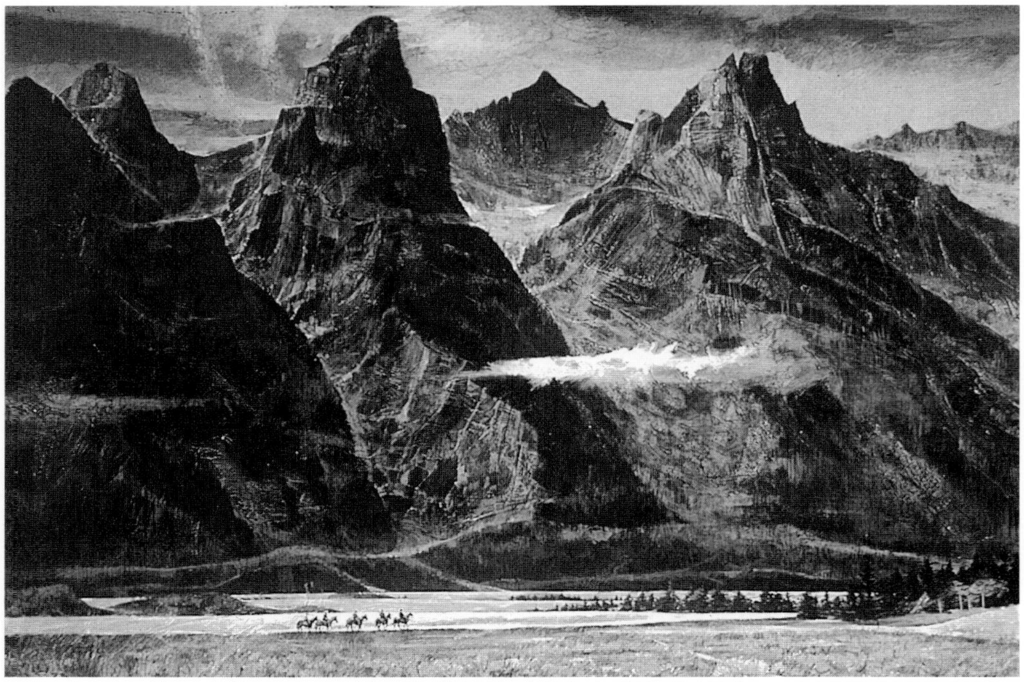

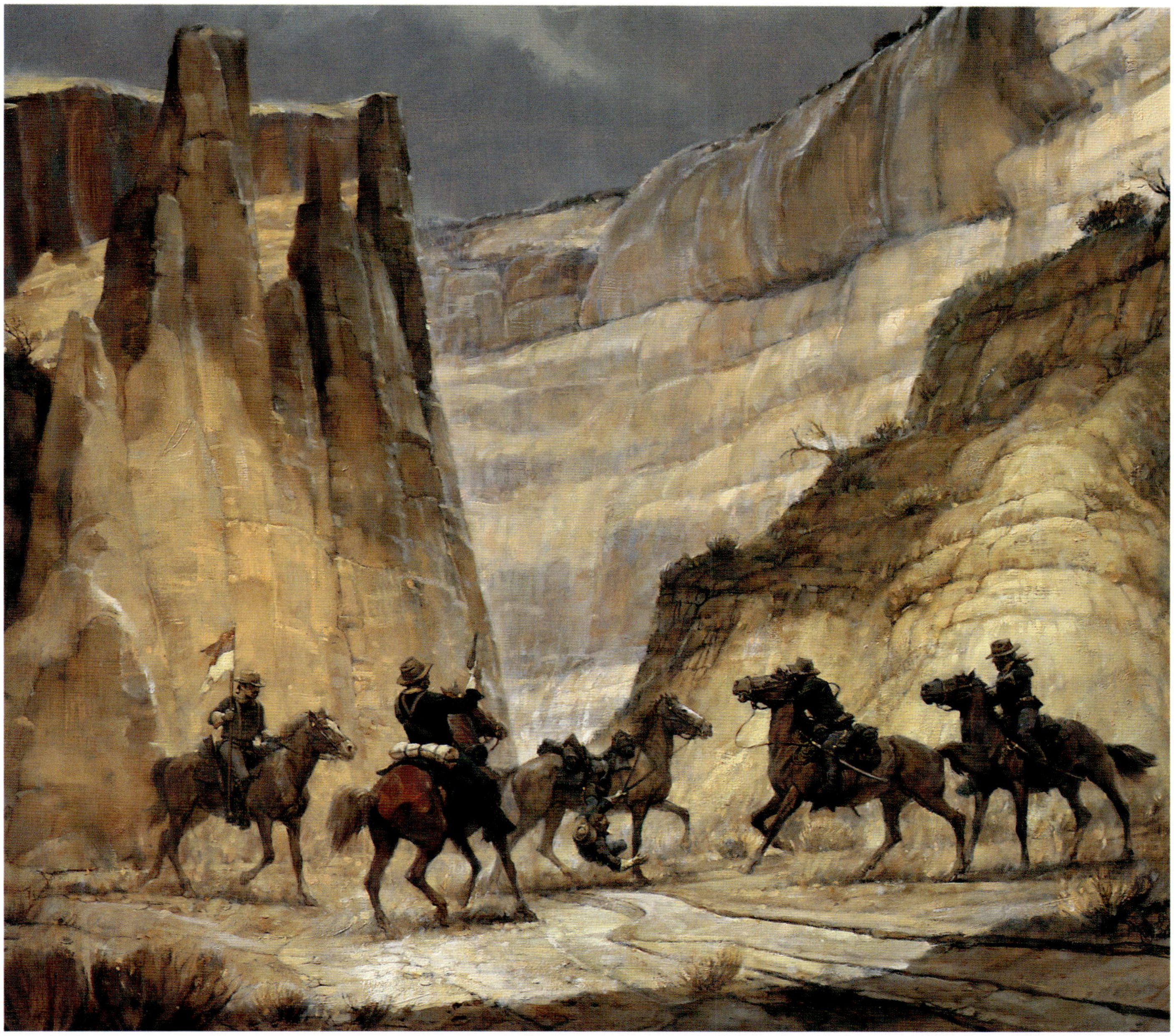

62. *Fired On*

ca. 1984

oil, 18 x 20

In the field, the cavalryman was a compact, self-contained unit. Outfitted with a poncho, blanket, water, hardtack and weapons, he was expected to ride for days and to fight on short notice. Here he finds himself in a vulnerable situation having just drawn fire from an undetermined angle.

63. *The Source*

1984

oil, 39 x 36

The theme of a "water source" has been depicted throughout the history of art. It was a natural subject for a painting of Apaches, however, since water was (and still is) one of the most important resources in the desert Southwest. The Apache, who were capable of surviving on plant moisture, would have reveled in a secret spring. Their stronghold at Apache Pass was situated there because it was the only place in the area with a constant supply of water. For the same reason, the cavalry and stagelines submitted to the terror of the pass on their travels through the frontier.

discovery. "It turned out to be an Oreodont or prehistoric pig. No relation to today's domesticated creature, the fossil was nonetheless of some significance to the park ranger who followed me back to the spot."

Riley painted his Badlands experience as if it had been a journey to the moon. A lone camper negotiates a winding road that slices through a staggering panorama of orange, brown, pink and green projections illuminated by the late-afternoon sun. The vehicle seems alien to this carnival of capricious forms. Yet the rocks are strangely nonthreatening, especially the two stone sentinels in the foreground which appear to mark the progression of the route. Painted in oils on canvas, ***Badlands National Monument [60]*** is signed "Kenneth Riley"—a signature he reserved for his fine art. But before he actually signed the painting, the arrow marking the road to Riley's tomorrow pointed in yet another direction.

Since studying with Reuben Tam, Riley had been casting about for a subject or place that might inspire him to paint for himself. Early in 1968 he thought he found it. The small clapboard house that he and MarCyne purchased at Five Islands along the coast of Maine offered not only a gorgeous rock-and-pine studded shoreline but a romantic escape on the edge of a little fishing village removed from the commercialization of the day. Riley built a studio next to the "Blueberry House," as they called it, and a deck for taking in the view of derelict lobster boats and their crusty owners—a subject recorded ad infinitum in the local galleries. "Maine was beautiful and we enjoyed it tremendously," says Riley of the house they owned until 1973. "I assumed I would uncover much about the waterfront to paint, but I simply couldn't find anything to say that was fresh or new about lobster traps and buoys."

While building the deck on Blueberry House, Riley got a call from the art department at Brigham Young University. Earlier in the 1960s, he had been commissioned by the Mormon Church to do a series of eight paintings for the Visitors Center in Temple Square in Salt Lake City. The success of these paintings and Riley's reputation as a first-rate illustrator resulted in an invitation to teach advanced art students in the summer of 1968. Though he anticipated his first teaching experience with some trepidation, Riley couldn't pass up yet another invitation to work in the West.

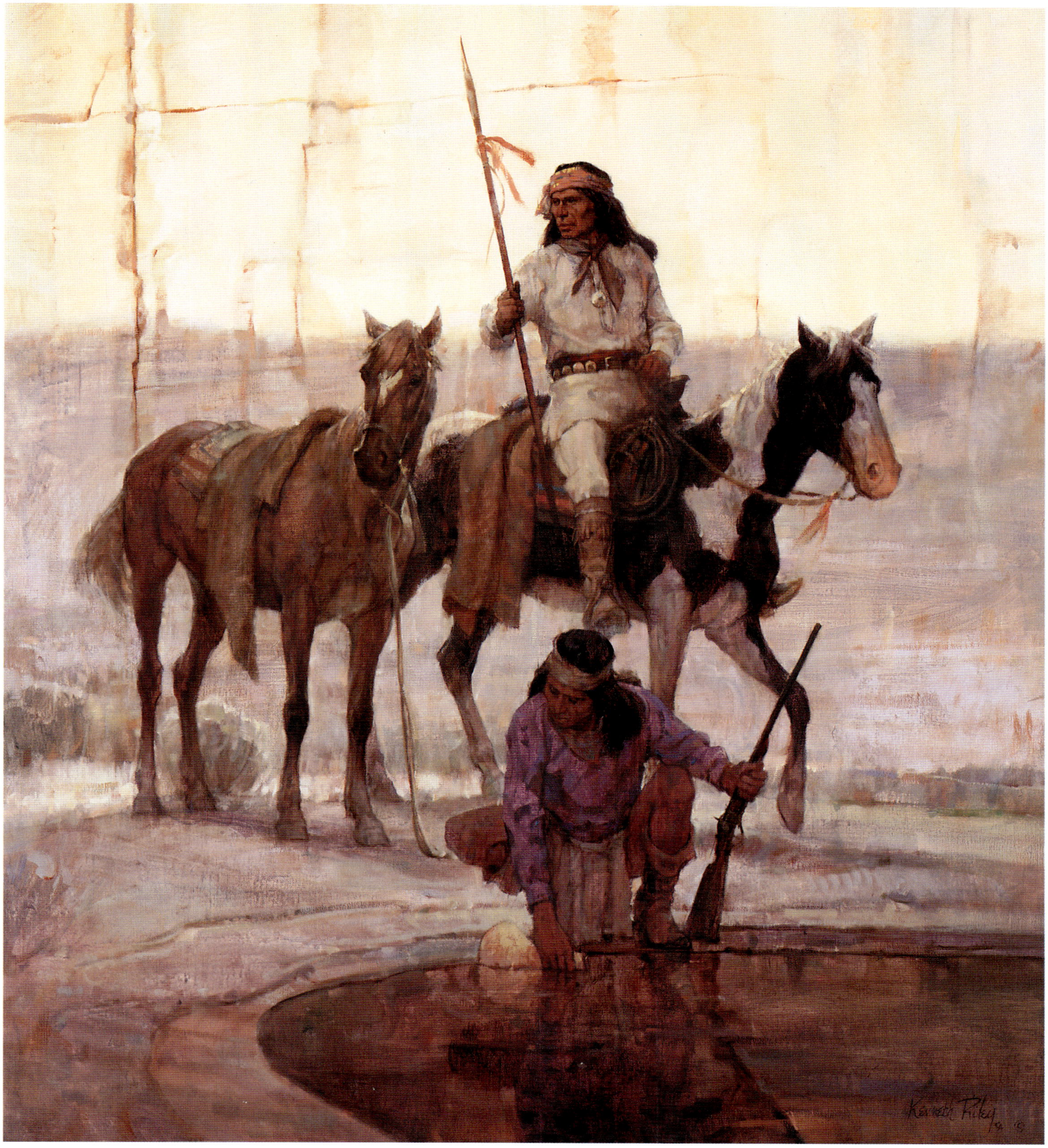

Avoid painting incidents because your subject will only become incidental because of it. Aim for the epic. —KR

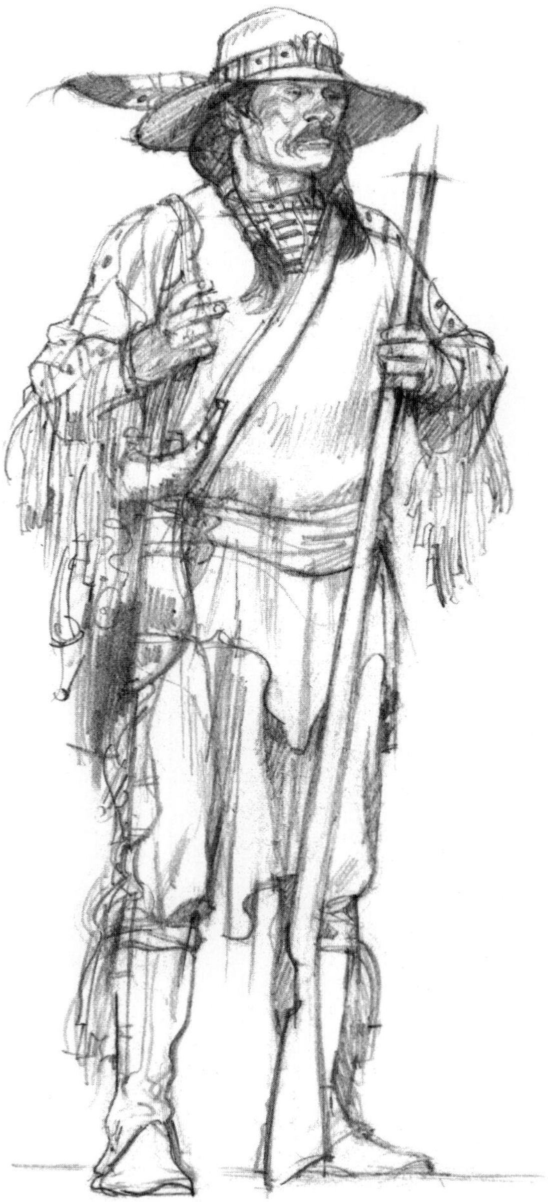

For two months Riley focused on setting up half-day modeling situations for his students. "They were bright, sophisticated kids, many having already been on religious missions overseas." On the weekends, he and MarCyne became itinerants, hiking amidst the canyons, buttes, mesas and valleys of the Wasatch Mountains and the four corners area of Lake Powell and Monument Valley. Mesmerized by the geological splendors, Riley absorbed history which presented itself at virtually every bend in the road. "It was unique history, definitely not based on European influences, and when you visited the sites, it was as if the events had just happened."

Equally important was the quality of light that Riley found to be missing in the East. "I was used to focusing on local color that looked rich on the page. When I came out West, however, I saw color with light coming through it—dramatic, broken light that created rich shadows. That got me excited and I was determined to make my life in the West." Riley was truly ready to move on to more meaningful statements than those incidental to a story. Though he had derived satisfaction from a number of historical calendars done for Humble Oil and a series of boldly graphic paintings advertising the USF&G Insurance Company, Riley was anxious to listen to his own heart and record its murmurings in paint. Luckily the new life he envisioned over the horizon wasn't without models for success.

John Clymer, who had been living in Jackson since 1964, reported that he was making a living, and more importantly, having a great time establishing a reputation as a history painter focusing on the Upper Northwest. Similarly, Bob Lougheed, who had been visiting New Mexico each fall for over a decade, was planning on moving to Santa Fe. His involvement in the nascent Cowboy Artists of America exhibition group at the National Cowboy Hall of Fame in Oklahoma City, had convinced him that there were buyers eager to acquire his on-location paintings of ranchlife and wildlife.

The enthusiasm of Clymer and Lougheed fed Riley's own hunger for a future in painting the epic of the West. "It couldn't have been too bad an idea since greater minds had thought of it before me!" Riley says. "Becoming a gallery artist meant I no longer had to be concerned with reproduction at all —it was a big release." The "big release" would likewise facilitate western

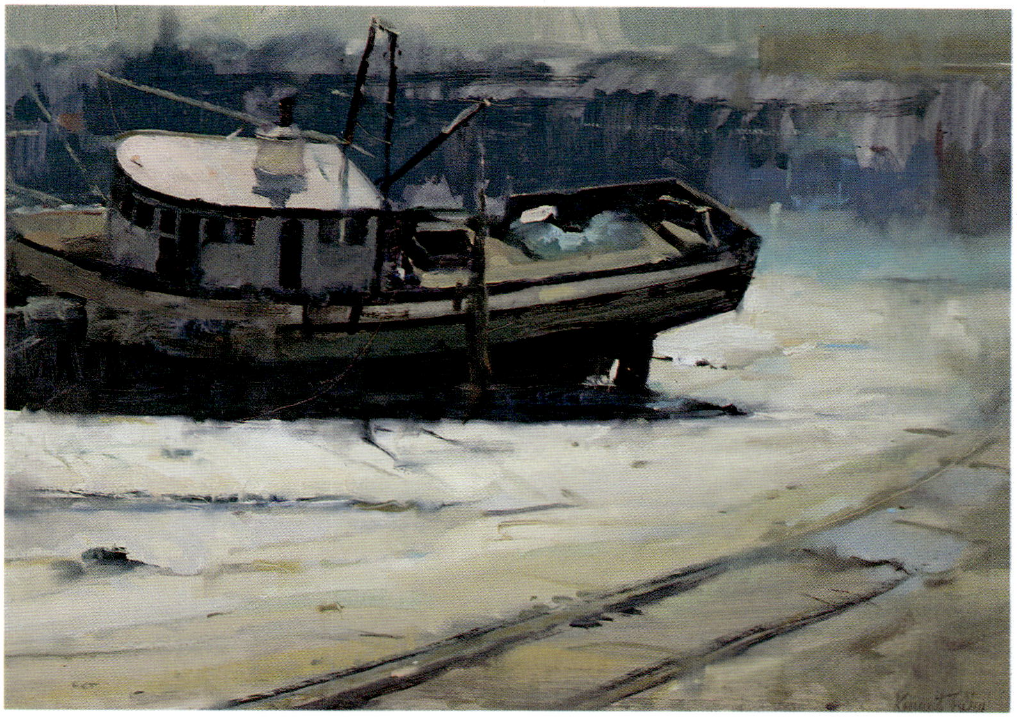

64. *Rocky Point, Mexico,* field sketch, oil, 13 x 18.

moves for a number of Riley's illustrator cohorts, including Howard Terpning (1927—) and Frank McCarthy (1924—), both of whom moved to Arizona, and Clark Hulings (1922—), who moved to New Mexico.

With his decision made, life moved quickly for Ken and MarCyne. Riley renewed an old friendship with Leonard Leone, art director at Bantam Publishing, who offered to tide him through the transition by commissioning a couple of book cover illustrations a month. In 1971 their Danbury home sold almost overnight, furnishings and all. Riley gave up his golf clubs and the set of English drums he played during jam sessions with a local group of doctors who called themselves the "Bandaids." "We made a big bonfire and burned up the rest," Riley says of his scrap file, which met a similar fate to the suitcases of old letters that MarCyne saw no need to take with them.

The successful 52-year-old illustrator who had matured among the deep forest greens of the Northeast was ready to begin his metamorphosis to full-time fine artist in the naked, sun-drenched Southwest. "We felt like pioneers heading out to a new land," Riley recalls of the journey westward. The drive that took him from Connecticut to Arizona coincided with the annual migration of monarch butterflies. "The monarchs were caught up in the after-drafts of the big trucks, then thrown down to the roadways where they were crushed under the tires. I hoped my fate wouldn't follow them."

65. *Discovery*

1977

oil, 24 x 42

In 1540, Coronado sent twenty-five horsemen out from Zuni Pueblo to explore rumors of a great river. With Zuni guides they traveled for almost three weeks and suddenly came out on the rim of a great chasm. The river at the bottom of the Grand Canyon appeared to be a "mere trickle." After three days climbing down to it, however, the explorers returned to report that rocks, which seemed the height of a man when seen from the rim, were in fact taller than the highest towers of Seville.... History does not record what the first Japanese visitors said when they saw the canyon.

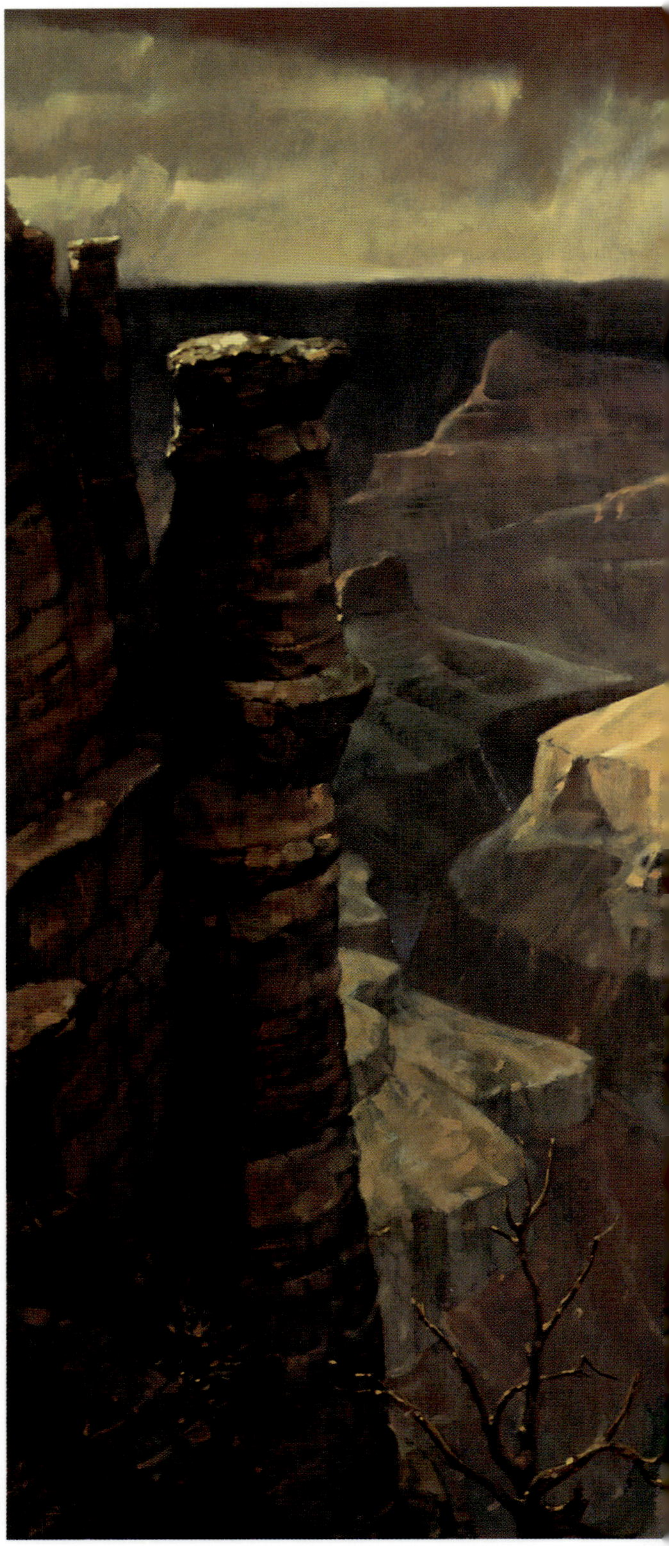

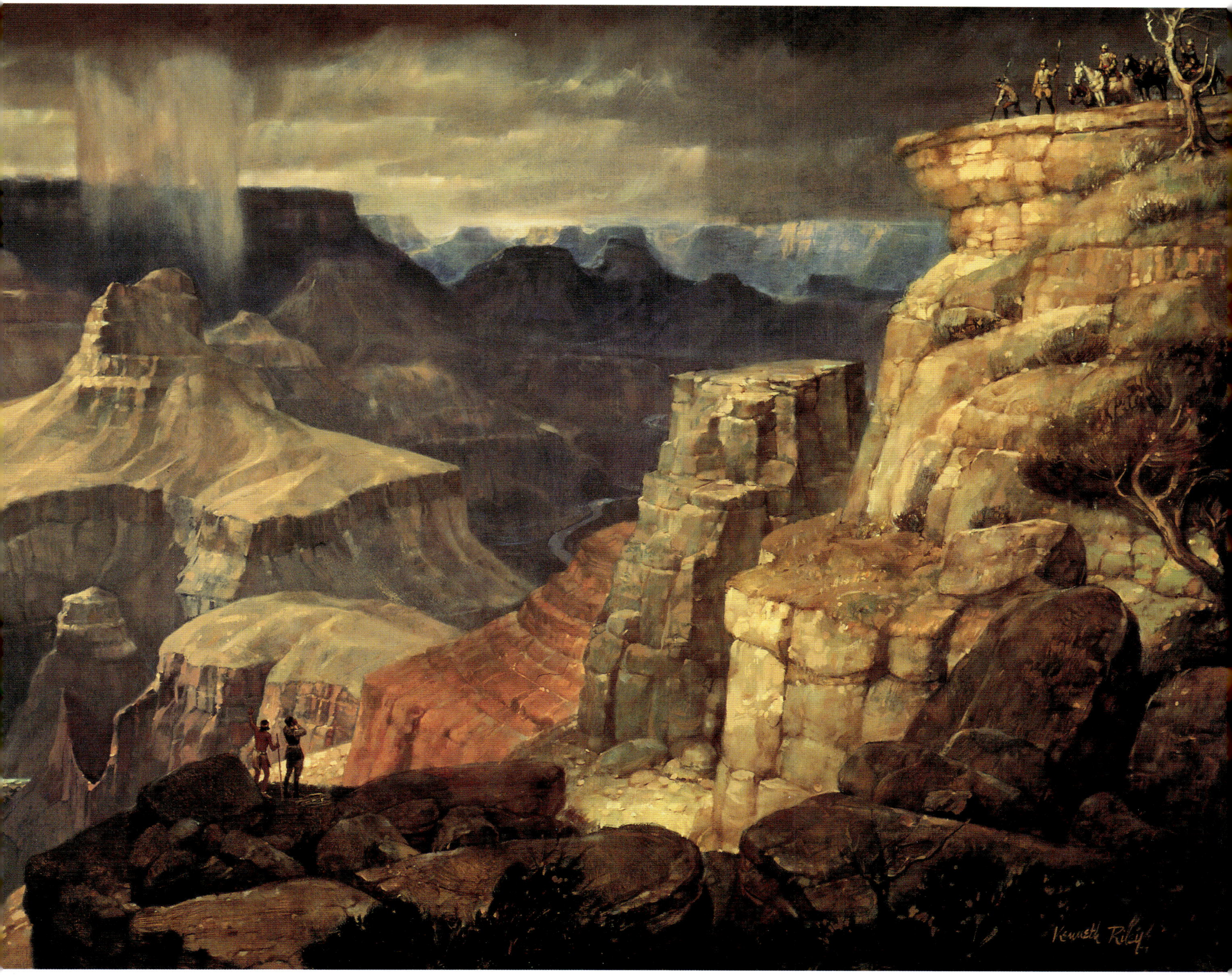
Kenneth Riley

RESURRECTION IN TOMBSTONE

Southern Arizona is a place of geological and climatic transitions. Head uphill from the Rileys' Tucson home into the Santa Catalinas, for example, and within an hour you climb through dense saguaro and paloverde, into lush grassland and chaparral, then pine and oak woodlands that give way to montane fir before climaxing in a subalpine fir forest at 9,100-foot Mount Lemmon. The temperature, warm and dry on the desert floor, becomes frigid and damp, turning the light, steady "female rain" of winter (as the Indians call it) into a snowpack ideal for skiing.

A similar geological change takes place an hour south of Riley's home, where the Santa Rita Mountains separate the spiny cacti-dominated Sonoran Desert on the west from the yucca-grasslands of the Chihuahuan Desert on the east. Here, in the valley between the Santa Rita and the Dragoon Mountains further east, a place nicknamed "The Town Too Tough to Die" tells its own tale of transition.

Site of a major silver mine discovered in 1877, Tombstone sprang up literally overnight and in less than a decade grew to twenty thousand people before the silver ran out and the water table reclaimed the mines. Once the biggest metropolis in the area, Tombstone's population went the way of quicksilver, dwindling to somewhere around a thousand in 1972 when Ken Riley drove his station wagon into town towing all of his and MarCyne's possessions in a trailer.

Despite its size, Tombstone's reputation was big. Declared a historic landmark in 1962, three-block Allen Street boasted Victorian facades such as the Bird Cage Theater and the OK Corral, where legendary tales of gambling, drinking and shoot-outs resulted in the town's claim to fame: Boothill. Riley drove right past the cemetery whose crosses acknowledge the demise of many a pioneer. Though he would reside in Tombstone for nearly three years, he never felt compelled to visit the headstones that marked suicides and murders, mine-shaft accidents and hangings. Rather, Riley focused on the legends etched in the canyon fortresses and granite palisades that the Apache called home. In the Dragoon, Whetstone, Peloncillo, Huachuca and Chiricahua mountains Riley experienced a landscape that author Elliott Arnold described

66. Detail of *Apacheria [67].*

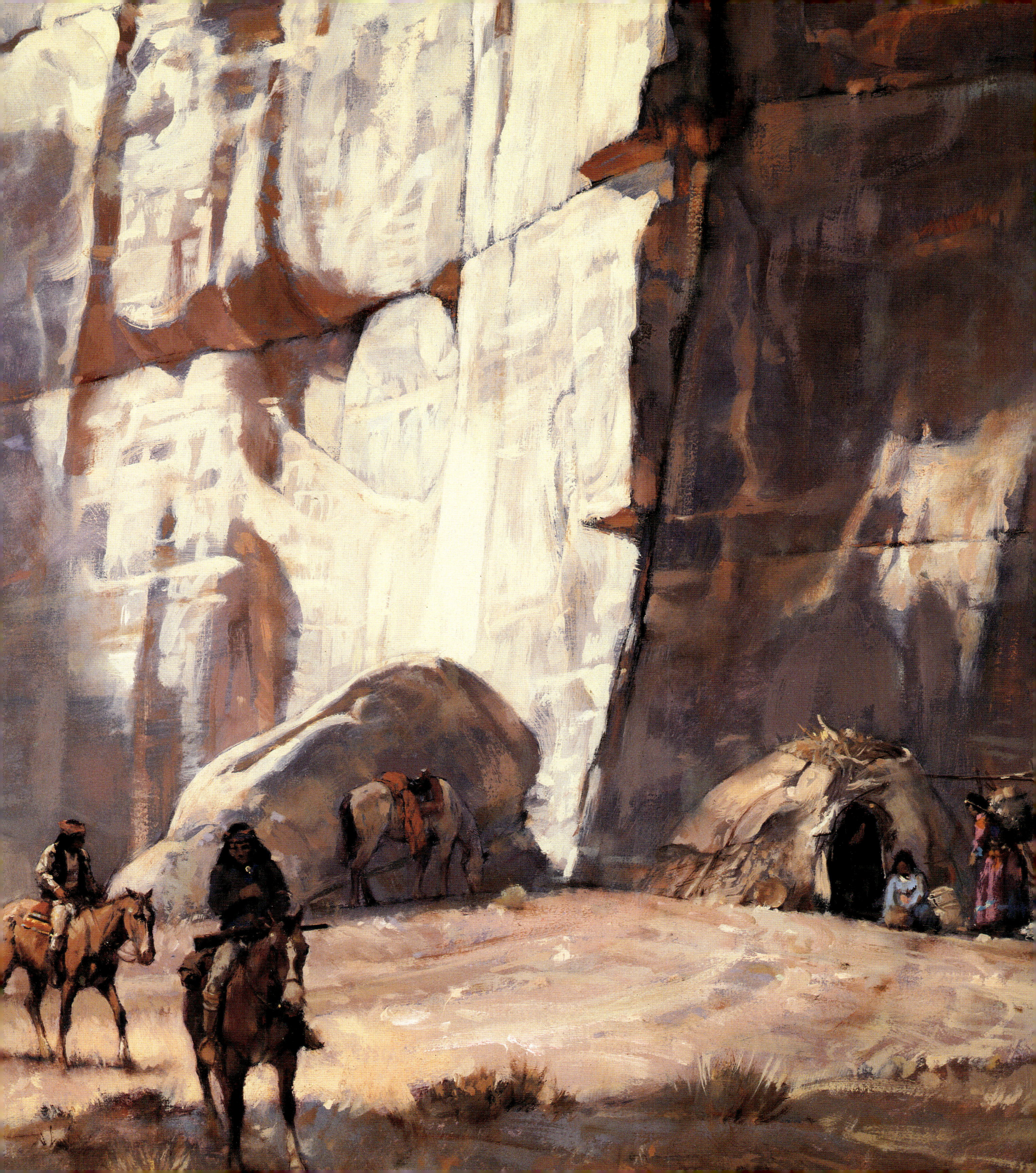

67. *Apacheria*

ca. 1981

oil, 20 x 24

Various bands of the Apache were located in a wide swath of the Southwest, from Arizona through New Mexico into Texas. Some, like the Jicarilla, were farmers. Others, including the Chiricahua, Coyoteros and Tontos of the desert Southwest, were nomadic hunters and raiders. The Apache's tenacity in surviving the harsh desert environment is legendary. Small enclaves of their people could be found in the canyons and mountain strongholds where they set up wickiups made of pole frames covered by twigs and brush. These could be hurriedly erected or, in impending danger, set afire once the owner escaped with his family's belongings.

in *Blood Brother* as "Big country.... It's a different kind of bigness ... that always seems to be away from you as if it didn't like people."

Having moved into a duplex, half of which they lived in and the other half they turned into a studio, Riley could walk to the post office where book cover assignments appeared twice a month, including one titled *Fadeout* by Joseph Hansen. Riley illustrated the cover with a guitar player, carousel horse and severely foreshortened body stretched out in the foreground. The caption may well have been inspired by Tombstone itself: "A thriller about a special kind of private eye and a corpse that wouldn't stay dead."

The Rileys had selected Tombstone in part because they had kin there. A year before their arrival, they had assisted MarCyne's brother in setting up a gift shop on Allen Street next to the Bird Cage Theater. Christened "The Silver Burro," the shop soon became the focus of MarCyne's marketing savvy when she started buying and selling the first Indian-made jewelry to be

68. *McElmo Canyon,* field sketch, oil, 16 x 20.

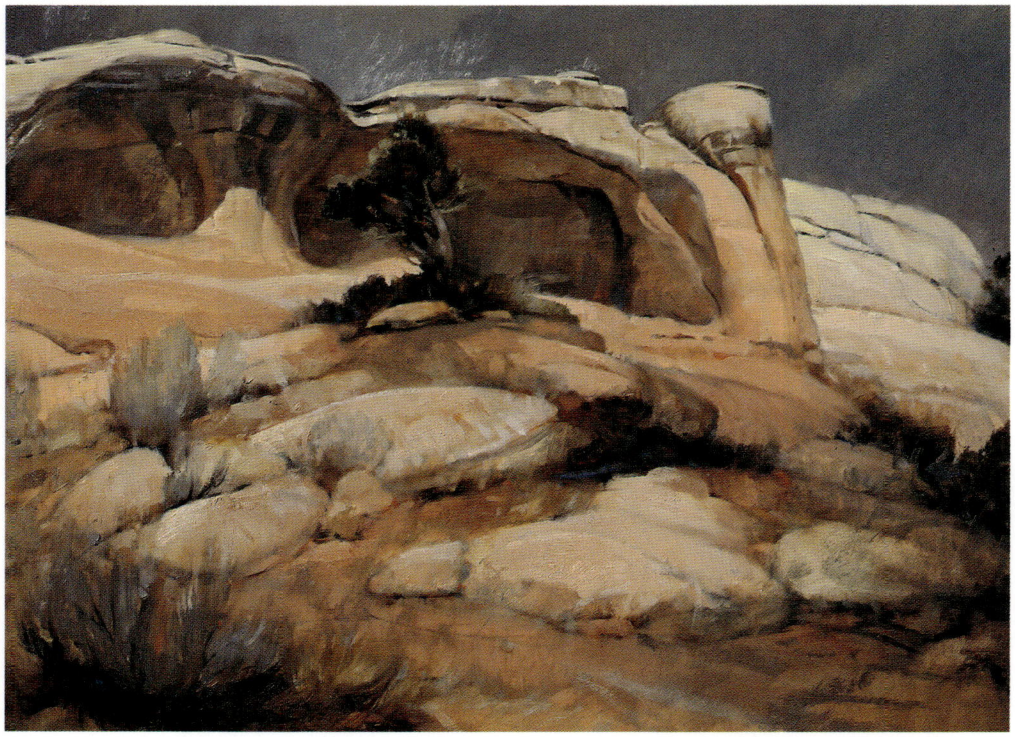

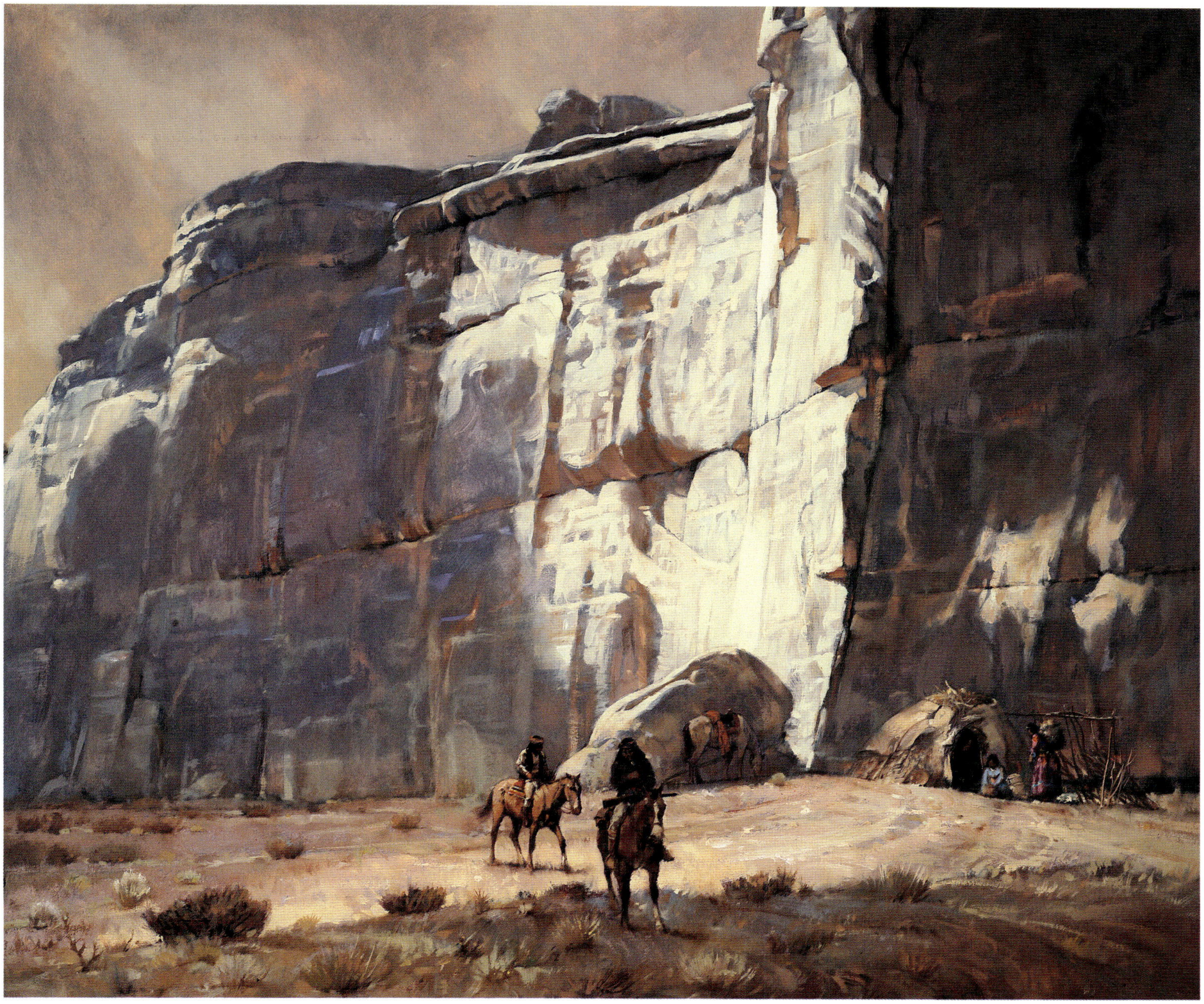

offered in town. Next to cases of jewelry, ceramic weed-pots and dresses designed by MarCyne, artist Kenneth Riley hung the first of his paintings.

Paintings of what? Of all his many illustration assignments, Riley most enjoyed the research that went into painting American history. His introduction to the American Indian as a topic had come in the early 1960s when he was commissioned to do storyboard vignettes for a picture map of *The Last of the Mohicans.* Then, in 1965, Riley received a commission to do a painting

69. *Comanche Twilight*
ca. 1984
oil, 32 x 40

Because of their proximity to the sixteenth-century Spanish Conquistadors, the Comanche of the Texas Plains were among the first Indians to acquire horses. The most talented of all the horse-mounted Indians, the Comanche were athletic riders and expert breeders. They maintained the largest herds of mustangs, which were viewed as symbols of wealth and prestige.

for the Department of the Interior to be placed in the visitors' center at the Little Bighorn Battlefield.

Titled ***Fruitless Victory [70],*** the subject matter and tone of the work were prescribed by Russell J. Hendrickson, of the Eastern Museum Laboratory, who requested a "mood piece" that illustrated this caption: "The Indians won a dramatic victory at the Little Bighorn, but they gained nothing. Within less than a decade, they either voluntarily returned to the reservations or were forced to do so by the military. The battle had been their 'Last Stand' as well."

Riley showed several Indians on horseback with a horse-drawn travois. As with the Mohican map, he created the landscape not by visiting the battlefield but by drawing upon library archives for site information and costuming and then imagining the emotional turmoil that filled the hearts of a people who won the battle but lost the war. Since the commissioners were part of the federal government, they offered the Library of Congress, National Archives and the Smithsonian as resources for "historical accuracy and fidelity to

70. *Fruitless Victory,* 1965, oil, 30 x 48, U.S. Department of the Interior, National Park Service, Crow Agency, Montana.

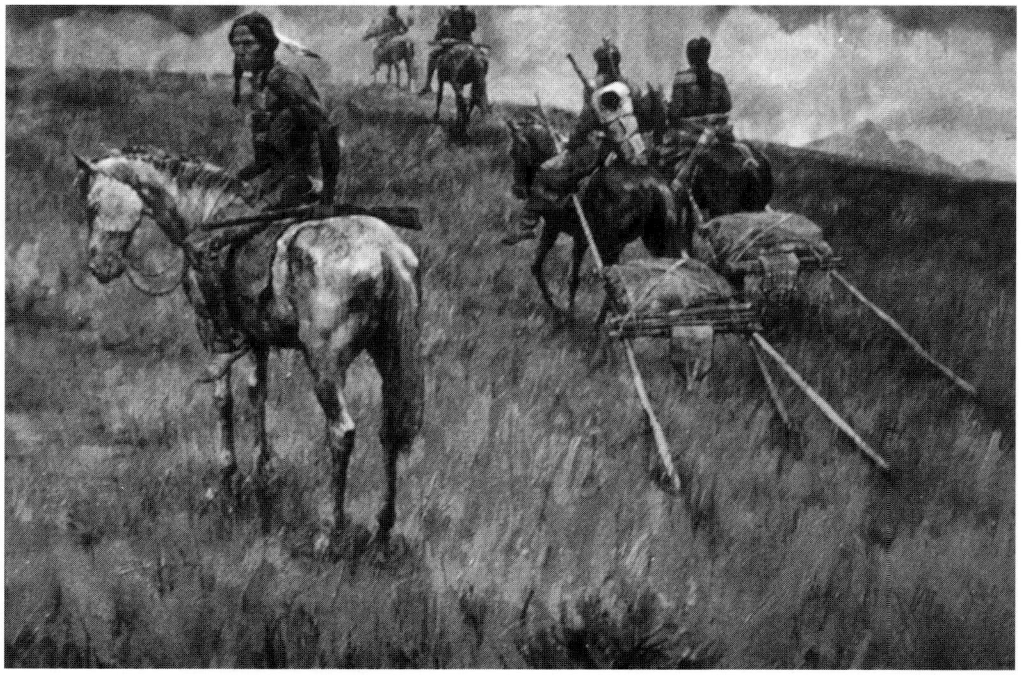

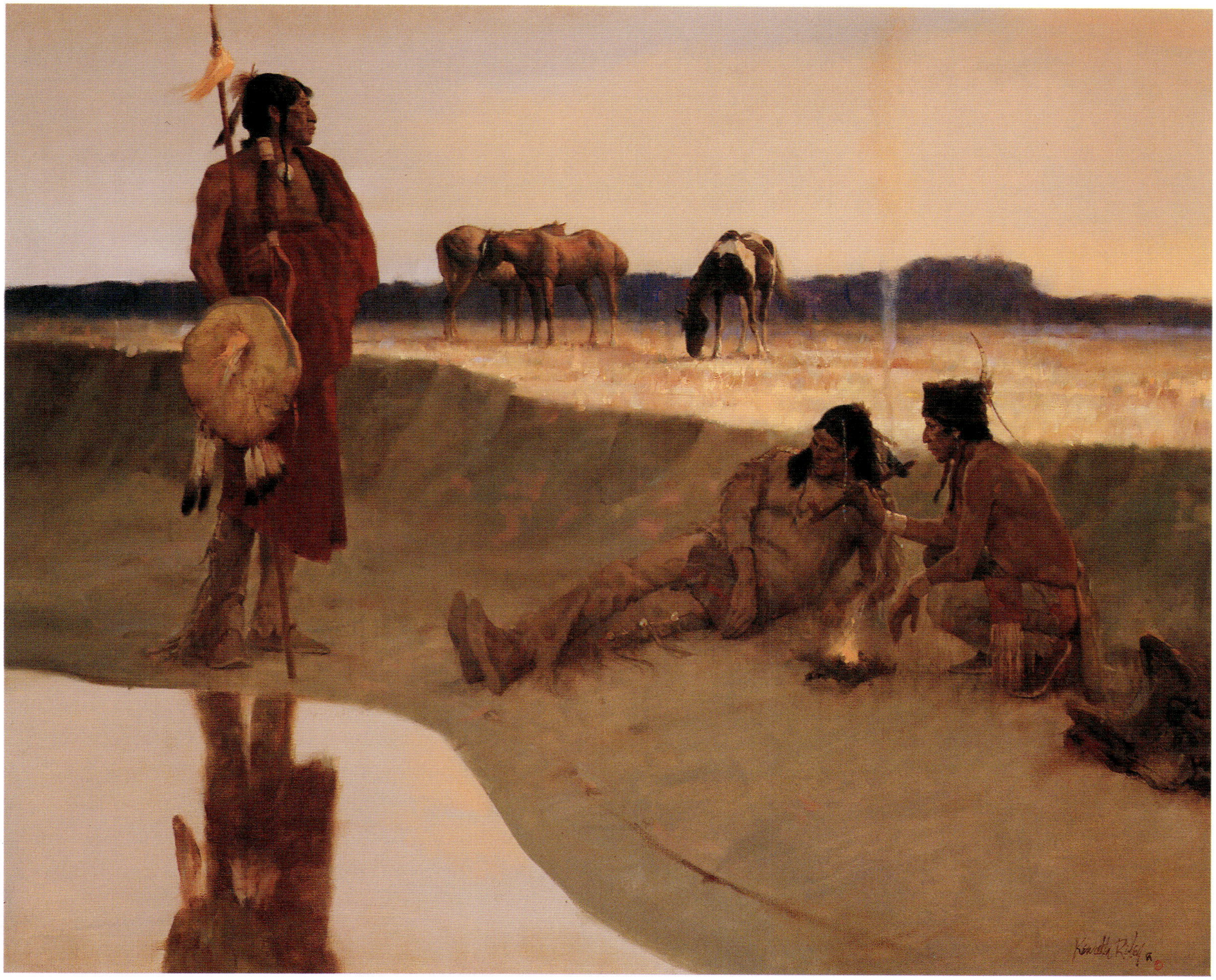

detail. We do not intend to do violence to either," wrote Hendrickson, "but on the other hand the purpose of the painting is not to emphasize either quality. The purpose is to illustrate the caption, which I feel sure we can do without perpetuating any historical inaccuracies." The fee for the painting, which was delivered in December 1965, was $1,000.

Four years later, in 1969, Riley received another assignment calling for Indian subjects from the *National Geographic*. The illustrations created for an article detailing the 1704 raid and massacre of a small Massachusetts

71. *The Trackers*
1984
oil, 30 x 26

In a maze of canyons, Apache guides could follow the most elusive of trails. The high-keyed light of Arizona bounces off the red rock, creating reflections that open up the shadows. The trooper is at the head of a patrol still out of sight.

village called Deerfield required extensive research into Woodland Indian dress and weaponry. Riley found the comparative history of the tribes and the exotic costuming intriguing. Moreover, the potential for focusing on anatomy and multiple figures was enormously rewarding.

The romance attached to these ghosts of history became real once Riley settled into Tombstone. Within a sixty-mile radius there was a mother lode of information to be gleaned from the crumbling barrack walls of Fort Bowie, the cabinets of artifacts at old Fort Huachuca and well-worn paths followed by the legendary Cochise. Hiking through the Dragoons, Riley could see the ruts that once guided the Butterfield Stage Line from San Francisco through Apache Pass, Dragoon Springs and on to Fort Smith, Arkansas. He wandered among the boulders where ancient pictographs tell mysterious stories and retraced the routes detailed by Captain John G. Bourke in his diaries chronicling the campaign of General George Crook.

Then Riley met a rancher whose family had lived in the valley between the Dragoons and the Chiricahuas for generations. "We were invited to a cookout at the ranch, and the young man asked if we wanted to see the family museum. It was filled with items that several generations of amateur archaeologists had unearthed. There were baskets and pottery and a pair of rush sandals, probably dating back a thousand years. The charred remains of cotton and corn were evidence of a once-thriving Hohokam village. Antique rifles told about the days when the family routinely barricaded the doors against raiding Apaches. What made it all so personal, however, was the labeling. Each item was tagged with its location on the ranch, as well as the name of the family member who found it. The objects condensed time. That experience triggered my empathy with the history of the area and gave me this craving to visualize it."

News of Riley's early paintings traveled to Tucson. The art columnist of the Tucson newspaper noted that a well-known New York illustrator was painting Apache lore in Tombstone. Stuart Johnson, a 28-year-old entrepreneur who had recently opened an art gallery called Settlers West, read the review and decided to pay Riley a visit. "Stu called and made an appointment. He was such a fresh-faced kid that I couldn't help but be a little dubious. But then he went over to see MarCyne, and she got the feeling that Stu would do a good job. We've had a close relationship ever since."

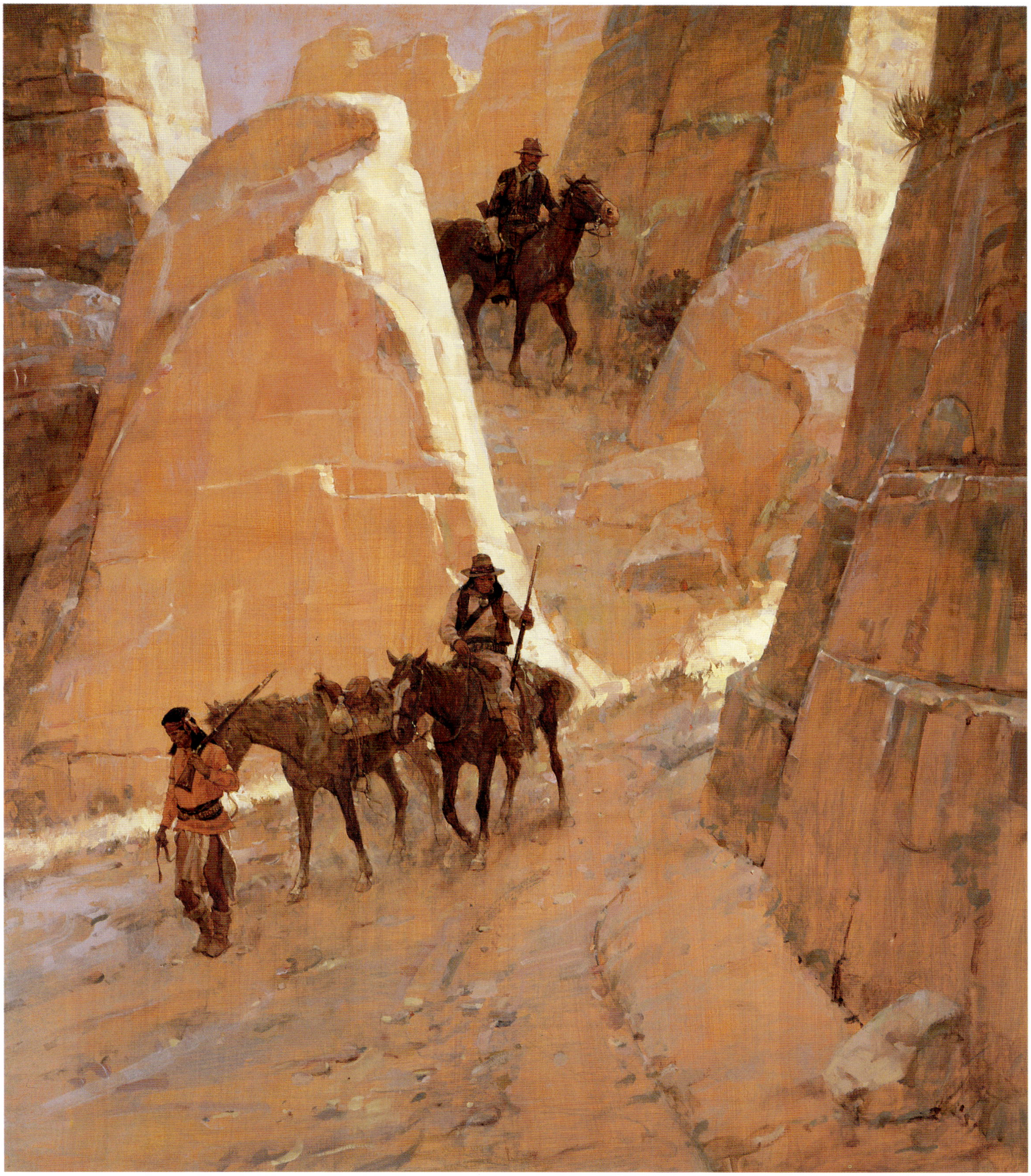

72. *First Breath of Spring*

1986

acrylic/oil, 15 x 30

Stage stops along the old Butterfield route were places of refreshment in more ways than one. Rustic, with a minimum of amenities, they supplied fresh teams of horses and respite to bone-weary travelers battered by wooden wheels which had jolted over miles of rocky roads. The first thaw would release moisture into the soil that turned the route into exacerbating mud—a far cry from the travel and lodging we've come to expect today!

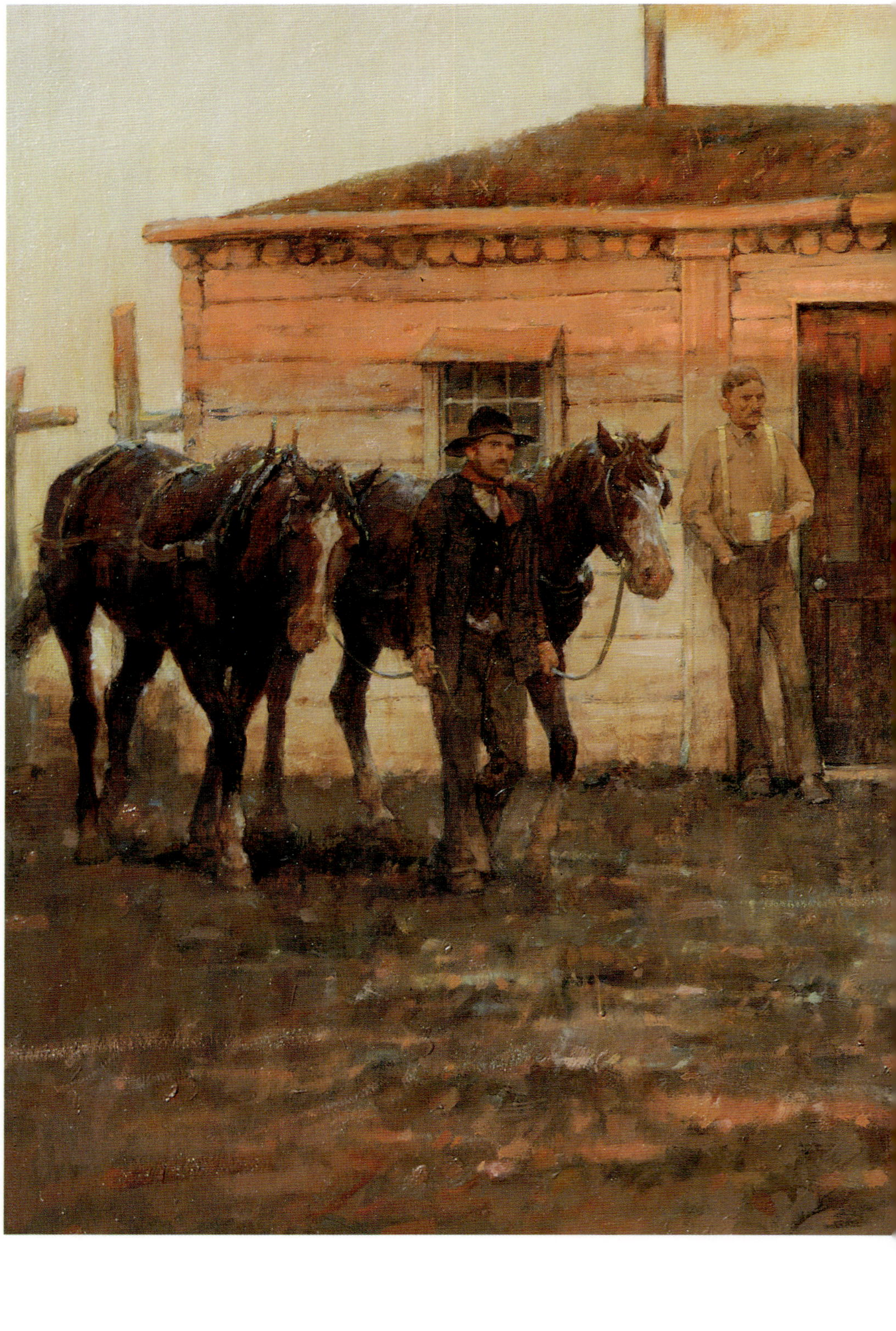

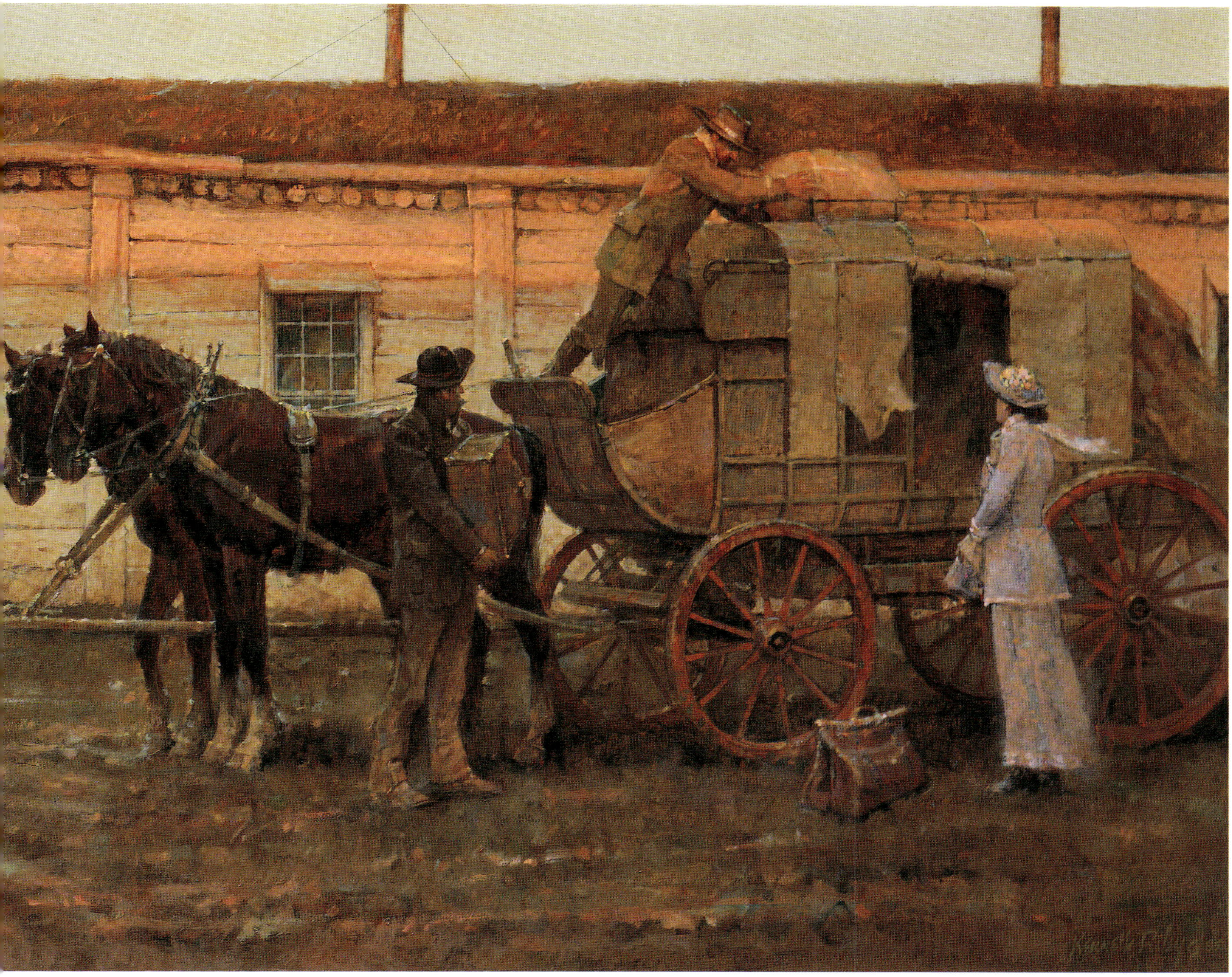

This was the spring of 1973 and Riley was working on several paintings for the inaugural exhibition of the National Academy of Western Art at the National Cowboy Hall of Fame in Oklahoma City. Formed as a replacement for the Cowboy Artists of America, which was moving its annual show from the Hall to the Phoenix Art Museum, NAWA was the brainchild of Riley's old badminton teammate Robert Lougheed. In June, Riley showed some of his first western paintings in an exhibit that included works by several of his former East Coast illustrator friends, among them John Clymer, Clark Hulings, Harold von Schmidt and Tom Lovell. "It was a marvelous coming together of artists who were as enthused about the West as I was," he says.

People ask how I paint a West that no longer exists. But had Rembrandt ever seen Jesus? Had Rubens ever seen an angel? Those who turn up their noses at history as a subject denounce a painting tradition that goes back several centuries. —KR

"The West is truly an American story," observes Riley. "And the setting for it is so phenomenal! So big! When Europeans visit, they can't believe the extent of the canyons, mountains and plains. I can still hike into areas so remote that I won't see another person all day—places where the land is unscarred by humankind."

73. *Ancestral Shelter*

ca. 1983

oil, 40 x 38

While camping in Utah's Canyonlands, MarCyne and I came across a wide, overhanging shelf in a rock formation. We ducked under it to get out of a passing thunderstorm and discovered a spring which nourished a maidenhair fern. Wandering back to inspect it, we looked up to find that the ceiling and walls were covered with handprints of all different sizes, surrounded by a storybook of pictographs. Obviously this had been the home of a family or tribe. I filed away this intimate experience for future use: what better backdrop for showing the winter shelter of succeeding generations of man?

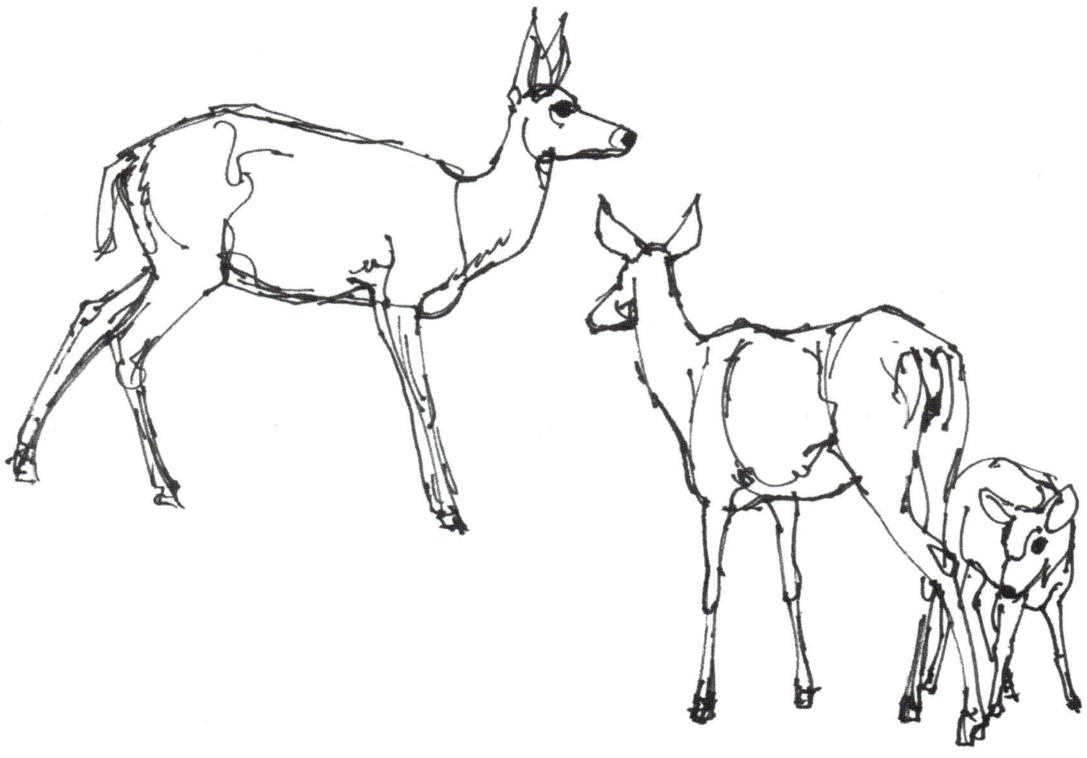

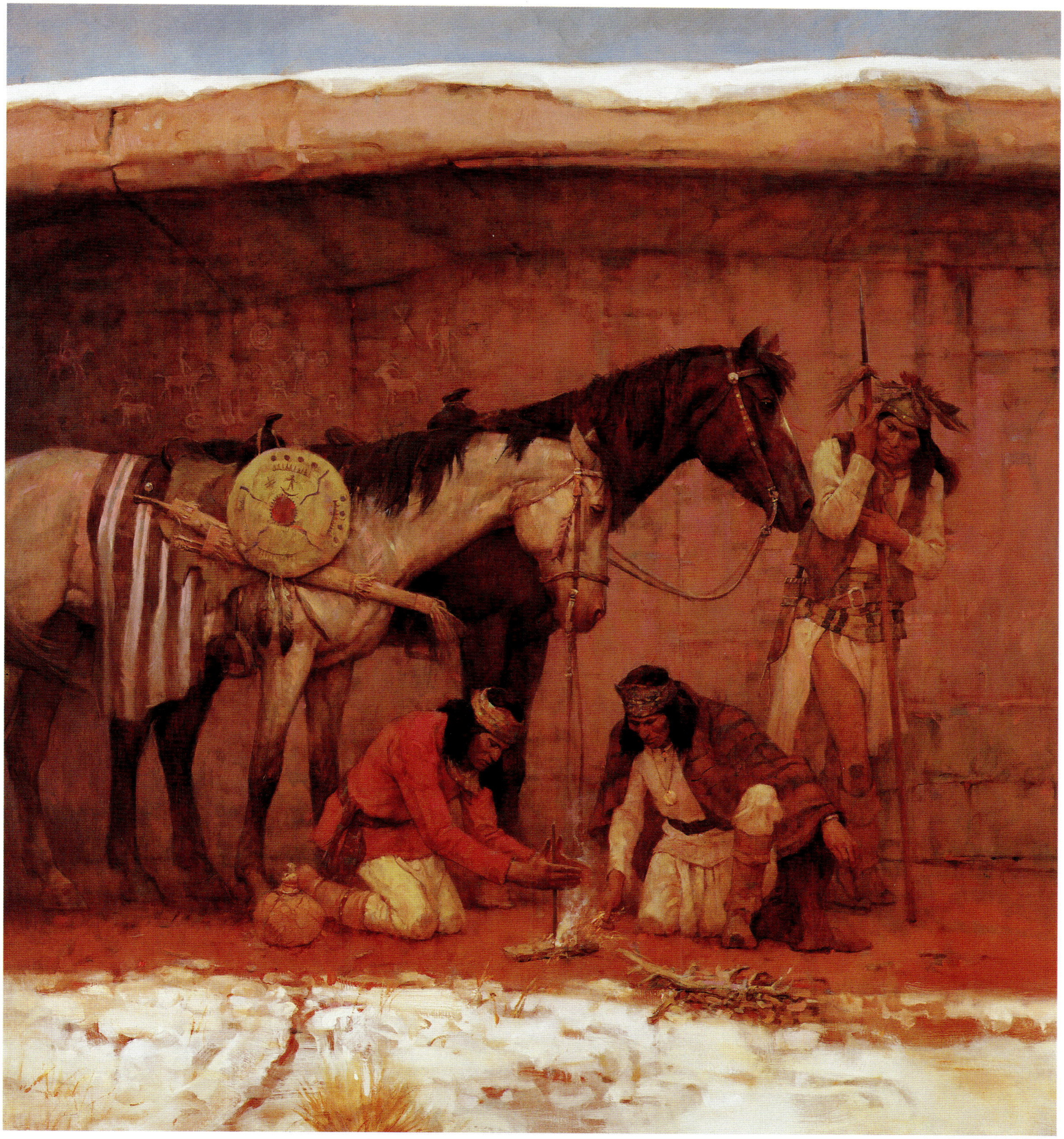

By 1975 Riley felt that his transition into western painting was complete and that Tombstone was too small and too remote for getting paintings to Settlers West and Husbergs Fine Art, Sedona. The decision to move into Tucson was facilitated when a home with a large studio came on the market. MarCyne closed the Silver Burro and the Rileys moved once again. The shift to a more urban setting, closer to friends such as Howard Terpning, introduced Riley to outside influences in more ways than one.

Throughout his illustration career Riley had been strictly a studio painter whose research methodology was based primarily on secondary resources. Given the deadlines he faced, he rarely had the luxury of visiting a site he was depicting. And since action and figures were generally the key to the illustration, the environment became incidental. In Arizona, Riley knew he had to change. In part at the insistence of Bob Lougheed, whose painting philosophy revolved around working outdoors, Riley was compelled to take on the heat

74. *Henry Mountains, Utah,* field sketch, oil, 12 x 16.

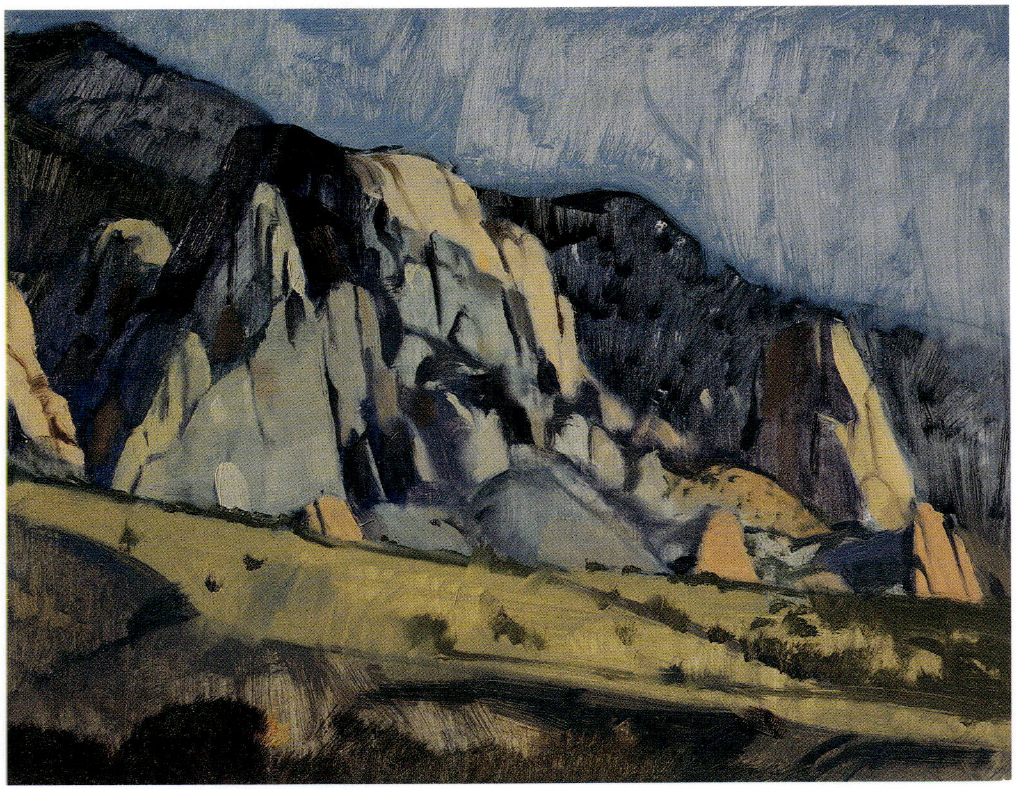

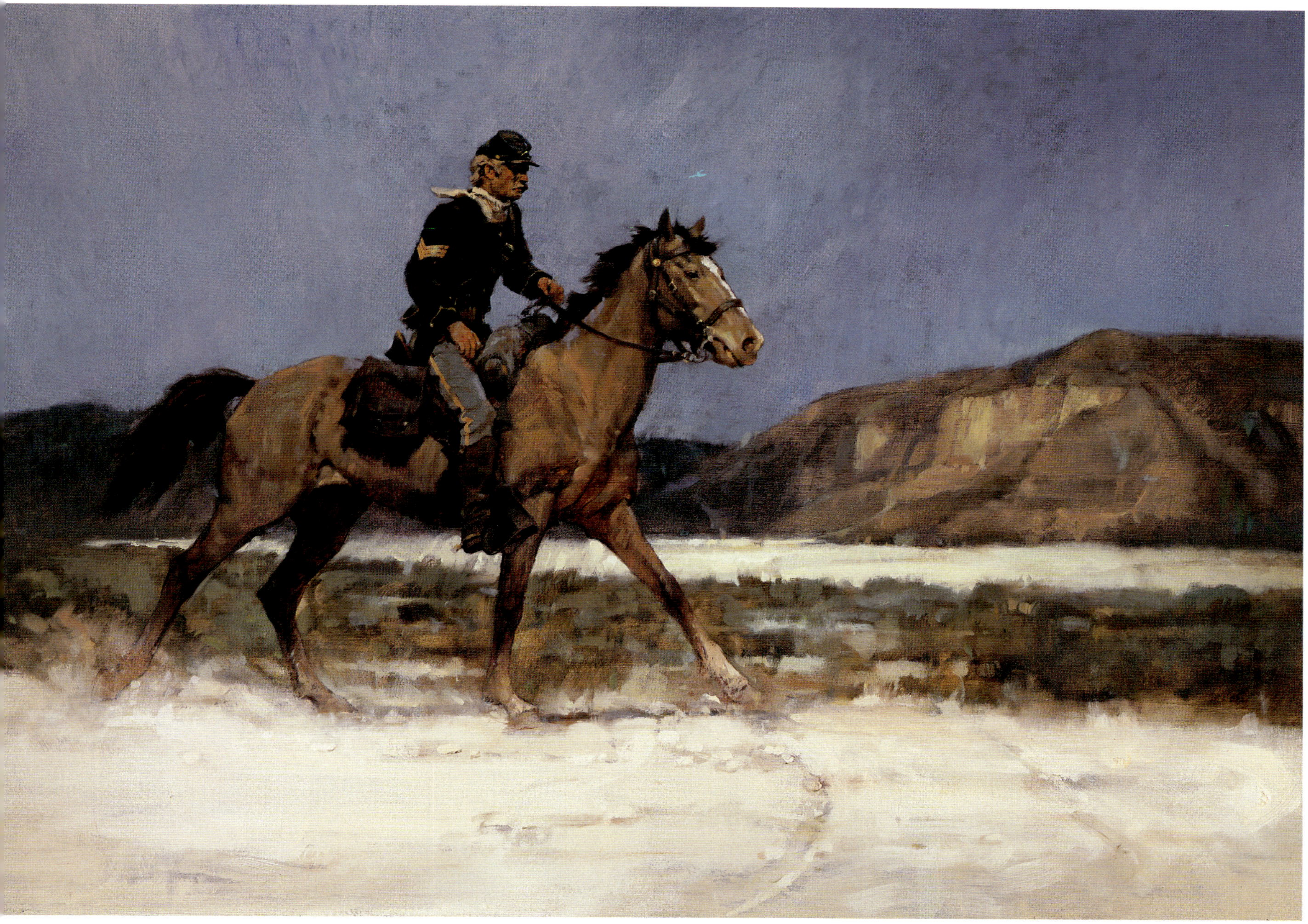

75. *Dispatch Rider*
1981
oil, 16 x 20

The dispatch rider had the unglamorous job of keeping the field units in touch with headquarters. In Apache Country the two most critical ingredients of his job were a sharp eye for ambush and a fresh horse with speed and stamina.

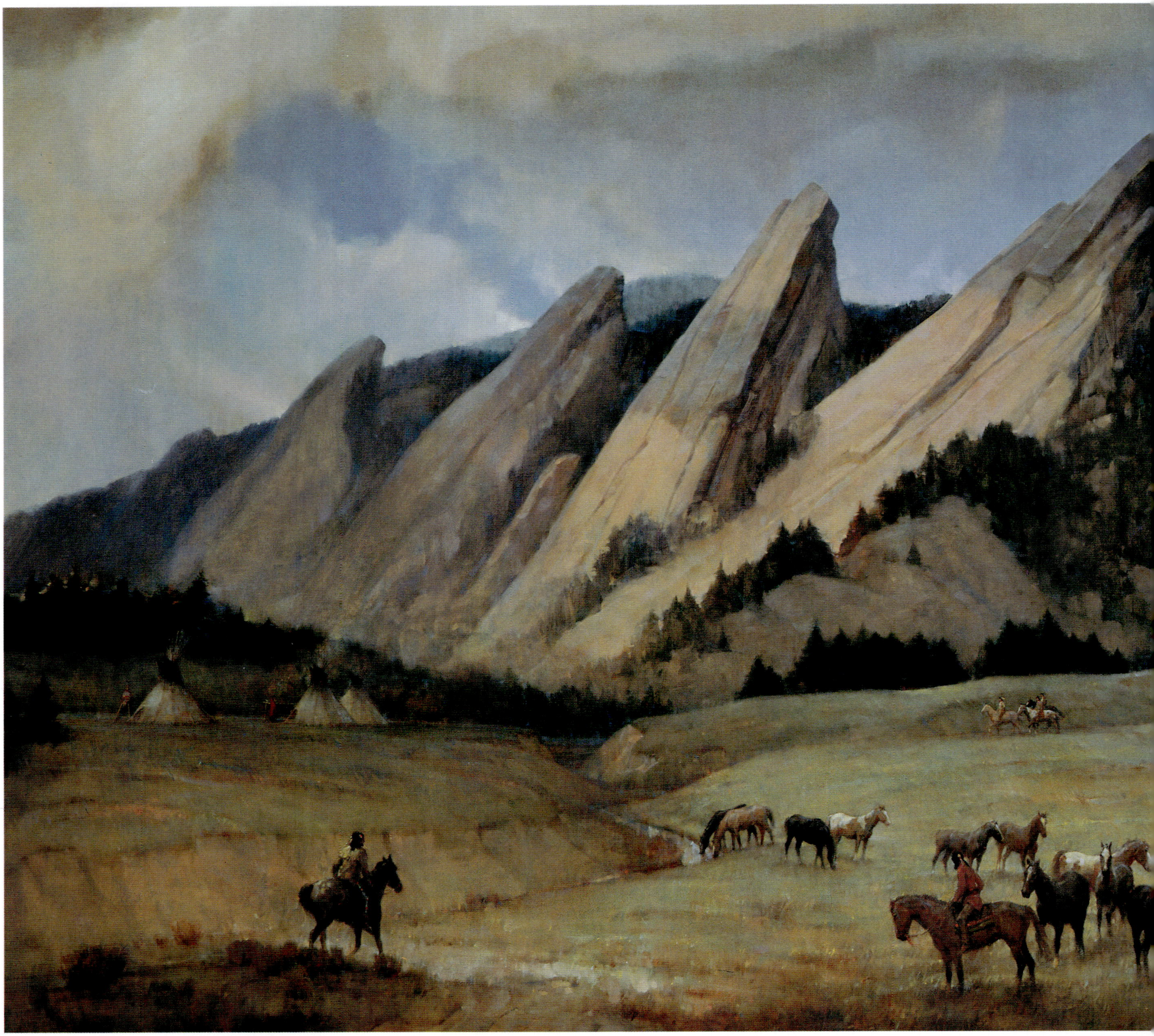

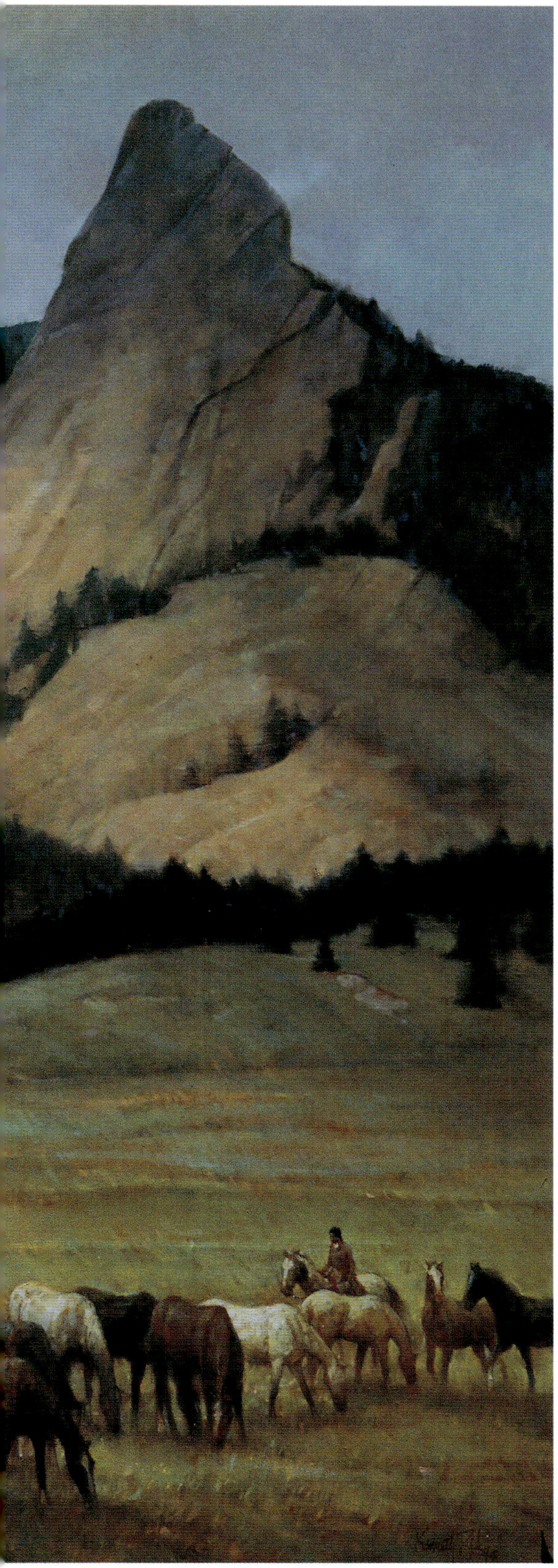

76. *The Flat Irons*

1990

oil, 60 x 72

The University of Colorado at Boulder backs up to a distinctive rock formation nicknamed the Flat Irons. It was a logical subject for this painting destined for the University Alumni Building. To give the mountains some scale, I imagined what it would have been like when the Arapaho camped in this meadow, long before roads penetrated the Rockies' Front Range.

77. *The Major's Mount*

1991

acrylic, 10 x 12

Capturing an officer's horse would have been quite a coup for this young warrior. Of course, we can only speculate if the horse was a runaway or what the fate of its former owner might have been. The evening sunset casts long shadows and reflects a shimmering hot pink on the fronts of the tepees—one of my favorite colors.

and wind, the bugs and clouds, and try his hand at painting in the field. He found the experience exhilarating.

"I learned that field sketches are the key to what goes on in the studio," he says. "They provide an understanding of light and the way colors work at different times of the day. And it was such a spontaneous happening as compared to the more controlled paintings done in the studio. To sit down in a beautiful spot and in a couple of hours produce a small but complete painting is a real joy."

Although he rarely uses his field studies as the basis for a painting, Riley relies upon them as reminders of how much variety there is in nature. "The sketches help eliminate the baggage of preconceived ideas, keeping your mind open to the limitless possibilities that exist in the landscape. I found that unless prompted by the real thing, the imagination returns to the same solutions. The field sketches remind me that the desert reflects the colors of the day and that rock walls aren't flat local color but infinitely detailed with irregular shapes, values, highlights and shadows—all of which change with every minute of passing light."

78. *Buffalo,* studio study, ca. 1974, acrylic, 10 x 10.

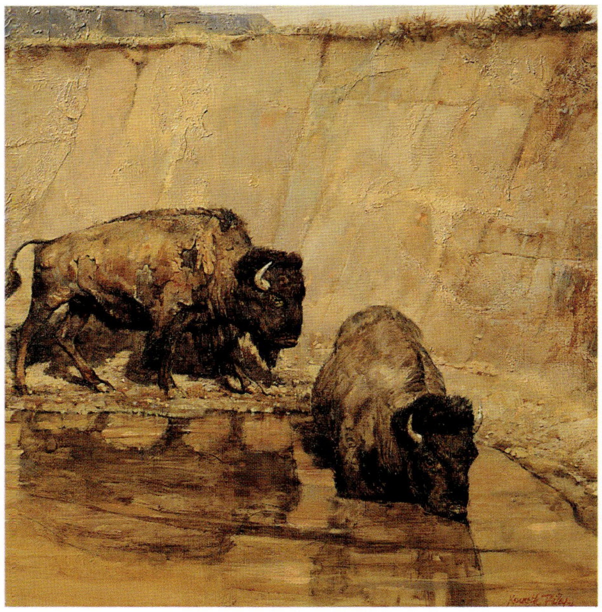

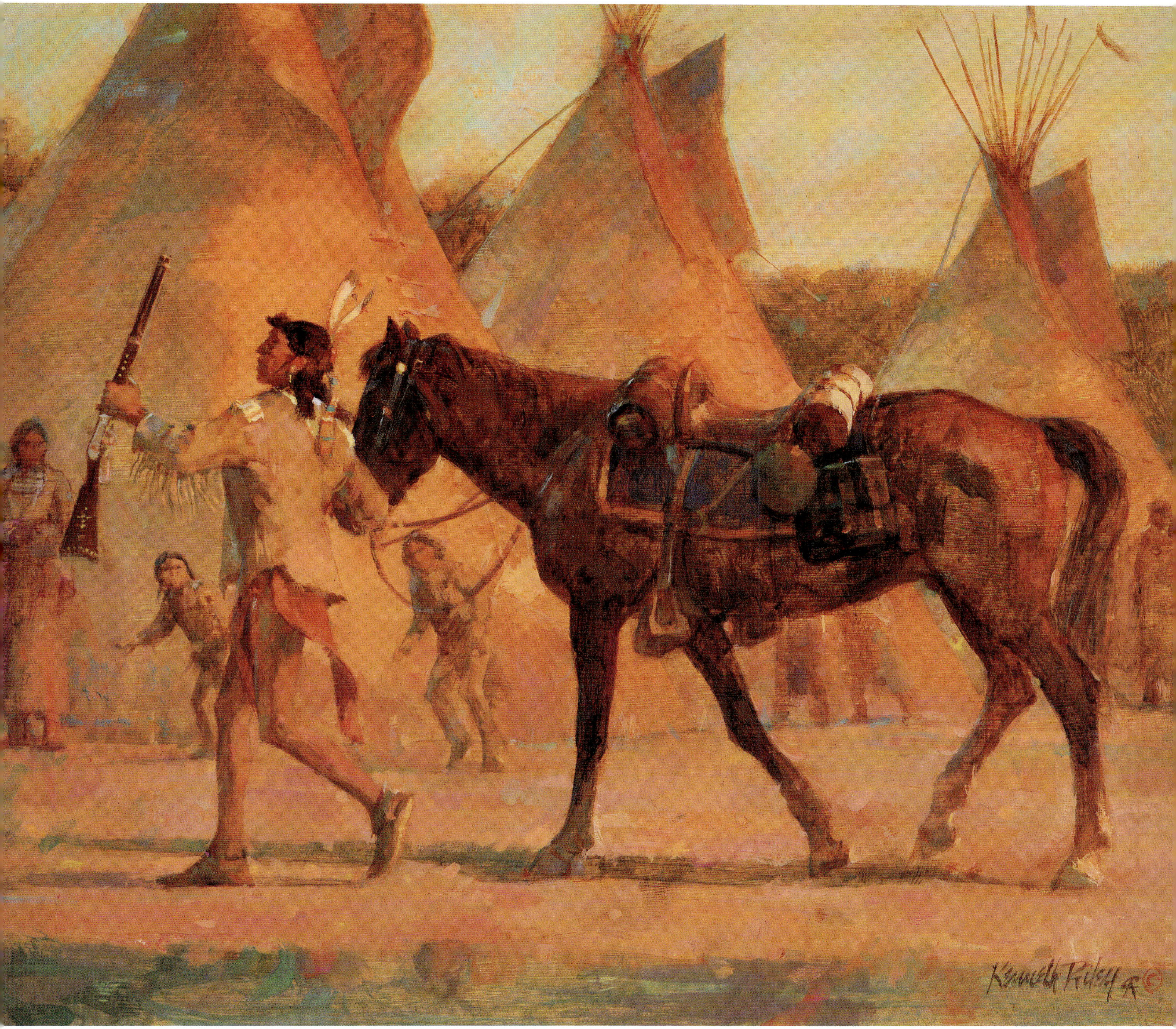
Kenneth Riley

Since his first experience painting outdoors, Riley has done numerous on-location paintings throughout the West and on his international travels. Several trips have been taken just to paint, including a 1978 month-long visit with Lougheed and twenty other artists to the Okanagan Game Farm in Penticton, British Columbia. "I'd never had the opportunity to paint directly from animals," Riley recalls. "After a while I got the feel of starting several sketches and then coming back to them once the animal returned to a position. Bob was such a great inspiration—he was a natural teacher and all of us hung on his every word. We developed quite a camaraderie, especially at night when we sat around the fire and exchanged ideas. So often we work by ourselves in our studios, isolated as far as any communication with others goes. With a group, however, you find that your problems are fairly universal and that you communicate using the same language."

In 1981, Ken and MarCyne spent the summer in the San Juan Mountains of southern Colorado. Painting in Mesa Verde and along the Delores River up

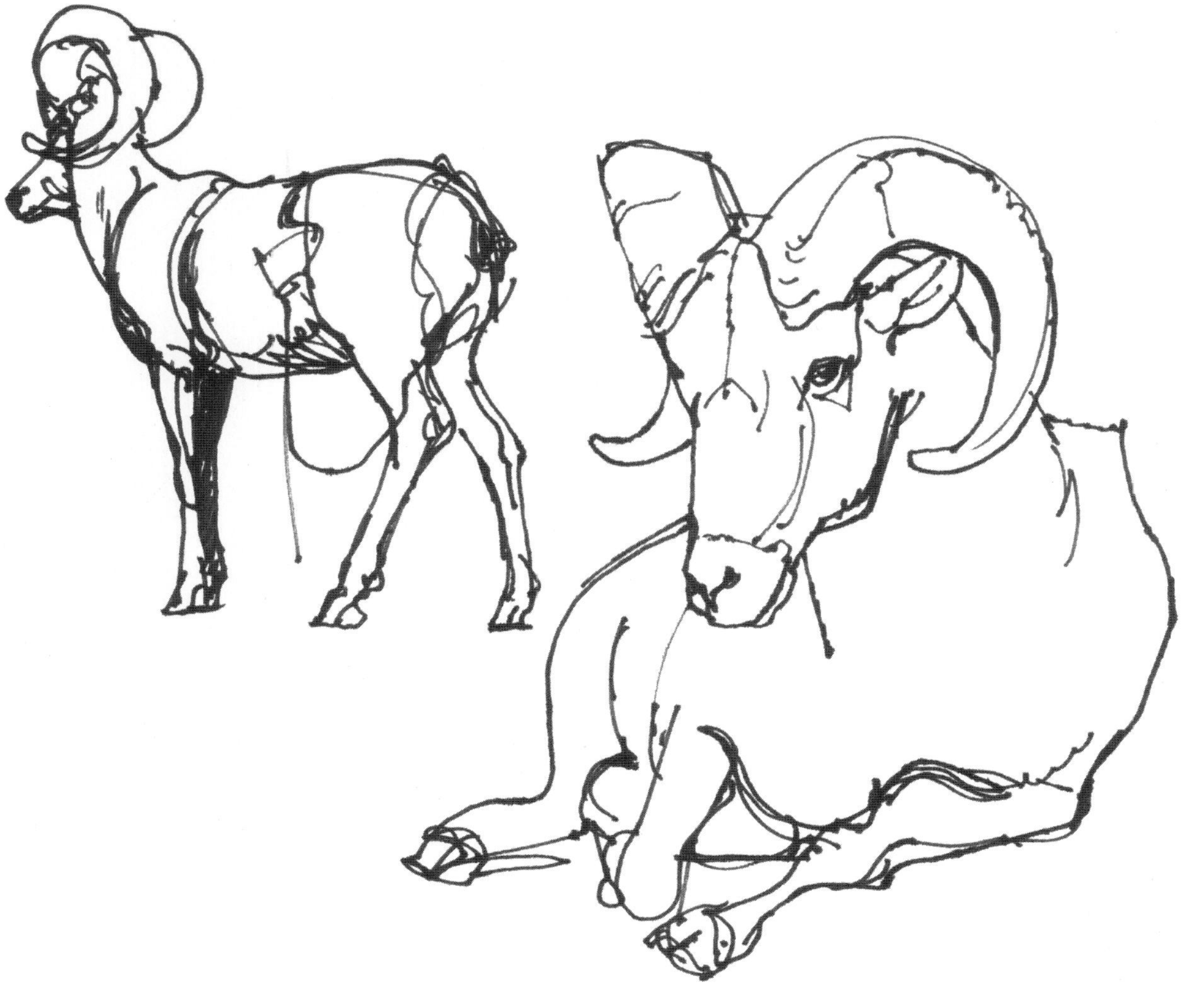

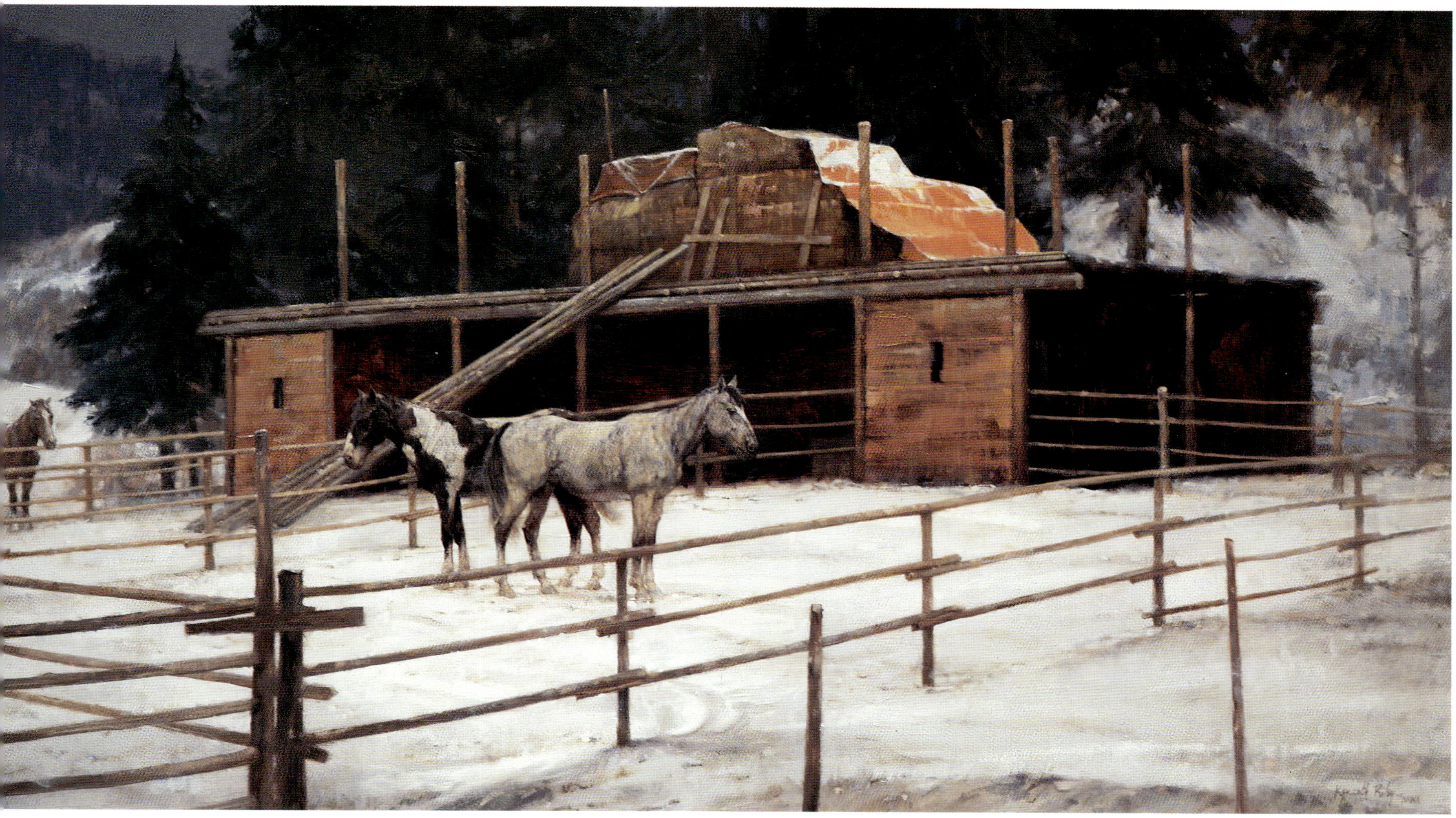

79. *Fresh Snow*
1979
oil, 22 x 40

While field sketching at the Okanagan Game Farm, I did an 8-by-10-inch field study of this shelter and corral. In an unusual move for me, I decided to scale up the sketch and do this full-size work. Perhaps it was the warm memories of that month with my good friend Bob Lougheed that caused me to tackle this cool winter scene, to which I added horses—Bob's favorite subject. Unlike the thick, juicy paint on my field sketch, the surface of my studio painting is more carefully managed. By applying transparent layers of warm and cool colors, I try for an overall richness that has visual depth as opposed to surface clutter.

to Telluride, he was exposed to a wide variety of terrain. Orange-and-pink canyons, expansive green meadows and snow-capped mountains vied with one another for attention. "To distill the character of the moment and hold the essence of your original idea despite changing light is the challenge of painting outdoors," he says.

Today, a small and a large version of a portable French easel sit packed and ready in his studio. They bear the scars of airplane baggage handlers in Portugal, where Ken and MarCyne spent three weeks painting in the country-side surrounding the medieval town of Obidos, as well as the spatters of paint applied during occasional hikes into nearby Sabino Canyon.

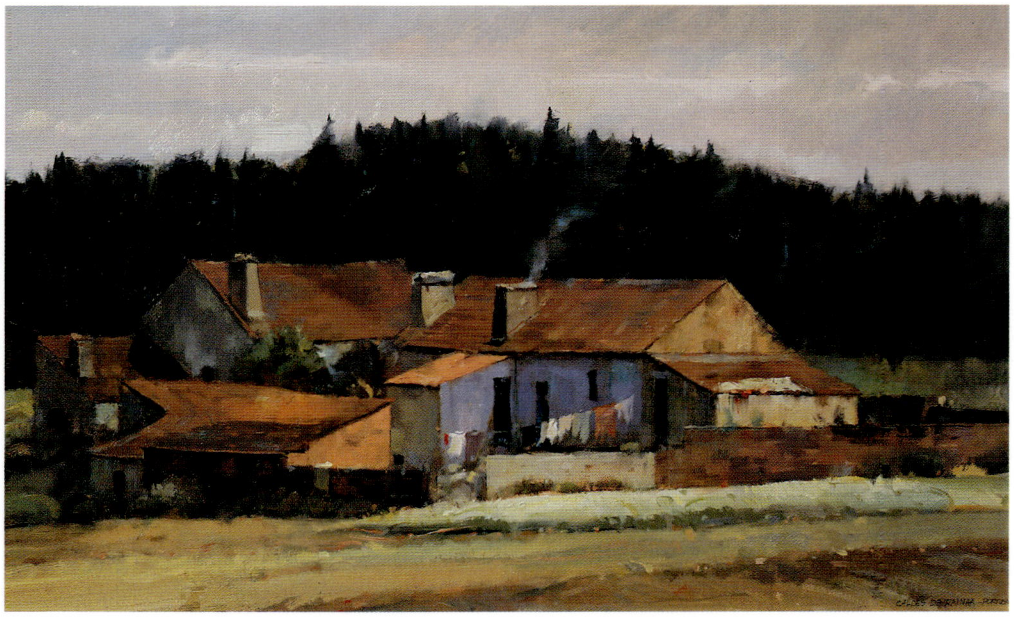

80. *Portuguese Farmhouse,* field sketch, oil, 12 x 20.

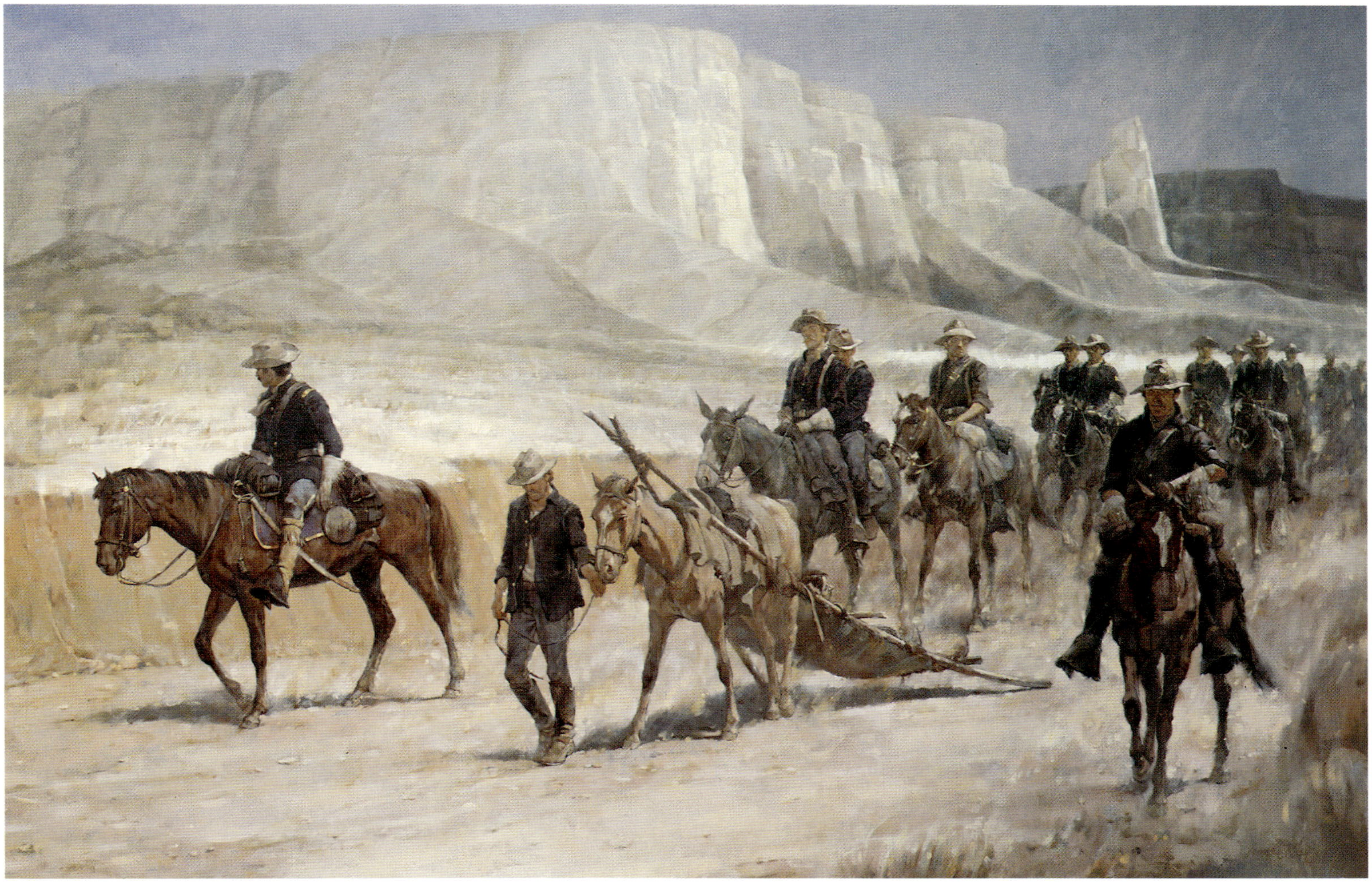

81. *The Long Way Home*
ca. 1977
oil, 30 x 40

I'm still amazed by desert light which bleaches color out of everything. The dusty atmosphere of a returning column of soldiers was an opportunity to take color out of the scene altogether—from delicate blues of the uniforms to the shimmering no-color light of the mountains. So many pictures show the glorious column riding out to battle but, as did Frederic Remington, I chose to focus upon the real-life fatigue that follows.

YIN AND YANG

Balancing the intellect and the emotions has been the crux of Ken Riley's work since he first encountered the divergent teaching philosophies of DuMond and Dunn. The process of achieving that balance has been facilitated in Riley's life and art by his close relationship to MarCyne, who is both wife and teammate, as well as a professional artist who signs her work MarCyne Johnson.

A successful painting balances the emotions and the intellect. The tendency to over-intellectualize in the studio can be mitigated by painting outdoors where intuitive emotions take over . . . or by asking your artist-wife to critique your work.—KR

To say that MarCyne's influence has been profound would be to understate a relationship built on over five decades of mutual love and respect. An art student when Ken met her, MarCyne painted throughout the years that they lived in New York and Connecticut. Her figural style evolved into abstraction in the mid-1960s after studying with Reuben Tam. While Ken never gave up the figure as a focus, MarCyne painted abstractly for over a decade, exhibiting her work in Manhattan and Danbury galleries. More intuitive than analytical, she focused on expressive colors and shapes, which became the foundation of her return to the figure in 1981 following their trip to Peru.

As MarCyne told Jackie Pontello in a 1987 article in *Southwest Art*, "The individual is the climax of creation and I could not ignore that.... I esteem women in my paintings, particularly Third World women. They are the traditional food producers, wood gatherers, water carriers and entrepreneurs who trudge miles each day to market any extra produce. For generations these women have struggled to scratch out a living and keep their families together ... yet they have no sense of their intrinsic value."

Despite the fact that Ken and MarCyne both paint the figure, their approaches to picture-making are very different, yet complementary. Ken's picture building is methodically segmented into steps. Beginning with an Idea, which may be a story, an allegory or an abstract concept, he designs

82. Detail of *Oaxaca Market, Mexico [84].*

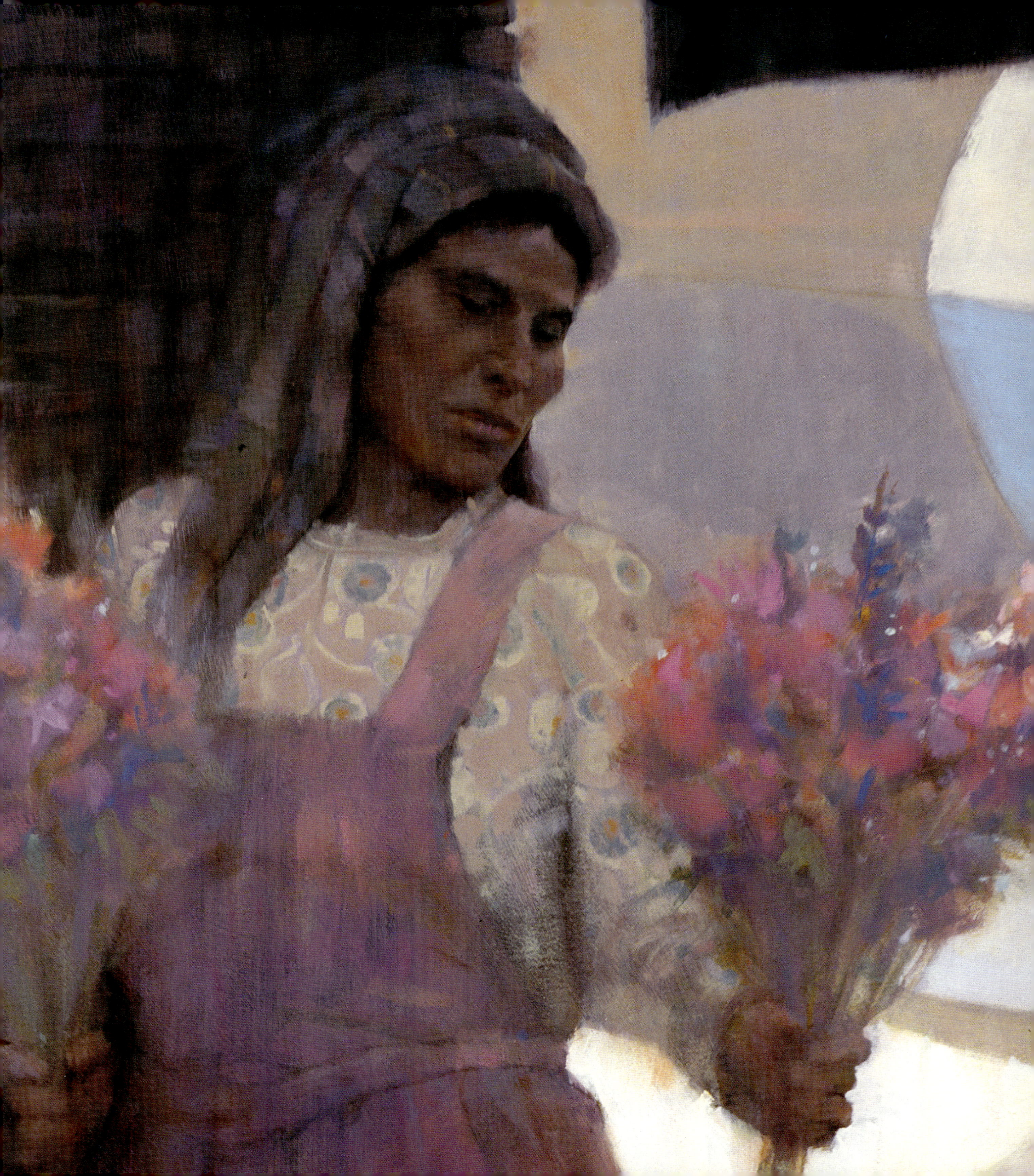

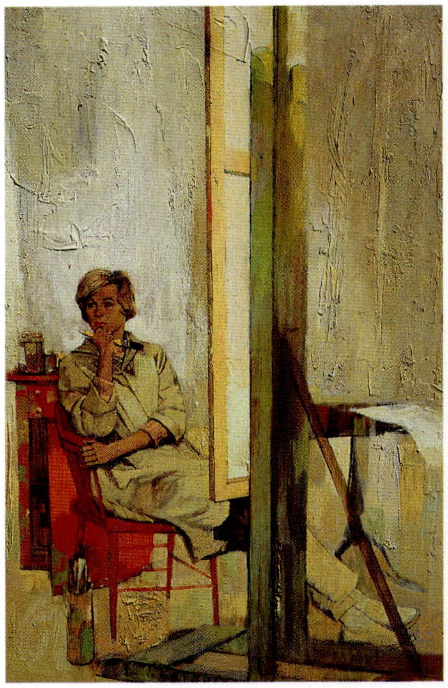

83. *MarCyne at the Easel,* ca. 1965, acrylic, 24 x 16.

84. *Oaxaca Market, Mexico*
1991
oil, 36 x 30

MarCyne and I often visit the open-air markets of Mexico. It is easy to be overwhelmed by all the colors, textures and shapes found in these busy places of commerce. In this scene I elected to focus on the three figures, which together form an axis. Around them luminous canopies spin like a pinwheel.

a foundation in thumbnail sketches. The sketch is turned into a small pencil drawing and color comprehensive, which is scaled up to a full-size drawing that is transferred to the canvas. Over the drawing he applies gauze-like layers of translucent color. Along the way, he controls the image, taking advantage of an occasional "happy accident" but generally trying to avoid them.

MarCyne, on the other hand, is highly experimental. Drawing inspiration from the unresolved tension of similarity and differences in color combinations and textures, she composes intuitively, responding to what is before her. Particularly attracted to materials, she collects handmade papers throughout her travels, experimenting with their absorbency of acrylic pigments. Like Ken, she uses color as a means of suggesting light, but unlike him she has no tried-and-true technique, no rules. "Color is a resource with great dynamic power," she said in a 1986 *Southwest Profile* article. "My intention is to arouse sensation and emotion through color."

Their varied approaches to picture-making are acted out in individual studios on opposite sides of the living room. Both spaces have north-facing windows and are open and uncluttered. Shawna, the German shepherd, sleeps in one corner of Ken's large studio/sitting room. Choco, the personality-plus *bichon frise,* bounces through when the spirit strikes him, dashing into MarCyne's more intimate space, which is shared with two Siamese cats. Her process of layering painted papers necessitates a second work area where a stash of papers offers colorful inspiration.

Ken and MarCyne's differing approaches have produced a dissonance that resolves into a resonating harmony in their married life. Always willing to critique one another's work, they respect the differences that make each unique. "Being an artist gets in your blood," Ken concludes of his and MarCyne's life together as artists. "At times I get jaded and worn out, ready to walk away from the studio. But after a few days, I get this itch to paint. Art becomes a way of life. It is a privilege to live the life of an artist and to share it with the wonderful gal I've been married to all these years."

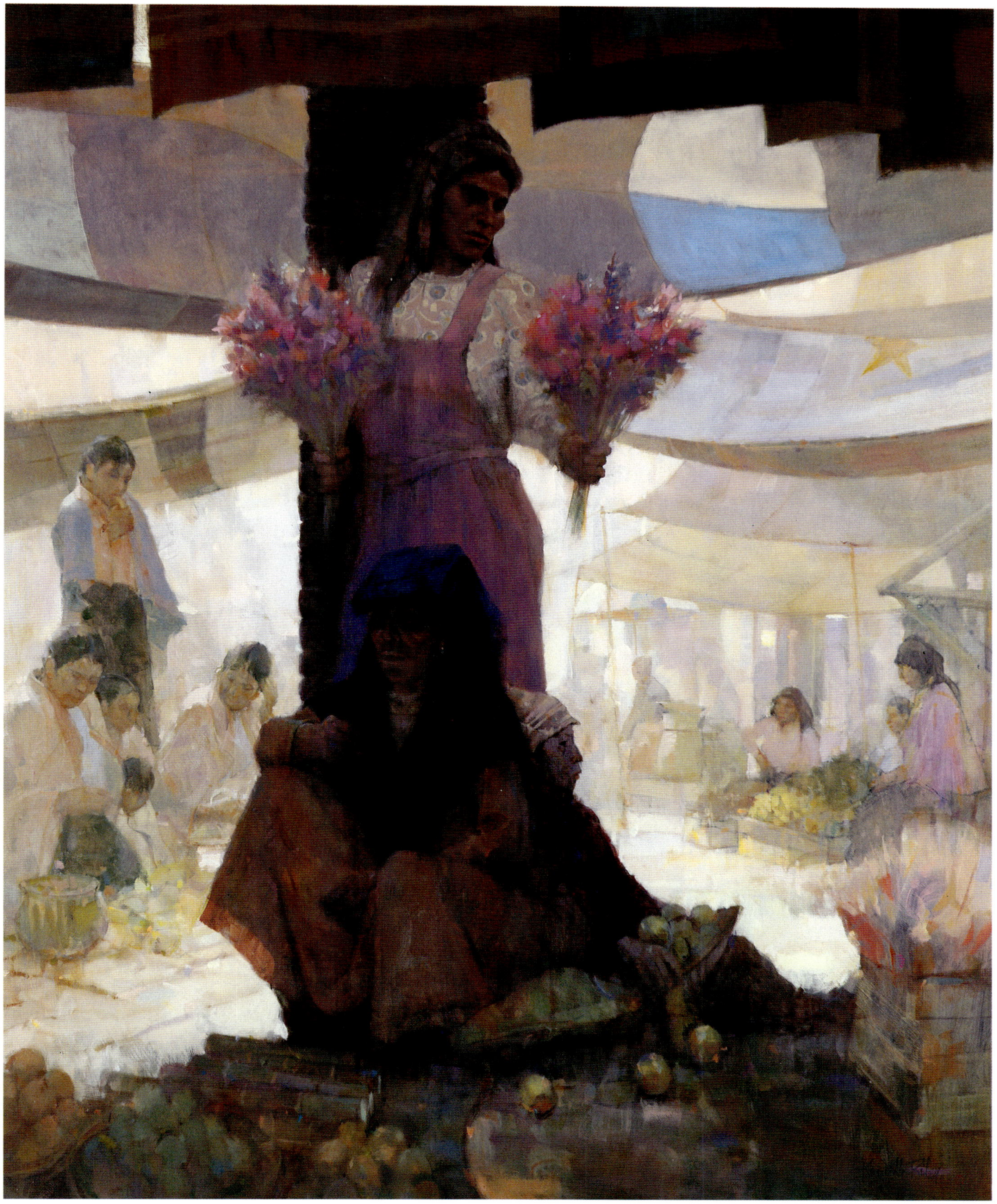

HISTORY PAINTING AS STORYTELLING, ALLEGORY AND POETRY

"History is an artifact. It does not exist until it is remembered and written down; and it is not truly remembered or written down until it has been vividly imagined. We become our past, and it becomes a part of us, by our reliving of our beginnings."
—Wallace Stegner (foreword to A. B. Guthrie's *The Big Sky*)

Ken Riley has always enjoyed the respect and admiration of his peers. Regularly included in the Society of Illustrators annual juried exhibitions in New York (see "Chronology"), he has more recently been identified as an "artist's artist." The description affirms Riley's narrative skills in relating the story of the West. More significantly, it applauds his risk-taking approach to color and design: By challenging rules, Riley makes the result an exciting work of art.

In recognition of his prowess, Riley has been invited to participate in all of the major western American exhibitions and sales that have taken place in the last decade. He is also a member of the two oldest, most prestigious exhibition groups in the West: the National Academy of Western Art and the Cowboy Artists of America. In the decade Riley has exhibited with the CAA at the Phoenix Art Museum, he has consistently won both gold and silver medals (see "Chronology"). He has also been accorded four Stetson Awards, which recognize the best overall exhibition as voted on by the artists themselves. "The CAA has influenced me," says Riley. "Unlike NAWA which has diversified and turned much of its attention to the landscape as a subject, the CAA remains mostly figure painters, an area in which I like to compete."

Though the figure is ultimately the focus of Riley's work, it is not the impetus to paint. Rather, the figure becomes a vehicle for expressing an Idea (a concept described at greater length in the chapter "Communicating the Idea"). The following thematic discussion of his subject matter introduces three Idea concepts that shape Riley's work and contribute to his philosophy. While the areas are not mutually exclusive, nor strictly chronological, certain aspects of them have been refined over time, resulting in ever-more concentrated and meaningful statements.

85. Detail of *Mandan Gold [86].*

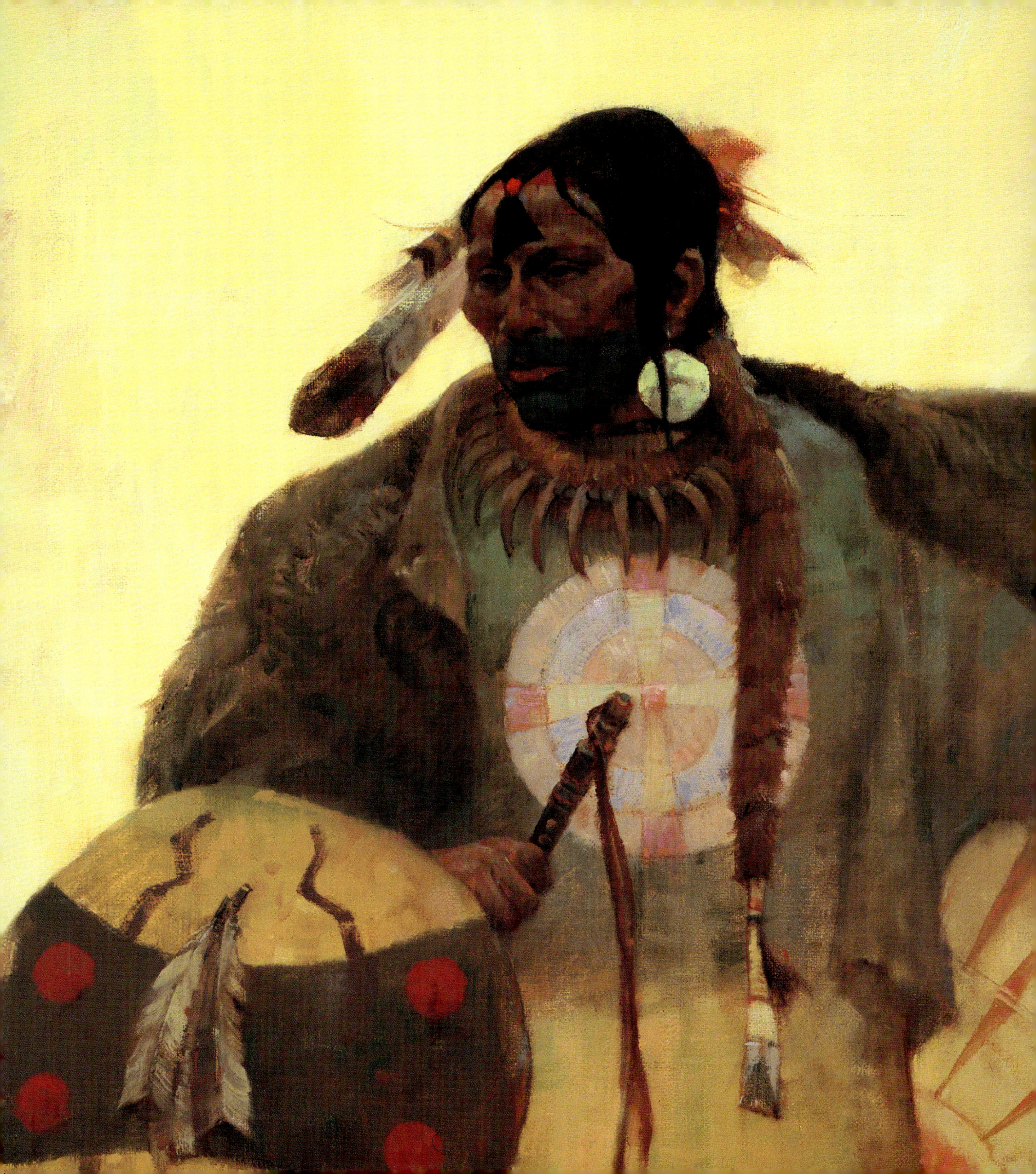

History Painting as Storytelling

When Riley began painting his easel art, he brought with him a love of the figure and an illustrator's desire to picture text. "Illustrators are uniquely qualified to paint the history of the West," he says. "Their basic training is to take subject matter that no longer exists and give it authenticity—to use their imaginations and empathy to transfer history into a context that becomes very believable."

Many of his narrative paintings rely heavily upon written accounts, notably first-person diaries. "Journals are especially inspirational since they are not watered down through successive interpretation," says Riley. "It's almost as if you are experiencing the event as it happens." In picturing historical anecdotes, Riley is sensitive to the details of costume, accouterments and geography. The importance of the latter is noteworthy. In the narrative paintings, especially the early ones, Riley positions his figures as small elements dominated by expansive horizontal or vertical vistas. Using a fairly traditional vocabulary of atmospheric perspective and natural horizon lines, the panoramas are breathtaking views that Riley has actually seen.

Though one might be tempted to call these works "historical illustrations," they are fundamentally different from the images Riley created for the page. "When I was illustrating I rarely had a subject that was meaningful to me personally," he explains. "Instead, I was picturing dramatic moments in someone else's script. In my own narratives I select topics that hopefully offer greater universal human interest, reflecting man's relationship to himself, to the land and to other men. It's a whole different approach—you might call it a respect."

The narrative paintings often deal with actual people—individuals whose deeds contributed to the evolution of American society. They come from a period during the nineteenth century when Anglos and Native Americans encountered one another on the western frontier. "It was a violent period, not only between two cultures but among the Indian tribes themselves," says Riley. "The Indians had their dignity. They lived quiet lives unless they were bothered or had to go into the wild to get what they needed to subsist. Their philosophy of living close to nature and respecting the land and animals was more enlightened than our attitudes today. I think those aspects influence the way in which I paint them."

86. *Mandan Gold*
1984
oil, 48 x 40

Simplifying an image to the fewest elements needed to make the statement has become increasingly important to me. In ***Mandan Gold*** I concentrated on the monumental quality of the Mandan culture. I eliminated any details that might draw your attention away from the snaking line that begins in the foreground shield, moving upward in a series of circular switch-backs that culminate in the drape of the robe over the man's extended arm. An extended buffalo robe offers many interesting possibilities in terms of shape. It also enlarges the person wearing it, contributing to the sense that these figures truly dominate the space.

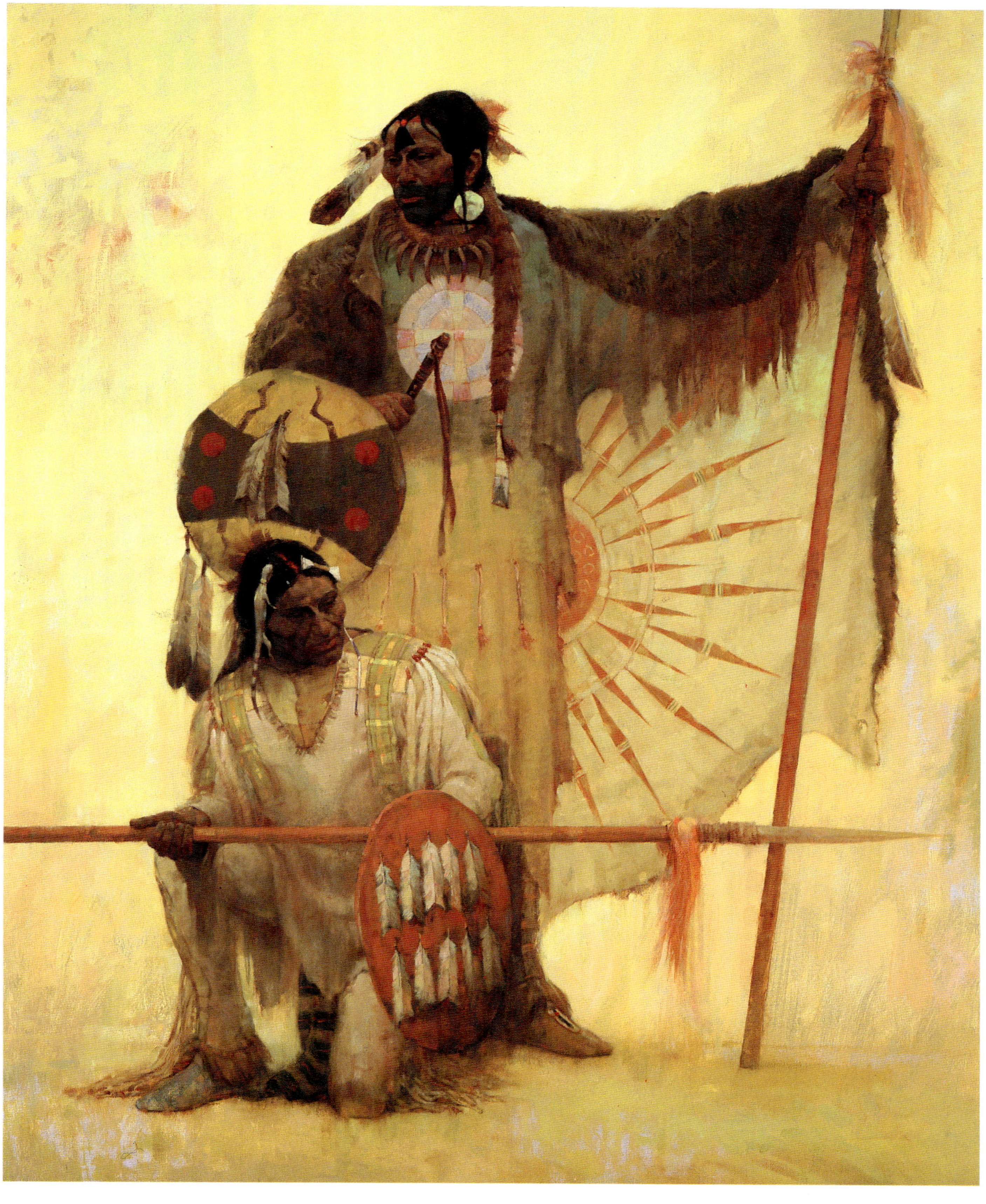

Among the southwesterners that piqued Riley's curiosity were the combatants in the Apache Wars: the Chiricahua Apache led by Cochise and later Geronimo, the cavalry and the Apache scouts under the command of General George Crook. Each of the players in this melodrama, which lasted from the 1860s through the 1880s, has been featured in scenarios where survival is not simply a matter of being the fittest but also the smartest. Rarely, however, does Riley show the two sides fighting. Instead, he prefers the more quiet, introspective moments when men are alone with their thoughts.

In many respects, the land also becomes an antagonist in the Apache War paintings. From his experiences painting in the mineral- and lichen-colored canyons, Riley creates works showing cavalrymen or Indians dwarfed by overwhelming rock walls, treacherous trails and scorching heat. In ***Dry Camp [87],*** for example, he noted in the 1984 NAWA catalog that "the sun-parched canyon country of the Southwest was part of the field of operations. Many a night's bivouac took place under cliffs reflecting the heat of the day and with no water in sight. The deep shadows of day's end exaggerate the diminished scale of man to his environment."

Set in the Chiricahua Mountains, the horizon line in ***Dry Camp***, as in many of Riley's narratives, is at the top of the painting, where textured canyons give way to a sliver of sky. Created by volcanic eruptions and eroding waters, the rock formations of the Chiricahuas sport arches and primeval, undulating faces topped by an odd assortment of rondels and turrets. Even in the shade, the pink-and-rose colored walls sizzle. And as poignant evidence of the inhospitable environment, a tree, bleached white, stands petrified in a once-wet wash.

Rarely is there much of a mid-ground in Riley's narrative paintings. Rather, the rocky promontories loom forward pressing themselves against the individuals. Such is the case in ***The Secret Place [105],*** where the dominating force is the pinnacled landscape. Cut into the east face of the Dragoons, the sublimely vertical canyons provided Cochise's warriors with countless natural vantage points for watching the dust of army operations at Fort Huachuca. Civilization has done little to challenge these age-old fortresses. Riley emphasizes the fact with a scraggly bush endeavoring to find life-sustaining moisture in a crevice of this formidable facade.

87. *Dry Camp*
1984
oil, 32 x 48

The sights and sounds of a cavalry patrol settling in for a night's stay in a desert canyon were reason enough for attempting this painting: picketing horses, cooking meals, preparing to bed down—everything but a shower. The rock walls were still radiating heat from the day's sun. Time to post the sentries.

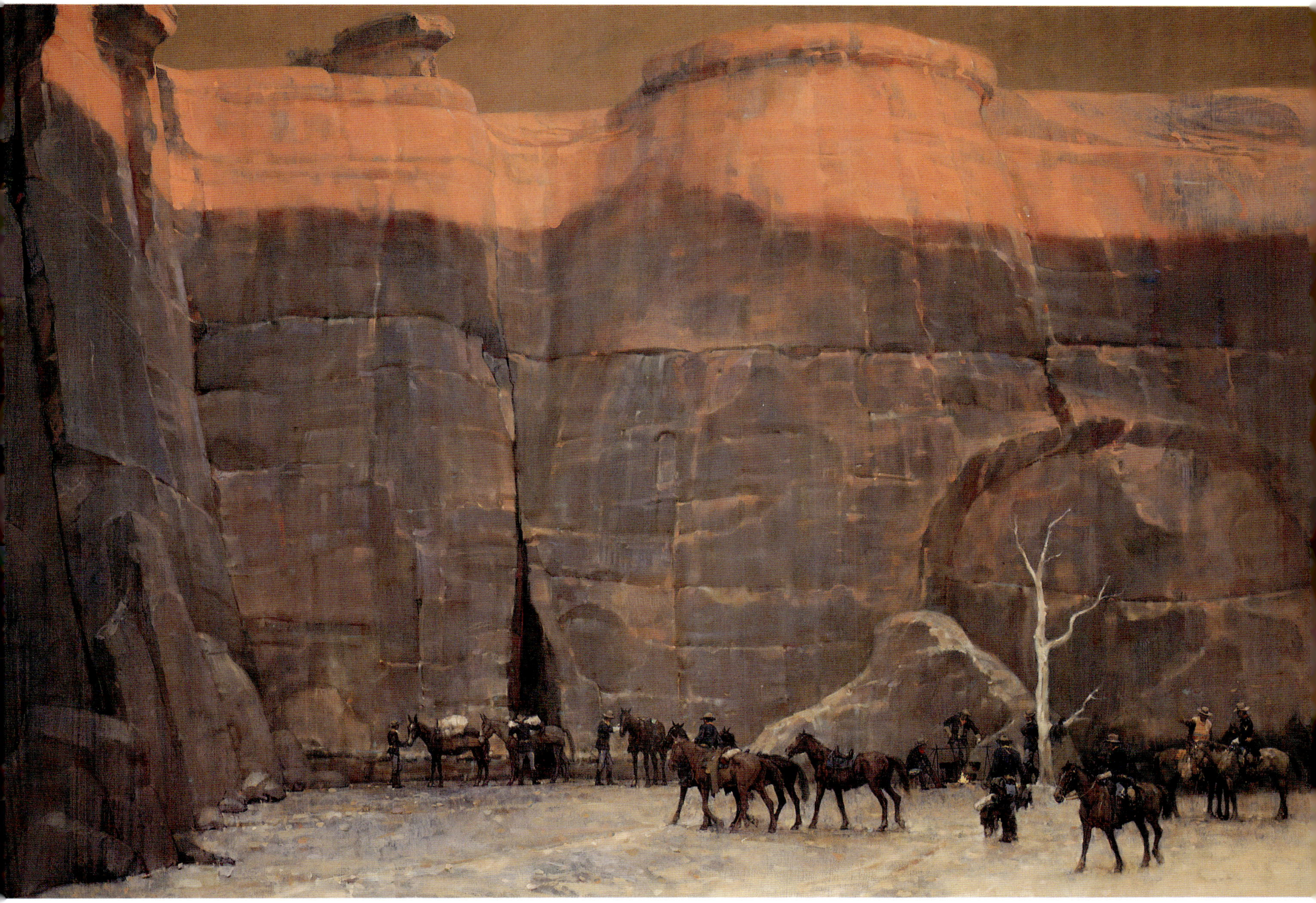

Confronting the force of the landscape are cavalrymen whose duty to country is conducted not with the pomp of the parade ground, but rather the inventive opportunism of firsthand experience. As Riley told Dan Blanchard in a 1978 Creative Crafts television program, "The field soldier is my main concern, not the parade soldier." In ***You Take What's Issued [91],*** the body language of the beleaguered soldier reflects the toll taken by the heat, which soaks a man's uniform with sweat, then covers it with dust. The soldier is a survivor if only through the combined strength of man and horse, individual and military unit. Likewise, the men depicted in ***Apache Scouts [113]*** reflect not the paradox of Apache chasing Apache, but the ennui of men relaxing in the shade, waiting for orders. Even the illustrious General Crook, whom Riley pictures riding a mule, has the look of "modesty ... and aversion to pomp and circumstance" that Bourke described in his journal.

I look for the universal viewpoint or mood—some emotion with which the viewer can bond. I don't think I could live with having my art be pure self-indulgence. —KR

88. *The Warriors*
1980
oil, 40 x 24

Of all the Indian tribes, the Mandan impressed me most with their strength, intelligence, determination and spirituality. When I read about their reverence and admiration for the calumet eagle, I felt I had found a symbol that would add strength to this picture of a warrior. Combining the two forms of man and bird created a large irregular shape that dominates the canvas. Everything else in the picture is a foil enhancing the warrior's monumentality.

Riley's narrative works include a series depicting Plains Indians. Initially inspired by the journals of Lewis and Clark, who explored the Missouri River to the Pacific Ocean in 1804–1806, Riley made several research trips into the upper Northwest during the late 1970s. Two memorable adventures included fellow painter Howard Terpning. On the first trip, in 1977, Riley and Terpning flew to Calgary. There artist Harley Brown (1939—) joined them in watching the centennial celebrations commemorating the Treaty Seven site where, in 1877, the Blackfeet Nation, Sarcee, Chippewa and Assiniboine tribes ceded their lands to the Canadians. On the second trip, in 1978, Riley and Terpning followed Lewis and Clark's travels through Montana. They also made a side trip to the Madison River where mountain man Osborne Russell confronted the Blackfeet in an incident Riley read about in Russell's *Journal of a Trapper*.

During his travels Riley studied the journals of two explorer-artists who were the first to travel up the Missouri River: George Catlin (1796–1872) who made several trips between 1830 and 1836, and Karl Bodmer (Swiss,

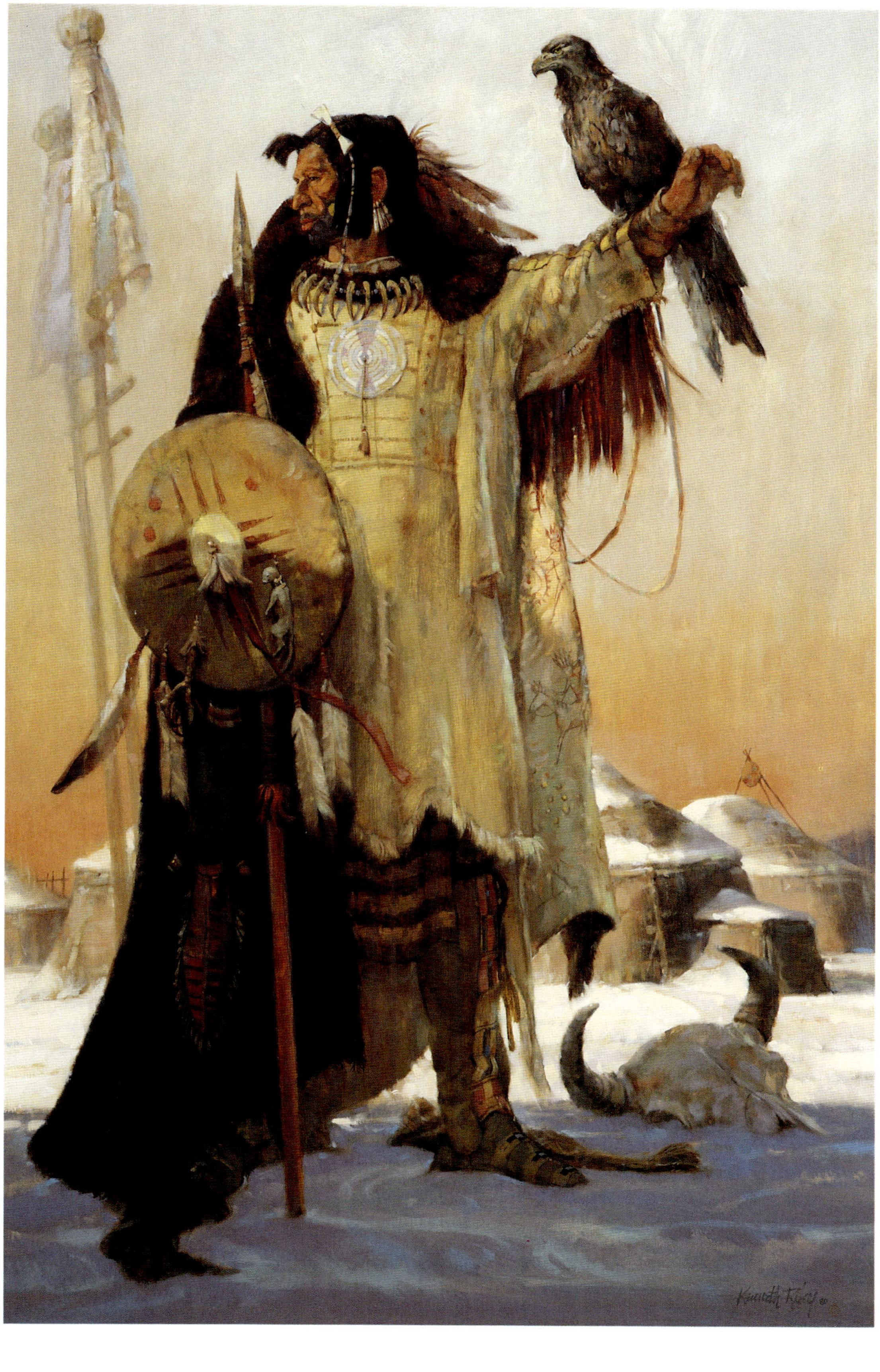

1809–1893) who accompanied amateur naturalist/ethnologist Prince Maximilian von Wied from 1832 to 1834. Both artists left pictorial and written accounts of the people inhabiting the Northern Plains. In particular they described the Mandan, a tribe originally located in present-day North Dakota. The Mandan have become a favorite of Riley's, resulting in several paintings, including four that depict artists Bodmer and Catlin painting portraits of Mandan warriors and chiefs.

While Riley does not go so far as to see this series of paintings as a metaphor for his own role as a historical painter, he and Catlin clearly share a mutual respect for the Mandan culture, most of which was lost to small pox in 1837. "I love the Mandan," echoes Riley. "They were such a pure tribe at the time of contact with the white man. Every part of their costuming was natural and crafted individually. And all the objects they wore were not only decorative but had meaning. When you read Catlin's account you just get wound up in it. Bodmer and Catlin captured the Mandan's statuesque dignity and their aversion to warfare. Those aspects of the tribe appealed to me most."

Tales of Medicine Bags [90] shows Catlin as a small element in the lower right hand corner. Feverishly painting, he is enraptured with the magnificent sight of Mandan Chief Four Bears holding his medicine bag and spear adorned with the scalps of his enemies. Based upon a painting by Bodmer, Riley faithfully renders the interior details of the Mandan lodge. But Riley goes beyond mere documentation. His painting is a study in figure groups whose interaction guides the viewer from Catlin to the far left of the canvas and finally to Four Bears, whose presence as the focus is emphasized by support beams which point directly to him. Described by Catlin, the medicine or "mystery-bag" of the Mandan was "the key to Indian life and Indian character.... Every male in the tribe carries this, his supernatural charm or guardian, to which he looks for the preservation of his life, in battle or in other danger, at which times it would be considered ominous or bad luck and an ill fate to be without it."

Riley's picture of Catlin shows an eery light that pours in from an opening at the top of the Mandan lodge, casting the entire scene in an antique patina, while highlighting the white accent of the buffalo skull atop a pole directly above Four Bears. A somewhat ambiguous symbol, the skull signified to the Indians a rejuvenation of their food source, while to Anglo audiences it has

89. *Crow Chiefs Visit the Minnetarees*
1980
oil, 36 x 60

The Minnetaree Indians were a sedentary tribe living in earthen-lodge villages on the upper Missouri River. As with their neighboring Mandan, the roofs of their lodges were made of thick willow boughs, covered with rock-solid clay. Supported by interior poles, the roof became an "upper deck" where the family could lounge during good weather. Since the Minnetarees were related to the more mobile Crow Indians, the roofs were probably a good place to watch for the relatives to come riding into town.

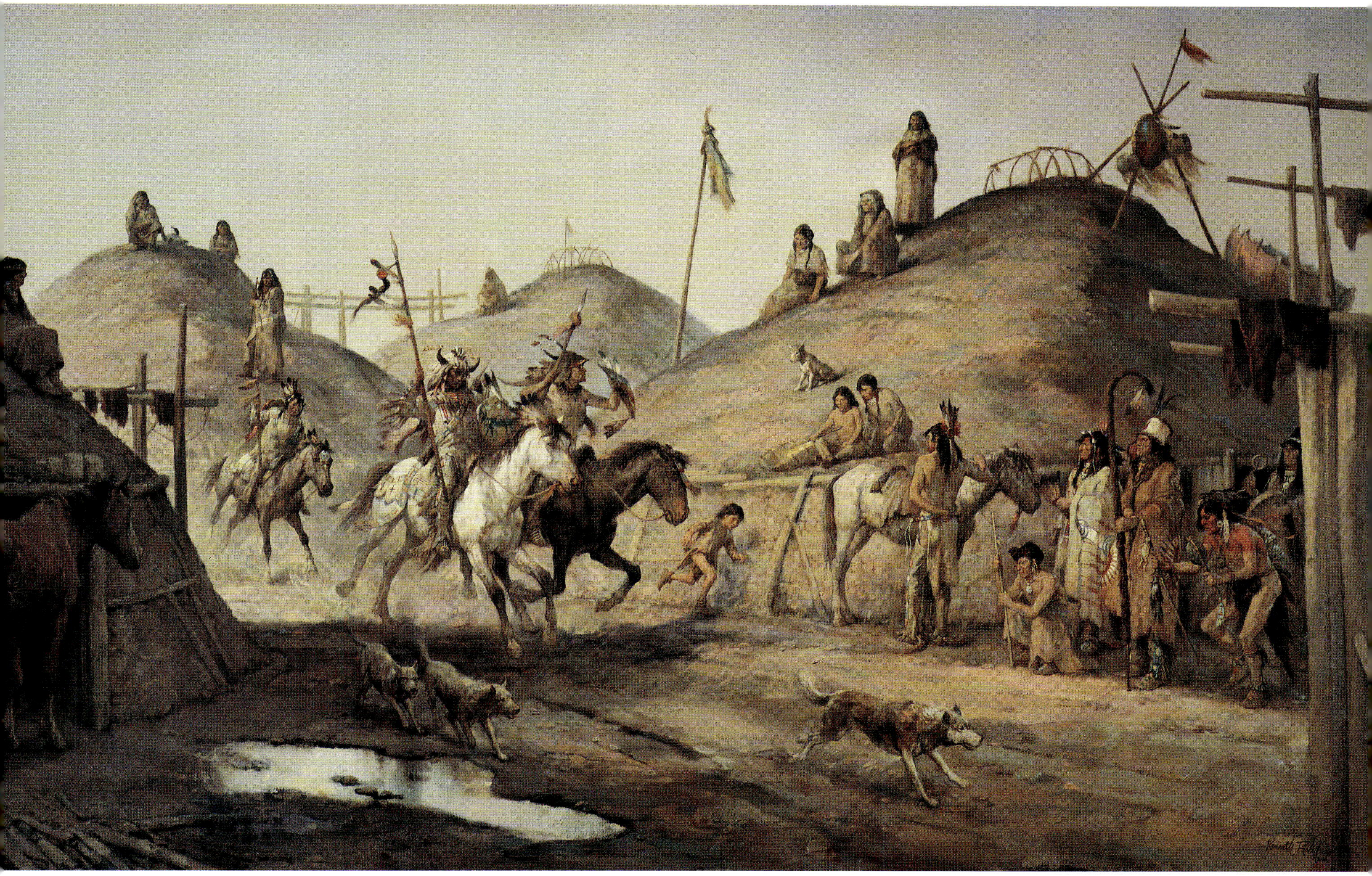

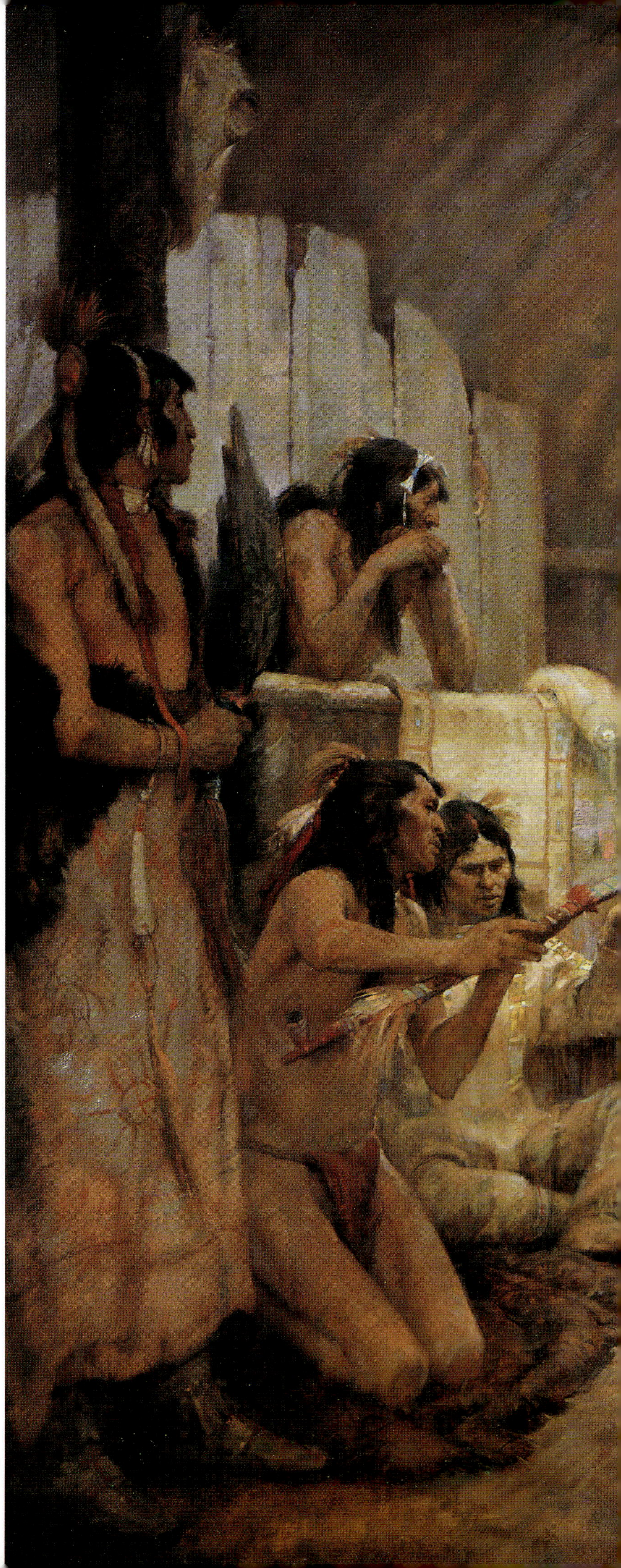

90. *Tales of Medicine Bags*

1980

oil, 30 x 36

When wintry winds howled, the Mandan sought the warmth of the fire pits and the comfort of the communal pipe in their earthen lodges. There, warriors relived tales of horse raids and enemy encounters, or they posed for curious artist-explorers like George Catlin, who lived with the Mandan during the winter of 1833. Impressed by the structure and cleanliness of the lodges, Catlin described the roof support as a place to hang everything from medicine bags to war clubs. Atop it, a buffalo skull was placed "as if by some conjuror or Indian magician, to guard and protect the spell of wildness that reigns in this strange place."

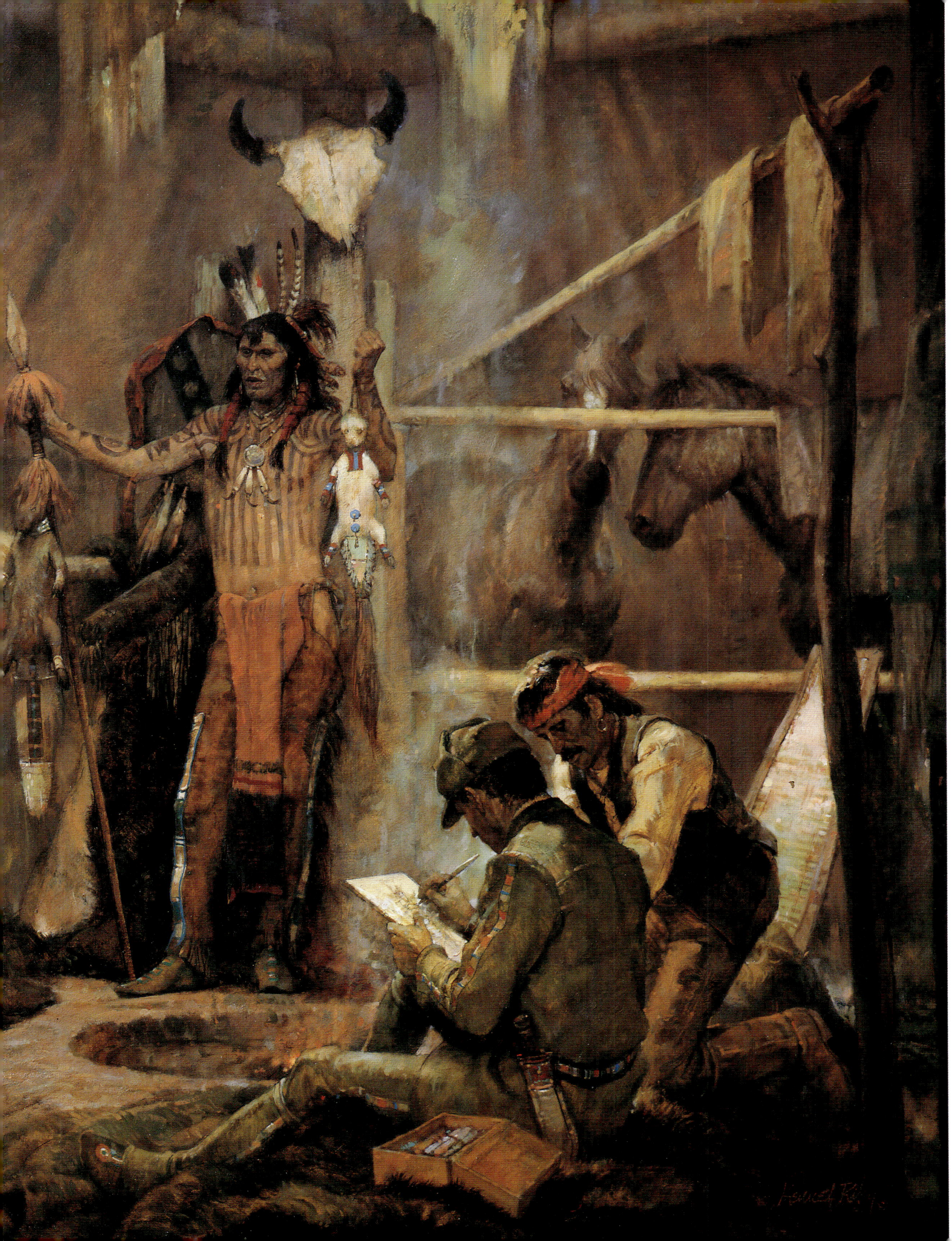

91. *You Take What's Issued*
1983
oil, 16 x 24

Stories abound about unscrupulous horse dealers who were well-paid by the government for pawning off less-than-desirable animals. One can only hope that the heart is bigger than the chest of this poor animal. In many ways, it was the heart and health of horses that won the West.

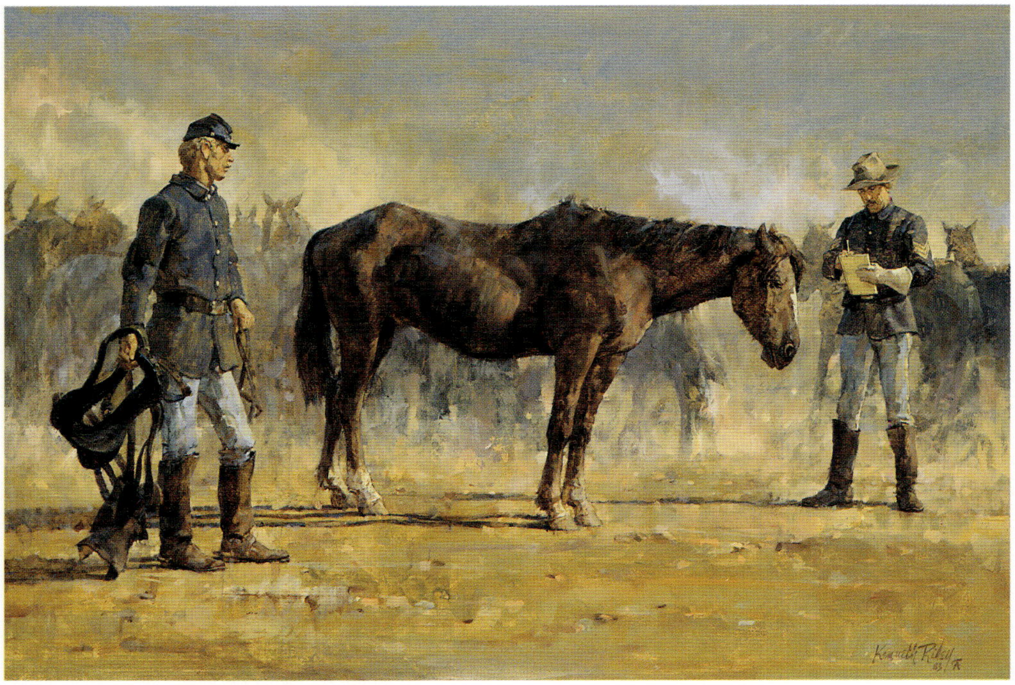

alternatively been used to represent the extermination of the buffalo herds (and Indians) as well as the freedom of the pre-reservation Indian. Riley has no doubt used it here as a reminder of the fate of the Mandan tribe whose collective magic, in the end, was unable to save them.

Two paintings done in 1983 reflect Riley's evolving desire to turn the facts of Mandan history into symbols of the demise of a lifeway. In ***Visit of Lewis and Clark [54],*** Riley drew upon the explorers' journals which outlined an encounter with the Mandan in October 1804. Still attached to the narrative, Riley has shown Lewis and Clark as small figures moving up a hill to meet with the Indians. But it is not the meeting that Riley is concerned with here. Rather, it is the Mandan tribe represented by the figures on the left, who are compressed into a shallow foreground space commanding our attention. The three warriors, who form a sequential movement from kneeling to standing, merge into a fourth, hydra-like shape. This fourth figure brandishes a spear, lifts a ceremonial rattle and displays a peace pipe. The fate of this "warrior, supplicant and negotiator" is spelled out in the buffalo skull at the bottom left and the ant-like intruders on the right who represent the trickling source of a never-ending stream of conquerors.

In ***In the Mandan Lodge of Four Bears [92]*** the narrative is again overtaken by a selection of objects that reflect the Mandan's fate. Painted in

92. *In the Mandan Lodge of Four Bears*
1983
oil, 50 x 36

According to Catlin, the most prestigious part of the Mandan warrior's dress was the tail of a war eagle or juvenile golden eagle which "conquers all the other birds in the country." Also known as the calumet eagle, the tail feathers were dyed red and used to ornament pipes. The shape of these stunning fantails was the inspiration for this portrait of Chief Four Bears whose headdress of ermine tails and buffalo horn signifies his importance.

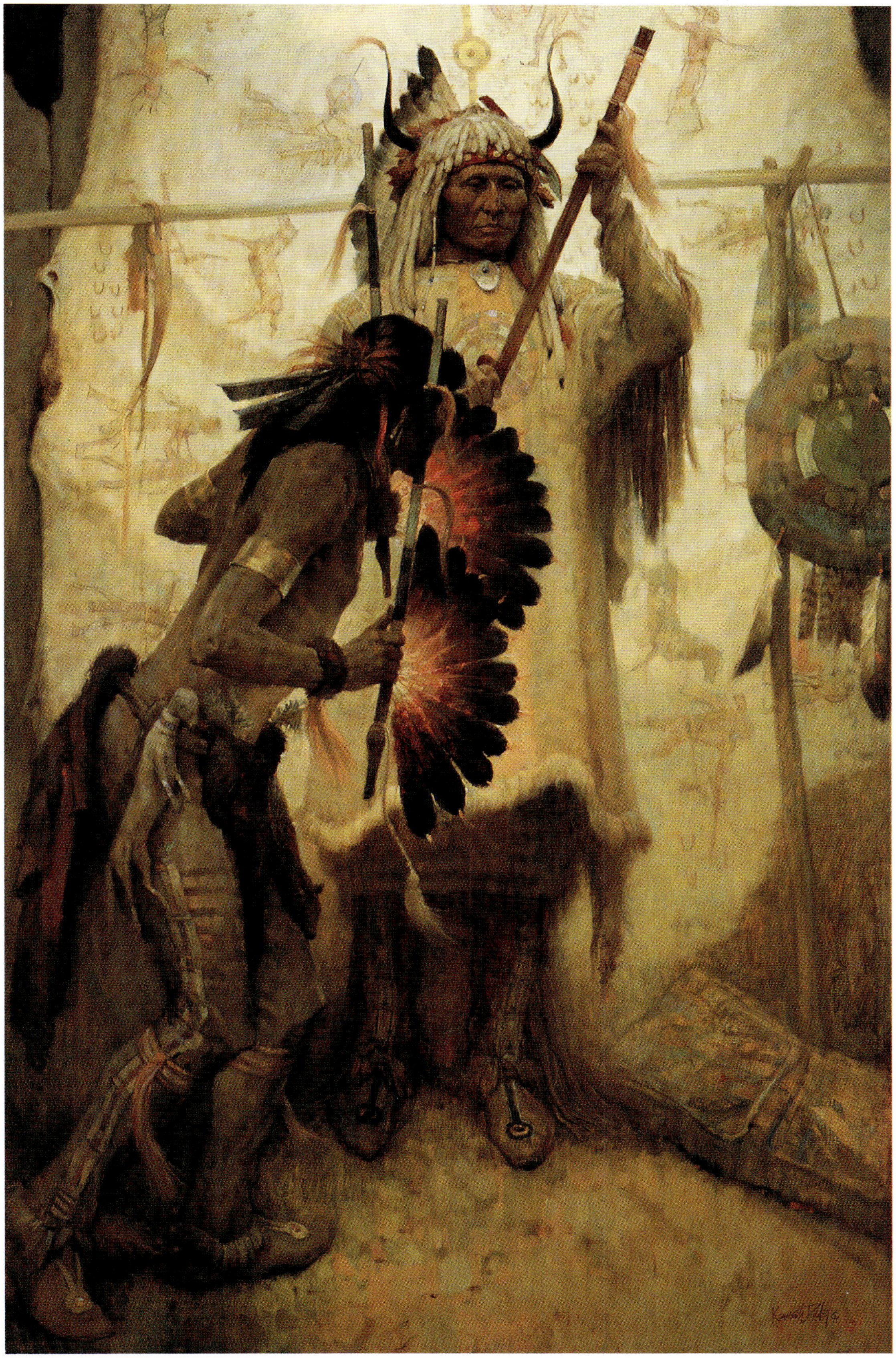

haunting, somber tones, the image shows Four Bears in his finest regalia sandwiched between a robe depicting his victories and a medicine man whose eagle-fan calumets glow with a supernatural light while he chants a song of healing. "I was concerned with the monumental quality," says Riley. "By positioning the foreground figure so he rises into Four Bears I created a much longer, more monumental vision of the man."

"Monumental" is the key to how Riley comes to view the Mandan experience. In 1984, he painted ***Mandan Gold [86],*** which won the gold medal in oil and the Best of Show at the CAA exhibition, and ***Wood Gatherers of Mih-Tutta-Hang-Kusch [93].*** These two paintings show in very divergent ways the monumental quality of which Riley speaks. In ***Wood Gatherers***, which was based upon a painting and several drawings by Bodmer, Riley offers a scene that looks like a chapter from the history of medieval Europe. Prince Maximilian had been particularly impressed with the weight of the bundles and described in detail how a woman laid down on a bound pile of wood, strapped it across her back with tethers, then was helped up by another woman. Quite unlike Bodmer's painting which diminishes the size of the figures in relationship to the landscape, Riley has turned the women laborers into the focus of the work. Bent under the weight of their burdens, they tend to their duties like oxen in yokes. Riley does not pity them, however. Instead, he salutes their tenacity. The wood gatherer who stands before us, her staff forming a cross against the wood bundle, is both an individual and a symbol of the dignity of laborers throughout the ages. Though she turns her gaze away, we embrace her in warm, earthen tones that entice us into the frigid winter scene.

Mandan Gold reduces the tribal experience to two figures juxtaposed as if they are united in mass and in thought. Draped over the standing figure's outstretched arm is a buffalo robe whose decoration radiates like the rays of the sun. The entire painting is suffused with a celestial light that permeates the standing figure. The figures are compressed into a narrow stage that is further delimited by the lances and by a series of repeating circles that cadence upward from the war shield at the bottom, into the face and upper shield, on to the quillwork decoration, bear-claw necklace and earring, and finally into the implied circle of the sun. This is a full-circle painting of death to eternal life, giving substance to Catlin's lament: "The tribe of red men of

93. *Wood Gatherers of Mih-Tutta-Hang-Kusch*
1984
oil, 24 x 42

In mid-winter when the Missouri River froze deep, Mandan women crossed to the other side to forage for food and wood. The women's role in sustaining the tribe was not much different from that of the women MarCyne and I have encountered on our travels into Third World countries. Whatever their burden, they convey themselves with dignity and pride.

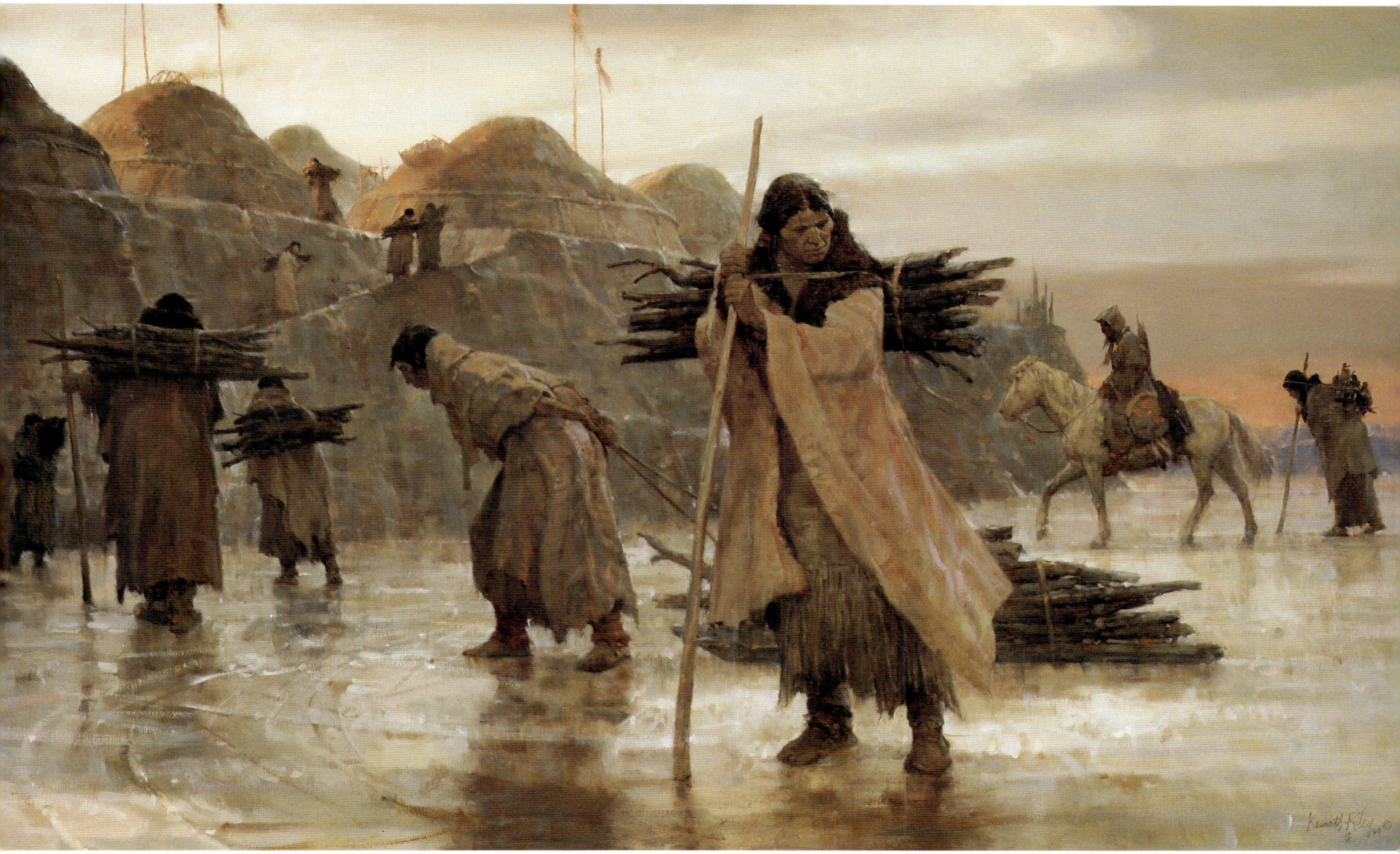

North America, as a nation of human beings, are on their wane; that (to use their own beautiful figure) 'they are fast traveling to the shades of their fathers, towards the setting sun.'"

Significantly, when Riley returned to his artists series in 1986, his approach to the narrative was very different. ***Bodmer Paints the Piegan Chief [6],*** which is in the permanent collection of the Phoenix Art Museum, reduces the number of figures and increases their scale in relationship to the picture space. Recession into the log building is held in check by the robe behind Iron Shirt, a Piegan Blackfeet Chief whose countenance and dress are taken directly from Bodmer's portrait. The composition zigzags from the still life of the painter's gear in the foreground, up to Bodmer and over to Iron Shirt, to whom Riley has given a pensive, vacant expression that noticeably contrasts with Bodmer's animated gestures. The resignation of the standing figure who looks down to Bodmer redirects our empathy to Iron Shirt. Riley shows us the "god of a nation" to whom Bodmer appears to be paying homage. The depiction of this "recording ritual" catapults both Bodmer and Iron Shirt into the realm of legendary heroes, to whom Riley himself pays respect.

History Painting as Allegory

"Art is a universal language because it is the expression of the feelings of man.... When you're painting a picture you are not defining a form but symbolizing an idea." —Harvey Dunn

94. *Cochise*
1984
oil, 48 x 40

There is no known photo or portrait of this famed Chiricahua leader who tried to accommodate and make peace with the whites. Falsely accused of kidnapping, Cochise and his family were placed under arrest in January 1861. When Cochise escaped to his stronghold in the Dragoon Mountains, he triggered the Apache Wars which were the scourge of Arizona territory for years. To stand at Cochise's mountain hideaway is to begin visualizing events that took place 130 years ago.

Though Cochise was one of the first western heroes Riley encountered both in his reading and in the landscape surrounding his Tombstone home, he did not paint a portrait of the man until 1985, in a work simply titled ***Cochise [94].*** The term "portrait" is a misnomer, however. For Cochise is not a real person in Riley's painting but an archetype whose values are the antithesis of settled America.

The irony of Cochise's sincere attempt to make peace in the face of an unjustified accusation of kidnapping adds to the perplexing combination of good and evil that he came to represent in Elliott Arnold's novel *Blood Brother.* Riley's painting, which was used on the cover of a recent edition of the story, reflects this betrayed honor. Cochise appears as a horseman at

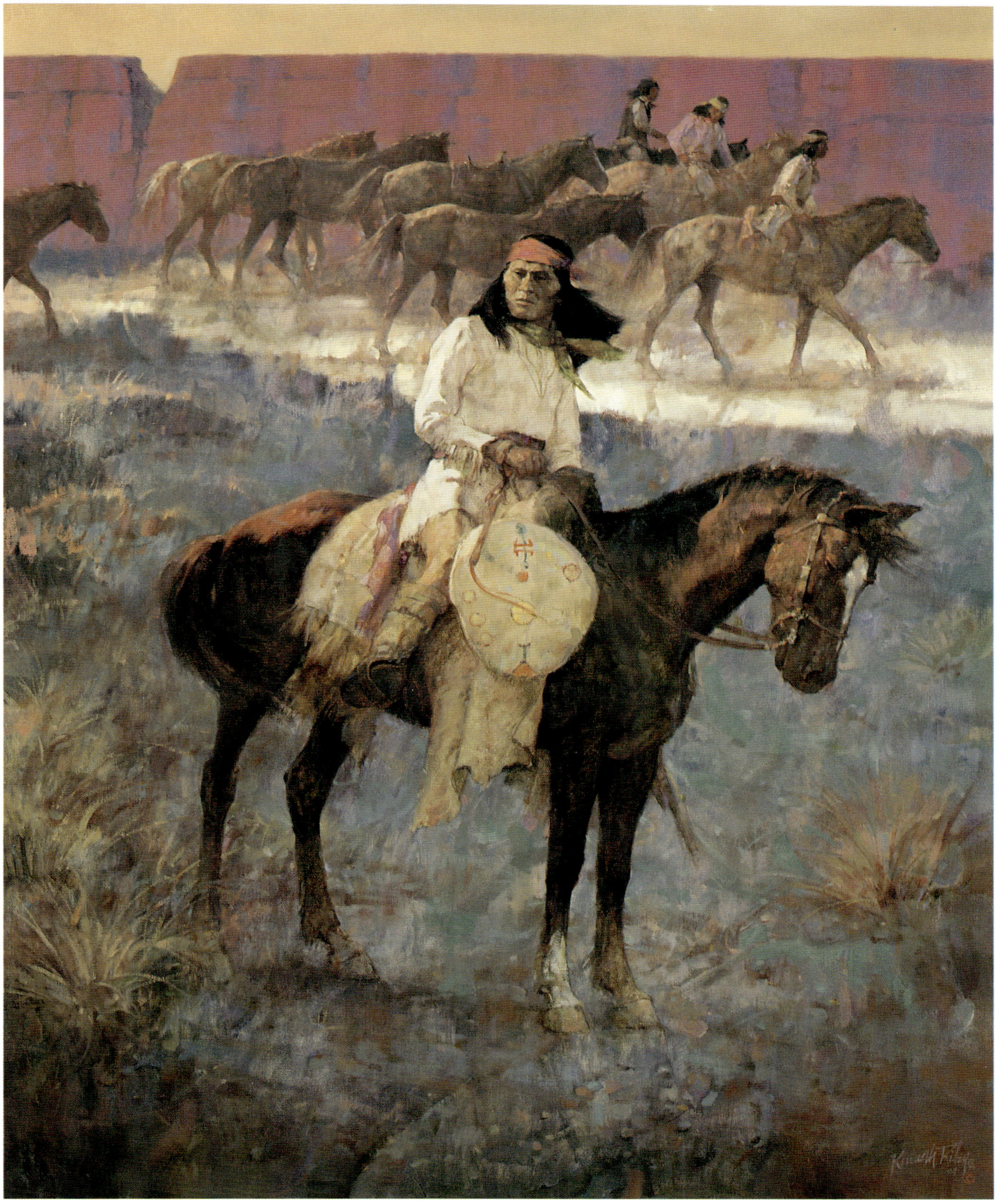

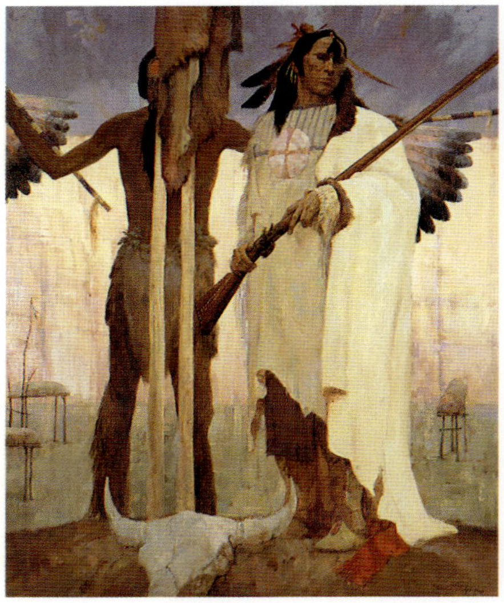

95. *Ancestors,* 1985, acrylic, 48 x 40.

the center of a tapestry of colors, from jade-green grasses to blood-red mesa to pale-orange sky. Soberly staring into the distance, his face is empty of emotion. Behind him, as if issuing from the depths of his memory, horses run free, led by warriors who dissolve into a band of white light. The wind blows hair and manes, body and soul, in the direction of disintegration. Cochise, who managed to evade the eye of the camera as he did the scrutiny of the cavalry, symbolizes a nation of people who could not cope with the paradox of being "given" lands they had long called home. Freed from the unknown details of Cochise's face, Riley gives artistic vision to the mythology of a nation.

"Freed from the details," as far as Riley is concerned, tops the list of the Artist's Bill of Rights. While he insists upon knowing as much about his subjects as possible, he refuses to be a slave to the particulars. "I don't tie myself to an object," he says. "I want to be able to enlarge or diminish—to play with the colors and shapes on my own terms. I do a lot of reading and looking in museums with the goal of absorbing what is there. Then I let it come out, not as ethnological re-creation but as an aesthetic statement."

The allegorical possibilities of the objects that make up the pageant of the West have always held a fascination for Riley. In ***Ancestors [95],*** for example, the slender poles of distant Mandan burial scaffolds appear like hieroglyphs etched on an ancient white wall. The vertical standards form a motif exaggerated in two foreground poles which hold back the specter of a ghost whose embrace gathers a warrior into the shroud of eternity. "The painting is allegorical," wrote Riley in the 1986 NAWA catalog. "The burial scaffolds in the background represent his lineage to that point in time when he symbolically becomes the last of his people."

Many of Riley's paintings focus on lineage and on the continuum of humanity that links one generation to the next, one tribe to another, the earliest culture to our most recent. A painting titled ***Sisters [96],*** for instance, was created around the "continuity of a culture—the tie between people of the past and present." Simplifying the idea down to two women, one looking backward, the other to the future, Riley mingles yesterday, today and tomorrow in a darkly flowing river of memory that forms a third element in the center of the painting. The cool and warm colors on either side represent, he says, "the passage of time." Tranquil and mysterious, ***Sisters*** is a hypnotic meditation

96. *Sisters*
1987
oil, 42 x 36

The term "global humanity" has almost become a cliché these days. Nevertheless, the concept behind it—that we are all linked not only to the planet but to past and future generations—has validity. This painting was an attempt to portray that linkage within the context of time. I used the same model for a mid-1800s Native American woman and her present-day self. The dark, abstract shape separates and joins these women in an eternal bond.

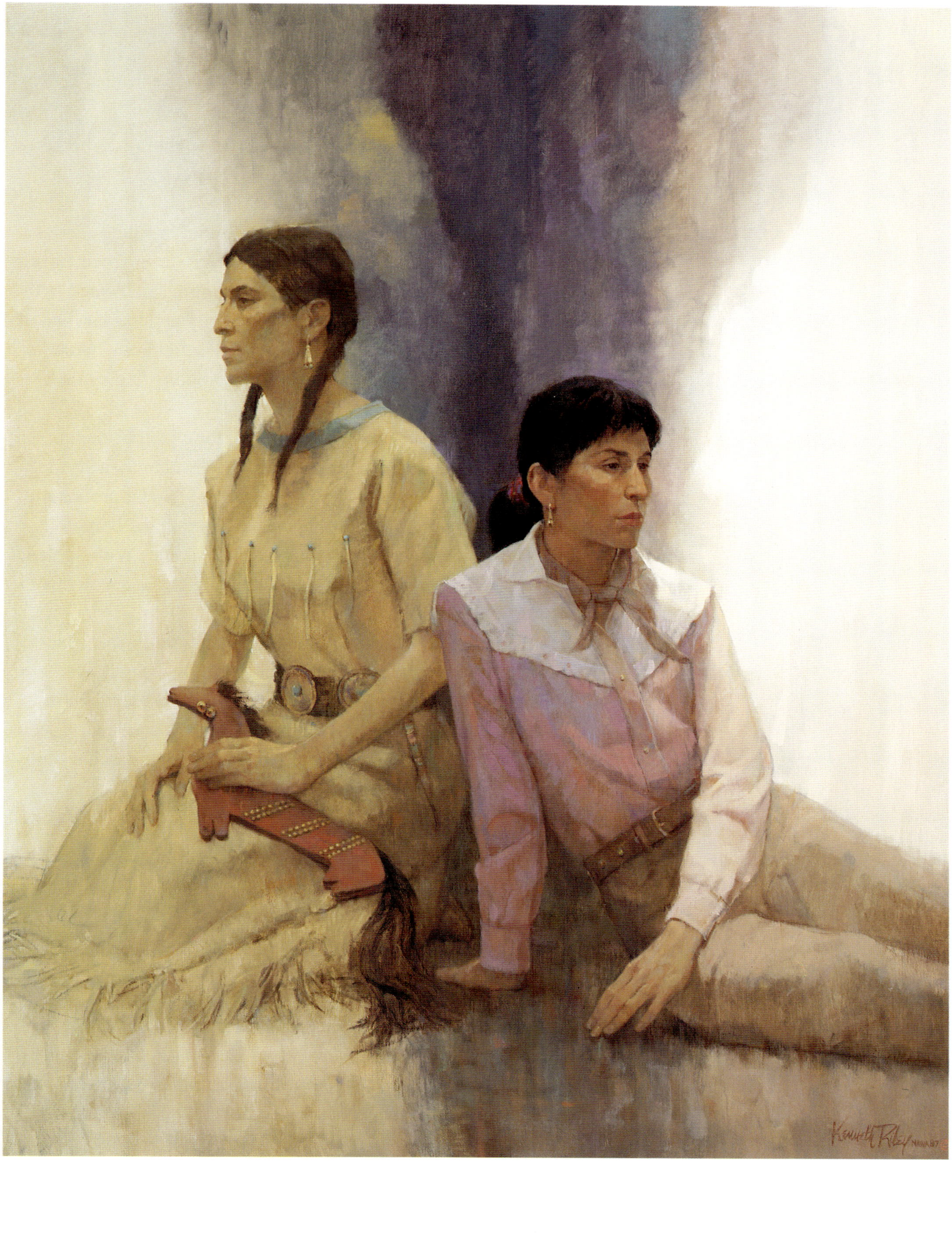

97. *General Crook and Geronimo*
1983
oil, 24 x 42

When it came to "media mentality," Cochise and Geronimo would seem to have been a breed apart: Cochise was never photographed, while Geronimo was photographed so many times that his face is familiar to one and all. Geronimo's capture was in the hands of General Crook who, along with two companies of Apache scouts and one company of white soldiers, went into the Sierra Madre of northern Mexico in pursuit of the renegades in the winter of 1886. After several skirmishes they caught up with the Apache leader and a one–on–one meeting was arranged. The agreement dissolved when an American bootlegger sold Geronimo $30 worth of liquor and he fled with twenty warriors, women and children.

on the cycles of history—cycles that Riley describes as "calming ... the same things have taken place for centuries. They occur over and over again, but with each one we build gradually to a higher state."

The timelessness of the women in ***Sisters*** has a parallel in Riley's series on the peasant women he and MarCyne have encountered during their travels. Influenced in no small way by MarCyne's series of paintings dedicated to the role of Third World women in the morality of community and the survival of culture, Riley has painted the women of Mexico, Bolivia and Peru. Most often he shows them in market situations where they proudly display their craftsmanship and produce.

The objects in ***The Witches Market, Bolivia [14],*** for example, are no doubt critical to the medicine-woman who sells them. Even in their panoply of shapes and colors, however, they are incidental to the stalwart profile and massive form of the seated figure whose shape is repeated in the bundles behind her and in the arrangement of the crates in front of her. With her hand officiously holding a cane, this woman has all the stature of the queen of England and the perpetuity of the Great Earth Mother.

Oaxaca Market, Mexico [84] similarly monumentalizes a flower seller whose form is elongated by merging into two other figures—possibly a daughter and mother—in a unit similar to that used in the Mandan paintings. Like a saint in a Mexican shrine, the standing figure holds a bouquet on each side. It is as though we are viewing an altar dedicated to a matriarchal trinity out of which the world spreads in a whirlwind of canopies whose triangular shapes capture the eternal breezes.

The curious combination of figures in ***Pisac Market, Peru [98]*** offers a similar commentary on the pageant of life. The peasant couple in the shadow of a wall that has seen many white-washings are of the here-and-now. Solid and complacent, their rosy-pink costumes merge with the reddish under-painting of the turquoise doorway through which we witness an event in a blaze of sunlight. The ambiguous figure in a long, dark dress appears to be from another culture and time. Like an apparition, she floats among the vendors silhouetted against a light that shatters into prisms of pink and pale-yellow. Of his and MarCyne's 1981 trip to this market, Riley recalls that they were "thrust into it and seemed to become a part of it all." The painting is a record of personal experience, projected through the lens of time and memory.

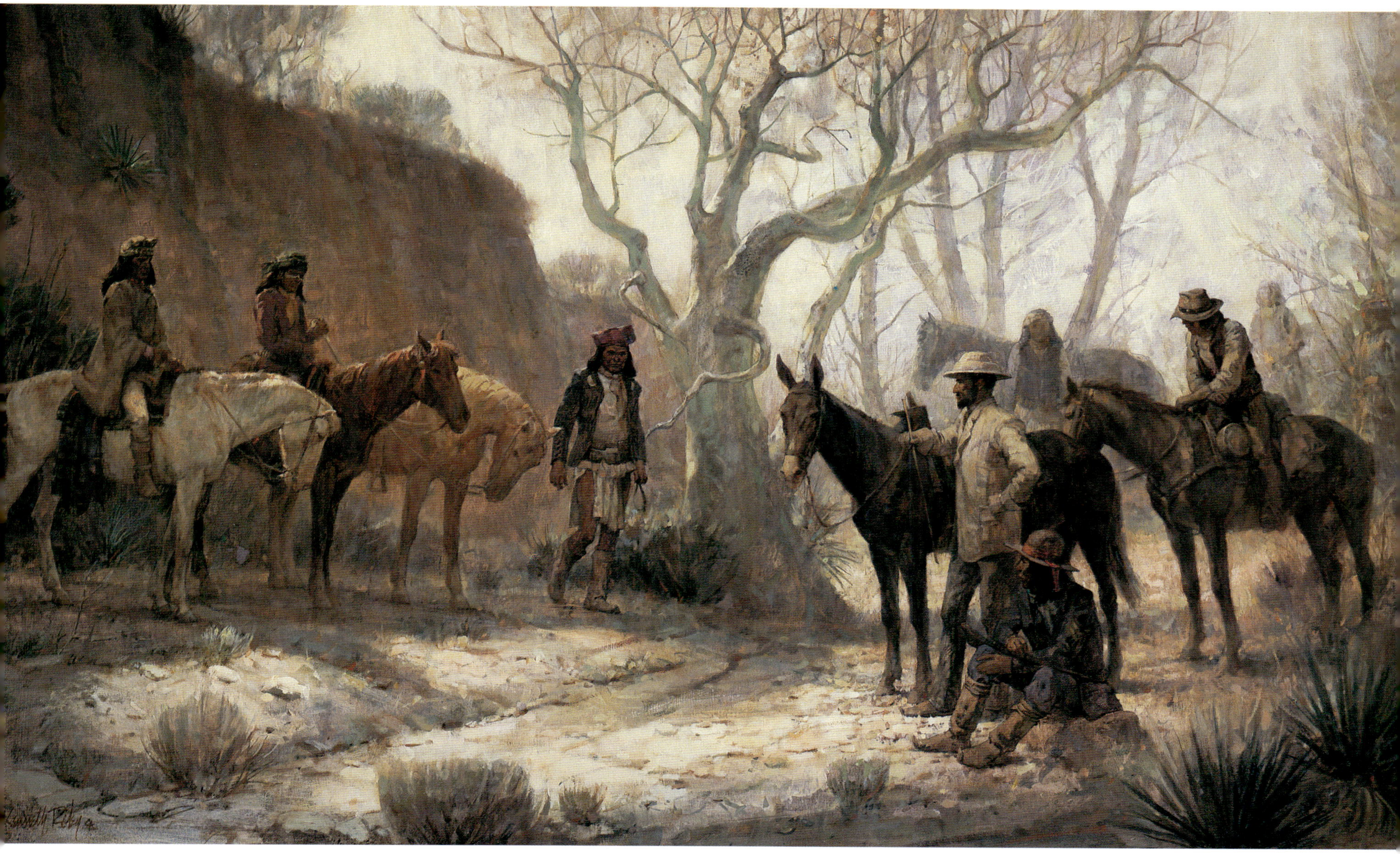

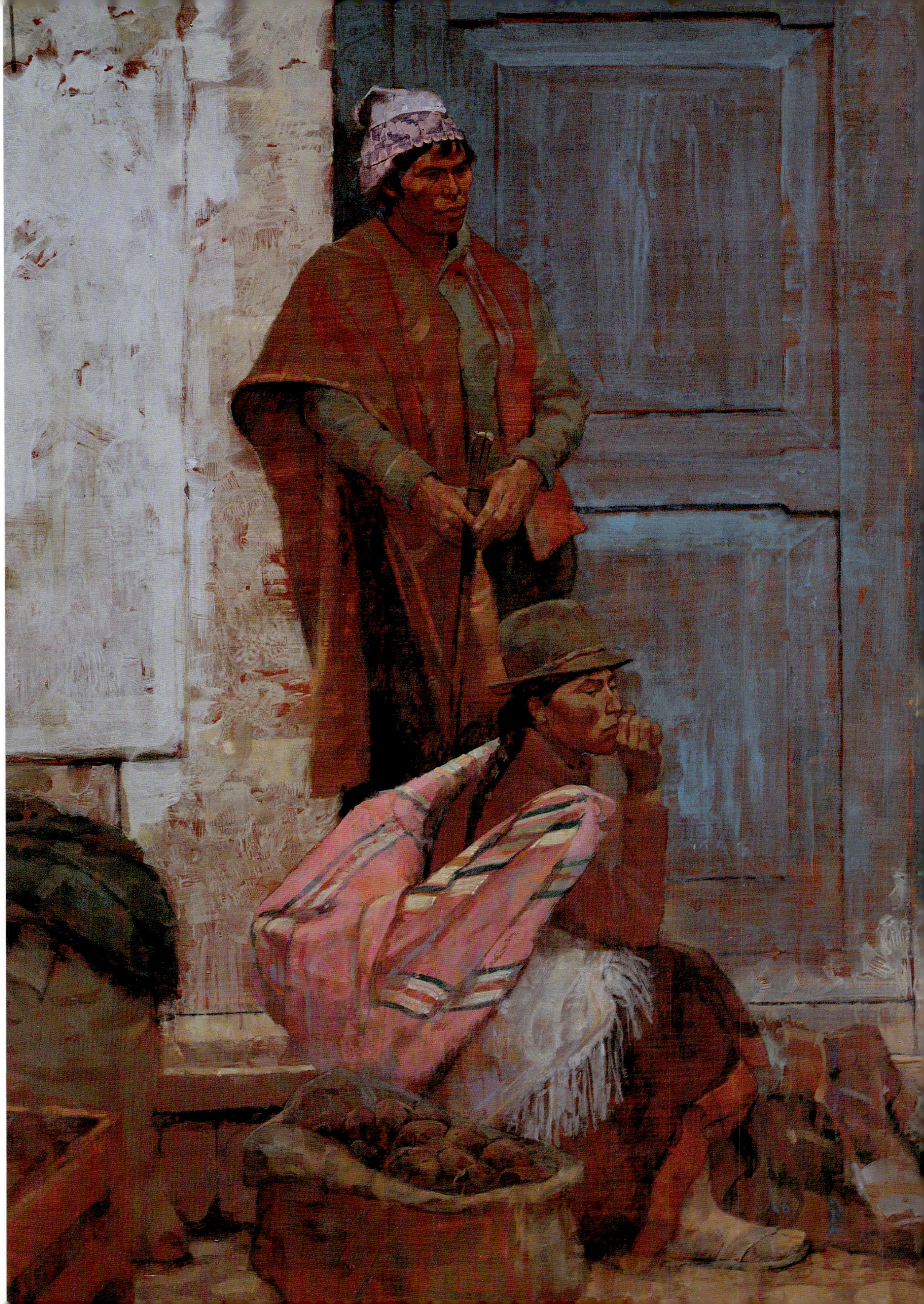

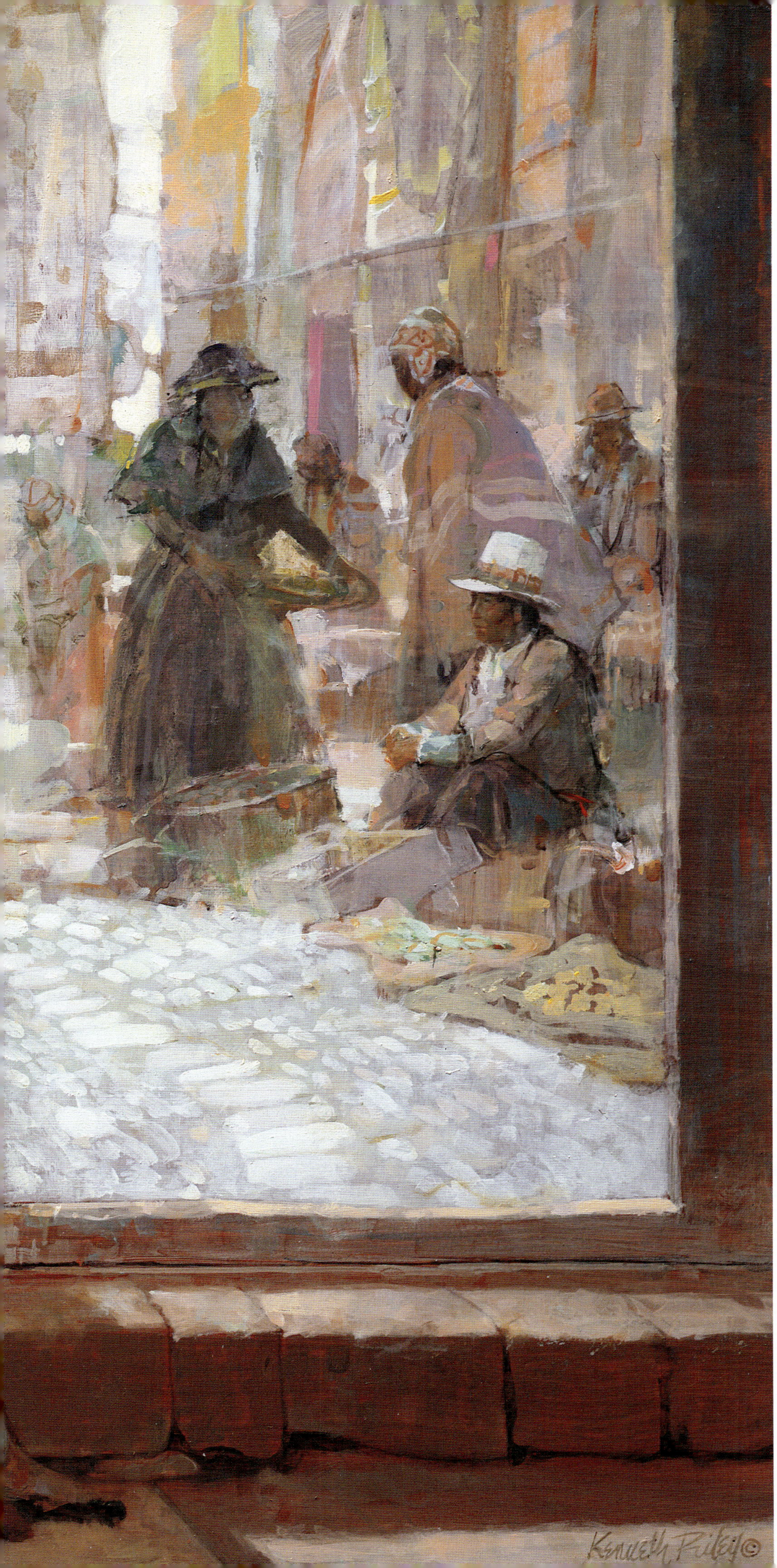

98. *Pisac Market, Peru*

1982

acrylic/oil, 24 x 30

We had planned our 1981 trip to Peru around attending this once-a-week event. But as luck would have it our flight from Lima to Cuzco was delayed several days. When we finally took off it was the morning of the market itself. As soon as we landed we hired a car and drove into a kaleidoscope of colors and sounds. People streamed into the plaza dressed in the various styles of the surrounding communities. With them they brought handwoven fabrics, pottery, crafts and produce of all kinds. Since it was a fairly small plaza, we were thrust into the melee of activity, sensing we had somehow become a part of it all.

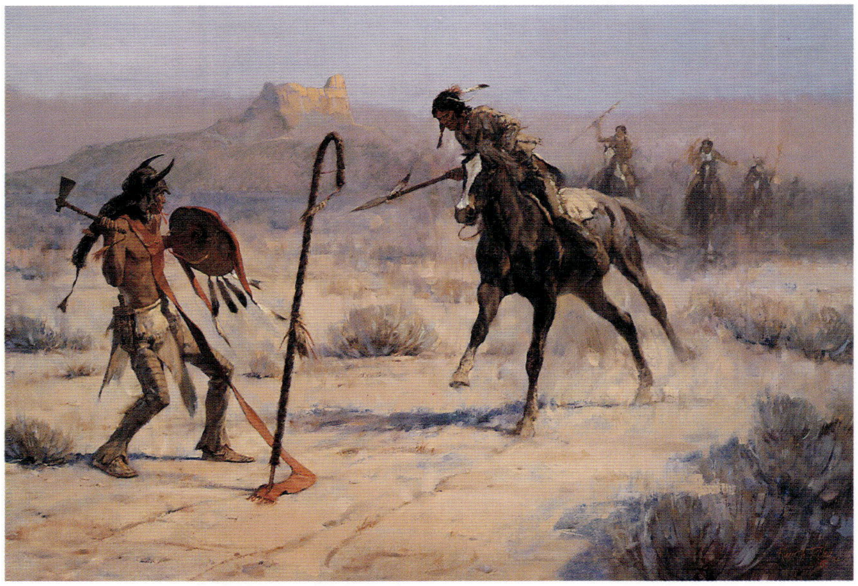

99. *Staked Out*
1981
oil, 24 x 36

In a final act of bravery, a Plains Indian warrior pins his sash to the ground with his lance, prepared to fight. Many tribes had warrior societies whose code of honor included care for the community and, if necessary, the sacrifice of a warrior's life to save that of his fellows.

100. *Gathering of Eagles*
1990
oil, 42 x 50

George Catlin was one of the more sympathetic of the early Indian observers. He lived with and wrote extensively about the fair-skinned, light-haired Mandan, believing them to have descended from a group of early Welsh explorers. The friendly treatment Catlin received from the Mandan corroborated his "fixed belief that the North American Indian in his primitive state is a high-minded, hospitable and honorable being."

The correspondences Riley finds between cultures and times are viewed in an unabashedly romantic light. "I look at history through rose-colored glasses," he says. "I see it all in a positive way." The pinks, blues, beiges and whites that swirl and dance in the painting titled ***Camelot [4]*** are an excellent example of what he means. "The parallels between the elaborate costumes, bannered lances and decorated horses of the Native American and the fabled Knights of the Roundtable inspired this work," he says. Richly embroidered, ***Camelot*** is fact and myth interwoven into the fabric of history.

History Painting as Poetry

If we were to categorize Riley's narrative works as time-specific history and the allegorical works as timeless mythology, then the third category could easily be called eternal poetry. A poem, writes Lynn Alterbernd, is "not an idea carried in a basket woven of sentences. It is an organism whose substance does not exist separate from the shape that it has."

The third Idea that motivates Riley to paint has little to do with a place on a map or a moment in time. Rather it emerges from his years of picture-making and is intrinsic to the process itself—namely, the challenge to make art about art. "Ignoring the subject matter altogether in my works, the paintings are intended to be exciting compositions and arrangements," he says. "Their value is not in the external image but in what I've brought to the

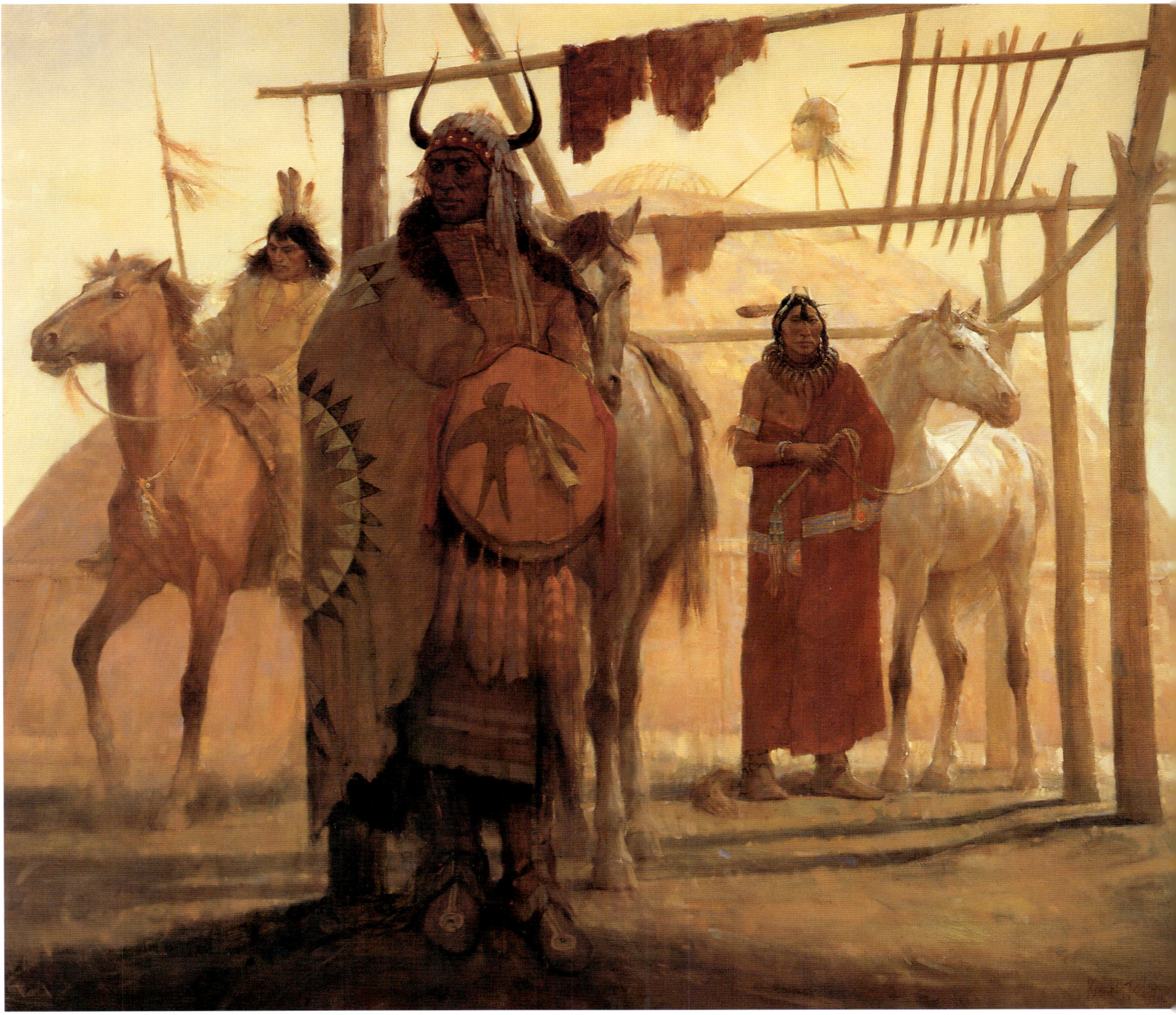

two-dimensional surface in terms of form, light, line, color and every combination thereof."

The integrity of the two-dimensional surface—the flat rectangle that is completely under control of the artist—is important in all of Riley's paintings and paramount in this third realm. "Everything becomes a design tool," he explains. "Manipulating viewers is what art is all about ... and of course, it is the artist's goal to manipulate them in his favor!" While relying upon his standard repertoire of people, landscape, animals and artifacts, the inspiration for these paintings is more conceptual than perceptual. They also share an unnatural (even anti-natural) space and an inventive utilization of negative shapes which become as important as the positives. Colors are subjective, chosen less for their fidelity to reality than for their ability to evoke a mood. And the light typically emanates not only from an outside source but seemingly from within the painting itself.

One of the earliest paintings driven primarily by abstract compositional elements is ***Shadows [102]*** done in 1983. Recalls Riley, "I was going through the photographs I had taken at the Treaty Seven site when I came across one of a tepee decorated with this big abstraction of an antelope. The shape triggered the entire painting. I started playing with it, asking myself what other shapes would complement and enhance it. The repeating pattern at the bottom of the tepee adds a rhythm to the static scene, while the grazing horse is a downward balance complementing the antelope's neck. The figure was added to stop or anchor the three triangles found in the overall tepee shape, the sunlit portion of the tepee, and the figure and horse. I loved cutting off the top of the tepee, creating the inverted triangles in the corners. The lances repeat the larger triangular shape in a more complete context."

The mood of ***Shadows*** is one of serenity and formal harmony. In it one senses a classical order that resists identification with any particular place or time. A sequel to ***Shadows*** was created four years later when Riley submitted ***The Red Tepee [108]*** to the 1987 CAA exhibition, for which he won a silver medal. Nominally inspired by the mention of a red tepee owned by the Comanche-Kiowa Chief Satanta, who fought in the Red River War of 1874–75, the painting is an exercise in triangular shapes and colors. "The goal was solidity," says Riley. "I wanted to show the three forms in a monumental, solid way. But the red color, as it always does, kept advancing in the

101. *Power of the Shield*
1991
oil, 48 x 36

A warrior's shield was an object of accumulative power and spirituality. Its design and colors were usually revealed in a vision. The objects attached to it had personal meaning and were viewed as "medicine" that would protect the owner from harm in combat. In religious ceremonies the shield's power was reflected in its circular shape which symbolized the eternal continuity of life.

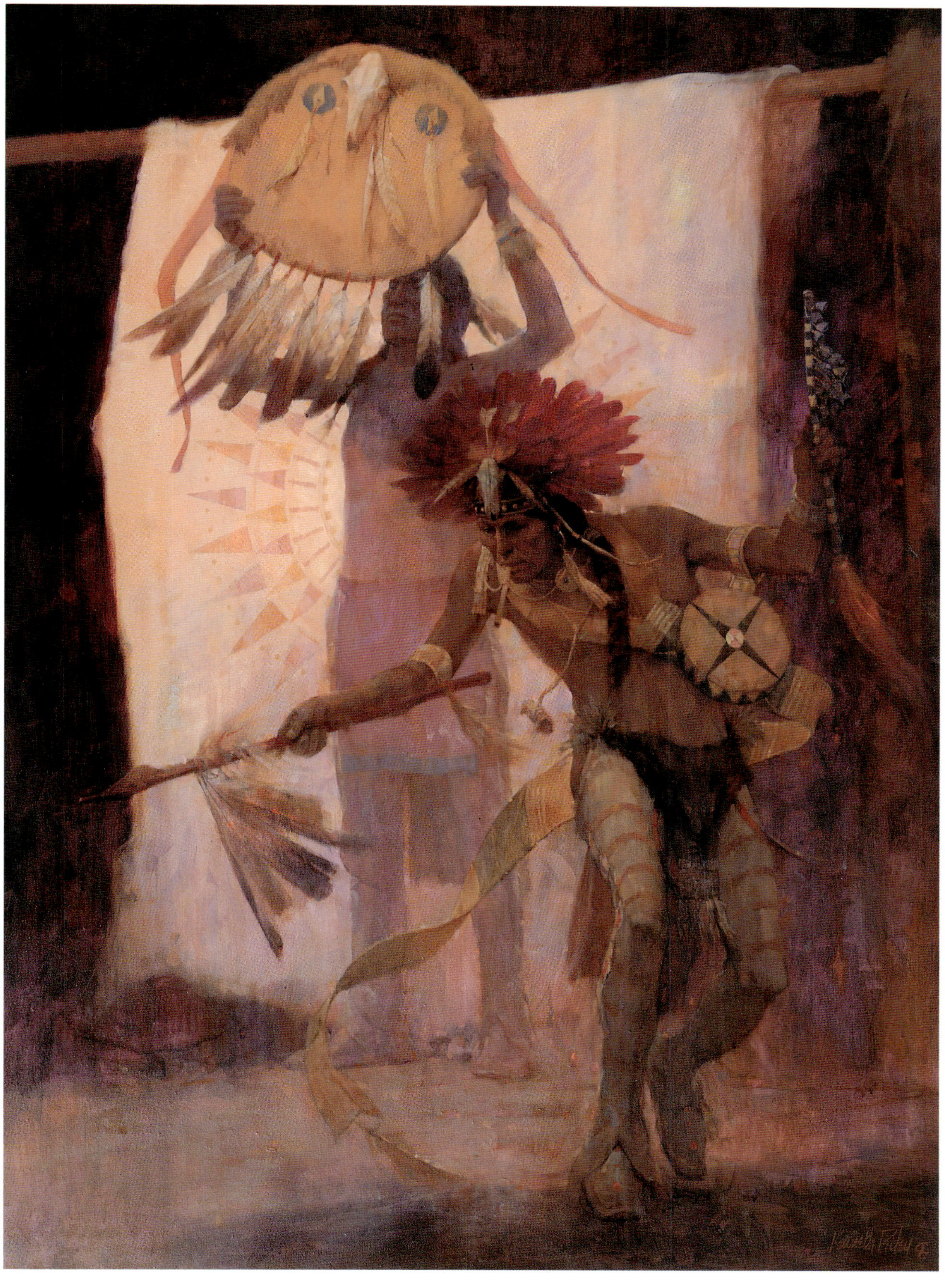

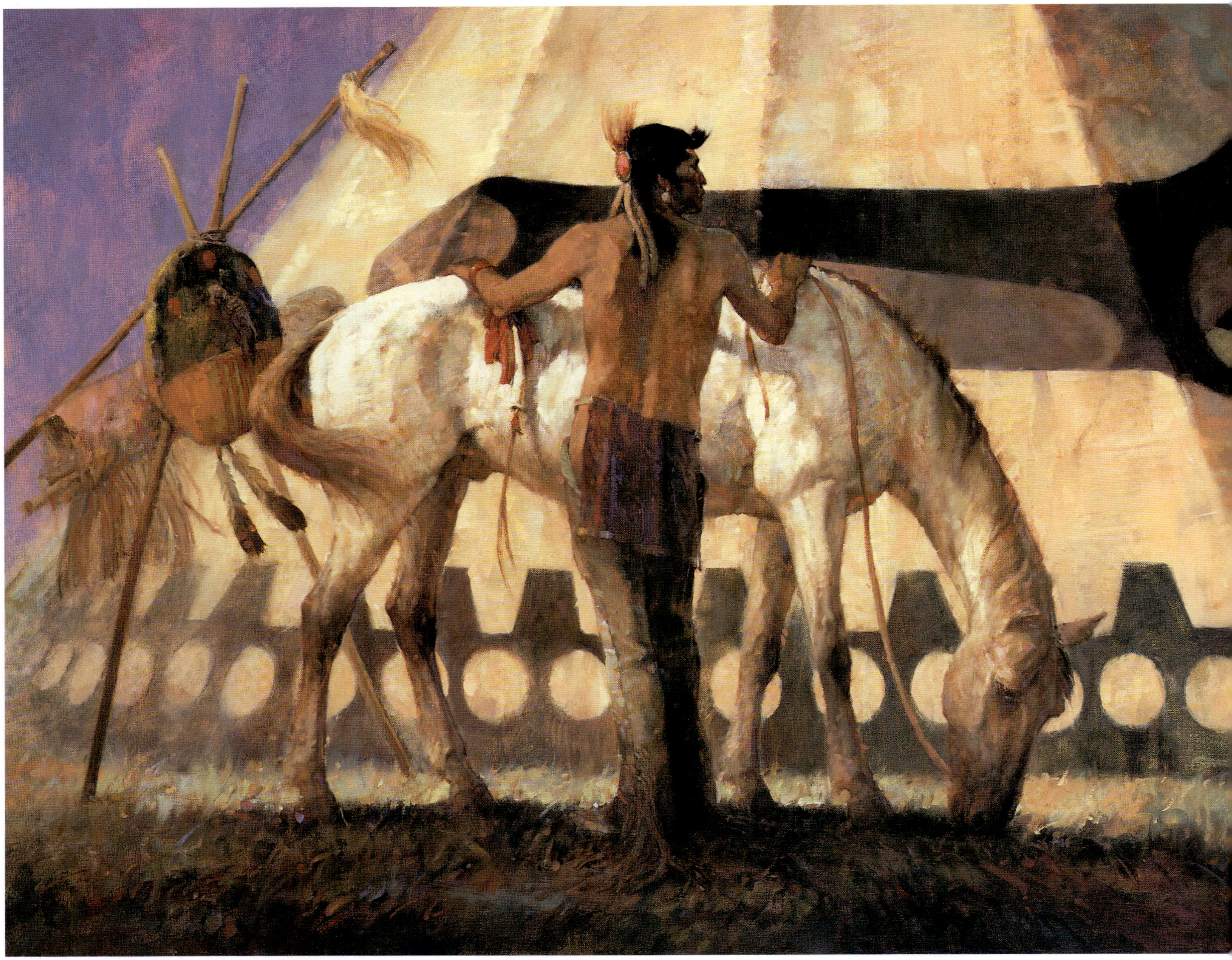

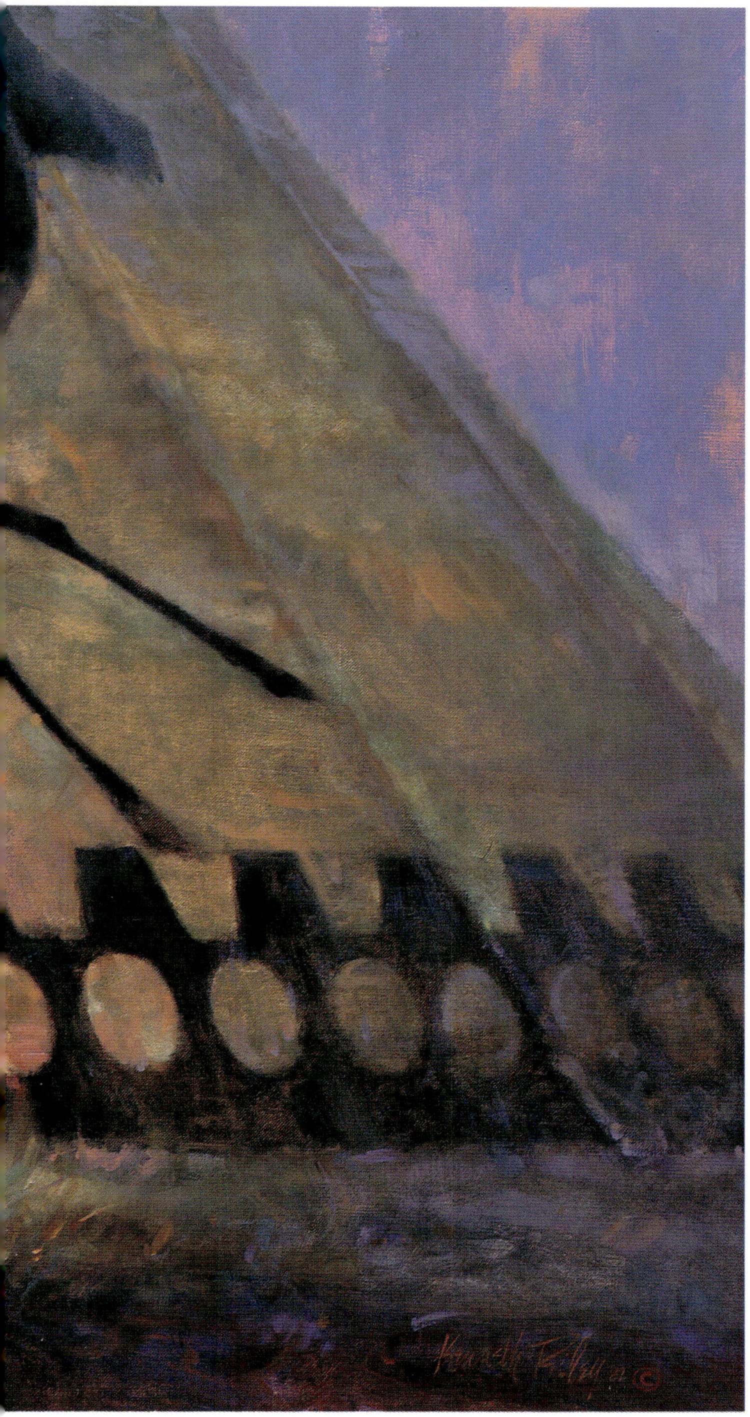

102. *Shadows*

1982

oil, 25 x 48

The Plains Indian aesthetic of appropriateness to purpose and harmony could be found in their tepee decorations which often showed large symbolic shapes, such as this antelope, against smaller, busier shapes at the base of the tepee. The inspiration for this work was a Blackfeet example I had seen at the Treaty Seven site in British Columbia. With his mode of transportation, this Plains Indian lords over his castle, just as a modernday suburbanite might oversee the car parked in his driveway.

space and I wanted it to recede. The challenge was to find the combination of cool, bluish-reds that would make the tepee stay in place."

The inverted triangular shapes which balanced in the corners of ***Shadows*** are here replaced by a more active upper register broken into inverted triangles that contrast with the restful horizontal baseline paralleling the picture frame. The diagonal ribs of the tepee sweep from right to left, finishing at an implied point of meeting directly behind the shield of the warrior. Using Thomas Hart Benton's favored device of composing a series of movements rotating around a real or implied central visual pole, Riley places a feathered lance at the front of the composition. The pole combined with the warrior becomes a fulcrum around which the entire composition turns like the spokes of a wheel. Active on the left, restful on the right, there is continuing eye movement in the composition, despite the fact that we are looking at what might otherwise be described as a static scene.

Riley's fresh approach to designing his subject matter comes from endless doodling in thumbnail sketches where he searches for elemental responses to the movement of line, interplay of shapes or drama of dark and light. "No matter how tritely you begin—a man leading a horse, for instance—the goal is to bring it around to something that has a different feel." ***Absaroka [103]*** is an excellent example. "I was looking for an interesting shape that would hold the elements together. A gnarled tree with raking arms seemed like a good solution. Placing the man and horse at the trunk area turned them into a single unit. I wanted it to be simple, so I kept the background light, flat, and the horse, man and tree integrated in the same values."

103. *Absaroka*
1988
acrylic, 36 x 27

The Crow Indians are a Siouan tribe whose own name, *Absaroke* (or bird people), gave name to the Absaroka Mountains that edge the Yellowstone River in south-central Montana. In many ways the Crows were the "dandies of the Plains." Their pre-contact clothing decorated with quillwork was replaced by colorful beadwork in the 1840s. Combined with exotic hairdos and elaborate horse bridles, Crow warriors were a vision of shimmering color, softened and blended into a unified, luminous harmony in the bleaching Plains sunlight.

The pressing together of these three elements states in formal terms the covenant between Indian, animal and earth. When a warrior died, his horse was sacrificed with him in order to convey the spirit into the afterworld. Together with the tree, whose roots dig into the earth while its limbs touch the heavens, the man and horse become a triadic symbol of the Native American lifeway.

Riley also uses trees as vertical motifs that contrast with the curved human or horse shapes. Simultaneously, the trees reinforce the two-dimensional nature of the picture plane. Such is the case in ***The White Pony [51]*** where the "landscape" is three horizontal value patterns that move from the darker, textured bottom up to flatter diagonal bands suggesting a mountain and sky. Space is pulled forward by the wall of trees that part like a curtain to reveal

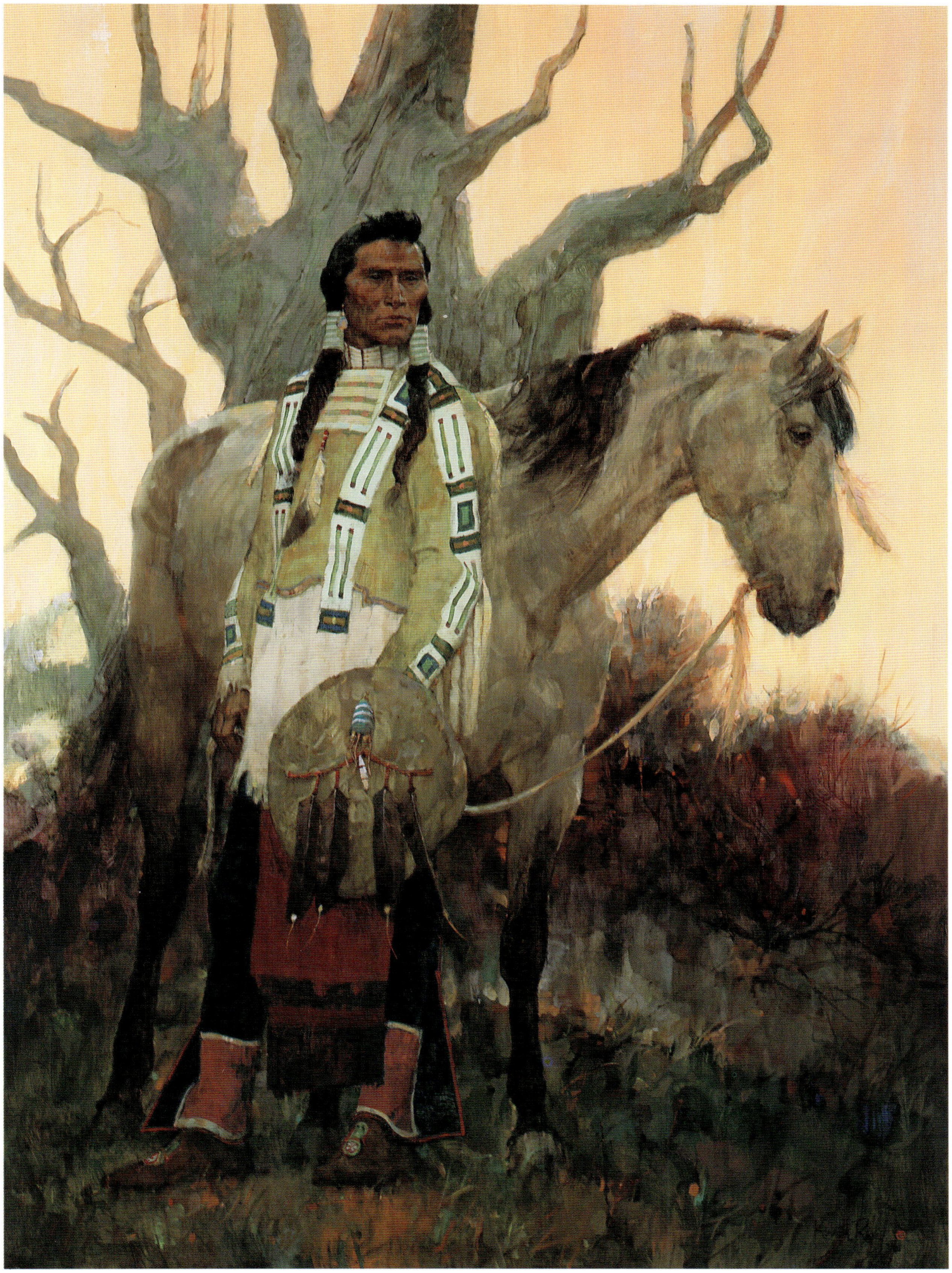

104. *Going to the Fair*
1987
oil, 13 x 18

Montana's annual Crow Fair has been taking place for over a century. Drawing tribes and tourists from throughout the United States, it is a wonderful celebration: a combination family reunion, carnival and hoedown. The music, dancing, food and competitions create something for the entire family, just as they did in the past when a Plains Indian mother showed off her skills in decorated clothing, horse gear and cradleboards. The travois—or "v"-shaped wooden structure which provided seating for the children—offers the artist a natural compositional element: The diagonal line leads into the painting and up to the baby's head.

the apparition of a dramatically foreshortened horse and a female figure. Everything is held on the surface, plotted into a muralesque serenity of subtle textures that envelop the viewer in a richness of surface, from leaf-covered forest floor to buckskin dress, horse hide and paper-white trunks. There is a tension between the close values in this essentially white-on-white painting—but in the end, the figure wins out. It is as if she is lit from within, a sensation reiterated in her expression which looks inward while the horse looks forward. Who leads whom? The ambiguity involves us in an elegiac dream.

Poetry, as in music, gains much of its primal attraction from rhythm and meter. The power of a drum beat has been close to Riley's heart since his days in Eddie Lain's dance band. No doubt his inner cadence quickened when he read George Catlin's account of the Mandan bull dance, a supplication to the Great Spirit performed by patriarchal men whose bodies were covered in black, red or white paint. Involving the entire tribe, the several days of drumming and chanting with wands and rattles, in the presence of the four cardinal points, climaxed in a duel between the powers of evil and good. "When the music and dancing stop, which are always perfectly simultaneous," wrote Catlin, "the whole nation raises the huzzah and a deafening shout of approbation."

Riley's red painting titled ***Four Lances [8]*** keeps time starting from the left where a neon-red lance establishes the foreground. From this vertical line we move into space through the opposing diagonal of a rattle which connects to the dancer's wrist, continuing the broken, angled line into the syncopated movements of every joint in his body. Headdress feathers and loin cloth lift to the cadence, as our eye moves up the lance, which rejoins the lance in the right background bringing us back to the foreground and straight up the figure into the light. The movement back and forth is reiterated by the use of warm and cool reds that advance and recede in the spirit of the movement.

Four Lances is motion personified. Riley took the concept to its ultimate conclusion when he painted ***Dance Progressions [44]*** for the 1991 CAA Exhibition. "My idea was the evolution of movement, a circle spiraling in space and coming out on the right-hand side. It is totally abstract, but I knew a figure could represent the idea of the line. Color came last. The red came at the end. It could be fire or sunset; it could be anything, but I wanted the final figure to stand out, so I thought, 'Why not white?'"

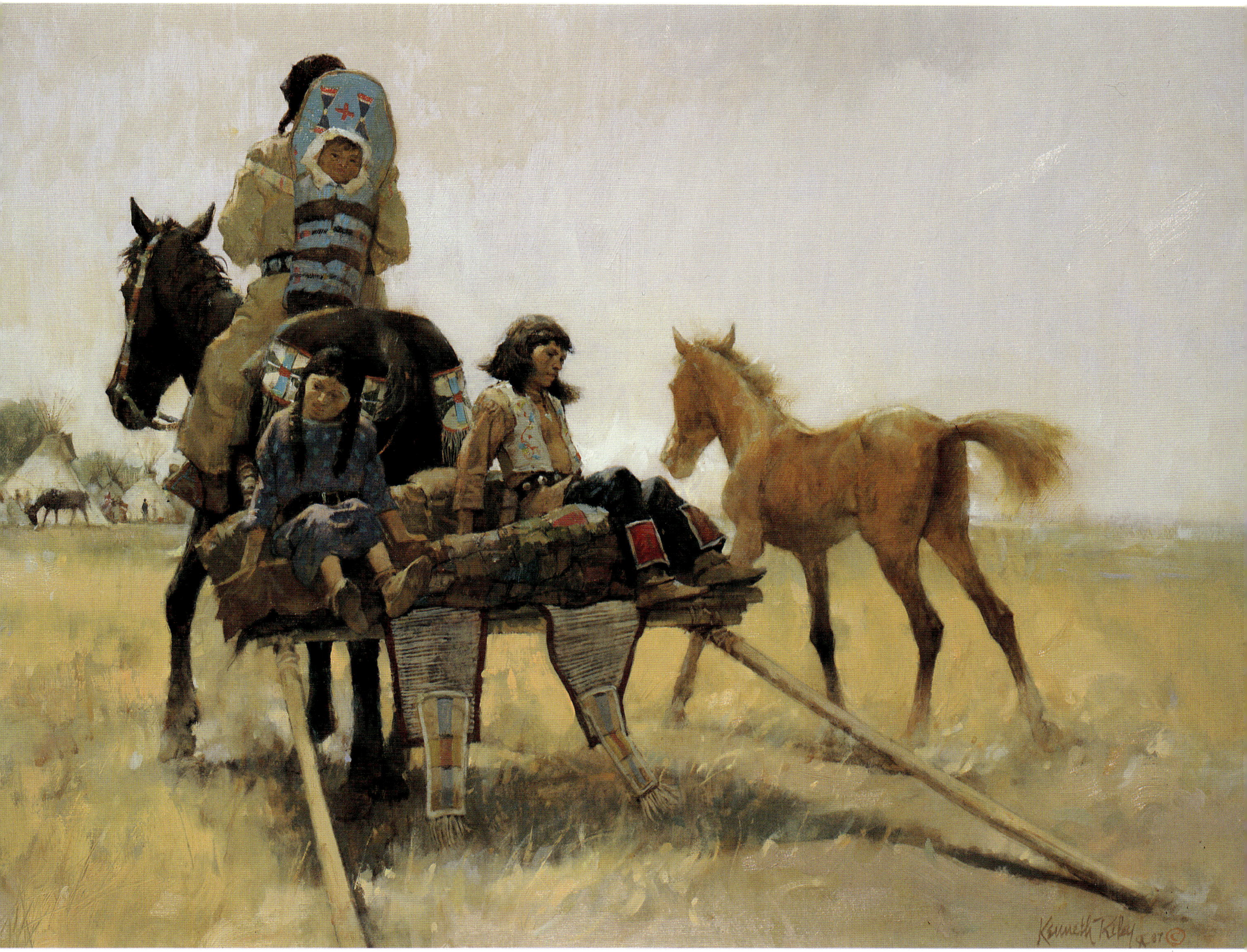
Kenneth Riley

Since studying Abstract Expressionism, Riley has been sensitive to the psychology of color. Though more instinctual than programmatic, Riley's theory of color trades on mood-evoking possibilities. "I don't copy color, I make it the color I would like it to be—the color that fits the overall context of the picture. Every color you put in, however, should have a relationship to the overall color feel of the picture. Once I've determined if it is a warm or cool picture—orange or blue picture—then I can distort the colors in order to create different contexts that add interest to what is depicted."

In ***Zapotec [106]*** Riley proves that lime-green flesh set against regal purple can work together in establishing the sensation of light and the idea of heritage. "I wanted the feeling of continuity between a present-day woman and her past as a Zapotec Indian. My model had this wonderful head that reflected all the connotations of her heritage. Purple, though it is difficult to work with, has a very contemporary feel, and it is everywhere in Mexico. I chose to make mine darker, more mysterious. A complementary cool against that warm lavender gave the flesh a different quality—not exactly realistic but a haunting feeling of the past."

The oscillation of the jewel-like colors in ***Zapotec*** causes a pulsing efflorescence, as if we are watching the northern lights against a screen of magical night. She is a figment of memory conceived on an immaterial surface. Riley succeeds in turning the surface into an insubstantial vehicle that offers to expand and guide the insights of the imagination.

Riley confesses that perhaps more than any of his paintings, these poetic works attest to his belief that the artist must paint for himself first and the public second. "If you start painting for some other reason, you've lost the whole meaning of your existence. It might sound selfish but I think you have to completely satisfy your own directions and objectives in order for the work to have meaning to someone else. I paint philosophically within an area that suits me, and I'm thrilled that it reaches out to others."

Reaching beyond the confines of a regional subject or a historical vignette, Riley speaks a universal language whose rich enfolding of fact and fantasy, the moment and eternity, representational with abstract, resonates in the human figure. Such works tell us as much about the person who paints them as about the individual or vignettes depicted. Not religious in a conventional sense, they are in fact spiritual—representing the intellectual and emotional synthesis of all that Riley has seen and felt.

105. *The Secret Place*
ca. 1982
acrylic, 48 x 24

One of the dividends of living in the Southwest is exploring relatively untrodden areas that trigger images for paintings. Hiking in a remote canyon of the Dragoons, I came upon a walled enclosure, open at both ends, but hard to detect unless you stumbled into it. Complete with fresh water, it was a perfect retreat for an Apache raiding party.

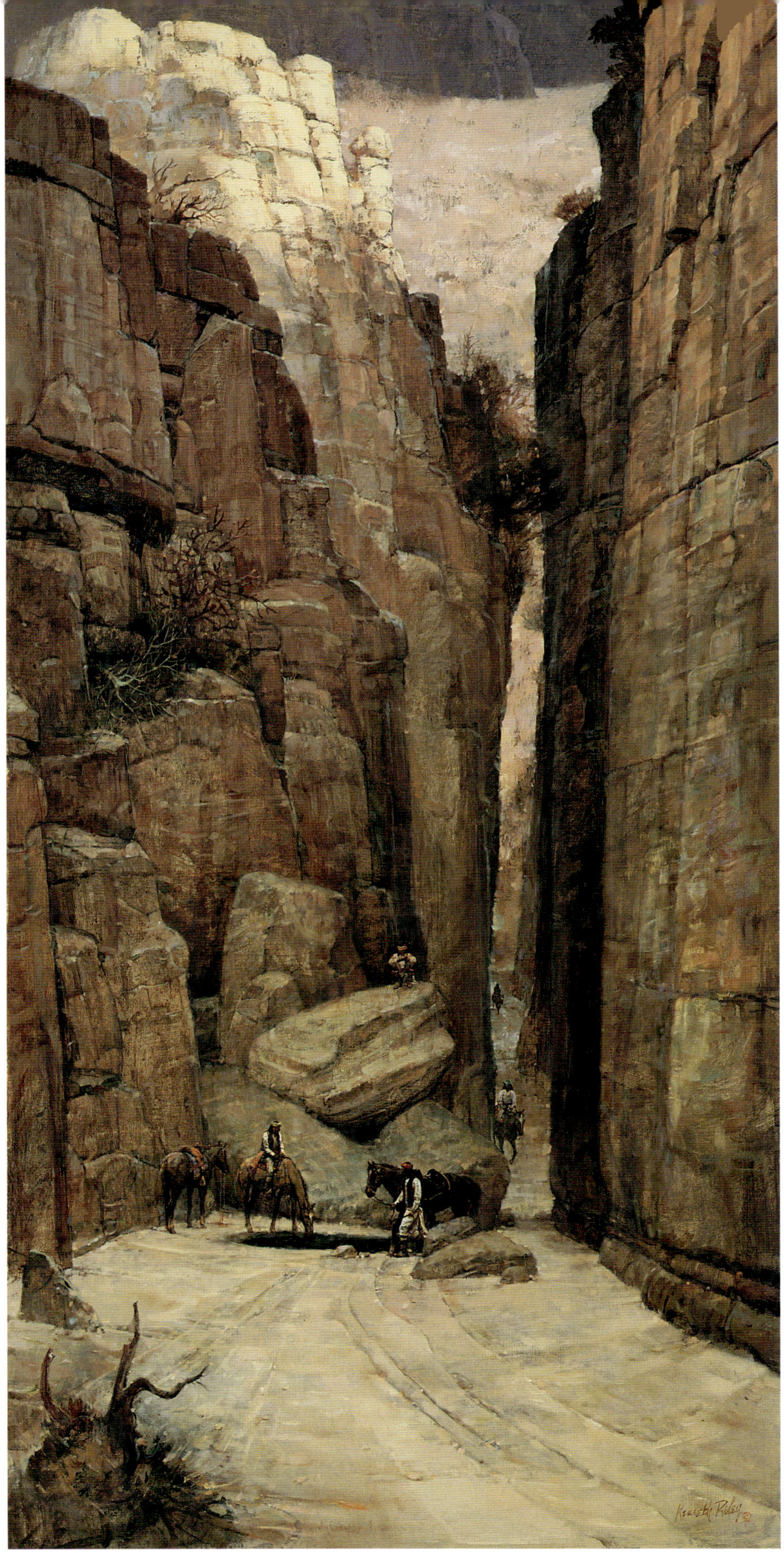

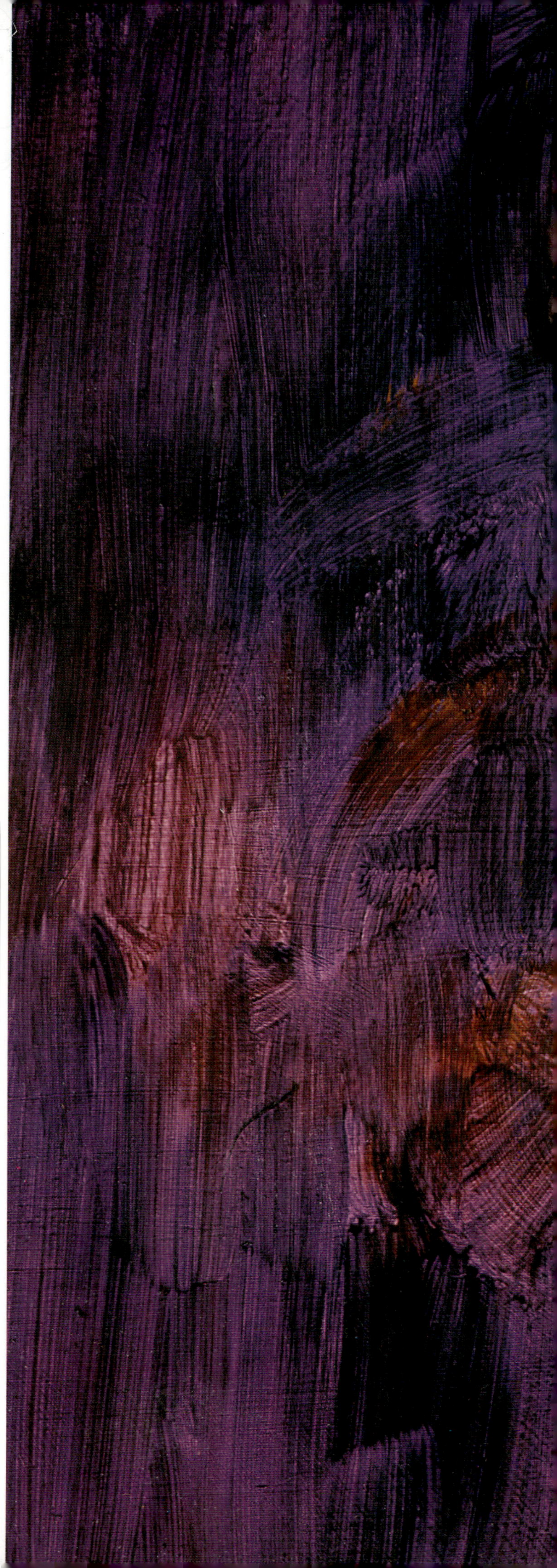

106. *Zapotec*
1990
oil, 9 x 12

I'm drawn to scenes that speak of the continuum that binds one generation to the next and each generation to the first. Women at looms, like this Zapotec weaver, create more than fabrics or rugs. They weave the threads of civilizations into the colorful tapestry of the universe.

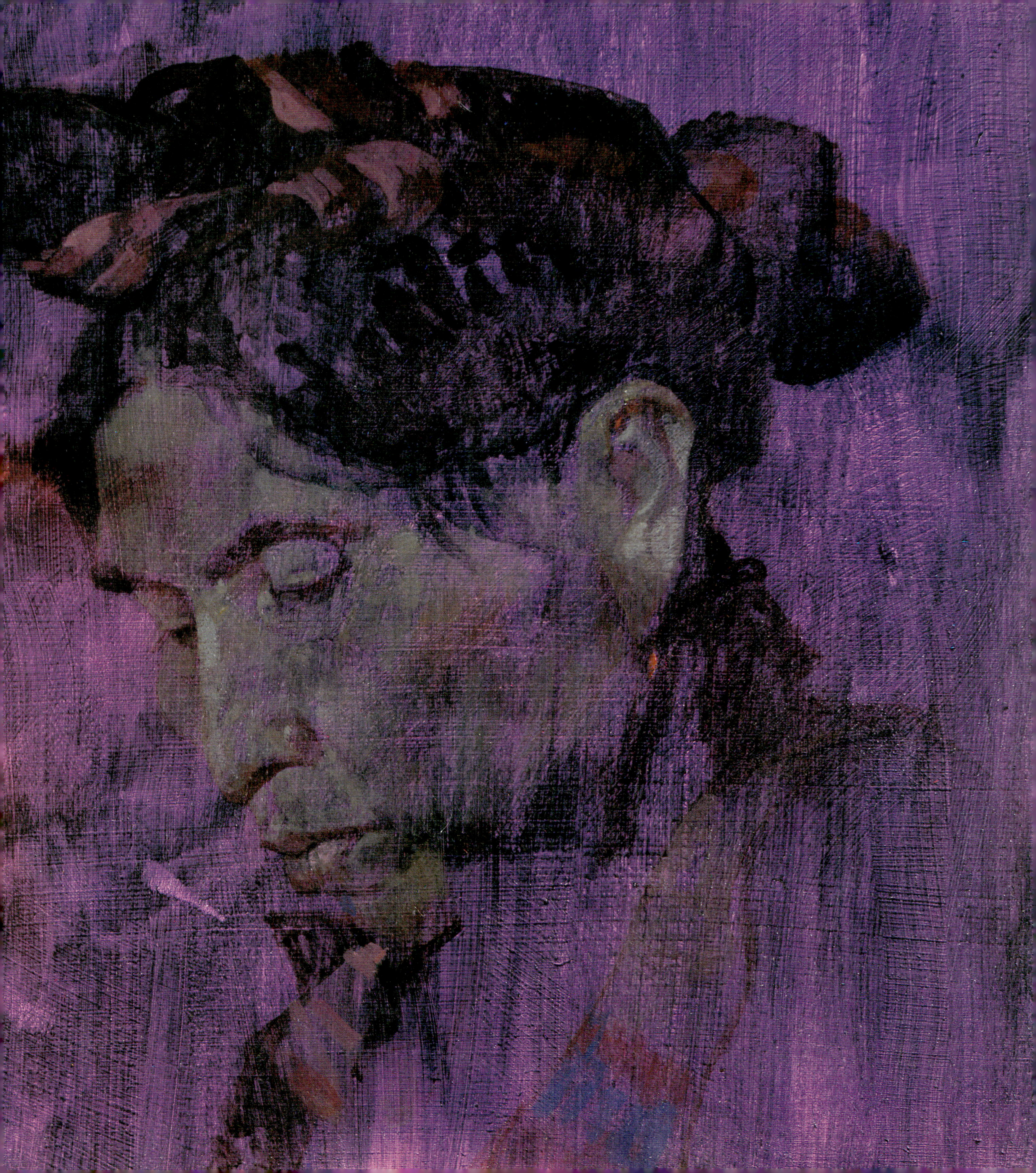

COMMUNICATING THE IDEA
NOTES ON COMPOSITION AND DESIGN

KENNETH RILEY

In the mid-1960s I became intrigued with the intricacies of composition and design. Design, I decided, was the skeleton upon which everything in a painting hangs. I spent several months jotting down my thoughts and trying to organize them into a lesson-plan for the beginning artist. The treatise that follows was digested from my notes. It is not intended to be a comprehensive list of rules. Rather it offers guideposts to self-criticism and aids to creativity. Whenever possible, I've referenced paintings reproduced within the pages of this book as illustrations of my points.

After nearly thirty years of putting these principles into practice, I'm more convinced than ever of the powerful role design plays in presenting an Idea and communicating it to the viewer.

I've never considered "developing a style" to be a yardstick of success. Rather, through constant referral and exposure to good art, music, theater, books—life in general—the artist's tastes, observations, needs and outlook evolve. Although unconscious of these things on a daily basis, they naturally affect your work. Through them your art takes on a distinction that sets it apart. —KR

In order to project an Idea or convey a feeling, an artist must be capable of a high degree of organization and an ability to present his Idea forcefully, yet simply and directly. The obligation the artist has to anyone viewing his work—whether an illustration for a story, still-life painting, portrait or mural—is to present the Idea in a fresh way. What will interest the viewer most is seeing something of the individual in the work.

An artist must study the history of the profession and learn his own likes and dislikes in order to arrive at an individual way of expressing himself. He must constantly develop his receptivity and sensitivity to line, form and color—for these are the elements that comprise composition.

Composition, then, is the arrangement or the organization of line, form and color. In composing, the artist must be conscious of the fact that the

107. Detail of *The Red Tepee [108].*

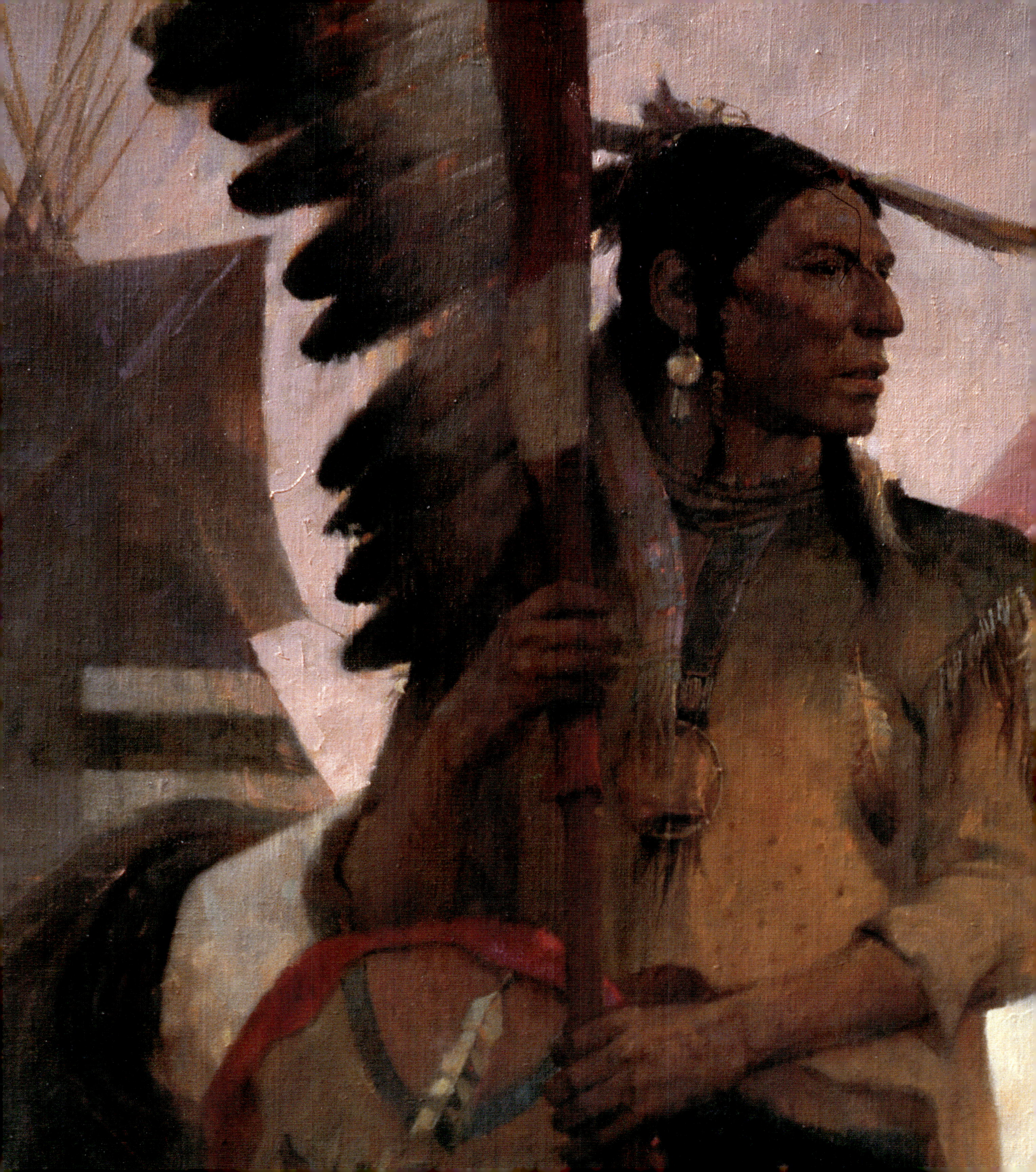

design—not the subject—carries the impact of the picture. As elements are introduced into the picture area, they must be related to one another and to the space they occupy.

Prehistoric cave people drew animals on the walls of their caves. As soon as they portrayed more than one animal, they were composing. By introducing a second element, a relationship was established, creating force, action or influence of each element on the others. With composition, the cave people became artists who were concerned with a central Idea.

The Idea

The most important element in any picture or composition is the Idea, or the reason why the picture exists at all. The Idea is the original motivation or point of emphasis. Without the Idea—or climax—there would be chaos.

The Idea is the means by which the artist imposes order. Through order comes clarification and communication. Everything in a painting subordinates to the Idea, which motivates all other elements, from the type of line, to the character of shape and the relationships of colors. Unlike the camera, which is limited to arrangements as they exist in space, artists arrange in order to present or dramatize an Idea. In so doing, design—not the subject—carries the impact of the picture.

A review of art history reveals that various elements of composition—line, form, value, color, movement, *et cetera*—are the foundation of memorable artworks. In the early cave drawings, for instance, simple, dramatic use of line carries the action and spirit of the Idea. Rembrandt van Rijn (Dutch, 1606–1669), on the other hand, used light as a means of dramatizing the Idea. Piero della Francesca relied on rhythm and pattern.

Most important, where the Idea is concerned, is thinking in the largest possible terms. In drawing the figure (which is in itself a composition) the artist thinks first in terms of movement and mass, then the details fall into place. The same is true with composing pictures: Resist becoming involved with details.

The artist usually begins the Idea phase of picture-making by drawing thumbnail sketches. These rough drawings explore movement and define the plastic possibilities of the composition. It is at this point that the artist

108. *The Red Tepee*
1987
oil, 48 x 48

Here I worked with a small number of elements that dominate the two-dimensional plane. The goal was to have both an interesting pattern across the surface as well as a suggestion of depth and atmosphere. I couldn't get things to gel until I happened upon a reference to a red tepee that Kiowa Chief Satanta was said to have owned. It gave me a dominant red shape upon which to hang my hat. Since the color red tends to advance, I threw in blue until I finally achieved a shade that made the tepee stay in the background.

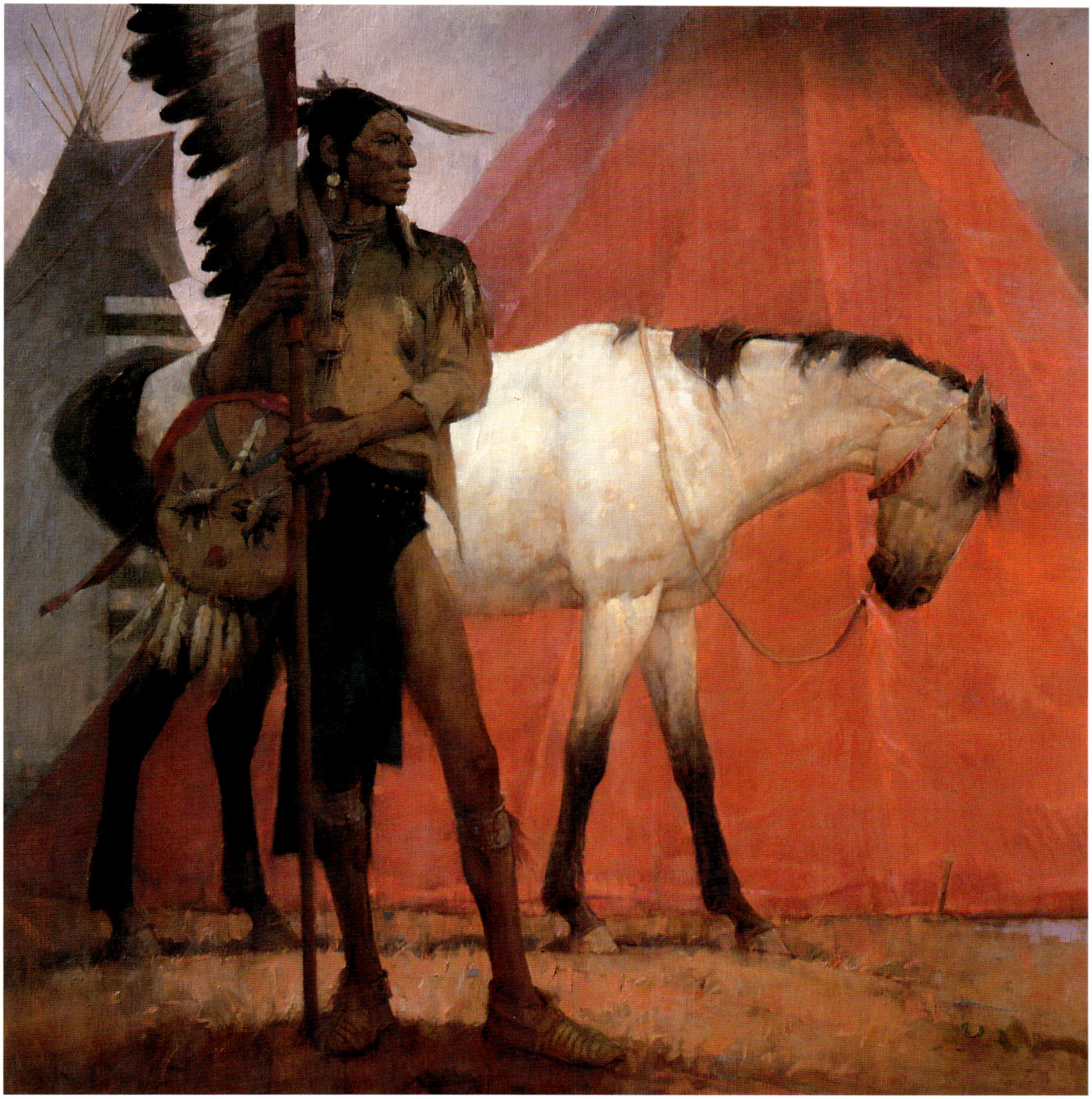

puts forth the most strenuous effort. To settle for anything less than the best possible arrangement of the Idea is to accept that the picture also will be mediocre.

When doing thumbnail sketches, the artist must constantly strive for movement and counter-movement. This interaction is a living quality. But do not confuse action of subject with movement. Even though the figures or objects appear static, there should be movement invested in line, form, color and value. Each gives mood or emotion to a seemingly quiet composition.

In exploring the Idea in thumbnails, instinctive reactions take place. This unconscious application is important, for it draws upon inner likes and dislikes. The early stage of Idea development should be free from formal restraint—the goal being to later review the thumbnail sketches and to evaluate the successes and failures of each.

Composition comprises the formal elements of line, form, value and color. Overriding these tools of composition, however, are three motivating factors that have to do with movement and the life of the picture: rhythm, balance and scale.

109. *Homage to Catlin*
1977
oil, 48 x 36
Leanin' Tree Museum,
Boulder, Colorado

I was introduced to George Catlin's journals in the late-1970s. The idea of an artist exploring the unknown and creating a record of his journey caught my fancy, and I decided to do a painting to honor his effort. In retrospect, my own emotional attachment to the Northern Plains Indian was largely influenced by Catlin's philosophy. I can't help but agree with his lament that "Art may mourn when these people are swept from their earth and the artists of future ages may look in vain for another race so picturesque in their costumes, their weapons, their colors, their manly games and their chases."

Motivating Factors

Rhythm

Rhythm is defined as the relationship between organized movement and predictable order, which is vital to the existence of any picture. Rhythm does not necessarily mean violent action on the part of the figures or objects in the picture. Rather it is the interaction of elements, such as line, form, value or color. Rhythm may also be expressed as a feeling of suspended action or mood. It can be achieved by such things as the directional thrust of the composition and the balance and counterbalance of line.

Rhythm is achieved by three means: Repetition, or the regular appearance of similar items, gives a picture direction or movement. In ***Mandan Gold [86],*** for instance, the poses are static, but a rhythm is introduced through a series of circles in the objects.

A second way to achieve rhythm is through progression, or the sequencing of elements in gradual degrees of importance. In ***Homage to Catlin [109]*** the

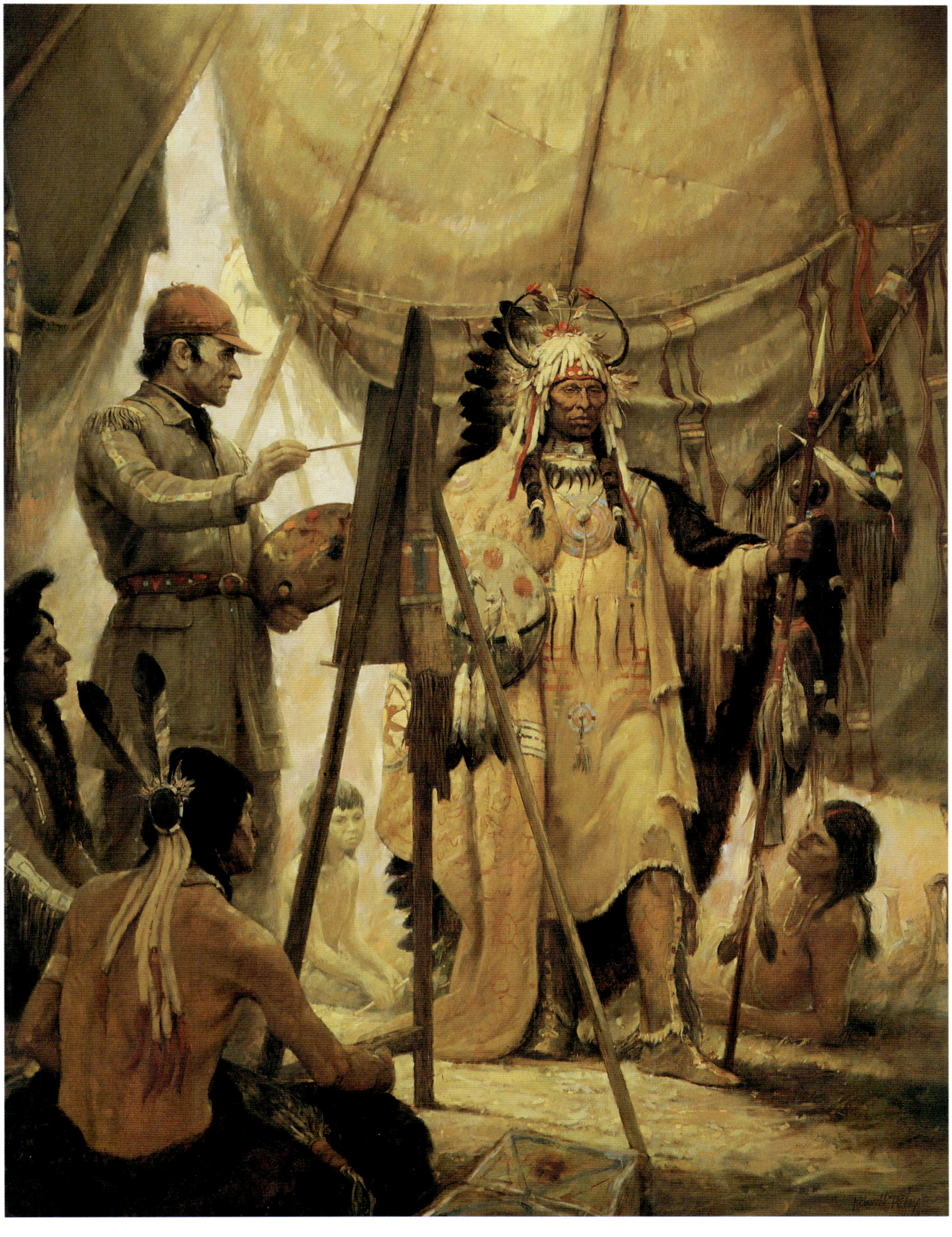

110. *The Doll*
1983
oil, 15 x 30

I had intended to do a conventional still life with this antique leather doll, but when I set it in my studio window to get a better look, what interested me most was the relationship of the doll to the larger, outdoor scene. That serendipitous placement spawned a number of thumbnail sketches of the doll on the inside edge of a tepee. The doll's relationship to the identifiable objects in the distance brought up an intriguing set of scale relationships and point of view. I leave it up to the viewer to create the story of how the doll came to this apparent abandonment.

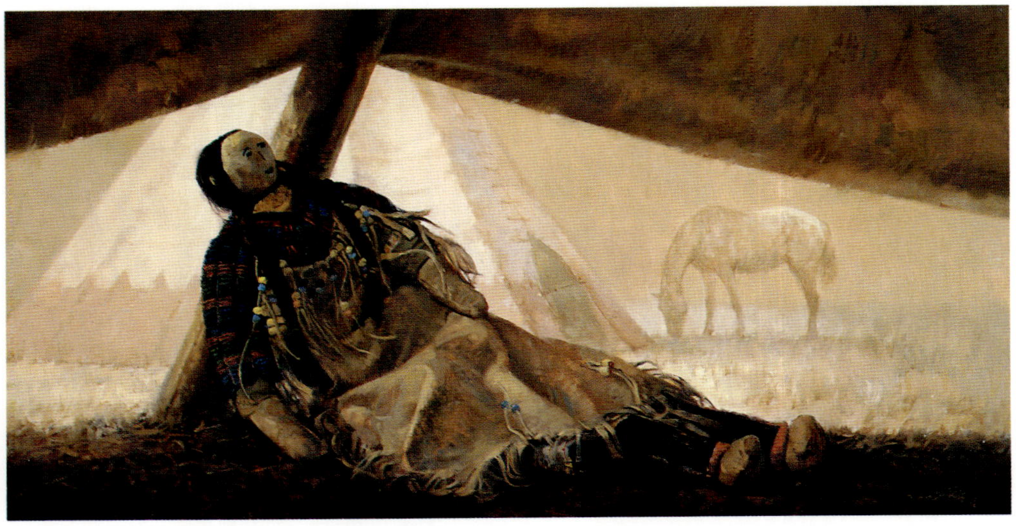

111. *Apache Moonlight*
1990
oil, 40 x 33

A high, full moon in desert country reflects off the sand, bathing everything with a cool light. It seemed like the perfect ambience for a trio of Apaches setting out for a raid. Described by journalists of the day as an elusive, shadowy foe, the Apache's physical appearance was spelled out by Captain John G. Bourke who wrote in his journals: "The Apache are strongly built, straight, sinewy, well-muscled, extremely strong in the lower limbs, provided with a round barrel chest, showing good lung power, keen, intelligent-looking eyes, good head, and a mouth showing determination, decision and cruelty. He can be made a firm friend, but no mercy need be expected from him as an enemy."

composition is based on a series of triangles, which vary in size from small to large. The triangular shape of the figure in the lower left-hand corner, the easel, the Indian figure and the thrust of the tepee poles all serve to dramatize the climax of the picture—namely, Chief Four Bears. The use of repeating shapes in picture-making gives strength and continuity to the structure.

The third method for achieving rhythm is continuity, or the flow of movement from one form to another. In ***Mandan Gold*** the circles create "s" curves that link into one another, climaxing in the standing-man's face. The action of line and form should carry the eye throughout the picture to the point of interest and then back into the picture again. The flow should never degenerate into a static state.

Balance

A complete statement of an Idea is well-balanced. It is a unit in which all elements (line, form, pattern, color, texture) are interdependent, and where the removal of even one element will destroy the total concept. Strong picture-making also demands an economy of means—never use more elements than needed to convey the Idea.

There are two kinds of balance: symmetrical or formal balance, and asymmetrical or informal balance. Symmetrical balance conveys a sense of order. The effect on the viewer is dignity and an impersonal, classical quality.

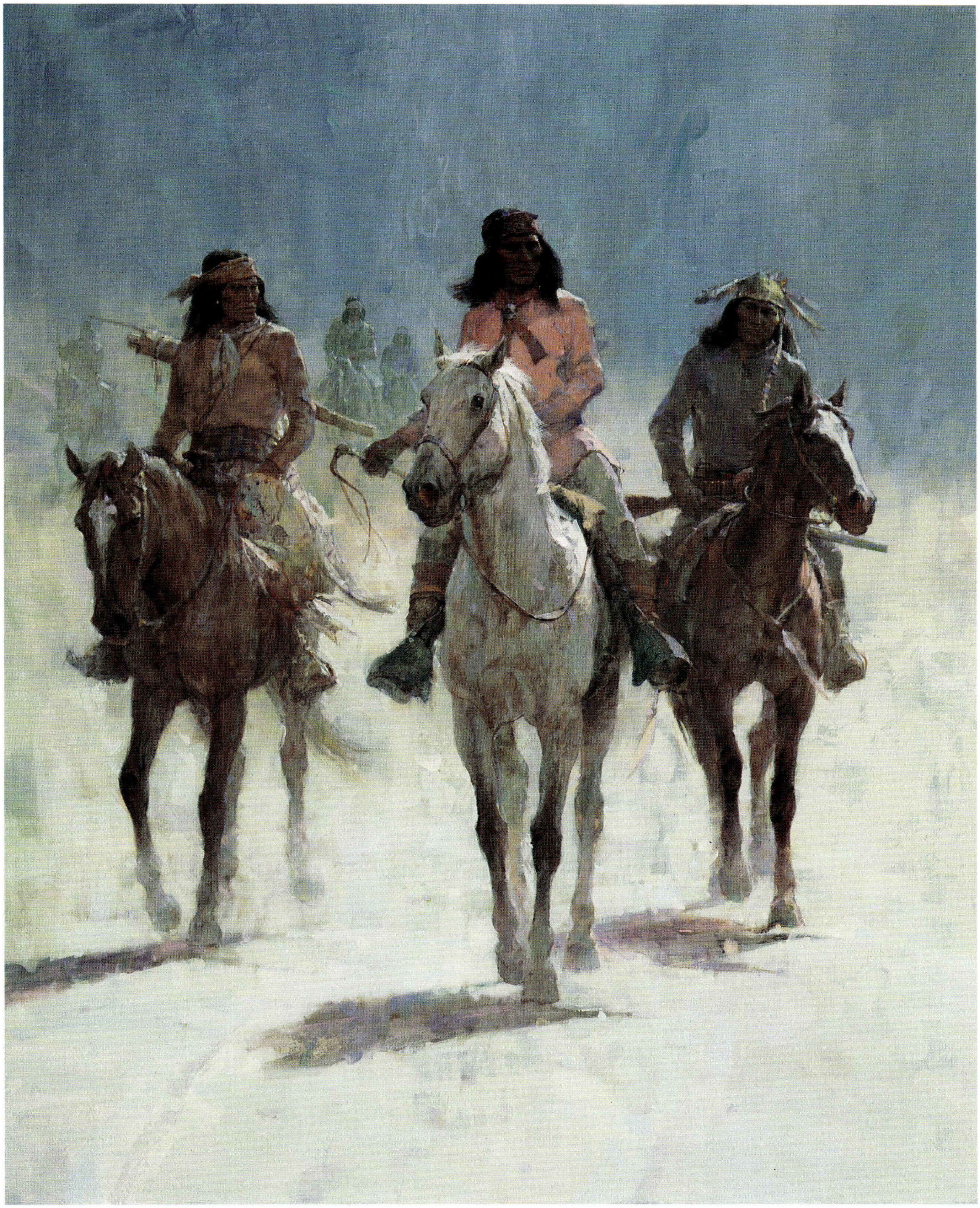

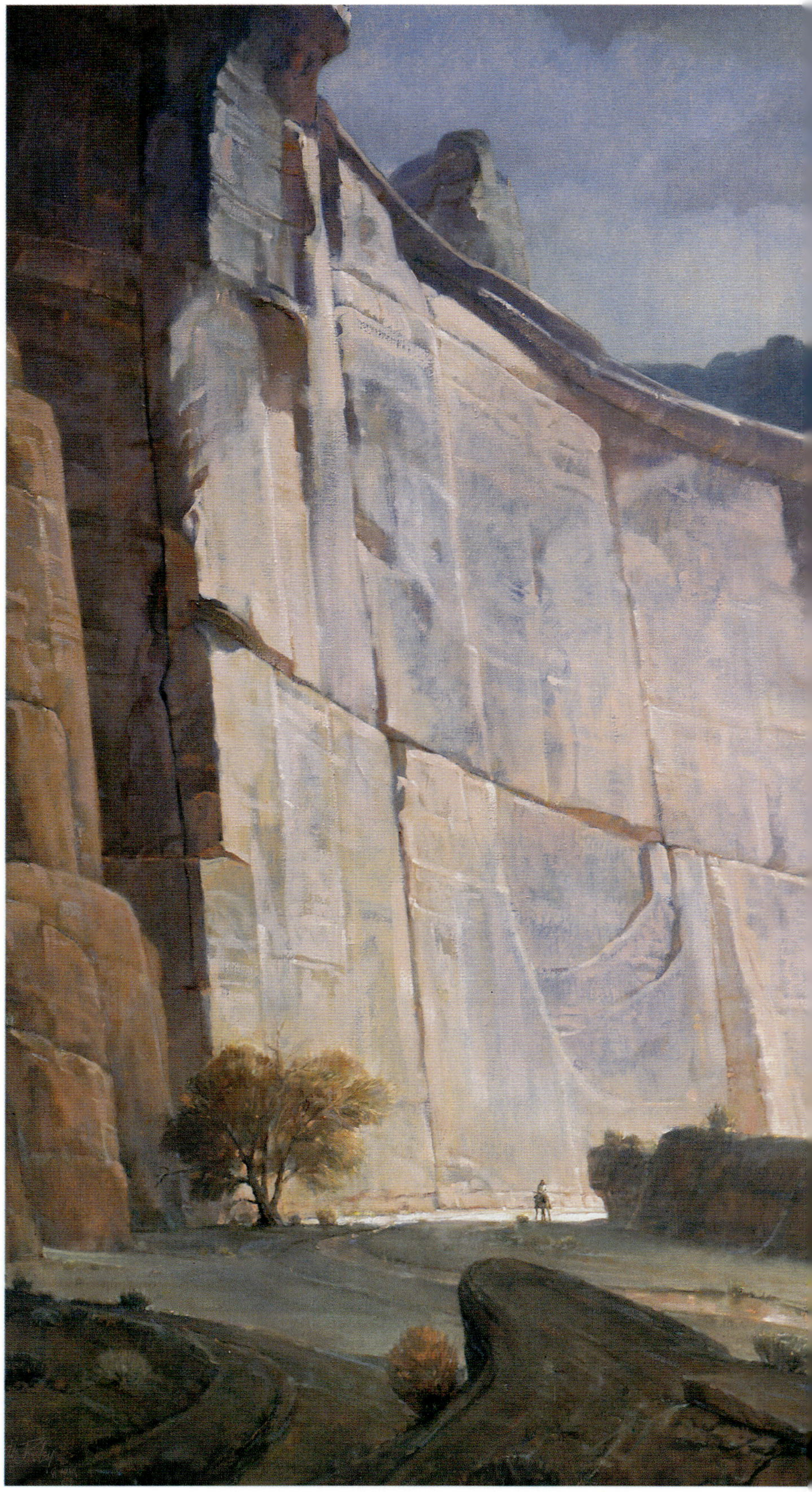

112. *Canyon Country*

1983

oil, 60 x 90

This painting was a private commission with the only stipulation that it be a scene with southwestern flavor. What freedom! A far cry from illustrating a story line. Generally similar to many locations in the Dragoon and Chiricahua Mountains, this landscape is one of the largest I've ever done. I enjoy working big: The paintings take longer but you can get inside them. Size alone can take an undramatic subject and give it meaning on the wall.

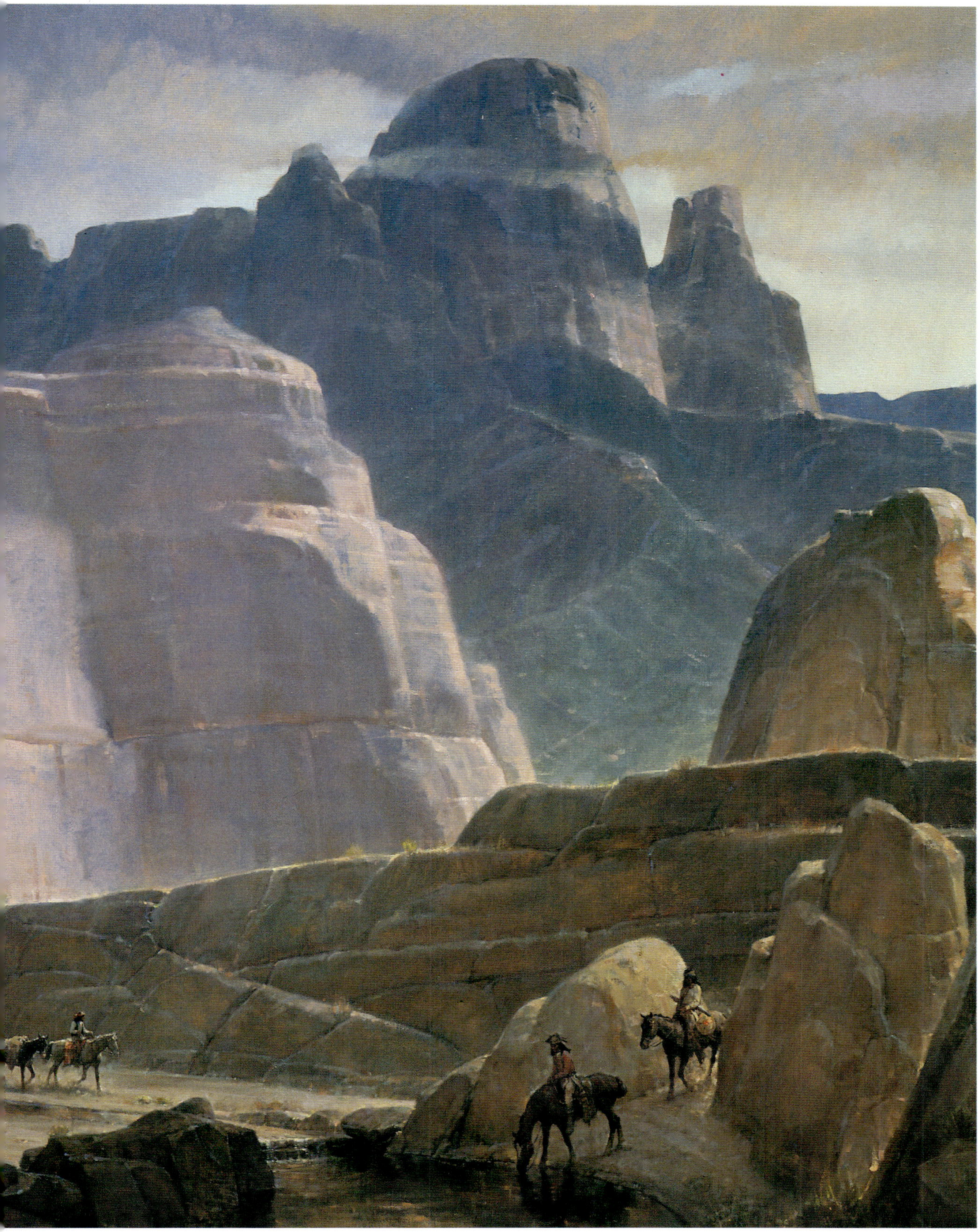

113. *Apache Scouts*

1991

oil, 12 x 21

From 1882 to 1886, General George Crook, a renowned Civil War veteran and Indian fighter, was given the job of keeping the Chiricahua Apache on the reservation in Arizona. He enlisted the help of men from among their own people to serve as scouts. Familiar with the mountains of both Arizona and Mexico, Apache scouts were instrumental in the surrender of the tribe. Intertribal rivalries and the boredom of reservation life made scouting for the enemy acceptable behavior.

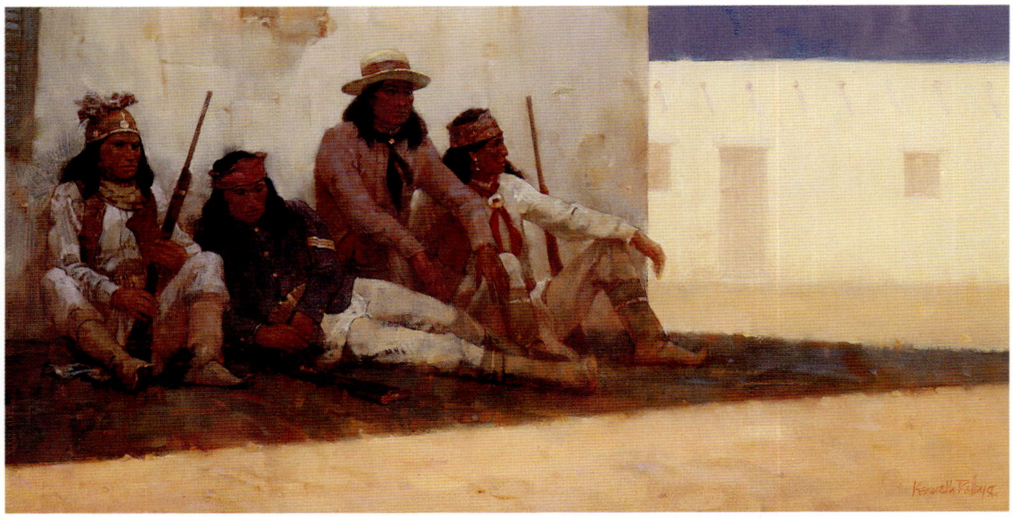

In symmetrical compositions the weight of forms within the picture are evenly distributed. ***Romancing the West [18]*** shows the three players in the drama of the developing frontier. The space is evenly divided and each fills his portion with a sense of pride and importance. Most early religious painters used a symmetrical, balanced composition, often based on geometric pattern, as the solution to conveying solemnity and majesty.

Asymmetrical arrangements, on the other hand, are purposefully composed to be startling and unexpected to the eye. Asymmetry creates pictures with tension and drama. Such pictures tend to elicit a more exciting response from the viewer. I used an asymmetrical composition in ***Pisac Market, Peru [98].*** The whole thrust of interest has been pushed to the left—seemingly creating an imbalance. I modified or balanced it and simultaneously kept the eye moving throughout the composition by the light that pours through the opening on the right.

Edgar Degas (French, 1834–1917) often used asymmetrical arrangements inspired in part by his study of Japanese art. Using a device of "occult balance"—or the practice of playing large empty areas against small busy areas—the Japanese encouraged the viewer to fill in the void.

114. *The Dandies*

1992

acrylic/oil, 36 x 42

I tried to convey an outdoor atmosphere and a sense of action in these three Indian riders who are engaged in a race to test stamina and establish rank. The artistic goal was to make the three figures come together as one large design and yet have each horse and rider be different enough to stand out as an individual.

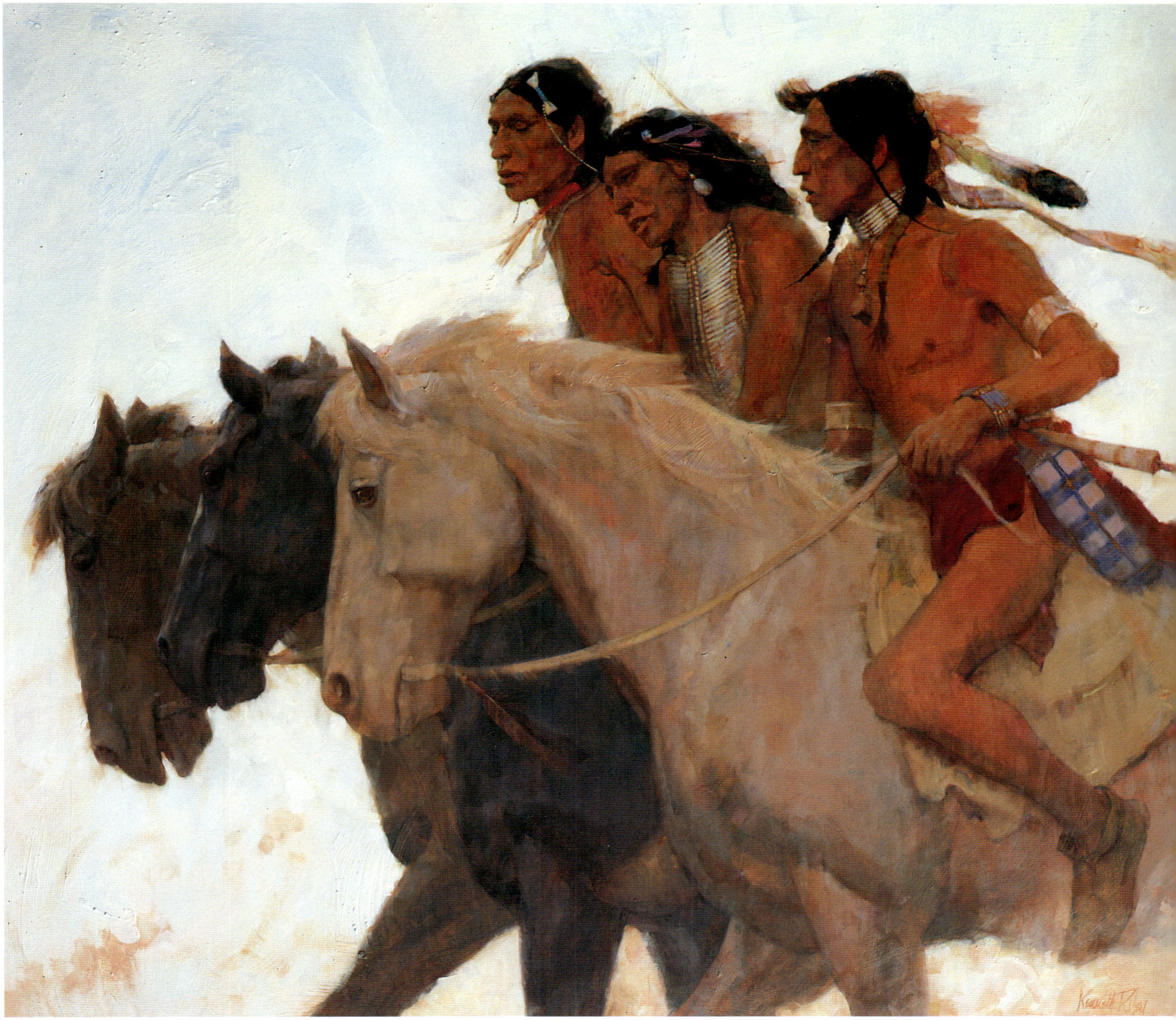

Scale

Scale is the proportion of objects in relationship to surrounding space or other objects. Scale is especially useful in establishing a mood, particularly as regards the human figure. Since we are familiar with the size of the human figure, it becomes a useful gauge of measurement. Put small figures in a vast space, as I did in ***Canyon Country [112],*** and the contrast produces a lonely feeling. Despair can be suggested by an extreme off center or crowding of the picture frame placement. Heroic moods can be established by having the figure dominate the space, overpowering the background, as is the case in ***Coming to Trade—Fort Union, 1833 [115].***

Scale in a composition can suggest volume. Crowding of the picture frame makes the figure seem larger and hard to contain. Movement that transcends the limits of the picture edge likewise suggests scale. It is important to look for this quality in thumbnail sketches. More often than not, if the feeling is not captured in the sketch, it will be apparent when the composition is brought up to working size. The scale of objects to their surroundings is relative, as long as the relationships are maintained.

115. *Coming to Trade—Fort Union, 1833*
1988
oil, 42 x 36

Fort Union was built by the American Fur Company at the confluence of the Yellowstone and Missouri Rivers, near present-day Williston, North Dakota. A supply station outfitting trappers headed into the wilderness, Fort Union also did a brisk business with area tribes who bartered furs for food, cloth and guns. Many early journalists described the colorful scene of tepees from various tribes surrounding the fort. The goal of my composition was to confront you with the excitement of a single figure who is so monumental as to be literally in the clouds. The curve of the horse's leg, head and lance coerce your view over to the other riders who descend into the camp.

Tools of Composition

Rhythm, balance and scale are the motivating elements of the Idea. Now we take up the tools for composing the Idea: line, form, pattern and color and their various adjuncts.

Line

Line in compositional terms deals with direction of movement within the picture. Line has several functions but primarily it guides the eye through and over forms at varied speeds, enhancing the climax or point of interest in the picture. When used to define a form, pencil or brush lines can take on a character that enhances the mood or imparts emotion. The language of line includes, among many emotive possibilities, the following: tranquil, wavy lines; emphatic thick or thin lines; nervous or irritable splintered, jagged lines; defiant, short choppy lines; dreamy, mysterious blurred lines; or playful, lilting lines.

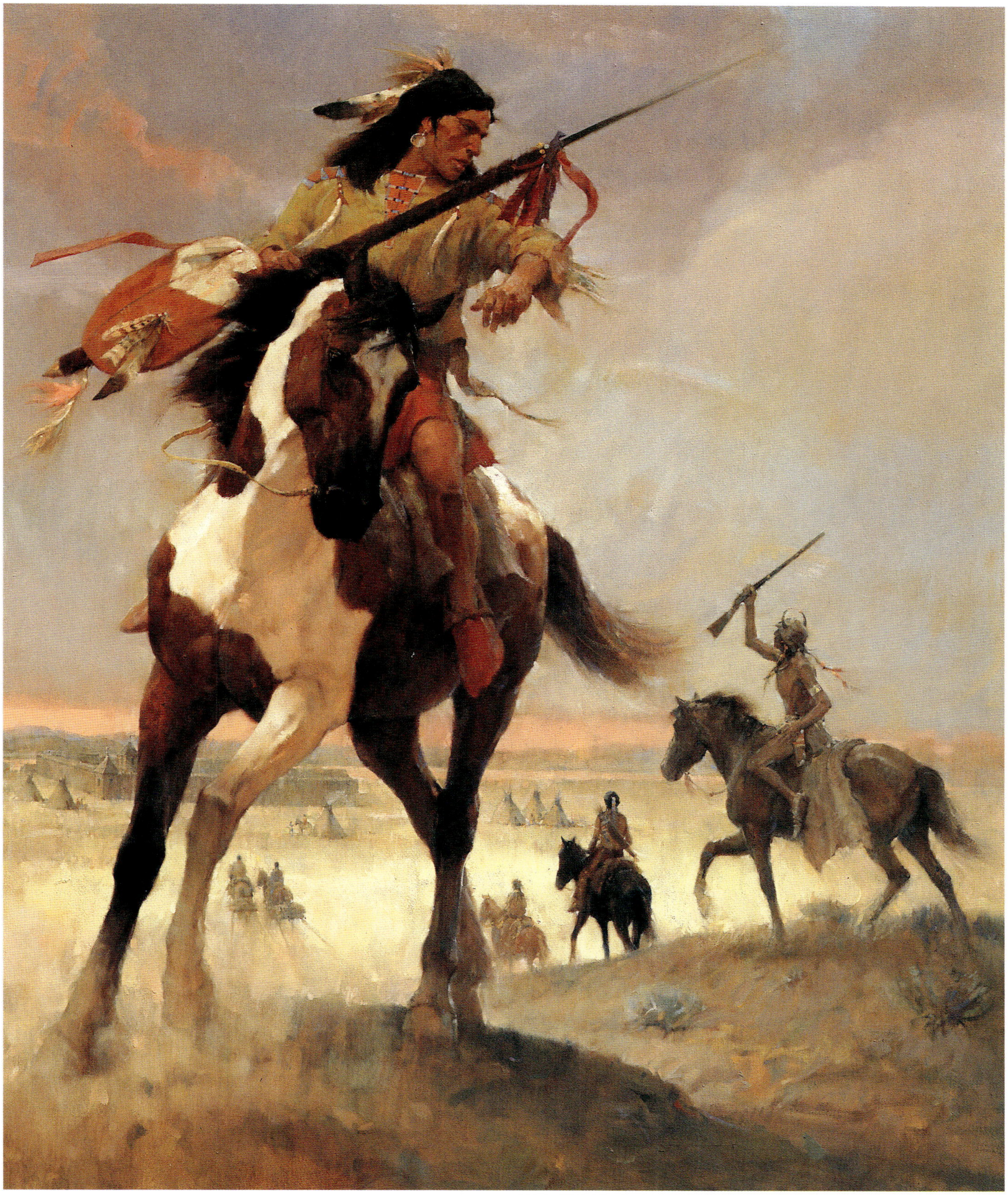

The picture itself may be based on a linear quality. The horizontal line of the horses' backs in ***Guarding the Herd [127]*** gives a feeling of repose and breadth. Vertical lines, on the other hand, suggest stature and dignity, an effect I was trying for in the noble trio of horsemen in ***Apache Moonlight [111].*** Diagonal lines indicate action, transition, unbalance. A diagonal line is a line of force with dramatic and powerful movement. I used a number of diagonal motifs in the ***Dog Dancers [126]*** to convey the Idea of movement—including the sunburst robe pattern in the background. Curved lines tend to pull the eye with them and can be manipulated into various speeds. In ***Dance Progressions [44]*** a strong three-dimensional circle served as my Idea. Beginning at the lower right-hand corner, the figure moves in a large loop that tightens and explodes in white light at the upper right.

Direction

Line can give direction and thrust, thereby drawing attention to the Idea or subject. Direction also creates space divisions, both vertical and horizontal.

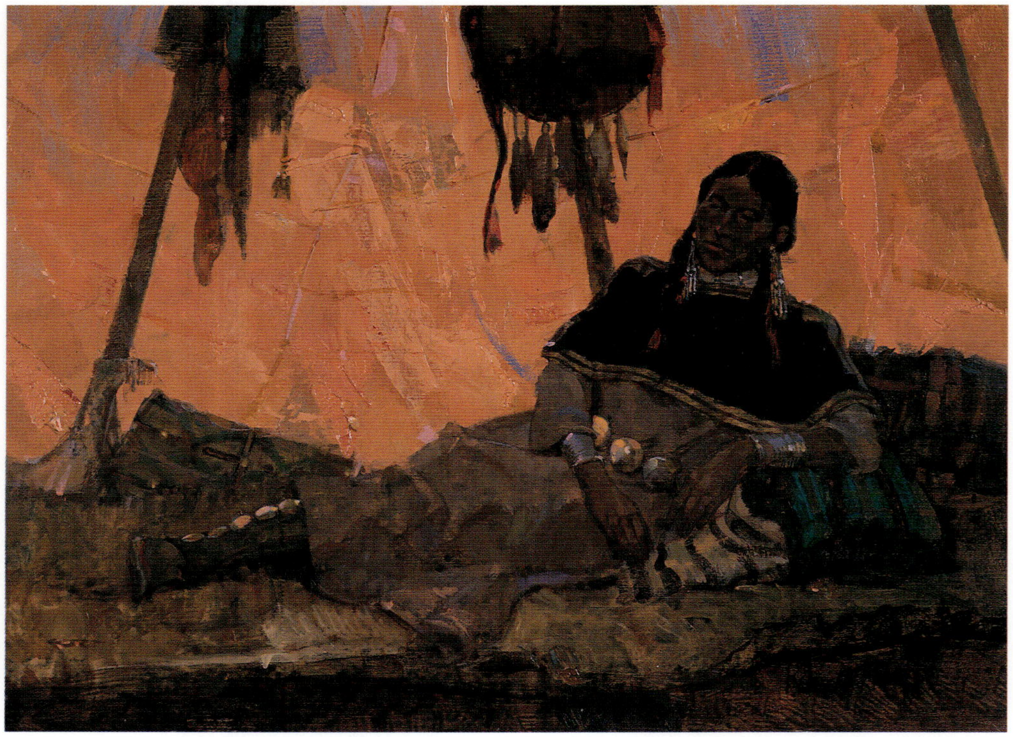

116. *The Princess*
ca. 1987
acrylic, 8 x 12

The daughter of a chief would probably have had the best tepee, appointed with ample furs and robes for lounging. It was an opportunity to create an Oriental or Moroccan type of scene, from unreal background coloring to opulent patterns and shapes. The accent colors were dropped in for balance and opposition—nothing too logical, really more for fun. This lady is a nod to Charlie Russell's treatment of a similar subject.

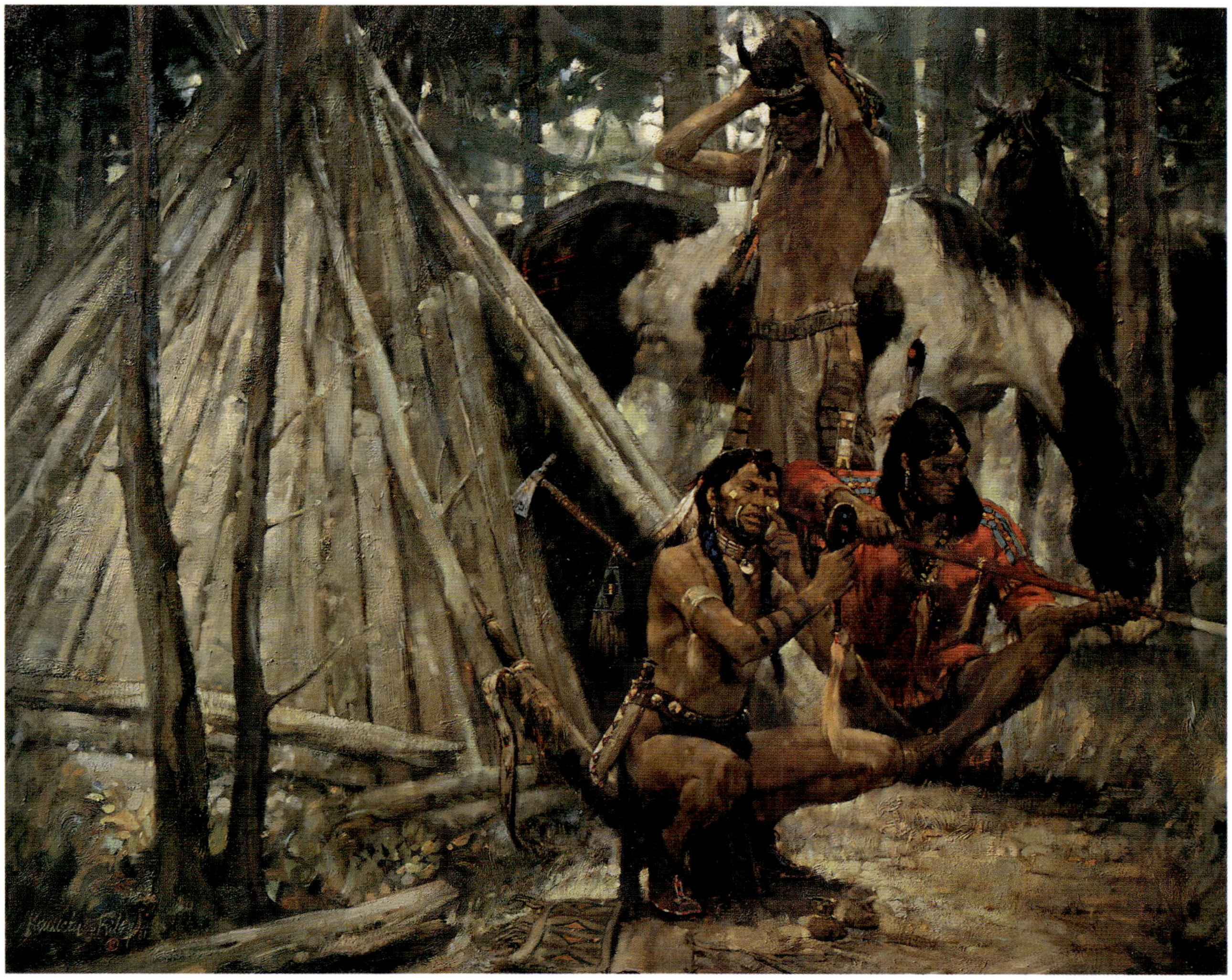

Division of the picture space may be achieved by use of a single line dividing the picture plane into two, preferably unequal, areas, or into several unequal areas that create exciting space relationships, as the small foreground and sky areas against the massive rock wall in ***Dry Camp [87].***

Thrust can also be diagonal, but if diagonal, it should be countered by some element to keep the force from moving out of the picture. In ***The Red Tepee [108],*** the thrust of the diagonal tepee ribs is counterbalanced by the vertical figure and pole.

Space may also be created by use of two directional lines such as vertical-horizontal, or vertical-diagonal, or horizontal-diagonal. In ***Mandan Gold [86]*** and in ***In the Mandan Lodge of Four Bears [92]*** I used lances and the interior poles of the lodge to create new, interesting spaces within the larger picture space.

117. *The War Lodge*
1981
oil, 20 x 25

On a research trip into Montana, a guide offered to take me into a remote area to see the remains of a century-old war lodge. Covered with moss, the lodge poles remained in position inspiring memories of a Blackfeet raiding party. Traveling many miles to contact their enemies, the raiders would set up a temporary lodge to stow excess gear and prepare themselves for the confrontation. Once they settled the score, they returned to the shelter, picked up their belongings and were on their way home.

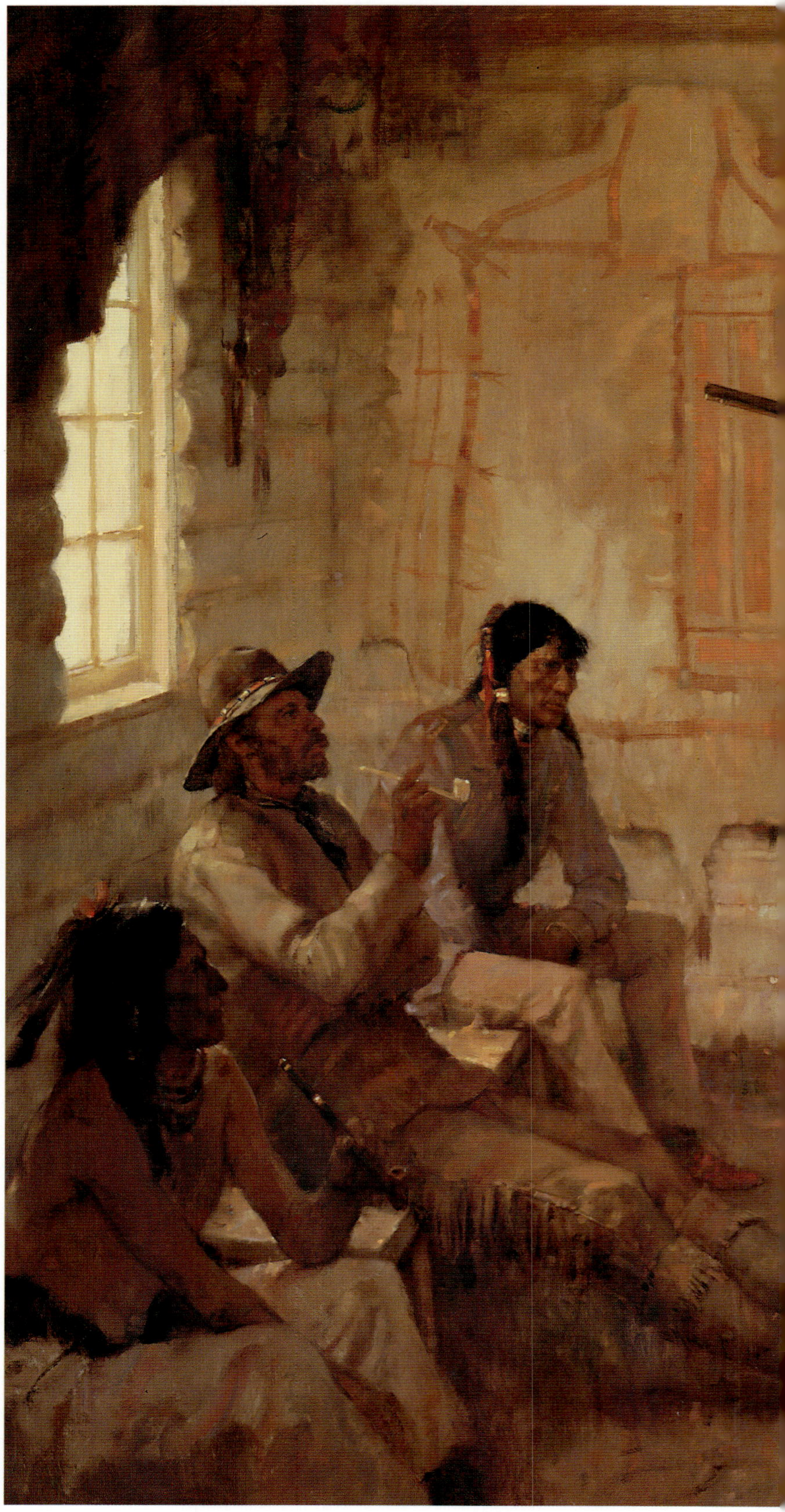

118. *The Robe Trade*
1984
oil, 28 x 44

During the period when trade in buffalo robes flourished on the Plains, small trading posts sprang up throughout Indian country. They were rustic structures made of logs or sod and stocked with knives, guns, blankets, cooking utensils, tobacco and illegal whiskey. I based this interior on a post preserved in Nebraska. The challenge was creating the sense of interior light with limited light sources. The window and doorway set up my value patterns and guide your eye throughout the figure groups.

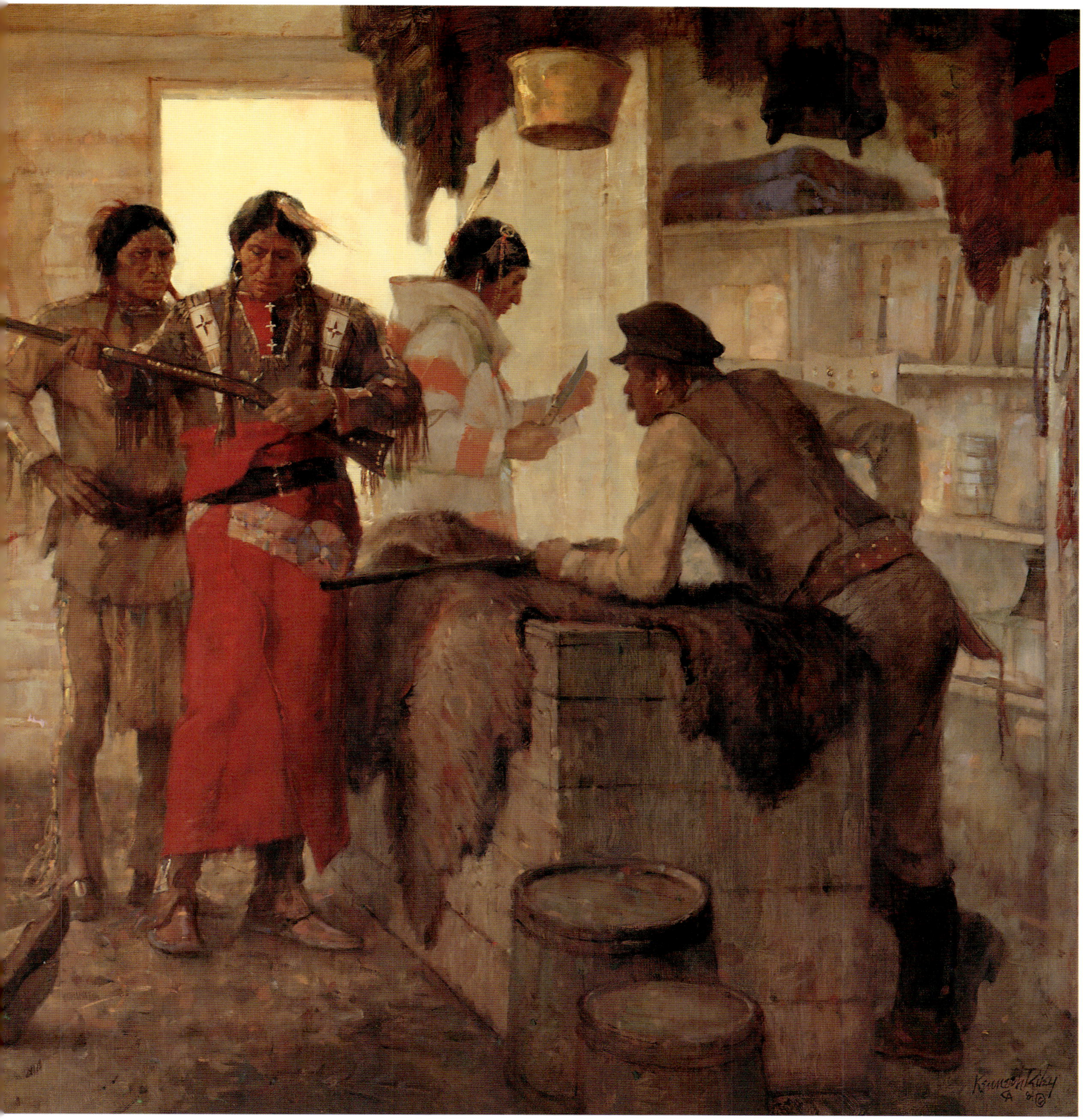

119. *Winter Hunt*

1990

acrylic, 16 x 18

Drawing upon the theories of Abstract Expressionism, I often begin a painting with color as my motive. The colors might be unnatural, as in the case of this Mandan scene, yet when combined with fragments of oppositional colors, the overall effect generates a mood as well as an environment that has sparkle and vibrancy.

Other directional devices that add interest to the picture space are light and dark patterns, contrasts of shape, and size relationships. The focal point of the picture may also be emphasized by contrasting value, movement, size or color. In ***In the Mandan Lodge of Four Bears [92],*** the movement of the foreground figure and his feathered pipes accelerates the eye to the principal subject. The red color along the route and the harder-edged silhouette of the Chief's face, as well as the lodge poles which point to his head, move the eye to the focus of this painting.

Likewise, lines can radiate out from a central point, as is the case with the tree branches used in ***Absaroka [103].*** The radiation outward is anchored in the contrasting solidity of the vertical of the trunk and figure crossed by the horizontal of the horse.

Paths and Stoppers

Changing the pace of the guiding line or line of direction adds interest to the composition. Some pictures place rest points along the route, stopping the eye as it seeks to find the central motif of the picture. This can be achieved by using an opposition line or form which slows or stops the flow of the action. In ***Tales of Medicine Bags [90]***, the composition begins with Catlin on the right and then makes a broad horizontal move to the crouched figures examining a pipe. Held in the picture by the standing figure, the eye stops at the man with his hands clasped who looks over to the focus of the figure holding a medicine bag. The corners of this composition are alternatively busy and quiet. I balanced the horizontal action on the right against the vertical action on the left.

Form

Form comprises shapes within the picture frame which combine to complete the statement. All shapes derive in theory from the triangle, circle or rectangle. These shapes may be comparatively two-dimensional, as in a painting relying on shallow space, or three-dimensional, where the forms move back into deep space.

The forms themselves are called positive shapes. The areas in between (or spaces) are negative shapes. In ***The Red Tepee [108]***, for example, the tepee is a positive shape while the inverted triangles of the sky area are

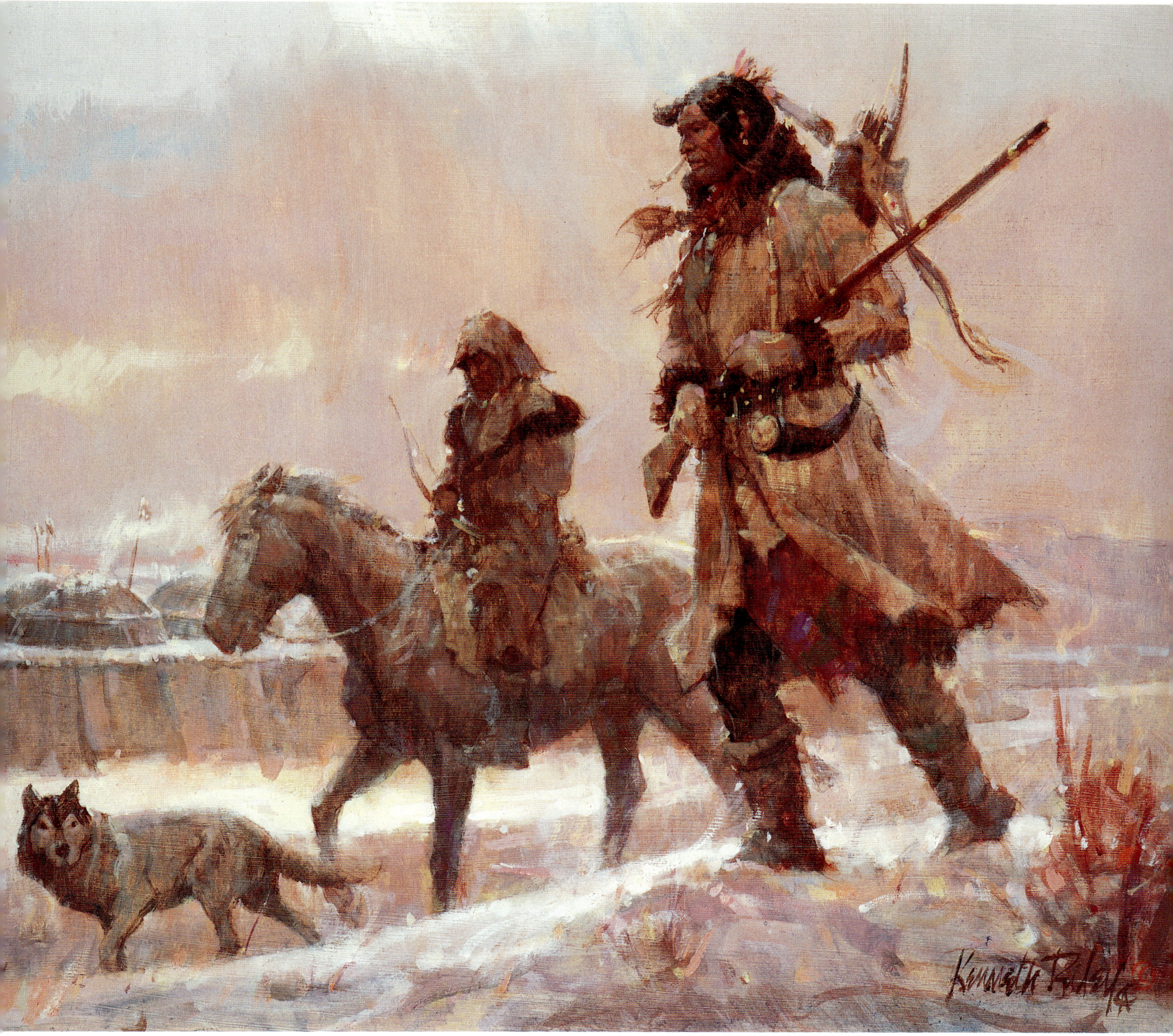

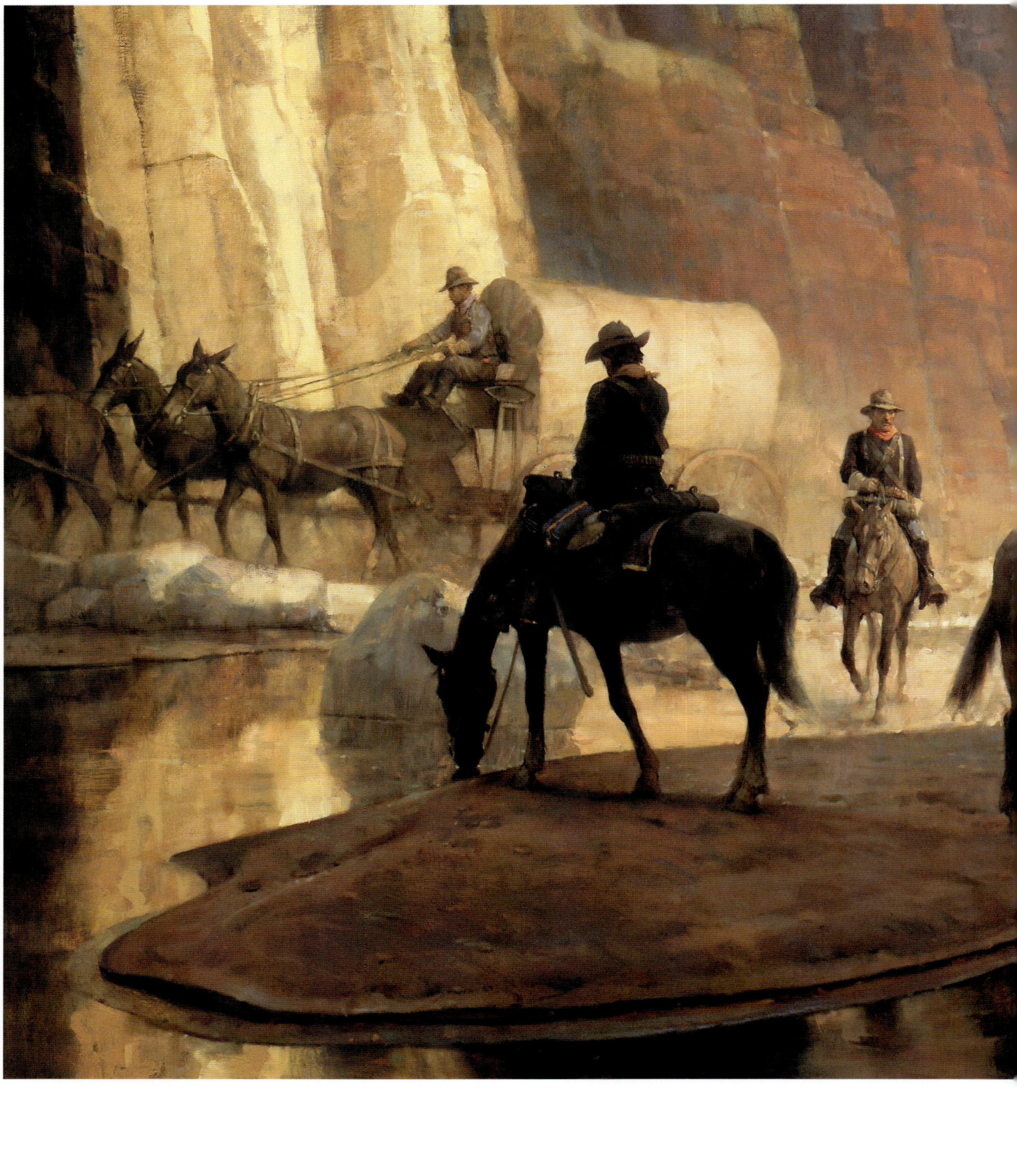

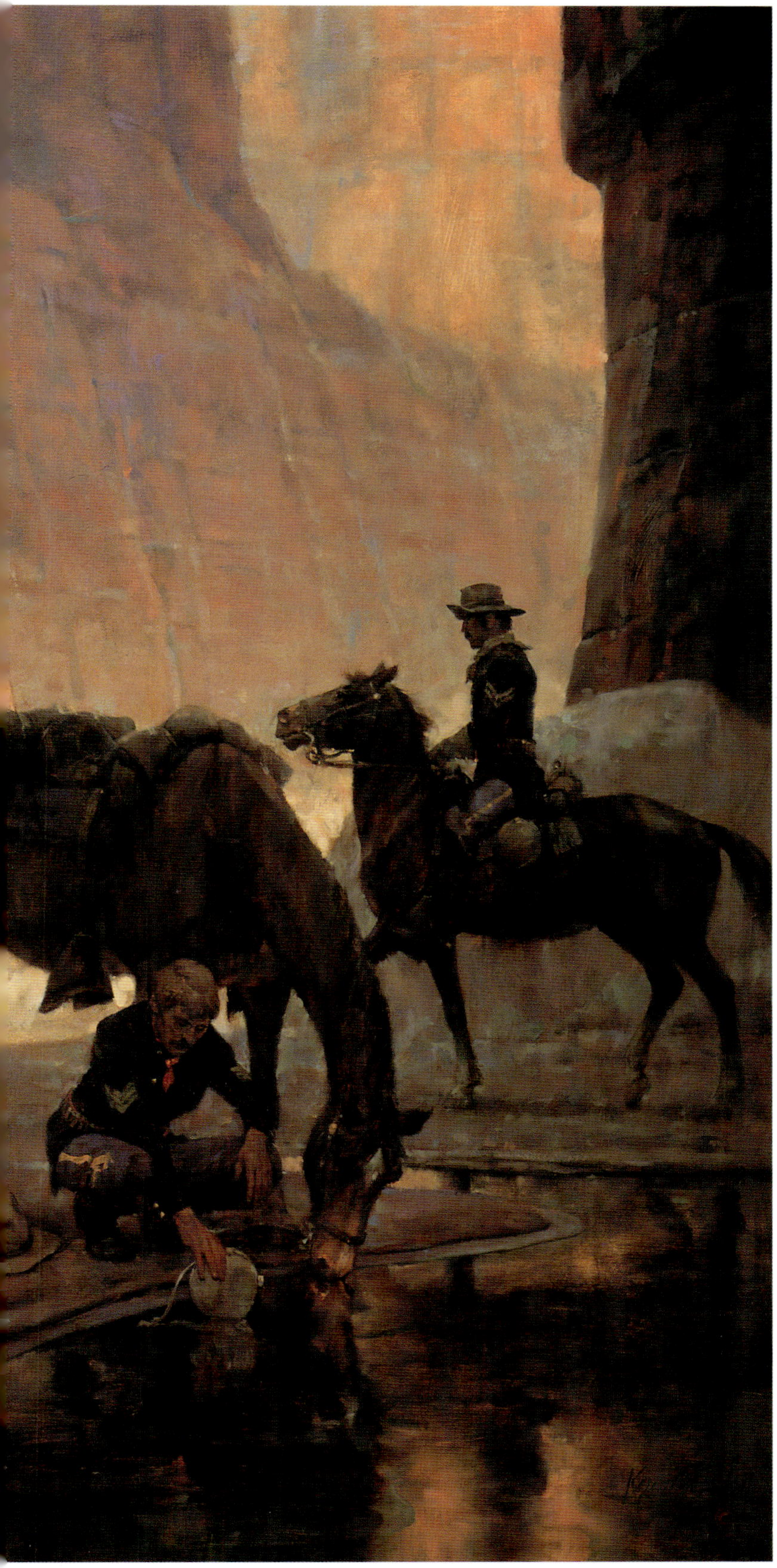

120. *Canyon Crossing*

1983

oil, 30 x 45

In the Southwest a cavalry unit on the move encountered a wide variety of terrain, little of which resembled a ride in the park. Vexing thorns, indignant mountain passes and rancorous boulders challenged all who traversed canyon country. Because of the scarcity of water, many treks were planned from one water hole or stream to the next. For me, the pool offered an opportunity to show reflected sunlight bouncing off the walls and creating large abstract patterns throughout the canvas.

121. *Cavalry Charge*
1984
oil, 24 x 48

Accounts of early wars often refer to the intimidating nature of a cavalry charge. To be in the direct path of a thundering mass of horse flesh and yelling riders caused many a foe to break and run. The same psychology has been applied to twentieth-century tank attacks. Although the result might be the same, the romance of elegant equine shapes would be missing.

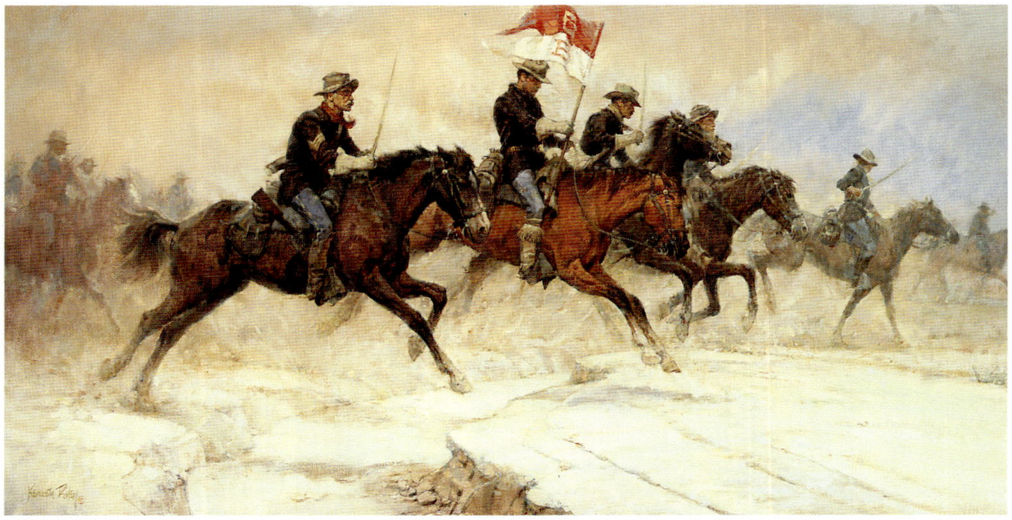

negative shapes. Negative shapes have form and affect the picture space as much as positive shapes. The arrangement of positive and negative shapes contributes to the rhythm, balance and scale of the Idea.

Shape is one way of establishing a center of interest, particularly if it is the most interesting shape or a sharply contrasting shape. Shapes repeated, like the crouching figures in ***Apache Scouts [113]***, set up rhythm, balance and direction, and give a picture a theme. Shapes can also become foils, one against the other (as with the triangular shape of the shadow in ***Apache Scouts***) creating tension, force or opposition to the subject.

In composing the large forms, rhythm and pattern should be established first, and the secondary shapes then fit into the larger scheme in a way that strengthens the whole. This may be thought of as a large plane of positive shapes balanced against the negative space or background. In ***Cochise [94],*** the horizontal line of running horses behind Cochise provides a foil for his static pose. This is an example of a strong horizontal shape balancing a central vertical shape.

122. *The Elders*
1991
oil, 12 x 9

Our youth-oriented society has lost sight of the philosophy that age should be venerated. In Indian society, on the other hand, an elder's accumulated experience is considered a reference point for the young. The elder's wisdom is sought as both a record of the past and a vision for the future.

Alignment

Some simple rules to consider in arranging shapes within the framework of the picture are: Edges of the shapes should not touch exactly. It is better to have them bypass slightly. Shapes that overlap one another halfway have a

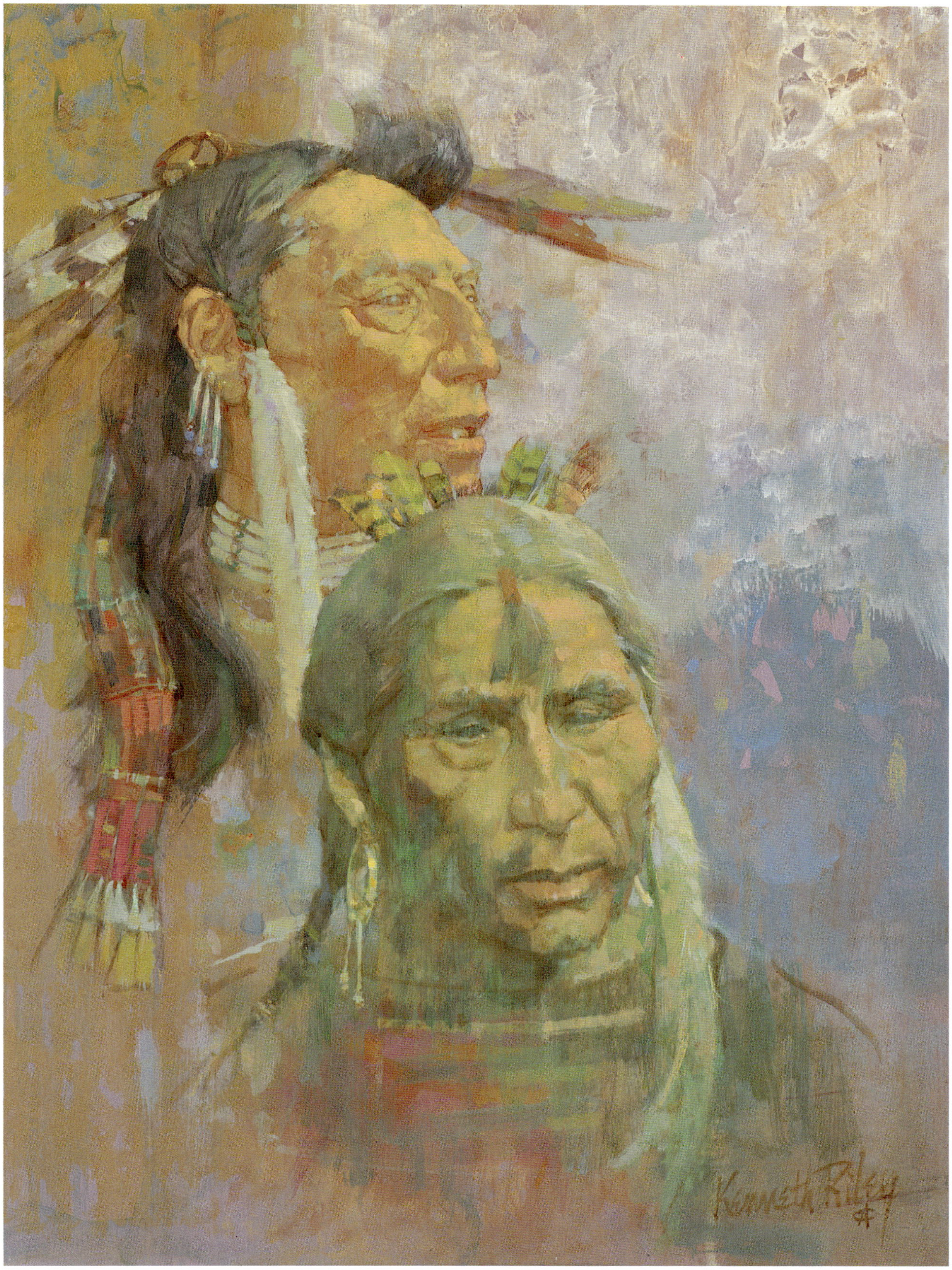
Kenneth Riley

123. *Chiricahua Warrior*

1980

oil, 24 x 20

Before the Apache acquired fire arms and white man's clothing, he dressed in a loin cloth made of soft leather topped by a Mexican white-cotton shirt. His moccasin boots had turned up toes and could be pulled over the knee to protect against cactus and rock. The bow, arrows and lance were made from desert plants. His scrawny horse was no doubt overworked and underfed from lack of good forage, yet the Apache made the animal leather boots to protect its legs from the harsh environment.

habit of canceling each other out. A shape should not be forced to the edge of the picture, nor should it cut the picture in two.

Plane

Plane deals with the forms of the subject or objects in relationship to the flat surface of the picture. The forms may be parallel to the observer/picture surface or at a diagonal or right angle to it. In composing, think in terms of flat planes that give direction or movement and three-dimensional planes that suggest objects moving into space. Flat planes and three-dimensional planes can also be worked in combination with one another. In ***The Source [63],*** which is a purposefully shallow-depth picture, the flat, circular shape of the pool leads back to the diagonal plane of horse and rider to meet up with the vertical plane of the canyon wall. Many pre-Renaissance painters simplified the method of constructing their paintings by dividing the picture into three planes—foreground, middle distance, background—and assigning different colors, values or objects to each. The approach is useful when planning a composition in depth. In ***Cottonwood Crossing [27],*** the foreground is a stream, the mid-ground includes figures, and the background is a wall of dark-blue mountains.

Pattern

The elements of line, form (shape), value and color produce patterns which should be arranged according to size, scale and angle in depth. Used only as a flat pattern, these elements move parallel to the picture plane, as is the case in ***Shadows [102]*** where the shapes are basically two-dimensional. In paintings with deep space, the pattern moves not only across the surface of the painting but also in depth. In selecting props for your pictures it is important to be conscious of variety in both flat and three-dimensional patterns, which adds interest to the total effect.

In setting up rhythm, movement, balance and scale, think in the largest terms first and organize a variety of sizes and characters. In ***The White Pony [51]*** I used two Ideas: a tonal, white-on-white coloration, combined with the vertical trees and figure. The balancing foil is in the diagonal of the horse. The space is also divided in depth by a large textured foreground that gives way to a distant diagonal background and thin strip of sky.

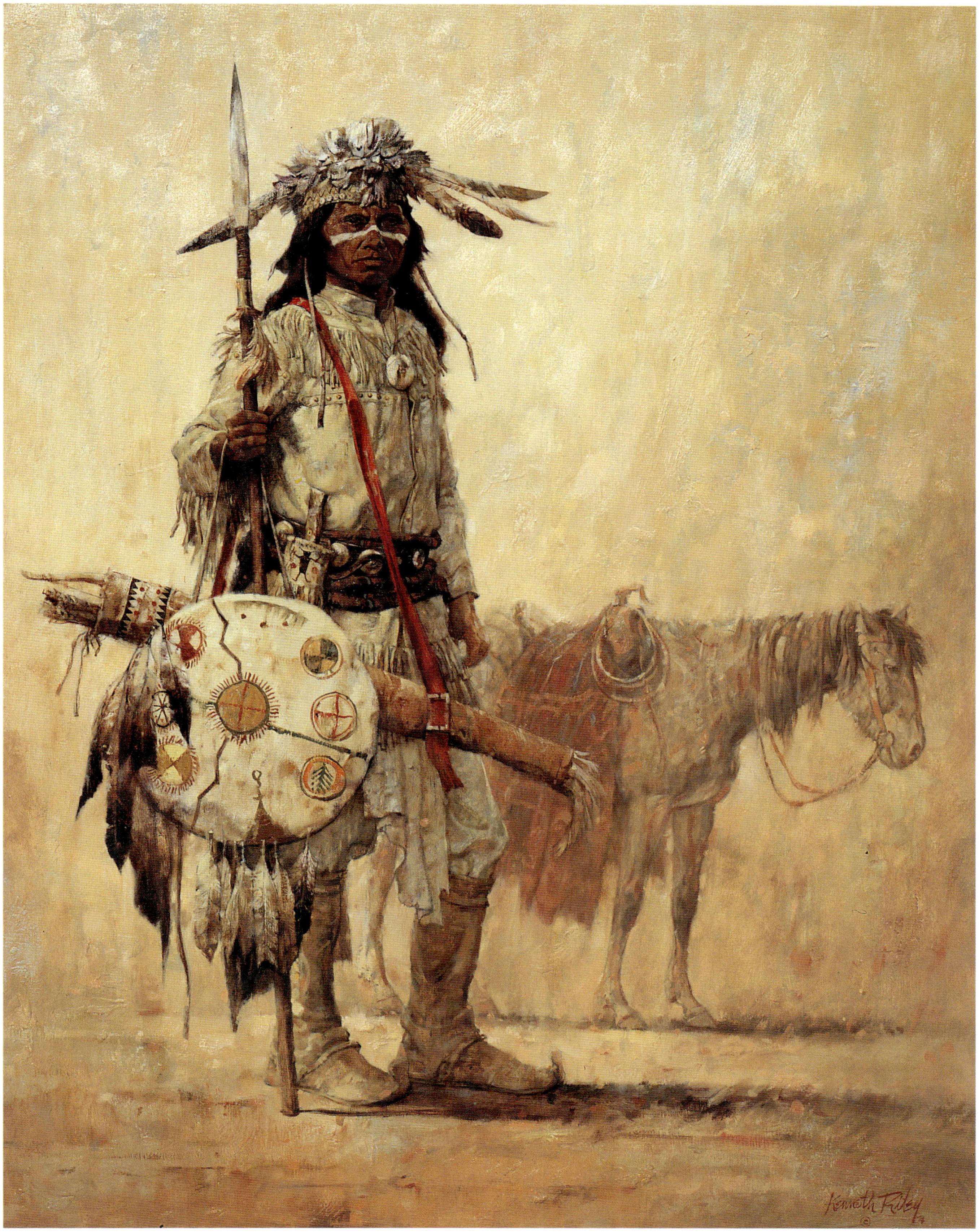
Kenneth Riley

Overlapping

In working with pattern, it is useful to use one shape in front of another to achieve depth or create more interesting larger forms. The three Mandan Indians in ***Visit of Lewis and Clark [54]*** overlap to create a larger and more interesting shape. The compression of their shape is balanced by the tiny figures in a large, open space on the right. Large shapes are often the point of interest. Overlapping shapes also create variety in volume by the amount of the shape that is exposed.

Forms contained by line create silhouettes in unlimited variety. The artist must be sensitive to relationships of various silhouettes and constantly play one against the other for variety, scale, balance, tension, movement—round against rectangular, regular against irregular, or hard against soft. Sensitivity to silhouettes—their abstraction and reaction to one another—adds dimension to the art of picture-making.

Closely allied with silhouette is a type of picture known as a "vignette." A vignette deals with the silhouette of an object or arrangement of objects against a white background. A large silhouette was the Idea in ***The Algonquian Family [59]*** which depicts people and horses compressed against a flat, slightly atmospheric backdrop. The artist must be aware of the shapes of individual units of the arrangement, as well as the outline of the large shape created by them. The contour of this large shape will first attract the viewer. Just as important, however, is the silhouette or contour of the negative space which likewise plays an important part in creating interest in the overall shape.

Value

Light produces values or gradations of brightness which in turn give the sensation of space. The range of value (or what is termed "key") depends on the intensity of light, whether it is high-key bright sunlight, middle tone, or low-key candlelight. In some pictures, high-key may dominate; in others, it may be the middle tone or low-key. Strong pictures focus on simplicity by using a basic tonal plan and an arrangement of value in a definite tonal range.

The full tonal range from black to white should be used in order to fully express the Idea. Emphasizing a particular tonality or value range, however, can contribute to the presentation, emphasis or storytelling qualities of the picture. The high-key picture, with major values in the top area of the

124. *Welcome Shade*
1980
oil, 36 x 24

This is a narrative painting for which any attempt at a description is only redundant.... I'm not alone among artists who wonder why we need critics to tell us the whys and hows of our pictures.

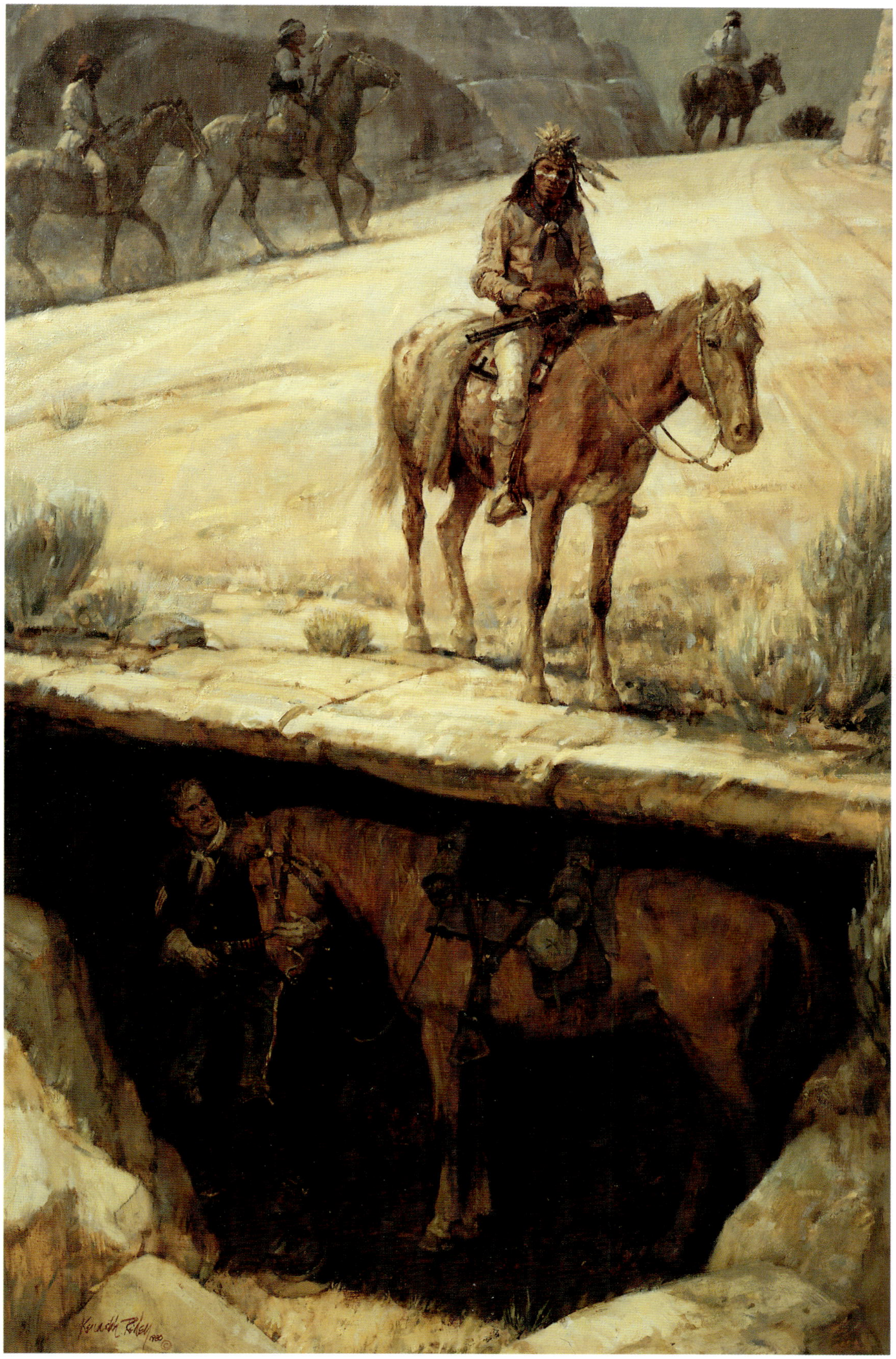

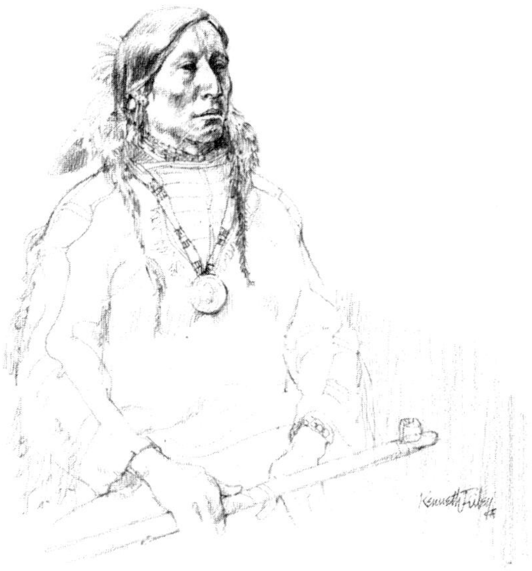

light-dark scale, can convey sunlight, the feeling of outdoors or a mood of gaiety ***[Camelot, 4].*** The middle range connotes elegance. Low key, that area from the half-tone to black, suggests night, interiors, mystery or richness ***[Zapotec, 106].*** A picture may be generally within a category while using accents of the other categories ***[Pisac Market, Peru, 98].*** It is important to remember that each area of a picture has a basic value key even though it contains accents. Holding a basic value supports the continuity of the picture plane and avoids a spotty look.

In order to arrange values in the simplest terms, we can reduce the range to four values: white, light grey, dark grey, and black. These provide an unlimited range of expression in four planes: greys and black on a white background, white and black on a light grey background, white and black on a dark grey background, or greys and white on a black background. Attention focuses where the greatest value difference is indicated, the extreme being black against white. Note the Indian's head silhouetted against the light of a doorway in ***The Robe Trade [118].*** This is a device to remember in forcing a center of interest.

Thumbnail sketches should reflect a simple value plan that eliminates detail. You can always elaborate later. Keep in mind that the tonal relationships have direction, rhythm, balance and counterbalance, and are related to each other as well as within their own areas.

Color

Color creates space, movement and the most immediate emotional response. It can soothe, startle, amuse, please or anger, as well as denote time (noon or night), place or thing.

We all possess both intuitive and educated color senses. These work together to create a personal use and response to color composition. The color of objects in relation to the whole sets a mood. The color scheme in ***Camelot [4]*** is festive. The color mood in ***Zapotec [106]*** is regal, while the color mood in ***In the Mandan Lodge of Four Bears [92]*** might be called somber. The play of one color against another can also carry the eye throughout the composition and thereby create movement.

Color is divided into two types: warm or cool. Warm colors advance, cool colors recede, giving depth to a picture. In general, a picture carries a predominant color scheme, either warm or cool. This decision must be

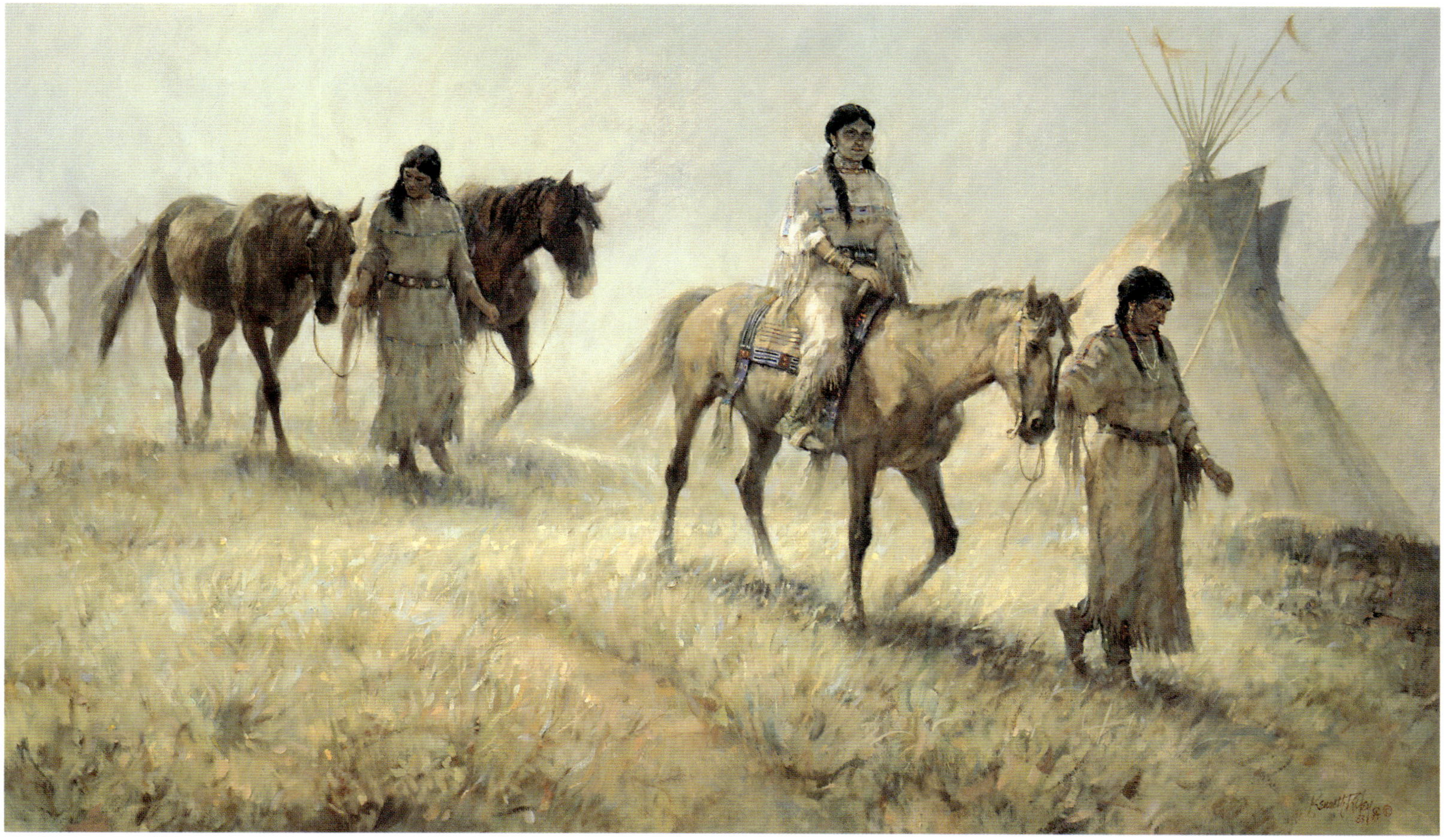

125. *The Dowry*

1983

oil, 26 x 45

One of the common threads in marriage rituals throughout time is the delivery of gifts from the bride to the groom and vice versa. In the instance of a Cheyenne wedding party, the bride was conveyed on horseback by her mother, followed by her sisters who led horses as gifts to the groom's family. Wearing a doe-skin dress, cured snow-white and silk-soft, the bride would no doubt be experiencing a joy tinged with sadness ... which is why I painted this scene in a warm, nostalgic light.

126. *Dog Dancers*
1981
oil, 36 x 30

The Dog Society of the Hidatsa Indians comprised the most courageous warriors whose success in battle allowed them to participate in specialized rituals. In this painting I drew upon Bodmer's documentation of costume elements to come up with my own version of the hypnotic dance. Since the designs and textures were my primary interest, I lit the scene with flat front lighting, which emphasizes the interplay of elements. What can I say but I just love all these patterns!

made in planning the picture, then the artist may select a dominant hue of red, yellow or blue. ***Bodmer Paints the Piegan Chief [6]*** is predominantly warm and yellow, whereas ***The War Lodge [117]*** is predominantly cool and blue.

The closer in balance the colors are the more quiet the picture seems. The colors in ***Absaroka [103]*** are all in balance and similar value, lending a feeling of quiet dignity. Excitement can be created by inserting occasional off-beat or strident color relationships, as in the progression from orange to blue in ***Romancing the West [18].*** It is wise to do color roughs in order to explore which color scheme best advances the Idea.

Texture

Although texture is primarily a surface quality, it can add interest and depth to a composition. Texture is a relief measure for the eye as it scans the surfaces in a picture. Texture also enlarges the language of the artist, enriching the response of the viewer by identifying form. Every plane has its own texture, whether smooth, rough, hard, soft, granular or slippery.

Texture can be broken into two categories: surface or local texture—the surface appearance of the object in real life; or, texture of the picture surface itself—brush strokes, their direction, size, thickness of paint, roughness or smoothness. (The latter should not be as much a concerted effort as a natural expression of the artist.) Texture can also help establish distance, since foreground textures are often more prominent than background—note the textured foreground contrasted against a flat background in ***The White Pony [51].***

Exercises

Pick up a good supply of variously colored and textured paper and/or cloth. Cut or tear the material into various shapes and then arrange abstract combinations on a sheet of cardboard. Use the principles of rhythm, balance and scale, and the elements of line, form, value, color and texture in your arrangements. The exercise will help strengthen the design of your realistic pictures.

In order to develop sensitivity to form, an excellent exercise is to take sheets of newspaper and begin tearing shapes at random, spreading them on the floor around you. Occasionally stop to compare and analyze those with interesting contours. Do this for ten minutes a day over one week and you

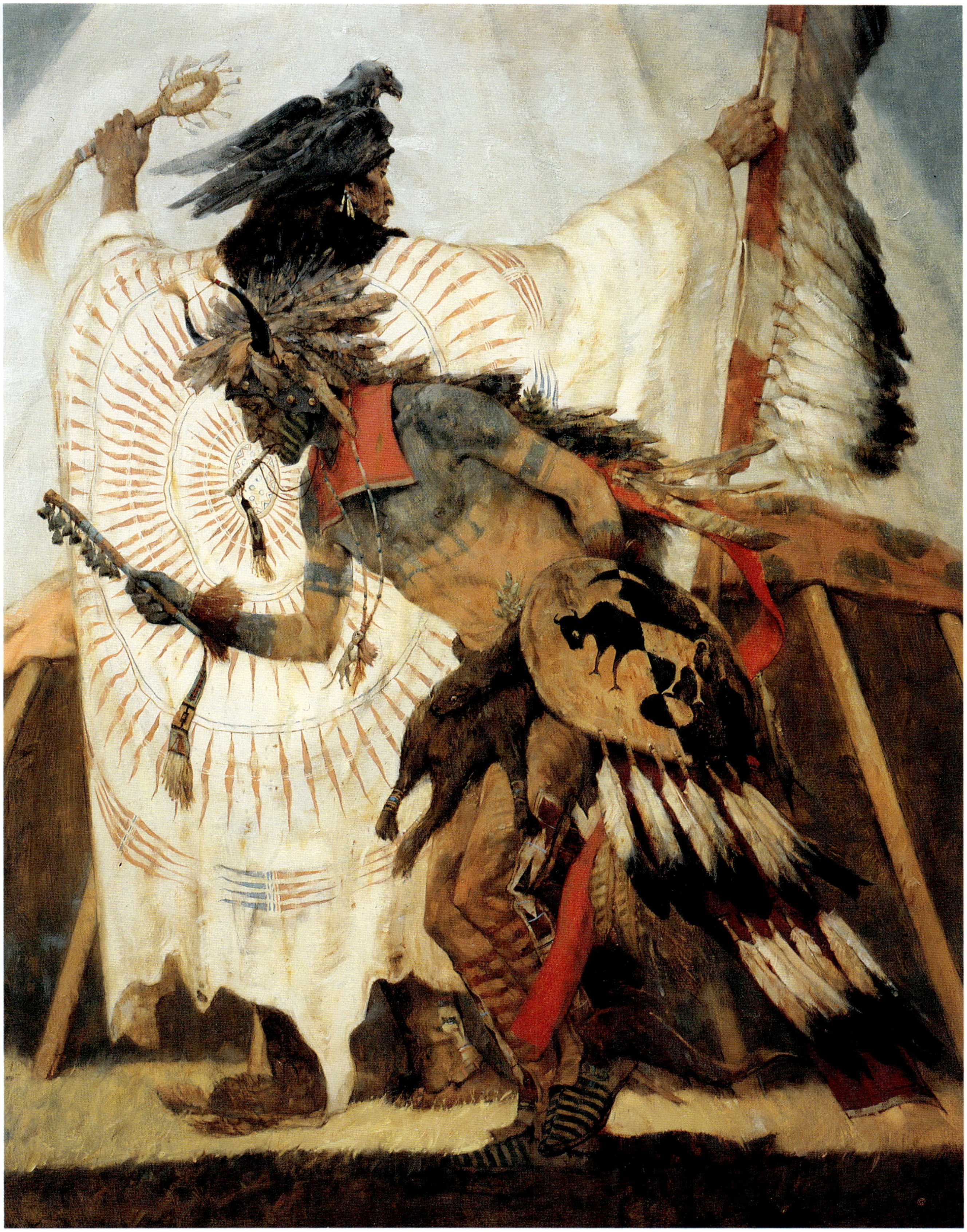

will become conscious of what constitutes a good shape and how to achieve it. Also, whether a shape falls into the category of circle, triangle or rectangle.

Unifying the Picture

Mood

Once you have your Idea in place, one of the first steps in conceiving and executing the picture is to decide what feeling or mood the picture should have to best project the Idea. Does the subject matter call for a happy or sad mood, delicate or brutal, peaceful or chaotic, mysterious or dignified? In creating the mood the artist brings into play all the elements discussed so far.

In ***The War Lodge [117]*** I wanted a feeling of pending action. The combination of verticals, triangular motifs and lost-and-found edges created an agitated, anticipatory mood—a feeling that these warriors are ready to begin their raid. ***Four Lances [8]*** on the other hand, creates mood with dramatic use of light, repetition of verticals and dynamic color.

Distortion

Distortion can be a useful and forceful means of making a point. It can be achieved by exaggerating perspective in order to accelerate or stall the Idea. The size of the canyon wall in ***Dry Camp [87]*** purposefully dominates the picture, stalling viewer involvement in the activities of the men below. Edgar Degas was noted for tilting his floor planes to gain immediacy, while El Greco (Spanish, 1541–1614) often attenuated his figures to emphasize elegance and anguish. Distortion is a powerful tool in composing the human figure ... so long as it is not an excuse for bad drawing!

Looking Angle

The distance from a subject and how much of it is in view is a design decision. In landscape paintings the artist might deal with deep space and scale, hence figures are generally small and at some distance ***[Red Flannel, 30].*** Whereas in portraiture the character of the head is all important with little or no background and shallow space ***[The Elders, 122].***

127. *Guarding the Herd*
1990
oil, 30 x 45

The Horse Culture of the Plains Indian revolutionized their mobility. In a very short time, Indians became dependent upon the animal, using them as transportation in search of food and in warfare. Horses were bartered and traded, coming to symbolize wealth and prestige. One of the highest honors was bestowed upon the warrior who managed to steal his enemy's war pony or buffalo runner. No wonder horses were so carefully guarded, even on a winter day when this man wears a trade blanket to keep himself warm.

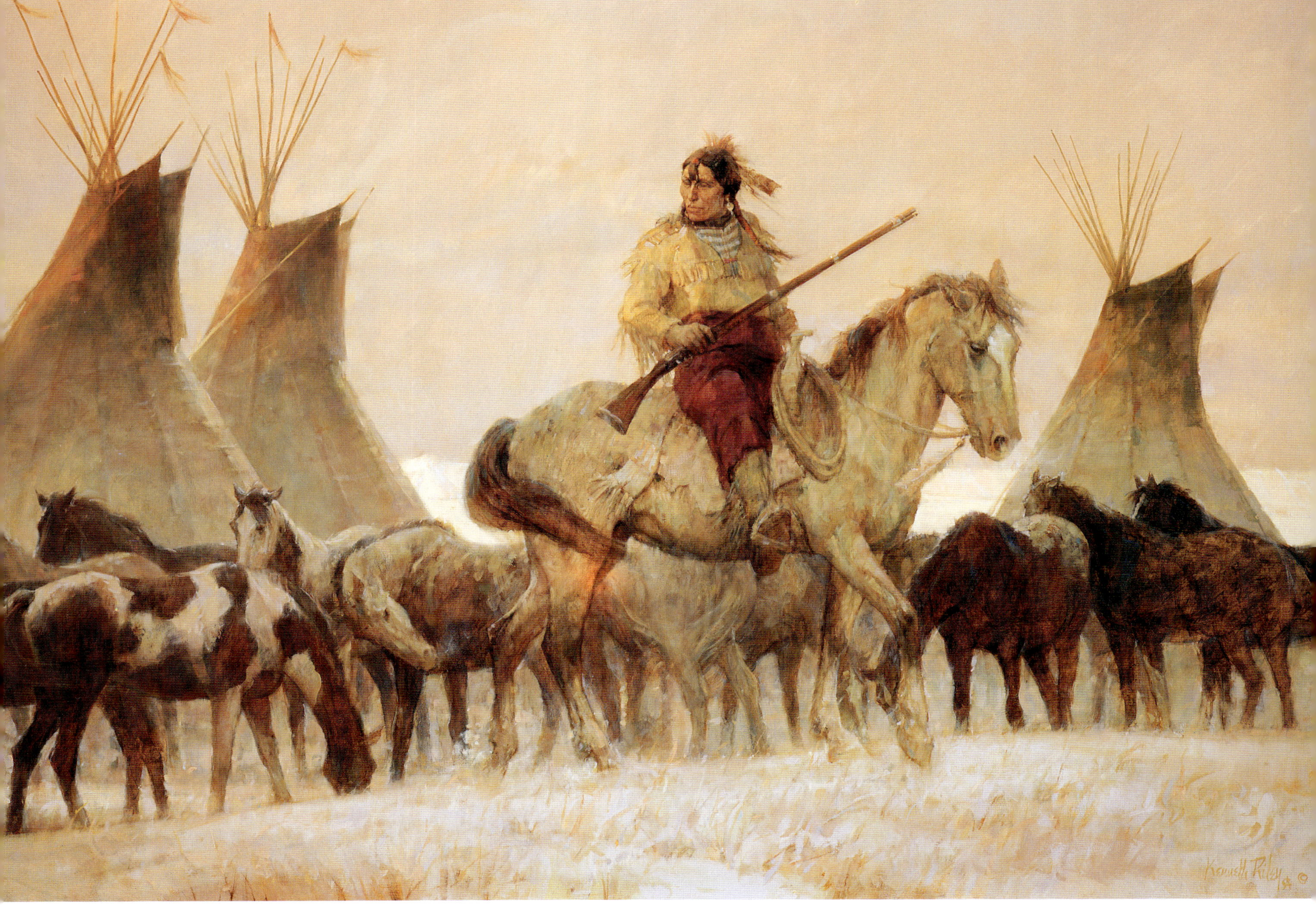

128. *Powwow Days*
1987
oil, 28 x 32

I often develop paintings around colors and shapes—all of which abound within Indian culture. The circle was a sacred shape for the Plains Indian, utilized in decorating both functional and ceremonial items. The circular shapes in this painting are balanced against the triangles of the tepees, with a variation on the theme appearing in the umbrella.

The artist must ask himself from which vantage point he wants to view the figure: front, back or side. Move around the subject mentally and decide which looking angle will best serve the Idea. The individuality of the artist is to a large degree determined by his ability to see the commonplace in a different way—to arrange the subject in space to make it seem fresh.

Horizon

Along with looking angle, the artist should consider the eye level or height from which the subject or scene will be viewed. This decision affects the horizon line, or that imaginary line to which objects in the picture would project in perspective.

Whether the scene is viewed from a high (bird's eye), low (worm's eye) or straight-on point of view enhances the storytelling, mood or Idea. Low horizons are dramatic and can become symbolic when used with large-scale figures ***[Chiricahua Warrior, 123].*** High horizons (at the top of the picture) offer more intimate views, compactness of shape and an affinity with surroundings ***[Cochise, 94].*** Avoid having the horizon line split the picture in the center, thereby creating two identical areas. In ***Welcome Shade [124]*** the use of the normal horizon for the top figure allowed me to get a dramatic downward view on the figure under the ledge.

Placement

"Looking angle" deals with the distance from viewer to subject and the amount of the subject to be included. "Horizon" considers point of view as to height. "Placement" regards the subject in relationship to the frame of the picture and to the other objects. The placement of the primary subject lends emphasis to it. The primary subject can be prominent in the foreground or set into the background, allowing the eye to find it. It can be tilted or pulled to the front. The exaggerated size and placement of the horse and rider on the left in ***Coming to Trade—Fort Union, 1833 [115]*** adds a drama that balances with riders going down a hill into a conventional landscape on the right.

A useful device for visualizing the Idea and stimulating creative placement is to approach the subject as if you are a stage director. Diagram a three-dimensional stage and then move the "actors" and "props" around the space to find out what arrangement best furthers the Idea.

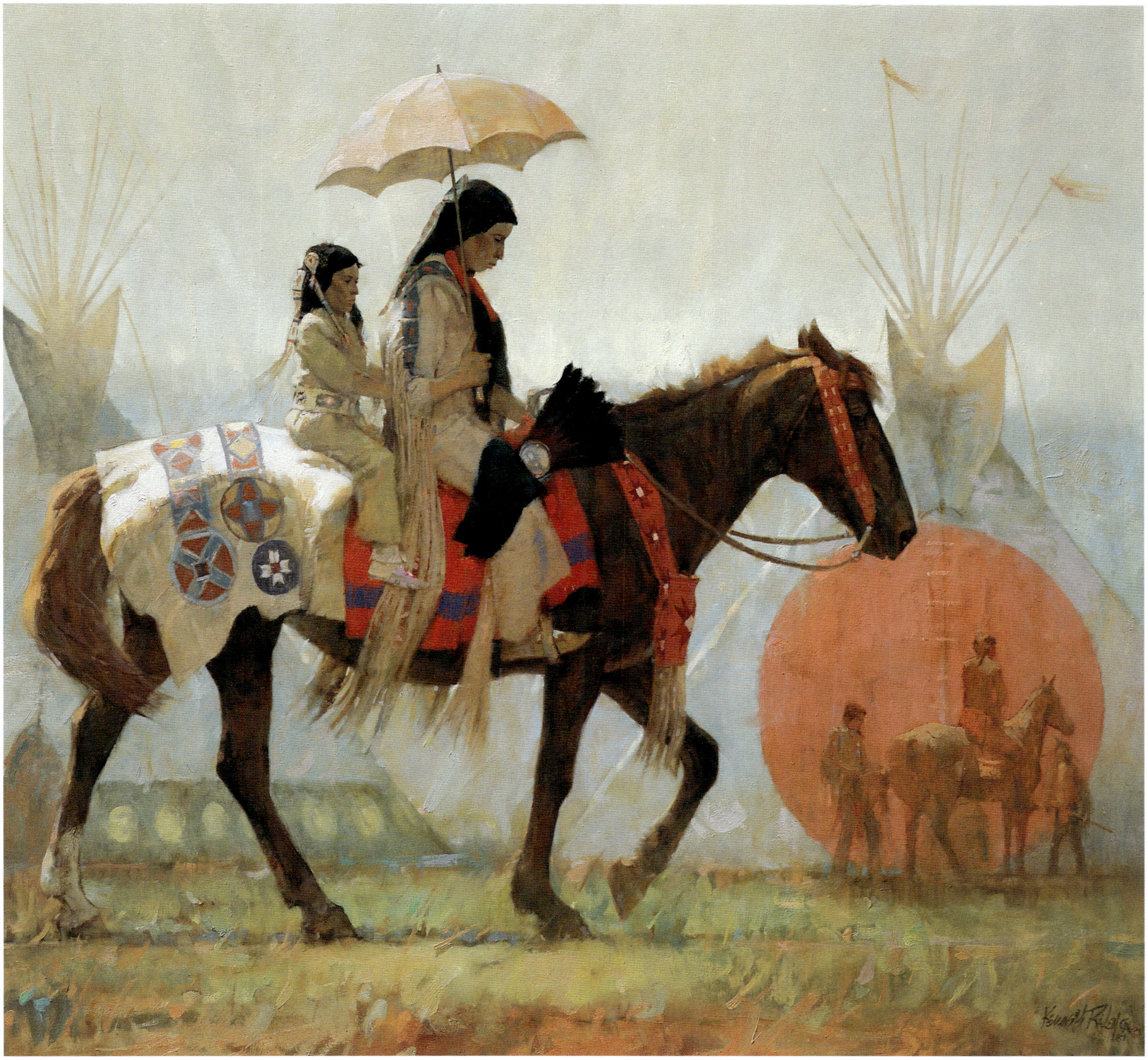

129. *Ceremonial Regalia*

1989

oil, 46 x 42

Leanin' Tree Museum,
Boulder, Colorado

The original idea for this work was to show the fore and aft of a costume along with a gun-stock war club. When I started composing the two figures with buffalo robes flung over their shoulders, however, I realized that a new form was created. This "third" entity came into focus when I placed the buffalo skull at the top. It also added the mystical connotation I had hoped to achieve in this work.

Lighting

While it is important to think in terms of the largest possible masses and tonal patterns in a composition, the way in which the subject is lighted also influences and determines pattern.

Flat light ***[Dog Dancers, 126]*** has a decorative, tonal or linear quality. It emphasizes local color, value and design. Back light ***[The Dowry, 125]*** calls attention to the silhouette or shape. Side light ***[Shadows, 102]*** provides volume by throwing form into strong relief.

The principles of rhythm, balance, movement, direction and emphasis are used to distribute the darks and lights of the composition. The tonal arrangements have their own abstract patterns as well as relationships and influences on one another. The strongest pictures are those in which the artist has made forceful, imaginative use of abstract pattern. A strongly designed picture with interesting patterns of darks, lights and middle values and bold thematic use of shape and color will stay in the viewer's mind for the longest time. If you can retain the placement of the abstract dark-and-light patterns as you develop the realistic elements of your original Idea in sketches, the abstract elements will show through, unifying and strengthening your picture.

All of these "rules" are but guides to decision making. The true test is understanding the rules and breaking them to the advantage of making a stronger statement and a picture with greater impact.

Keep worry and fear out of the picture. The joy is in the doing and that will come across to the viewer. If you don't love it, no one else will. —KR

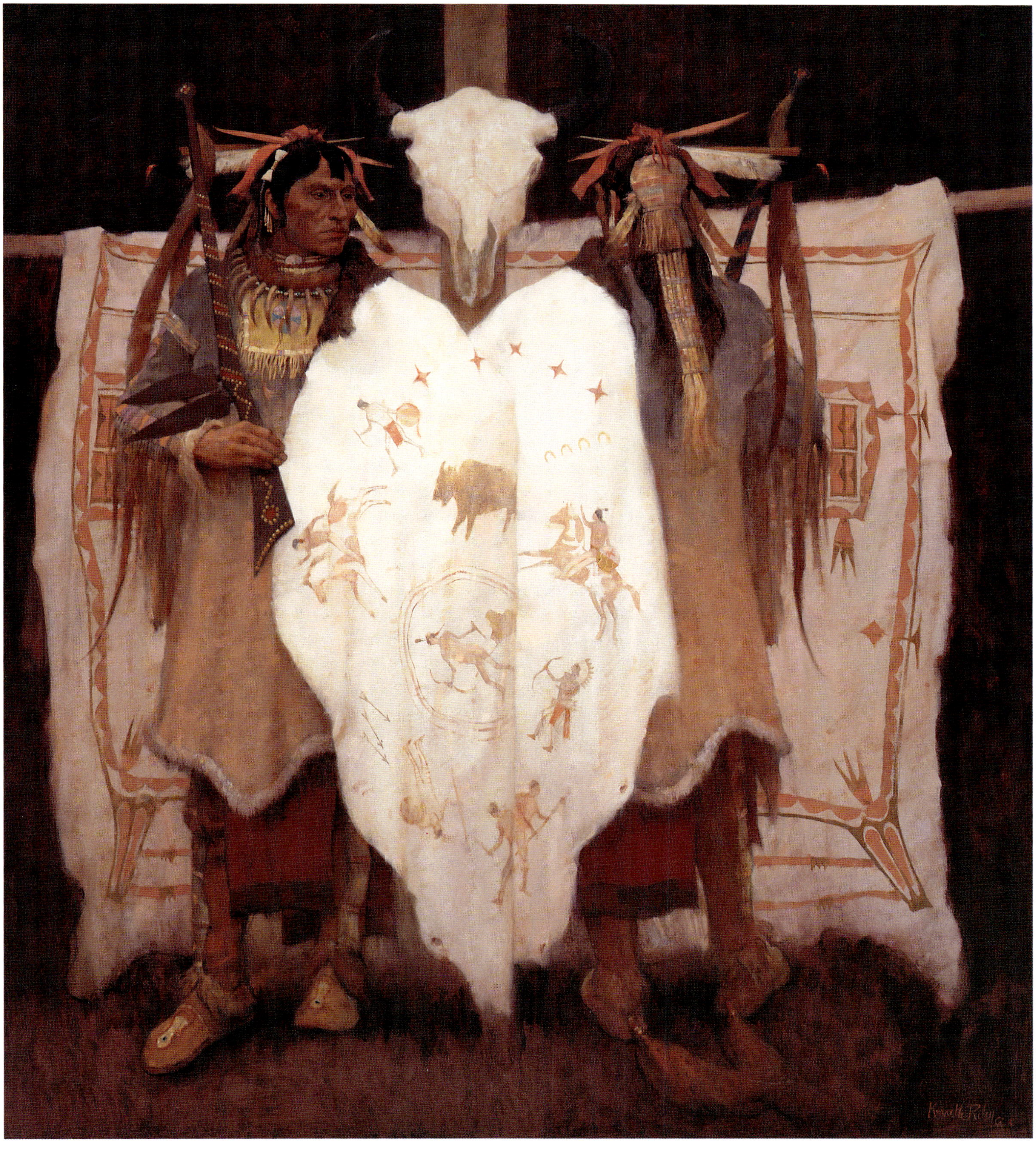

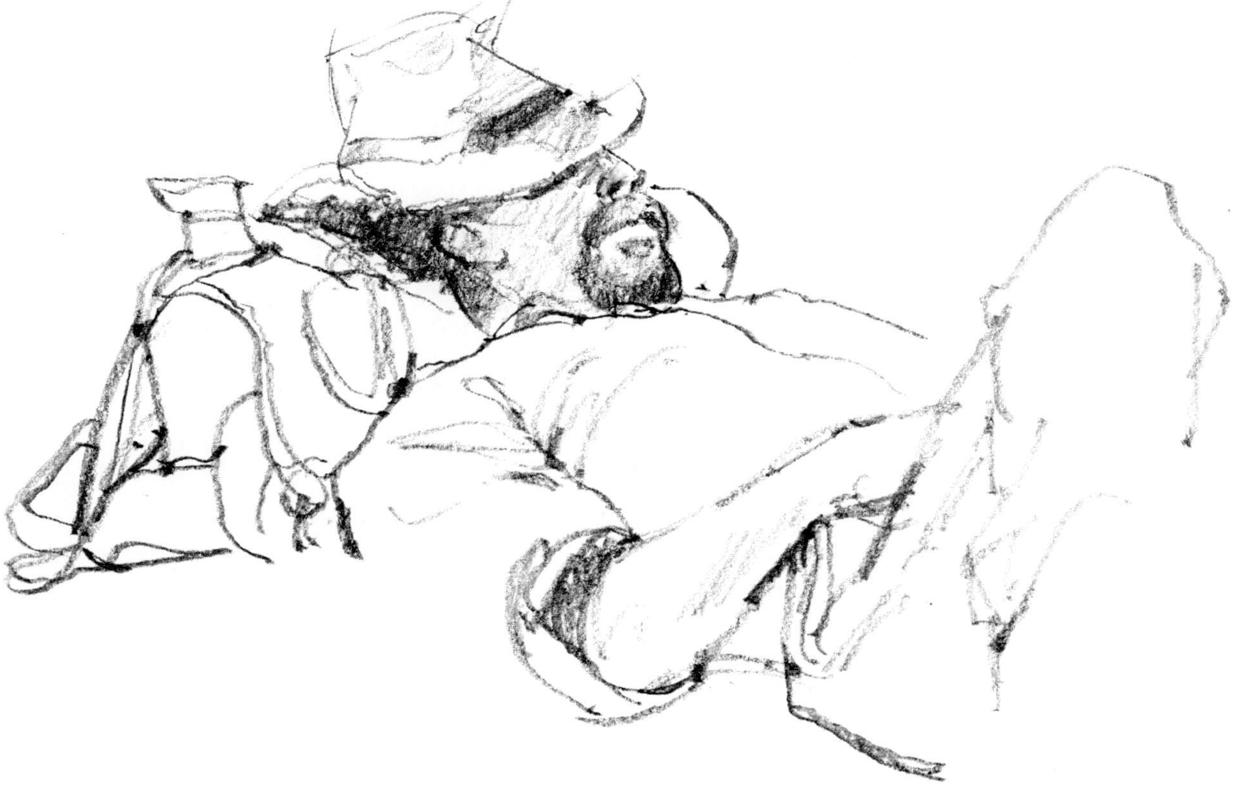

CHRONOLOGY

1919	Kenneth Pauling Riley born September 21 in Waverly, Missouri, the only child of Marie Pauling Riley and Elwin A. Riley.
1921	Riley family moves to Carrollton, Missouri. Ken spends weekends and summers at the farm of his maternal grandparents Edwin and Molly Pauling, near Blackburn, Missouri.
1925	Enters first grade at Carrollton Elementary School.
1926	Riley family moves to Parsons, Kansas. Attends Garfield Elementary School through fourth grade.
1929	Riley family moves to Blackburn, Missouri. Attends fifth and sixth grades at Blackburn School.
1931	Riley family moves back to Parsons. Attends East Junior High School.
1934	Enters Parsons High School. Plays drums with Eddie Lain and His Orchestra on weekends and summers through 1939.
1935	Takes first art/craft classes from Olive Rees.
1936	Wins award in a competition at Pittsburg Teachers College, Kansas.
1937	Graduates from high school. Enters pre-med program at Parsons Junior College.
1938	Enters a three-year art program at Kansas City Art Institute, Missouri.
1939	Begins dating fellow art student MarCyne Johnson.

Harvey Dunn put it best: Your good pictures belong to the world. Your bad pictures are all yours.—KR

1941	Receives scholarship to attend the Art Students League and moves to New York City. Marries MarCyne Johnson December 12. Studies with Frank Vincent DuMond at ASL. Takes evening classes with Harvey Dunn at Grand Central Art School.
1942	Enlists in the U.S. Coast Guard.

1943 Transfers to the Coast Guard Public Relations office, Seattle, Washington. Assigned as combat artist on the assault transport U.S.S. *Arthur Middleton* in South Pacific.

1944 Transfers to Coast Guard Headquarters, Washington, D.C. Exhibits in "Paintings and Drawings by U.S. Coast Guard Combat Artists," September 17–October 8, 1944, at the National Gallery of Art. Designs commemorative stamp for the Coast Guard. Wins grand prize at the 7th Annual Outdoor Art Fair sponsored by Washington *Times Herald.*

It would be wonderful if exhibitions could be held without prizes. Art is such a beautiful, individual accomplishment and not a competition. Prizes seem to be more for the sake of the patron than the artist.—KR

1945 Commissioned by David Finlay, director of the National Gallery of Art, to illustrate *War Letters of Morton Eustis* (Washington, D.C.). Discharged from the service in the fall. Moves to Ridgefield, Connecticut. Draws comic book vignettes for Simon and Kirby. Receives first illustration assignments for book covers and dust jackets for Doubleday Publishing Company, which later commissions illustrations for Fulton Oursler's *The Greatest Story Ever Told* (1950) and Anthony Trollope's *The Eustace Diamonds* (1951).

1946 Shows work at the Associated American Artists Gallery, New York City. Receives first illustration assignments for Bantam Books.

1947 Buys a cooperative apartment on West 75th Street in New York City. Receives first illustration assignments for *The Saturday Evening Post.* Illustrates fiction for the *Post* for fifteen years including the C. S. Forester series on Captain Hornblower beginning in the mid-1950s.

1948 Obtains agent Barry Stevens (later Frank Lavaty) to represent his work for fiction and nonfiction illustrations in *Cosmopolitan, Coronet (Esquire Publishing), McCalls, Redbook* and *Reader's Digest.*

1949 Moves to Peter Cooper Village, 23rd Street, New York City. Becomes part owner of a thirty-foot sloop called *The Whitecap.* Receives first assignments from the *National Geographic* to illustrate "The British Way" (April 1949). Additional assignments include "Raid on Deerfield" (June 1969).

1950 Purchases a cottage on Lake Candlewood, New Milford, Connecticut, for weekends and summers.

1952 Moves to an apartment in New Milford and begins building a home on a five-acre lot outside Danbury, Connecticut.

1953 Moves into Danbury home.

1956 Travels to Korea and Japan through the Society of Illustrators and the U.S. Air Force.

1959 Receives first assignment from *Life* magazine for a series of historical paintings of U.S. presidents. Additional *Life* assignments include a Civil War series 1961–1964, for which ***Surrender of Appomattox*** is now in U.S. Military Academy Museum at West Point, New York. Vacations five weeks in Europe, primarily Italy.

1960 Juried into the second annual Society of Illustrators exhibition. Also accepted in the 1962, 1964, 1967–68, 1971–74 exhibitions. Begins series of historical calendars for Humble Oil Company, New Jersey. Visitors Center of the Mormon Church, Salt Lake City, Utah, commissions eight paintings.

1962 National Guard Heritage Collection commissions four paintings of U.S. civilian militia in war-time activity, including ***The Battle of Bunker Hill*** which is presented to President John F. Kennedy in an Oval Room ceremony on September 25. Studies with Abstract Expressionist Reuben Tam at the Brooklyn Museum School, New York.

1964 Travels to Libya through the Society of Illustrators and the U.S. Air Force.

1965 Travels to Norway on commission for the Garrett Company and vacations in Sweden and Denmark. Commissioned by National Park Service to do the painting ***Fruitless Victory*** for the Visitors Center, Little Bighorn Battlefield.

1966 Travels to Grand Teton National Park and Yellowstone National Park for the Society of Illustrators Artists in the Parks program for the U.S. Department of the Interior.

1967 Travels to Mount Rushmore, the Black Hills and the Badlands for the Artists in the Parks program.

1968 Buys a summer home at Five Islands just outside of Georgetown, Maine. Conducts an eight-week seminar on illustration at Brigham Young University, Provo, Utah. Travels throughout Utah and the Four Corners area on weekends.

I think it was Degas who once said that at twenty-five years of age, everyone has talent. The problem is to have it when you reach fifty. —KR

1971 Makes plans to move to Arizona. Travels to Mesa, Tucson and Tombstone. Sells home in New Milford and moves to Five Islands.

1972	Moves to Tombstone and illustrates two book covers per month for Bantam. MarCyne runs gift shop "Silver Burro." Meets Stuart Johnson and joins Settlers West Galleries, Tucson, Arizona.
1973	Becomes charter member of the National Academy of Western Art, Oklahoma City, Oklahoma. Participates in the annual summer shows in 1973–1982, 1984–1988 and 1991. Settlers West hosts a two-man show for Riley and Joe Bohler. Makes first of many trips into Mexico.
1974	Shows work at Husberg Art Gallery, Sedona, Arizona, through 1977.
1975	Buys a home/studio on the northeast side of Tucson.
1976	Exhibits in the Royal Western Watercolor Exhibition, National Cowboy Hall of Fame, Oklahoma City, Oklahoma.
1977	Participates in centennial celebration at the Treaty Seven site, Calgary, Alberta, Canada.
1978	Spends a month at the Okanagan Wild Game Farm, Pentictan, British Columbia. Participates in Settlers West's annual "The Great American West" exhibition (1978-1992).
1979	Exhibits in "Tucson Collects: The West," Tucson Museum of Art, Arizona.
1980	Buys land near San Juan Peaks in southwestern Colorado. Exhibits in the Western Heritage Sale, Houston, Texas, through 1985. Exhibits in the Nita Stewart Haley Art Show, Midland, Texas, through 1982.
1981	Spends four weeks in Obidos, Portugal, and the summer painting in Colorado. Exhibits with the Driscol Collection of American Western Art in Beijing, China. Exhibits with the Artists of America, Denver Historical Society, Colorado (also 1982–1984, 1988, 1990). Spends three weeks in South America, primarily Peru and Bolivia.
1982	Joins Cowboy Artists of America and participates annually in the sale/exhibition at the Phoenix Art Museum, Arizona, through 1992. Exhibits with the Biltmore Celebrity Art Show and Sale, Los Angeles, California, through 1984. Participates in Settlers West's annual "The American Miniature Exhibition" (1982-1992).
1983	Awarded Silver Medal at CAA show for ***Visit of Lewis and Clark.*** Exhibits in opening celebration of Cowboy Artists of America Museum, Kerrville, Texas, and continues to exhibit in anniversary celebrations through 1992.
1984	Selected Artist of the Year, National Western and Wildlife Society, Minneapolis, Minnesota. Teaches design workshop at the Cowboy Artists of America Museum. Travels to Nepal, India and Pakistan. Awarded Gold Medal and Best of Show at CAA show for ***Mandan Gold.***

1985	Travels to Spain and Portugal with Western Heritage artists; takes sidetrip to Morocco.
1986	Builds a new home/studio on northeast side of Tucson. Exhibits with Cowboy Artists of America at the Missouri Athletic Club, St. Louis. Teaches as part of the CAA-Ten workshop at the CAA Museum.
1987	Awarded Silver Medal for ***The Red Tepee*** and Stetson Award at the CAA show. Exhibits with Cowboy Artists of America in "Images West," Old Pueblo Museum, Tucson, Arizona.
1988	Selected as Tucson Festival Artist of the Year. Awarded Gold Medal and Best of Show for ***Four Lances*** and Stetson Award at CAA Show.
1989	Awarded Gold Medal for ***Ceremonial Regalia*** and Stetson Award at CAA Show. Teaches a workshop on the human figure at CAA Museum.
1990	Exhibits at the Hubbard Award of Excellence Exhibition and Sale, Ruidoso, New Mexico.
1991	Receives Cowboy Artists of America Museum Roundup Award.
1993	Receives Eiteljorg Award for Excellence and given retrospective exhibition, July-September, at the Eiteljorg Museum of American Indian and Western Art, Indianapolis, Indiana.

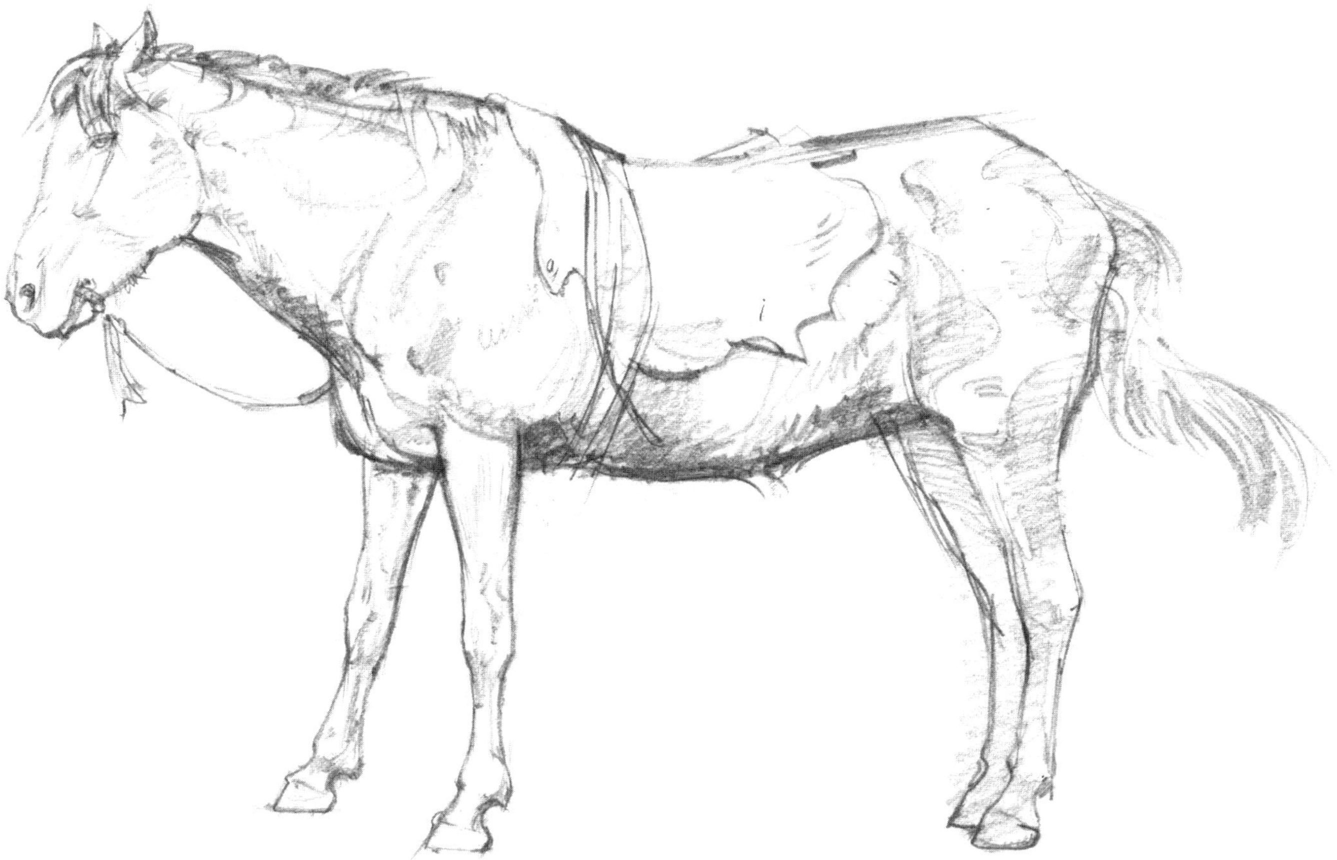

SELECTED BIBLIOGRAPHY

Abrams, Herbert E. "The Teachings of Frank Vincent DuMond: Penetrating Light." *American Artist*, March 1974, 36–45.

Adams, Henry. *Thomas Hart Benton, An American Original.* New York: Alfred A. Knopf, 1989.

Altermann and Morris Auction Catalogs. Dallas/Houston: April 1985, June 1985, December 1987, February 1990, November 1991, February 1992.

American Miniature Exhibition (annual). Tucson, Arizona: Settlers West Galleries, 1982–1992.

Anderson, Jeffrey and Charles B. Ferguson. *The Harmony of Nature: The Art and Life of Frank Vincent DuMond.* Old Lyme, Connecticut: Lyme Historical Society, 1990.

Annual, The. New York: Society of Illustrators, 1960, 1962, 1964, 1967–68, 1971–1974.

Arnold, Elliott. *Blood Brother.* Lincoln: University of Nebraska Press, 1979.

Artists of America Annual Catalogs. Denver: Denver Rotary Club/Denver Historical Society, 1981–1984, 1988, 1990.

Bartell, James. "Ken Riley." *Art of the West,* Jan/Feb 1991, 24–31.

Benton, Thomas Hart. *An American in Art—A Professional and Technical Autobiography.* Lawrence: University of Kansas, 1969.

————. *American Regionalism.* Lawrence: University of Kansas, 1969.

Blanchard, Dan, and Walter Gray (producer). *Creative Crafts.* Oklahoma City: Community Workshop of the Metropolitan Library System, KTVY-NBC, 1978. Video tape.

Bourke, John G. *On the Border with Crook.* Lincoln: University of Nebraska, 1971.

Buscombe, Edward, ed. *The BFI Companion to the Western.* London: The British Film Institute, 1988.

Catlin, George. *North American Indians.* New York: Penguin Books, 1989.

Cotterman, Dan. "Sagebrush Artist: Kenneth Riley." *Horse and Rider,* October 1987, 31–33.

Cowboy Artists of America Catalogs. Phoenix: CAA and Phoenix Art Museum, 1982–1992.

Cowboy Artists of America Museum Auction Catalog. Kerrville, Texas: CAA Museum in conjunction with Texas Art Gallery, Dallas, May 1985.

Dedera, Don. *Visions West—The Story of the Cowboy Artists of America Museum.* Kerrville, Texas: CAA Museum, 1983, 58–59.

DeVoto, Bernard, ed. *The Journals of Lewis and Clark.* Boston: Houghton Mifflin Company, 1953.

Dunn, Harvey. *An Evening in the Classroom.* New York: Mario Cooper, 1934.

Fielding, Mantle. *Mantle Fielding's Dictionary of American Painters, Sculptors and Engravers.* Poughkeepsie, New York: Apollo Book, 1983, 785.

Gerdts, William H. and Mark Thistlethwaite. *Grand Illusions—History Painting in America.* Fort Worth, Texas: Amon Carter Museum, 1988.

Goetzmann, William H., et al. *Karl Bodmer's America.* Lincoln: Joslyn Art Museum and University of Nebraska Press, 1984.

Great American West Catalogs (annual). Tucson, Arizona: Settlers West Galleries, 1978–1992.

Guthrie, A.B., Jr. *The Big Sky.* Boston: Houghton Mifflin, 1947.

Halsey, Ashley, Jr. *Illustrating for The Saturday Evening Post.* Boston: The Arlington House, 1951, 103–105.

Harvey, Betty. "Ken Riley." *Artists of the West and the Golden Rockies,* Spring 1976, 20–23.

Hassrick, Royal. *Western Painting Today.* New York: Watson Guptill, 1975, 30.

Jim Fowler's Period Gallery West Catalogs. Scottsdale, Arizona: Spring/Summer 1979, November 1979, 1980, 1982.

Johnson, Stuart. "Reflections of an American Artist." *Art West,* Fall 1978, 40–47.

Karolevitz, Robert F. *Where Your Heart Is—The Story of Harvey Dunn.* Aberdeen, South Dakota: North Plains Press, 1970.

May Galleries Auction Catalogs. Scottsdale, Arizona: March and October 1986; March 1987; March and October 1988; January, April and July 1990; January 1992.

Mayer, Kay. "Kenneth Riley." *Art West,* December 1982, 83–86.

National Academy of Western Art Catalogs. Oklahoma City: National Cowboy Hall of Fame, 1978, 1979, 1982, 1984–88, 1991.

National Finals Art Auction Catalogs (annual). Las Vegas: Settlers West Galleries and Drummond Gallery, 1986–1991.

Pontello, Jacqueline M. "MarCyne Johnson." *Southwest Art,* June 1987, 29-31.

Quinn, R.M. "Bringing History Alive." *Southwest Art,* July 1981, 50–57.

Reed, Walt and Roger Reed. *The Illustrator in America.* New York: The Society of Illustrators, 1984, 274.

"Riley Paints Western History." *Today's Art Magazine*, 1979.

Reynolds, Catherine A., et al. *Cowboy Artists of America*. El Paso, Texas: Desert Hawk Publishing, 1988, 113–115.

Samuels, Peggy and Harold. *Encyclopedia of Artists of The American West.* Secaucus, New Jersey: Castle Books, 1976, 400.

————. *Contemporary Western Artists*. Houston: Southwest Art Publishing, 1982, 440–441.

Schoolcraft, Henry R. *The Hiawatha Legends*. Autrain, Michigan: Avery Color Studios, 1990.

Sussmann, M. Hal. "Kenneth Riley." *Southwest Art*, October 1989, 78–85.

Texas Art Gallery Preview and Auction Catalogs. Dallas: June and September 1983; March, September and December 1984; March and September 1985; May 1986; June and November 1989; March, September and December 1990; March 1991.

Weller, Allen and Lee Nordness. "Reuben Tam." *Art USA: Now*. New York: Viking Press, 1962, 308–311.

Western Heritage Sale Annual Catalogs. Houston/Grapevine, Texas: Connally-Marchman-Pierce Association, 1980–1985.

PRINTS AND POSTERS

Algonquian Family, The. Poster image for Cowboy Artists of America exhibition, Phoenix Art Museum, Arizona, 1992.

Bitterroot Trappers. Photo-offset lithograph, 12 x $22\frac{3}{4}$, edition 350, National Print Galleries, Scottsdale, Arizona.

Blackfeet Chiefs. Photo-offset lithograph, $16\frac{1}{2}$ x 20, edition 900, Hadley Companies, Bloomington, Minnesota, 1984.

Bodmer Paints the Piegan Chief. Photo-offset lithograph, 20 x 16, Desert Hawk Publishing, El Paso, Texas, 1988.

Canyon Crossing. Photo-offset lithograph, $16\frac{1}{2}$ x 25, edition 999, Hadley Companies, Bloomington, Minnesota, 1984.

Cochise. Photo-offset lithograph, $20\frac{1}{2}$ x 17, edition 999, Hadley Companies, Bloomington, Minnesota, 1987.

Coming to Trade—Fort Union, 1833. Photo-offset lithograph, 28 x 24, edition 999, Hadley Companies, Bloomington, Minnesota, 1990.

Cottonwood Crossing. Photo-offset lithograph, $15\frac{1}{4}$ x $22\frac{3}{4}$, edition 350, National Print Galleries, Scottsdale, Arizona.

Discovery. Photo-offset lithograph, $14\frac{3}{4}$ x 27, edition 450, Tucson Festival Society, Arizona, 1989.

Dowry, The. Photo-offset lithograph, $16\frac{1}{2}$ x 29, edition 999, Hadley Companies, Bloomington, Minnesota, 1984.

Gila Sundown. Photo-offset lithograph, $16\frac{1}{2}$ x 27, edition 450, Cowboy Artists of America Museum, Kerrville, Texas, 1991.

In the Mandan Lodge of Four Bears. Photo-offset lithograph, 28 x $18\frac{1}{2}$, edition 850, Hadley Companies, Bloomington, Minnesota, 1988.

Lemhi Pass. Photo-offset lithograph, edition 350, National Print Galleries, Scottsdale, Arizona, ca. 1982.

Mandan Gold. Poster image for Cowboy Artists of America exhibition, Phoenix Art Museum, Arizona, 1985.

Mandan Gold. Photo-offset lithograph, $24\frac{1}{2}$ x $18\frac{1}{2}$, edition 999, Hadley Companies, Bloomington, Minnesota, 1986.

Near the Stronghold. Photo-offset lithograph, $13\frac{1}{2}$ x $22\frac{1}{2}$, National Print Galleries, Scottsdale, Arizona.

Red Tepee, The. Poster image for Cowboy Artists of America exhibition, Phoenix Art Museum, Arizona, 1988.

Robe Trade, The. Photo-offset lithograph, $17\frac{1}{2}$ x $26\frac{1}{2}$, edition 999, Hadley Companies, Bloomington, Minnesota, 1984.

Source, The. Photo-offset lithograph, $18\frac{1}{2}$ x 17, edition 999, Hadley Companies, Bloomington, Minnesota, 1984.

Tales of Medicine Bags. Photo-offset lithograph, 18 x 22, edition 350, National Print Galleries, Scottsdale, Arizona, ca. 1982.

Winter Traders. Photo-offset lithograph, $16\frac{1}{2}$ x $23\frac{1}{4}$, edition 999, Hadley Companies, Bloomington, Minnesota, 1984.

Yuma Connection. Photo-offset lithograph, $26\frac{1}{2}$ x $14\frac{1}{4}$, edition 1000, The Connally Collection, Somerset Publishing House, Houston, Texas, 1984.

ALPHABETICAL INDEX OF ILLUSTRATIONS

WITH PLATE NUMBERS

Absaroka 103

Algonquian Family, The 59

Ancestors 95

Ancestral Shelter 73

Annie Laurie 23

Apache Moonlight 111

Apache Scouts 113

Apacheria 66, 67

Badlands National Monument 60

Baseball in Tokyo 52

Basket Weaver, Mexico 53

Beach Scene, Engebi 39

Bodmer Paints the Piegan Chief 5, 6

Camelot 3, 4

Canyon Country 112

Canyon Crossing 120

Catch is Running, The 36, 38

Cavalry Charge 121

Ceremonial Regalia 129

Chiricahua Homestead 49

Chiricahua Warrior 123

Cochise 94

Comanche Twilight 69

All dimensions are stated in inches, height preceding width.

Coming to Trade—Fort Union, 1833 115

Competition, The 29

Cottonwood Crossing 25, 27

Coxswain 37

Crew Cut Aboard the U.S.S. *Middleton* 40

Crow Chiefs Visit the Minnetarees 89

Dance Progressions 43, 44

Dandies, The 114

Discovery 65

Dispatch Rider 75

Dog Dancers 126

Doll, The 110

Don Quixote 58

Dowry, The 125

Drawings .... pp. 4, 28, 42, 52, 54, 88, 102, 110, 184, 194, 199, 211

Dry Camp 87

Elders, The 122

Evening Calm 7

Farmyard 26

Field Sketches and Studio Studies
- Buffalo 78
- Henry Mountains, Utah 74
- McElmo Canyon 68
- Portuguese Farm House 80
- Rocky Point, Mexico 64

Fired On 62

First Breath of Spring 72

Flat Irons, The 76

Four Lances 8

Frederic Remington and the Buffalo Soldiers 50

Fresh Snow 79

Fruitless Victory 70

Gathering of Eagles 100

General Crook 48

General Crook and Geronimo 97

Going to the Fair 104

Guarding the Herd 127

Hidden Eyes 31, 32

Homage to Catlin 109

Illustrations for *The Saturday Evening Post*
  "Horatio Hornblower" 46
  "Mountain Woman" 45
  Untitled, man standing beside mantel 47

In the Mandan Lodge of Four Bears 92

Jackson's Big Hole 61

Kenneth Riley
  Drummer in orchestra 21
  Five-year-old, dressed as an Indian 16
  On his patio in Tucson 12
  Portrait of, by Harley Brown 1
  Sketching aboard the U.S.S. *Middleton* 41
  With his painting *For Thine is the Kingdom* 35

Legend of Manabozho, The 9, 10, 11

Long Way Home, The 81
Major's Mount, The 77
Mandan Gold 85, 86
MarCyne at the Easel 83
Mess Hall on the U.S.S. *Middleton* 42
Morning Call 24
Morning Delivery 19
Oaxaca Market, Mexico 82, 84
Peruvian Mother 2
Pisac Market, Peru 98
Power of the Shield 101
Powwow Days 128
Princess, The 116
Red Flannel 30
Red Tepee, The 107, 108
Robe Trade, The 118
Romancing the West 17, 18
Salt Flats at Wheelus Air Base, Libya 55
Saturday in Town 56
Season's End 15
Secret Place, The 105
Shadows 102
Signal, The 34

Sisters 96
Source, The 63
Spellbinder, The 33
Spring Song 20
Staked Out 99
Tales of Medicine Bags 90
Tea for Two 22
Tide pools on the coast of Maine 57
Trackers, The 71
Trinkets 28
Visit of Lewis and Clark 54
War Lodge, The 117
Warriors, The 88
Welcome Shade 124
White Pony, The 51
Winter Hunt 119
Witches Market, Bolivia, The 13, 14
Wood Gatherers of Mih-Tutta-Hang-Kusch 93
You Take What's Issued 91
Zapotec 106

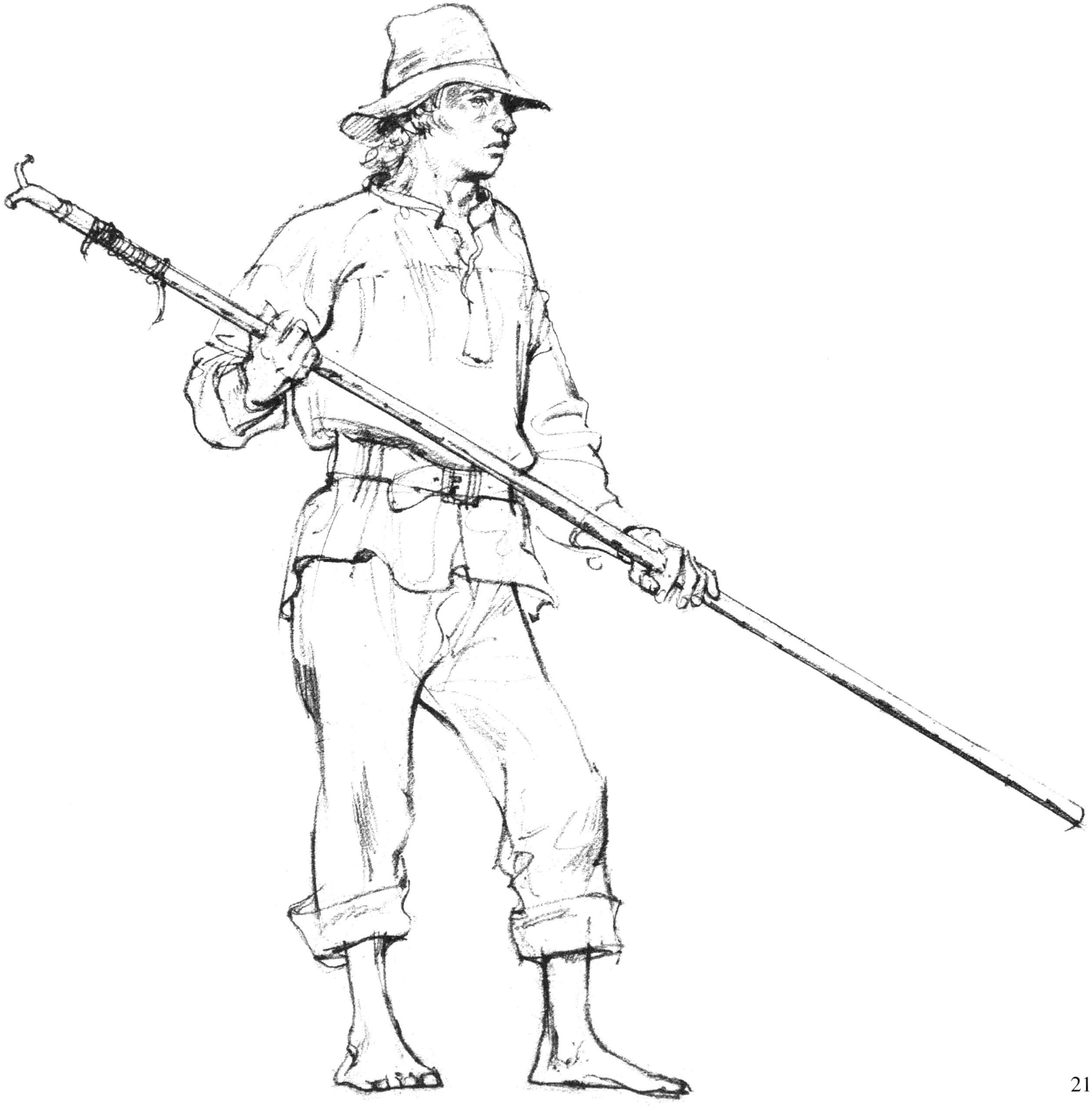

ACKNOWLEDGMENTS

Many people generously participated in the frustrating experience of reading a book about pictures without any of its pictures. Dan Blanchard and Walter Gray are especially thanked for candidly pointing out what was missing in the script. Jack Hines and Jack Morris each supplied professional expertise and encouragement, and Professor O. Walter Johnson offered the critical editing that helped put information into perspective. Ken and MarCyne Riley broke up the interviewing process with warm hospitality, fine dining and good company. James K. Ballinger brings insights only someone with his years of experience and knowledge can convey, as does Michael Duty. The sensitive organizational and design skills of Marla Dankert and Larry Samuels paired pictures and words with the dignity Riley's art so richly deserves.

Cooperation of the following people was essential to picture research: Kitty Deernose at the Little Bighorn Battlefield Museum, Valerie Kinkade at the U.S. Coast Guard Academy Museum, Susan Cadwallader of the U.S. Department of the Interior, and Alice Price at the U.S. Air Force Art Collection. And without the help of Maynard Harding, unofficial "town historian," I'd have been short on facts about Parsons, Kansas.

Lastly, but most importantly, a special thanks to Stuart Johnson, Settlers West Galleries, Tucson, Arizona, for having faith in my ability to tackle this project.

Designer:	Larry Samuels, Head of Exhibition and Graphic Design, Eiteljorg Museum
Editor:	Marla Dankert, Senior Curator for Art History, Eiteljorg Museum
Type:	Times Roman
Printer:	Regent Publishing Services, Corte Madera, California, and Hong Kong
	Hilltop Press, Indianapolis, Indiana